KIPPENBERGER

KIPPENBERGER

The Artist and His Families

SUSANNE KIPPENBERGER

Translated from the German by Damion Searls
Foreword by John Wray

⌐L

Kippenberger: The Artist and His Families
Susanne Kippenberger

This edition published in the United States by J&L Books.
Copyright © 2011 J&L Books and Susanne Kippenberger
Translation © 2011 Damion Searls

www.JandLbooks.org

Kippenberger: Der Künstler und seine Familien
Copyright © 2007 BV Berlin Verlag GmbH.
For Texts and Pictures by Kippenberger © Estate Martin Kippenberger,
Galerie Gisela Capitain, Cologne. All rights reserved.

The translation of this work was supported by a grant from the Goethe-Institut
which is funded by the German Ministry of Foreign Affairs.

ISBN 978-0-9829642-1-7

1. Kippenberger, Martin, 1953 – 1997
2. Artists – Germany – Biography

Printed in South Korea by Samhwa Printing Company

First English Edition

For my sisters,
Bine, Tina, and Babs,
and for Helena

CONTENTS

xi   Foreword

xv   Translator's Note

1   My Big Brother

16   Parents and Childhood

96   Hamburg

139   Berlin

215   Stuttgart and the Black Forest

237   Cologne Years: Beginnings

346   Cologne Years: The Turning Point

364   America

401   Frankfurt and Kassel

430   Cologne Years: The End

493   Jennersdorf

522   The Art of Being Human

539   Note to the American Edition (2011)

543   Acknowledgments

555   Index

563   Illustration Credits

ON UNDENIABILITY

Martin Kippenberger left a mark on my life twice, once as an artist, once as an ordinary man, without the two of us ever meeting. Unlike most of the medium-sized army of people who count themselves among his admirers these days, he was a person to me first—as a member, however attenuated, of my extended family—and as an artist only later. But it was as an artist that he marked me permanently.

Kurt Kocherscheidt, a well-regarded Austrian painter and my mother's cousin once removed, had been dead for four years when I learned that his widow, the photographer Elfie Semotan, had married again. Elfie's new husband, known to me at the time only by his last name, Kippenberger, (also an artist, apparently, and a heavy drinker, and—worst of all!—a German) was bound to be viewed somewhat critically by my family in general, and by my Aunt Elsa, Kurt's mother, especially. Aunt Elsa, then in her seventies, didn't think much of this new husband's art, and the rest of us duly took our cue from her. Those members of my family who'd actually met this interloper reported that he was a loudmouth; the one concrete description of his work that reached my ears featured a frog nailed to a cross. You didn't have to be a churchgoer (which my Aunt Elsa was to the end) to consider this a questionable aesthetic choice. I was living in New York City by then, a typically self-preoccupied twenty-four-year-old, far from my Austrian family. I filed the frog-crucifier away under Other

People's Business and focused my attention on paying the rent.

The 1990s were the years of Martin Kippenberger's ascendancy, however, and I couldn't help but notice—at first with indifference, then with a kind of semiconscious annoyance—that attention was being paid to his career, the kind of international, blue-chip attention that my uncle Kurt had been slow to receive. By that time I was working at the Paula Cooper Gallery in SoHo and was superficially acquainted with Kippenberger's art, at least to the extent of knowing that there was more to him than visual one-liners. I was aware of the prodigal extent of his output, and of its remarkable variety, because there was no way at that point *not* to be aware of it. Every piece that I saw—all in reproduction as yet, in *Artforum* or *Frieze* or *Parkett*—seemed to be the work of a completely different person.

I should have been prepared, then, for the retrospective that arrived at Vienna's Museum Moderner Kunst in 2003, but the truth is that it flabbergasted me. I visited it three times in one week, and it's still on my mind nearly a decade later. It served as an object lesson for me in, among other things, the extent to which a person can be wrong. I'd been wrong about Kippenberger: that much quickly became clear. There have been any number of artists whose artmaking has been similarly irreducible to a single approach or medium—Marcel Duchamp, Mike Kelley, Bruce Nauman—but none, at least that I know of, has demanded so emphatically to be judged on the totality of his or her life's achievement. Context is crucial to appreciating Kippenberger's art, and context is what, at long last, the *MuMoK* retrospective supplied.

At the periphery of my vision, as I went from room to room, from the early gray-scale paintings to the installations to the drawings on hotel stationery to the excruciatingly virtuosic self-portraits, a form began to coalesce—a kind of aesthetic and emotional afterimage, hulking and soundless—that disappeared if I looked at it directly. Self-subverting, ironic, and even flippant as many of the individual pieces seemed, the animus behind the body of work was austere and deliberate and (it seemed to me) boundlessly sad. Seen all together, Kippenberger's work was so human that it hurt to think about. Gifted as he undoubtedly was, his art appeared to have been made in the face of—and, sometimes, directly out of—his weakness and his fallibility, which may explain why it affected me so deeply. Dissembling as it often came across (and occasionally was, most likely), I'd never encountered art that seemed more naked. And I haven't in the antic decade since.

Susanne Kippenberger has managed to look directly, it seems to me, at what I could see only out of the corner of my eye, and she has described it with indefatigable calm. The Martin Kippenberger who emerges in the following pages may be recognizable as the man who satirized (and marketed) himself so unflinchingly, but we come to know him as a great deal else besides. No artistic self-invention, however extravagant, is ever *sui generis,* which is a part of what makes artists' biographies necessary. The straightforward tone of this book is a useful corrective to its subject's infamous extroversion and bluster, which cast an often harsh light on certain sides of his character while obscuring many others. Like a host of other artists, from Joseph Beuys to Andy Warhol to Jeff Koons, Kippenberger's persona was arguably his central creation, and it's a credit to Susanne that she transmits this clearly without allowing Kippenberger's version of Kippenberger to smother all the fascinating others. She has certain advantages, of course, being the artist's sister. Maybe no one but a sister could have managed it.

It's an embarrassment to me now, my family's knee-jerk and essentially defensive dismissal of a body of work that we were in ignorance of; and I imagine that all those (and there were more than a few) who reacted to Martin Kippenberger's art with prim indifference during his lifetime must feel as abashed as I do. It's ironic, of course, that I should be writing an introduction to this remarkable book, given the smug tenacity of my own resistance. But maybe that's also fitting. Martin Kippenberger's work broke down my resistance through mechanisms that remain largely mysterious to me: his brilliance played a role, of course, and his wit, and his shamelessness, and his relentless energy. But the true key lies elsewhere, in something much harder to put into words. I've tried to summarize it, but I can't do it justice, least of all in a single expression. The closest I can seem to get is undeniability.

— John Wray

TRANSLATOR'S NOTE

Martin Kippenberger spoke and wrote in a very, *very* irregular German and my translations in this book keep its idiosyncracies: crazy spelling, made-up words, and so on. (Translations of quotes by other people likewise use nonstandard English to represent nonstandard German.) I would like to acknowledge and thank the translators who have tackled Kippenbergerese before me, in particular the uncredited translators of the chronology "Martin Kippenberger: Life and Work" (in *Kippenberger*, Taschen 1997, reprinted in *Martin Kippenberger: The Problem Perspective*, MOCA 2008, pp. 349–52); the uncredited translator of Kippenberger's 1991 interview with Jutta Koether (in *Martin Kippenberger: I Had a Vision*, SFMOMA 1991, excerpts reprinted in *Problem Perspective*, pp. 310–340); Micah Magee (translator of the 1991 *Artfan* interview published in English as *Picture a Moon, Shining in the Sky: Conversation with Martin Kippenberger*, Starship 2007, rev. ed. 2010); and Ishbel Flett (translator of the catalog section of Uwe Koch, *Annotated Catalogue Raisonné of the Books of Martin Kippenberger: 1977–1997*, D.A.P. 2003). I consulted these translations and used them where possible, sometimes modified.

The titles of Kippenberger's works, exhibitions, and books present a different challenge, with their concise poetry, humor, and cultural references. Many of the titles have been translated before, sometimes in multiple ways, not always capturing their meaning and nuance; some of the titles were originally in English, and in those cases I kept them as Kippenberger wrote them (for example, *One Flew Over the Canarybirds Nest* or *The Happy End of Franz Kafka's "Amerika,"* not translating/correcting "Happy End" to "Happy Ending"). My thanks to Gisela Capitain, Regina Fiorito, and Lisa Franzen, from Galerie Gisela Capitain and the Martin Kippenberger Estate, for their help with translating the titles; I also found Diedrich Diederichsen's essay "The Poor Man's Sports Car Descending a Staircase: Kippenberger as Sculptor" as translated by James Gussen (*Problem Perspective,* pp. 118–56) helpful for several titles.

All the footnotes in this book are by the translator, not the author.

KIPPENBERGER

MY BIG BROTHER

He was my big brother. My protector, my ally, my hero. Whenever I got into a fight with my sister, I only had to yell "Maaaartin, Bine is..." and there'd be something, a "Cologne Cathedral" (Martin yanking poor Bine up by the ears until she was dizzy) or an Indian burn. He wrote me letters like this from his boarding school in the Black Forest: "Dear Sanni, How are you? I think about you every day. Are you baking cake yet? Don't snack so much, you'll get a tummy ache. Do you brush your tiny teeth every night? I hope so." He was ten at the time; I was six. Now I'm 54, ten years older than my brother was when he died.

It was on March 7, 1997. Almost exactly the same people came to Burgenland for his funeral as had celebrated his marriage with Elfie Semotan there a year before.

He was so looking forward to 1997—it was going to be his year, his big breakthrough at last. A "Respective" in the Geneva Museum in January, then a few days later the opening of *The Eggman and His Outriggers* in Mönchengladbach, his first solo show at a German museum since 1986. In March, the Käthe Kollwitz Prize and an exhibition of his *Raft of the Medusa* cycle at the Berlin Academy of Arts, then documenta in June, and the sculpture exhibition in Münster—but he didn't get to see those. Hepatitis, cirrhosis, liver cancer: six weeks after the diagnosis, he was dead.

Is it possible, advisable, permissible to write about someone so close to you? My first reaction, when asked if I could imagine writing about my brother, was No! No no no.

Yes.

Martin Kippenberger is a public figure. A pop star, a brand name, a classic contemporary artist. He is written about, spoken of, and judged. Newspapers and magazines that kept deadly silent at best about him while he was alive now praise him. And he—who let nothing escape comment—can no longer say anything. Night and day (especially night), he used to manage his image as an artist, but now he has lost control. That is what he was most afraid of.

He shows up as a character in novels, there is a hotel suite named after him, a play, a restaurant, a guinea pig (at least one). You can buy him as a notepad. Ben Becker dedicated a song to him: "Kippy" on the album *We're Taking Off.* His early death has turned him into a legend, especially for younger people—a kind of James Dean of contemporary German art. A devil for some, a god for others. The picture of the human being is fading away.

The picture we have of the artist, on the other hand, seems to be growing clearer and clearer. His work began to be taken seriously only after his death; now that it is finished, it can be viewed in peace, and connections within his body of work can be discovered and explored. Martin produced at such a pace that there was barely time to glance at his work when he was living. Now he has platforms he could once only dream of: the Venice Biennale, the Tate in London, the Museum of Contemporary Art in L.A., the Museo Picasso in Malaga, and the Museum of Modern Art in New York. But posthumous fame was exactly what he wasn't interested in. He wanted to experience and enjoy the success that he, in his opinion, deserved. He believed in himself from the beginning, in himself and in art.

People terrified of him while he was alive now say that

Martin is no longer here to get in the way of his art. The shock of his sudden death was a wake-up call for those who had only seen the humor, not the seriousness behind it—and who couldn't even laugh at that. Zdenek Felix, former director of the Hamburg Deichtorhallen, holds the humorlessness of German museum directors partly responsible for the fact that, between 1986 and 1997, Martin had solo shows at the Centre Pompidou in Paris, the Hirshhorn in Washington, the Museum of Modern Art in San Francisco, and Boijmans Van Beuningen in Rotterdam, but not one in a German museum. "He was too early," says Tanja Grunert, the gallerist, "Martin was always too early."

There are many different pictures of Martin Kippenberger, both public and private. He drew and painted lots of them himself, constantly had his picture taken, and put himself on display in bars and museums, at exhibitions and parties. He was often described as cynical, but he was a great moralist and humanist. In Berlin in the late seventies he was known as an impresario of punk and hard rock in the Kreuzberg club S.O.36, but in his studio he preferred to listen to the oldies: Dean Martin, Frank Sinatra. "My Way."

He is sometimes described as an autodidact, but he learned his craft at the Academy of Arts in Hamburg, and broke off his studies only when they got to be too boring. No, he wasn't an autodidact; he was a self-made man. He created himself rather than waiting to be discovered. "He was his own best salesman," said the gallerist Bärbel Grässlin. But not everyone was buying: "He was not a good person," the obituary in *taz* cruelly said.

For Martin everything, even his name, expressed his vision. As a boy, he was always allowed to ride on St. Martin's horse during the St. Martin's Day processions, and like the saint, he shared everything he had. Money, success, and influence; his sense of fun, his art, and his worries. When things were going badly for him, he got mean.

He knew how to hit home. "He saw through people like an x-ray," a girlfriend says, and found all their weak points. He attacked the bad and defended the good the way a lioness guards her cubs. There were people who hated him and people who loved him in the burning depths of their hearts—the innkeeper's daughter in Austria no less than the rich collector. Ever since Martin's death, people have quoted his line: "I work hard so that people can say: Kippenberger was a good time." And he usually was a good time, but woe to anyone around him when he wasn't.

The image of the jolly entertainer masks the shadows underneath, and the fact that he worked himself to death creating this image and his work. "When you face an abyss," he wrote on one of his pictures, "don't be surprised to find you can fly." His wild artist's life seems thrilling from a distance to fans. He himself called it "insanely strenuous to be on the road with absolutely no private life." Still, that's what he did a lot of the time—lived as fast as a driver on the autobahn. Then, for a few days or a week, he would stay with friends or acquaintances who made him feel looked after and cared for. He wouldn't constantly have to show off, but could show his weak side too, and be quiet.

In the early years he was constantly pulling down his pants, but few people ever saw him truly naked. How can I strip him bare now that he's dead, and reveal his vulnerability, his fear, his doubts?

The picture of him we need to draw is more complex than either his enemies or his fans would like. As complex as his art. Who was my brother? An anarchist and a gentleman, one of the boys and a friend to women, big brother and little brother, a sole provider who was anything but solitary—yet perhaps, in the end, solitary after all. He attacked and undermined the art scene while playing along within it; he was someone who "simultaneously rejected and thoroughly celebrated the role of the artist," as Diedrich Diederichsen said.

He was always something of a Rumpelstiltskin. He bounced through the art world as a collector, painter, impresario, museum director, installation artist, graphic artist, dealer, photographer, braggart, teacher, and puller of strings. For him, that was the freedom of art: to constantly overstep boundaries, including the limits of good taste. "Embarrassment has no limits." His rituals for getting under people's skin (the endless, pointless jokes; the swaggering, macho songs sung in groups that pointedly excluded women) were all tests: What are people willing to put up with, and when will they start to rebel? Do they know a joke when they see one?

The more horrible something was, the more he liked it as material for his art, from a flokati rug to Harald Juhnke, from a bath mat in front of the toilet to politics to Santa Claus. One critic said that Immendorff brought the German battlefields to the international art world, while Kippenberger brought German everyday life.

As he openly admitted himself, he made "kitsch" now and then. *Rent Electricity Gas* (the title of one of his shows) needed to be paid. He wanted to live well. The rhyme "*Nicht sparen—Taxi fahren*" (Don't save money, take a taxi) was one of his favorite sayings. He never saved; he invested all his money in life and art, not bank accounts and prestigious purchases. He only got himself a BMW once, when he went to Los Angeles. In Hollywood, he thought, you have to flaunt it. He wanted the biggest BMW, with a chauffeur, of course, and when he could only get the second biggest, he glued the missing cylinders on the back, as top hats ("cylinder" and "top hat" are the same word in German). Martin arranged and reframed everything, from matchboxes to invitations to hotel rooms, leaving his mark everywhere. Walter Grond called it "kippenbergerizing the world."

He farted at the table with important museum people—yet with Mrs. Grässlin in the Black Forest he behaved impeccably. Johannes Wohnseifer, Martin's last assistant, worshipped Martin's good manners, his "natural authority." Many people experienced his excessive lifestyle in Cologne and Berlin, Vienna and Madrid, but not his periodic retreats to the Black Forest, or a Greek island, or Lake Constance, to carry out his "Sahara Program." Every year he went to a spa for several weeks, where he ate only dry bread and drank only fruit juice and water. Afterward he could plunge back into his excessive life.

I wouldn't call these contradictions—I would call them extremes. F. Scott Fitzgerald, another heavy drinker and romantic, described it this way in his autobiographical essay "The Crack-Up": "The test of a first-rate intelligence is the ability to hold two opposed ideas in the mind at the same time, and still retain the ability to function." That was the intelligence Martin Kippenberger had, he who had never graduated high school. He always wanted everything—to have his cake and eat it too. *I is another* was the title of a major exhibition in which Martin was represented with several of his self-portraits, but "I am I," is what he would have said, "and I am many."

This book is not the full truth. It does not aim for completeness or uninterrupted intimacy, and certainly not for art-historical classification and interpretation. It does not fulfill the chronicler's duty to cover everything. It is a portrait, not a biography. But everything here is true—is *a* truth, but not merely *my* truth. It is the result of numerous conversations with family, friends, museum curators, gallerists, artists, and critics. *Truth*

*Is Work** was the title of his exhibition with Werner Büttner and Albert Oehlen in the Folkwang Museum in Essen, the city where we grew up. This book sets out to understand how he became who he was—how the Kippenberger System operated. And also to remember a time when the collectors who now pay hundreds of thousands of dollars for a self-portrait wouldn't have taken it for a fraction of that sum.

"Is the boy normal?!" his teacher asked, horrified, when faced with this child who did not see the world like a child—a nine-year-old with the wit and humor of an adult who still hadn't learned his times tables and had never learned to write properly. He would rather look out the window than at the blackboard. "Martin, Our Artist" was written on the kitchen wall in our house when he was a boy. He never had to play the artist, which is why he could play *with* the role of the artist. What can art and the artist do, and what should they do: that was the guiding thread of his life. He tried out every possible artist role; he took the famous line from Beuys, "Every human being is an artist," and flipped it on its head: "Every artist is a human being."

No, he was never normal. He burned like the cigarettes he seldom failed to have in his hand. "Howdy-do!" he said in the morning to the retirees at the Äppelwoi cider bar in Sachsenhausen, and with another "Howdy-do!" he stood in the door of Bärbel Grässlin's gallery a few hours later, looking for someone to join him for lunch. "Howdy-do!" he yelled into the telephone in the evening—after his afternoon nap, which was sacred—and so it went on: eating noodles, having a good time, working, and dancing until dawn. At 7 a.m. he was standing ramrod straight in the Hotel Chelsea in Cologne, saying his hellos in Chinese. He had already danced a little jig around the cleaning lady, and now he greeted the Chinese

---

* A rhyme in German: *Wahrheit ist Arbeit.*

hotel guests, hands folded across his breast, bowing to each one. They may not have thought it was funny, but he did. A few hours later he was back at work.

The people with him laughed and suffered. Anyone who went out with him at night knew there was no way they would get to bed—Martin was merciless.

He could never bear to be alone, except maybe during his afternoon naps or when he was painting. *Big Apartment, Never Home* is the title of one of his pictures. As soon as he moved somewhere—and he was constantly moving from one city to another: Hamburg, Berlin, Florence, Stuttgart, Sankt Georgen, Cologne, Vienna, Seville, Carmona, Teneriffe, Frankfurt, Los Angeles, and the Burgenland—he immediately sought out the local bar that would become his living room, dining room, office, museum, studio, and stage. His hometown headquarters was the Paris Bar. Its owner, Michel Würthle, was his best friend.

His hanging around in cafés was actually all about "communication, communication, communication," according to Gisela Capitain, his gallerist and executor. The "Spiderman," as he once portrayed himself, spun his nets everywhere, day and night: "Martin was always on duty." Truth Is Work: that was another boundary he crossed—the one between life and work, between himself and others. "On the whole and plain for everyone to see I'm basically a living vehicle." Every party was both a stage for his performances and a source of raw material for his new works. That is why it is so hard to answer the question of who my brother was. The person cannot be separated from the artist—he turned almost his whole life into art. Many people could not distinguish between the artist and the person, but still, it is important to avoid simplifying his art by seeing it merely as reflecting his life. (Anyone who thinks they can reconstruct the stations of Martin's biography with his drawings of hotels falls right into his trap: he drew pictures on the stationery of many more hotels than he actually stayed in.) The art was not a reflection of his life, it was his life.

He was an only son with four sisters; a boy who was not like other boys, who painted and cried and would rather play cards than play with cars (this would later bring in a fortune as an adult). He was the only one of us children who enthusiastically took part in our father's staged photographs, but at the same time he never took direction. He coquettishly struck a pose, arms flung around a lamppost and one foot pointing up in the air behind him. His eyes sparkled in the photos the way they always did: enjoying himself, giving off sparks of energy. He was like that from the beginning: funny and charming, difficult and uncomfortable, cocky and uninhibited and free.

Again and again he got into fights with his family. He suffered when our parents sent him to boarding school; he never felt sufficiently loved, acknowledged, and supported. But he was always attached to them. This terror to the bourgeoisie was a family man through and through; the *enfant terrible* rushing around the world also cherished the family traditions. Our mother died young, and he gave his daughter her name; our father's signet ring with the family coat of arms never left Martin's finger. He always insisted that we all celebrate Christmas together and clung tightly to the rituals: there had to be presents and a big Christmas tree and turkey dinner— and no question about who would get the drumstick. He even came along to church sometimes; he never officially left the church. He hated routine and tried something new with every exhibition project, yet he needed rituals the way a drunkard needs lampposts.

He always said he wanted a large family of his own, but he couldn't handle life as a paterfamilias for long after his daughter was born.

9

Martin never lived in a pure artistic sphere. He brought us, his thoroughly unglamorous family, everywhere—to tea with Rudolf Augstein, publisher of the news magazine *Der Spiegel,* when we were still practically children; to luxury hotels in Geneva, where he got us free rooms; to the wild party celebrating his opening at the Pompidou Centre. "Are you coming?" read the invitation, and woe to those who didn't. He would feel as hurt as a little boy. He had our mother stay in his substance abuse halfway house, and showed work with our father.

The *enfant terrible* really was a child his whole life, one who gathered families around him: friends, collectors, landlords and landladies, fans. He could beam with pleasure, sulk, run rampant, lose his temper, and be unfair, like a child—but then, the next day or next year, own up to it like a man and publicly apologize. He threw himself at our grandmother during a summer vacation once—through a glass door that he was too excited to notice—and would later throw himself into ideas and projects the same way, sometimes causing as much pain as the broken glass did back then.

He could be greedy, jealous, and egocentric, but also proud, of himself and of many other people, of their art, their craft, their cooking. He didn't just brag about himself. And he wanted presents like a child, too. For his fortieth birthday, an orgy of spending and dissipation, he wanted a Carrera slot-car racetrack; he would stand under the Christmas tree with shining eyes. "Childhood never really ends," he said in an interview with artist Jutta Koether.

He was extremely intelligent but never an intellectual. He read the *Bild* tabloid and Mickey Mouse comics, not Roland Barthes and James Joyce. He drew his material from popular culture. He let someone else read Kafka and tell him about it, the way he let others travel and draw and build sculptures for him. He would discover things lightning-fast, seize on ideas, and assimilate them. If there was something he couldn't do in the morning, he would show people that he had learned to do it by the afternoon: make etchings, play the accordion, speak Dutch. It wasn't real Dutch, of course, but it sure sounded like Dutch.

"Think today, done tomorrow" was one of his most well-known sayings. It was only half true. His major projects, such as *The Happy End of Franz Kafka's "Amerika,"* percolated for a long time before they were ready. One year he would paint three or four pictures; the next year, forty or fifty.

He overflowed with ideas that no one else had, or if someone else did have them, he simply appropriated them, whether they came from Picasso or his students or his daughter, Helena. He was as generous in taking as he was in giving, and he always demanded from others what he himself offered: everything. "You had to take care not to turn into a Kippenberger slave," Bärbel Grässlin said.

He wanted fries and croquettes served at the opening of his exhibition at the Boijmans Van Beuningen Museum in Rotterdam because that's what we ate on our summer vacations in Holland, every night for six weeks. The museum would have preferred tomatoes and mozzarella but Martin had nothing but contempt for such things. He hated the prevailing fashions—postmodern architecture, arugula, shoulder pads, video art. Whatever was "in" was "out" for him—good only for material. Political correctness disgusted him. He built postmodern houses out of plywood and glued lighters all over them, or produced a multiple for documenta: a white plate with a big hole in the middle, *"Ciao rucola mozzarella tomate con spaghettini secco e vino al dente."*

He likewise discarded his hippie look early and cut his hair short, put on a tie—unheard-of in Kreuzberg in the seventies—and wore only the finest suits and most expensive shoes, even in the studio. Clothes, too, were a costume. He wanted to be a walking contradiction to everything people expected from a crazy artist. Aside from that, he liked to look good, at his best like the Austrian actor Helmut Berger. He loved to hear people remark on his similarity to Visconti's leading man. He would have loved to be famous as a movie star, or a poet. Opera and theater didn't interest him. But movies! He knew the Hollywood classics by heart, even years after he'd seen them, and could recall scenes in the most minute detail. "Anyone who saw him in action, ranting and raging, swinging his mic onstage at 5 a.m., could see his genuine, abiding star quality, a charisma which happened to have been diverted into the art world," said the obituary in the *Independent*.

In his worst periods he looked like a shabby artist: unwashed, drunk, and fat. So he pulled his underpants up over his belly like Picasso, stuck out his paunch, had a photo taken, and turned it into an exhibition poster, or a painting, or a calendar. Every weakness became a strength when transformed into art, even if the pain remained. When punks beat him up in Berlin, he had his picture taken with his bandaged head, swollen face, and crooked nose, and later painted himself like that, too. He titled it *Dialogue with the Youth*, part of a triptych called *Berlin by Night*, and he also used it as an admission ticket; he loved repurposing things as many times as he could.

He was a child of the Ruhr District, the industrial center of Germany that gave him his directness, fast pace, and dry humor. He liked how people there interacted with each other naturally and honestly. They were raw and unsentimental, always aboveboard, never stuck-up. He was an absolute master of the notes on the social keyboard, but he didn't divide people into important and unimportant. When his neighbor, a good, honest photographer, didn't understand Martin's art, Martin explained it to him seriously and in detail. He met everyone at eye level, whether millionaires or children, neither looking up at them nor looking down on them. That is why children loved him so much. They also often understood his humor better than the critics and curators, and didn't automatically feel offended by his outrageous sayings and provocations, which, in his friend Meuser's view, were "just his way of saying, 'Hello, so who are you?'"

He liked to quote Goethe and our mother: "From my darling mother my cheerful disposition and fondness for telling stories." From her also came his generosity, social conscience, and pleasure in meeting new people no matter where they came from—the ability to see what was special about others no matter what form it took. From our father he inherited artistic talent, a tendency to excess, lack of inhibition, and love of enjoying himself, self-presentation, staging scenes. Artist Thomas Wachweger coined a word, *Zwangsbeglücker* (someone who forces others to have fun), that fit both father and son.

He was full of longing. He craved drugs, then alcohol; recognition and attention; love, TV, and noodle casserole. Martin asked lots of mothers to cook him our mother's noodle casserole, and of course turned it into art, too. *Kippenberger in the Noodle Casserole Yes Please!* was the title of one of his first exhibitions, in Berlin. "Addiction [*Sucht*] is just searching [*suchen*]," he explained to Jutta Koether in an interview. "I reject everything and keep searching for the right thing."

"Man Seeking Woman," along with his photograph and address, was printed on the sticker the size of a visiting card that he put up all over Berlin in the seventies. It was more than a good joke—behind the irony was a deeper seriousness. He called one of his catalogs *Homesick Highway 90,* and on the title page was a picture of him with our father crammed into a photo booth. Homesickness and wanderlust; longing for a place to call home and running away to be free of all ties, obligations, and labels; the desire for peace and quiet and the restless curiosity and dread of boredom; the paradox of wanting to be recognized, wanting to belong, but not wanting to be pigeonholed. That was his lifelong struggle.

In the sixties, little girls used to stick glittery roses, pussy willows, and forget-me-nots into friendship books and copy out little didactic verses alongside: "Be like the violet in the grass / modest and pure in her proper station, / Don't be like the prideful rose / always wanting admiration." My brother drew a caricature in my album of German chancellor Kiesinger ("big") on the left, de Gaulle ("bigger") in the middle, and on the right, at the top, on a victory podium and with a wide grin on his face, a beaming man with elephant ears and a crew cut: unmistakably Martin. His little poem: "Love is like an EVAG city bus / It makes you wait and doesn't care / And when at

Self-portrait in friendship book, 1966

14

last it hurries by / The driver yells 'Full!' and leaves you there /
Your [and then in a heart:] big brother, Martin."

Everything about Martin is here: the humor, the mockery,
the irony (directed at himself, too). His poking fun at pretense
and his lack of respect for power, along with his own ambition
and boastfulness. His linking the banal with the elevated,
and kippenbergerizing an existing rhyme with a personal
detail ("EVAG" stands for Essener Verkehrs AG, the Essen
transit authority). The longing for love, and the fear of being
excluded from love and remaining alone. The draftsmanship,
the tenderness, and the pride he had in being a big brother.

CHAPTER ONE
PARENTS AND CHILDHOOD

"He was running away."

The answer came before I even asked the question: How did it happen that he went and stayed with you when he was so young, just nine years old? His first long trip away from home, going with total strangers all the way from deep in the Ruhr on the western edge of Germany to deep in the Bavarian Forest in the east, near the Czech border—what was that like?

"He couldn't wait," she says.

He wasn't coming to see her—he was leaving where he was.

Our parents and Wiltrud Roser barely knew each other. Our mother had written a letter to the artist just six months earlier, the first of many that would travel from Essen to Cham. "Dear Wiltrud!" she started the letter—to a woman she didn't know, and didn't know anything about except that she illustrated beautiful children's books. All she knew was Waldemar, Roser's illustrated dog.) "I'm addressing you by your first name because it's right either way: I don't know if you're a Miss Roser or Mrs. Roser, and you'd be offended (actually you probably wouldn't be, but you might be) if I wrote the wrong one." Our mother definitely didn't want that, since she wanted something else from this stranger: a picture. She wanted to surprise our father for Christmas with a family portrait just like the one in *Waldemar*. He might well have come up with the same idea himself—"that happens to us a lot, that we plan the same surprises for each other"—and if so, Wiltrud should say yes to her and no to him.

Instead of a photograph for Wiltrud to copy, she sent short descriptions:

Dad: broad-shouldered and stocky
Mom: no distinguishing characteristics, like all mothers
Barbara ("Babs"): 11 yrs old, thin, bangs, strawb. blond
    short hair, freckles & a very critical look
Bettina: 10, strong, long dark blond pigtails, maternal,
    head usually tilted
Martin ("the Boy"): 8, short hair, lots and lots of freckles
Bine (Sabine): 6, short and stumpy, blocky head like Dad,
    light blond pigtails & an electric socket in the middle
    of her face
Little Sanni (Susanne): 4, dark blond pigtails, clever

"Will you do it? It would be great! We are such a crazy and fun family that we would probably give you a ton of material for more children's books." Our mother wrote that she had already met many Munich artists in similar fashion and had become friends with them. "I think you'd be a good fit with us too." Would Wiltrud ever have the chance to come to Essen for a visit?

Wiltrud Roser drew the picture, which still exists, and she came to our house for an artist party. The next morning the two women sat at the breakfast table coming up with plans for everything Wiltrud should do in the big city: plays, museums, and more. And then our mother said she didn't know what she was going to do, Martin simply refused to go to school anymore. He was sick, too. "Incredibly pale" is how Wiltrud Roser remembers him. He was suffering from what our mother called the proletariat sickness or Ruhr anemia: a sallow, bloodless face. "The sky was yellow in the Ruhr"; the chimneys in Essen still spewed smoke then—fresh-washed clothes were black if you left them hanging on the clothesline for a few hours.

In Bavaria, the sky was blue.

"Why doesn't he come with me?" Wiltrud Roser said. She had a son, too, just a year younger than Martin, and the school year was almost over anyway.

"Martin, would you like to come home with me?" she asked him when he came into the kitchen.

"When do we leave?" he answered.

So that was that. No more plays, no museums, no shopping trip to the big city—Martin was determined and didn't give Wiltrud any peace. They left the next day for practically the outermost reaches of the German world, a little town where teachers and students were often transferred as punishment.

The address couldn't have been more perfect: 1 Spring Street (Frühlingstrasse 1). He liked the old house with all its

Our family as drawn by Wiltrud Roser

18

nooks and crannies, right on the Regen River, with a sawmill out back—a giant, adventure-filled playground. It was a house like ours: cold in temperature but warm in every other way, full of pictures and books, with little wooden figures standing around everywhere, even in the bathroom. Albrecht, the father, was only a distant figure—he worked as a puppeteer in Stuttgart; the aunt was a Chiemsee painter; Wiltrud worked on her picture books; the grandmother took care of the children. Martin did what he would so often do later in life: he got other people to work for him, hiring Wiltrud's son Sebastian to do his homework. His grades in math and writing improved, though only temporarily—school remained torture for him and for everyone around him. The boys spent a lot of time with Wiltrud in her studio, each one busy with his own picture. One time, "with a fabulous gesture," Martin swept everything in front of him off the tabletop.

"Martin, what are you doing?!"

"Making room."

And, she thought, he was right. Other people might have called it naughty. She called it kingly. "He was never bad, just kingly: bossy but generous."

He sat for her as a model, too, and our mother said that when the book with those drawings came out, he showed it "to everyone, whether they wanted to look at it or not."

Martin was "terribly easy to take care of," a darling boy, and Wiltrud, a short woman with short hair, cheerful and sassy and always a straight talker, was certainly right for him. At eighty she can still laugh about the gaudy kitsch in the Cham Catholic church. She has lived in Cham her whole life, in her parents' house at the edge of a small town, but has few ties with the locals. She just lives there.

She told me that Martin wasn't homesick, "not at all," but that he made presents for his sisters the whole time he was there. Martin stayed six weeks; it seemed like months and months to her. And at the end of the stay he went back to Essen just as eagerly as he had left.

The thank-you letter that our mother sent to Wiltrud Roser sounds euphoric: Martin regaled the family with his stories, like the one about Vicar Bear and his cane, until we cried with laughter. "Already on the first morning he danced the polka, around to the right and around to the left, in his long nightshirt, it was a scream. He can sure dance, and paint too!" He'd been painting what he had seen in Bavaria, including Sebastian ("it couldn't have been any more like him") and Vicar Bear ("who looks terrifying"). "His stay with you was so good for him, in body and mind and spirit, that I can't thank you and everyone else in Cham enough."

Delight over his scholastic progress didn't last long, in any case. After summer vacation Martin went back to school in Essen-Frillendorf to repeat third grade. Everything was like the old days again, and soon he would be sent off to a boarding school in the Black Forest, and from there to the next boarding school, and so on.

The Rosers were his first "second family," and he kept in contact with them. Cham was the beginning of his life far away from home. One of his most haunting self-portraits is called *Please Don't Send Home*: Martin peers out like a little runaway child, with no home any more, imploring the viewer to take him in because there is no going back. He wanted to move forward, get ahead, achieve something, conquer ever-new territory.

Still, according to his friend Michel Würthle, there was one place among all the many places in his life where he was always happy to return: "Childhood. The family house. Mama and Papa."

OUR PARENTS

A person doesn't create himself out of nothing, after all.

—MK

[Did your parents play a part in your personality?]
Massive, massive, massive. I have to admit it. A huge
part.... Both parents. Both extremes.

—MK

They fell in love with each other through writing. Writing
letters.

Actually, they had already known each other for a long
time: they were in the same dancing school without really
noticing each other. Their parents moved in the same circles
in Duisburg. And long before he received letters from her
himself, he had read her letters.

It was during the war, in Hungary, and the doctor in
his regiment, one Wiechmann, always showed him what
she'd written. Wiechmann didn't know what to make of the
dry letters and couldn't understand why he wasn't getting
anywhere with her. The young lady just wouldn't catch fire.
Our father gave him good advice but it didn't help.

Later, after the war was over, our father's father invited her
over to dinner—not without thinking, perhaps, that she might
make a good match; he would have known that as a manager at
Deutsche Bank. After a stroll in the woods, our father took her
to the streetcar: "the only thing I remember was her unusual way
of walking. She just galumphed along." He found it touchingly
awkward. And that was that, until he wrote to congratulate her
on her recent graduation from medical school, just to be polite.
She wrote to thank him for his thanks, "and from that bungled
thank-you-no-thank-*you*" arose an exchange of letters.

21

He gently accused her of maybe being too cold to the other man, Wiechmann, and our mother got furious: she had only written to him on the front in the first place out of pity! But then, wounded in his masculinity, this Wiechmann had started insulting her, accusing her of being a "sexless workhorse"—her, Dr. Lore Leverkus, a young doctor who had just started her first job at the Göttingen Clinic for no salary because the paid positions were reserved for the men returning from the war. "I don't care to answer letters like that."

The two of them debated the meaning of love and discussed art. She told him about Beethoven concerts she had heard, live or on the radio, and he told her about the pictures he was painting and the classes he was taking. "A ten-page letter two or three times a week," our father said later, "no one can withstand that." For his twenty-sixth birthday, March 1, 1947, she typed up their letters, bound them, and gave him the volume, illustrated with the little pictures he used to send her to accompany his words. She wrote as the dedication "You for me and me for you." And next to the dedication was a bookplate he had drawn for both of them to use: someone sitting in an armchair and reading a newspaper that said "Lore" on one side and "Gerd" on the other.

They called each other "Little Man" and "Little Mouse." She sent him care packages with oatmeal, bacon, textbooks, ribbons, brushes, and Rilke poems. He, a mining student in Aachen, sent her stockings, and also work: reports to type up and send on to the senior office. He sent her drawings and watercolors, which she tacked to the wall of her room. Whenever he painted, "burning with zeal," he forgot everything, including the stove he was supposed to keep hot while she cooked for him and did the laundry. Sometimes she read to him while he was painting. Art, he would later say, was what he had really wanted to study, really wanted to do. If only the war hadn't gotten in the way.

When she was offered a position in Odenwald, she turned it down: "There's not the slightest intellectual stimulation there, I'd go brain-dead." She liked to go to concerts, to the theater—a Shakespeare production in a ruined cloister, for instance. She was an enthusiastic reader of what people were reading in those days (Manfred Hausmann, Frank Thiess), and she liked telling him, a "specialist in the field," her impressions of various art exhibitions in Wiesbaden. She worshipped the Old Masters (Dürer, Grünewald, Bosch) and complained about contemporary artists: "All their works have nothing to say except 'Me, me, me.'" Within six months, she had revised her opinion and said she recognized genius in modern painting; she didn't want to "label it as smears of color on the wall any more."

In one of his early letters, Gerd had told her that he was more afraid of marriage than of the war. But on August 2, 1948, the banker's son and the factory director's daughter were married: Gerd, son of Gertie née Oechelhäuser and Hans Kippenberger, and Dr. med. Eleonore "Lorchen" Augusta Elena, daughter of Otto and stepdaughter of his new, third wife Dr. med. Lore Leverkus. Despite taking place in the lean postwar years, it was "a real peacetime wedding," thanks to various bartered items (coal for wine, for example), care packages, cured meats from the black market, and ration cards contributed by all the guests. There had been several small engagement parties rather than one big party, and now the wedding itself was celebrated in style for three days: guests marched through the village singing miners' songs on the first night, carousing until nine the next morning; the written schedule for the second day said "Sleep late!"; finally came the ceremonies on the third day, first at the registry office and then in the church. After lunch on the third day, according to the program: "Catch your breath," then coffee, and finally dancing.

The groom himself had illustrated the "wedding newspaper" that was handed out to all the guests, and had written most of the poems in it as well. Like so many other family occasions to come, this festive day was recorded for posterity: "Mother-in-law Lore greeted the guests at the front door in her slip. Father-in-law Abba stood in the bedroom in his long underwear, unashamed, while Little Mouse had a wreath pinned up in her hair. Meanwhile little female cousins of every shape and size shuttled back and forth through the house, being either fed or put to work. The sexton didn't want to let us into the church until we paid the marriage fee."

Their honeymoon was in the Bergisches Land: hiking in the mountains. He shoved rocks he found geologically interesting into her backpack, and she secretly took them out again and dropped them. Almost as soon as they got home— by boat to Düsseldorf and from there by streetcar—he was off again, for a month in England with his fellow students. She had a job by then with a country doctor, near Aachen, and she supported her husband while he was in school.

DAD

He was born on March 1, 1921, the oldest of four brothers, so in 1939 he had just graduated high school and finished his time in the national labor service. He began his hands-on training in the mines: "I had chosen the career of the old Siegerland families: coal miner. But then, of course, came the war."

Later, when he would tell stories about the war years, they were almost always comic. He was determined to see the beautiful side of things and refused to let even a war quash his worldview. His memoirs of the time read like stories of adventure tourism: when he transferred in Berlin on the way to Poland as an eighteen-year-old soldier, for example, he felt "a tingly sensation from being abroad, not knowing what to expect." In Poland, he went to bars and enthused about the Masurian lake country; in France, he visited Joan of Arc's birthplace, flirted with a little French girl from Dijon, came to love Camembert, climbed the church tower in Amiens, and held hands with a girl named Adrienne in Nahours, drinking a glass of wine with her father. He named his horse in Pommern "Quo Vadis" and used him to reenact scenes from Karl May, the beloved German writer of American-style Western novels. In Russia he jumped naked into the icy water. Then things got unpleasant. "We woke up from the dream of playing at war into the reality. Commands, orders, standstills, eyes left, eyes right, dismissed."

The CV that he later wrote up for an exhibition makes it sound as though the only thing he did during the whole war was art: diary sketches, landscape pictures, illustrations; invented scenes, real events, horses, people, caricatures, village idylls, Hungarian scenes, transferring ordnance maps onto three-dimensional sand-table models, and whittling with a pocketknife while a prisoner between May and July 1945.

He would later write to his young fiancée that he was rarely in a bad mood. "My recipe for the war is: whistle a tune whenever you get sad." He must have had a lot of opportunities to whistle. There was a period when no one wanted to be in the same regiment as him because he was always the only surviving soldier from his last regiment.

He never spoke of the horrors—only dreamed about them. Well into the 1950s he would scream in his sleep at night, according to our mother. Later, in a letter to us children, he would write that he was not allowed to yell at the guys in the mine, even when he got angry at them: "If I did, they'd report me for rudeness, which they call bad personnel management now and really frown on. Nowadays they want only good personnel management. I can understand that—good personnel management is actually a beautiful thing. When I was still a soldier, I always craved some decent personnel management, but it wasn't in fashion at the time. On the contrary. We had to yell and scream if we wanted to impress our superiors—whoever screamed the loudest was automatically the best. You can see from this how attitudes change over time."

After a few months in an American prisoner-of-war camp, he returned home and started to study mining in Aachen. It was a booming industry after the war: the mines smoked and reeked, and "everyone was clamoring for coal," as he wrote in 1950. The miners were the heroes of the postwar period—they provided warmth for the freezing Germans—and they were thanked with the annual Ruhr theater festival in Recklinghausen. Our parents would see many plays there over the years.

It was backbreaking work under ground: dirty, hot, and dangerous. "The mine shaft is the dairy cow of the place," he wrote about his first workplace in Altenbögge, "except that it's sometimes not quite as docile." He would often experience just how hard it was to control this wild cow. "Sometimes I feel like the annoyances never stop." There were explosions in the pit, or water would flood in; he often had to spend all night in the mine. But the worst was bringing dead bodies up out of the pit. He attended many funerals. Once, when Martin wrote from boarding school for our father's birthday, he wished him three cheers: "once for luck in the mine, once for a very happy day, and third, most important, that you stay healthy."

Still, maybe because of the danger, he found the work

"The Mine," Gerd Kippenberger

fascinating. "It's important to be possessed in a way by your job." Our father, as a young man, discovered in mining "all the oppositions and dualities of life itself": cruelty and solidarity, friendship and backstabbing, crudity and humor, tradition and innovation. At a time when the Ruhr region was officially ashamed of being the Ruhr (it would later call itself "Rustia," punning on "Russia," in a self-deprecating publicity campaign that was heavily criticized), he saw the beauty in the ugliness: the austerity of the industrial architecture, the coexistence of shafthead frames and meadows, and especially the people— the workers' direct and natural ways, their warmth and humor and pride. In the Ruhr region, he would later write, he, the Siegerlander, found his second homeland.

27

He had barely started his first job, in Dortmund, when our oldest sister, Babs, was born: July 28, 1950. "Barbara" was what most miners named their firstborn daughters, after their patron saint.

Mining turned out to be a feudal world. "We live on Mine Street, the royal road of Altenbögge, so to speak," our father recorded. "The senior officials—the highest caste in the place—live there, so we are only tolerated and suffered." But soon he himself belonged to that highest caste: he was made director of the Katharina Elisabeth Mine in Essen-Frillendorf in 1958 and given a giant house as a residence, with a huge garden, tended by gardeners. Sometimes our father had a chauffeur, Uncle Duvendach, who took trips with us.

But no sooner had he arrived in Essen than the great crisis in the mining industry began, as did worrying, anxiety, and fear for his job. "Now we need to get tough," he wrote in September 1963 to friends in Munich. "The coal crisis continues, and whoever doesn't go along (with the crisis) gets fired. Whoever fires the most people is the champion marksman." His mine was shut down too; he was transferred to a desk job and eventually let go. In September 1972, just back from vacation, he got the news: "early retirement," at fifty-one. A few months later, just days before Christmas, he had a heart attack. Only after several frustrating attempts to secure a foothold in the construction industry—likewise in crisis—did he find another position: as a manager at a plastic tubing company in Mülheim.

His fascination with mining and its traditions only grew in this period. He continued to do research, reading books on mining's history and practice in other countries. When he died, he was buried in his miner's tunic, meant for special occasions—the same one he had married our mother in.

He could be crude as well as charming and tended to find

the shortest path from one social blunder to the next. He loved provocation and making fun of people. Once, introducing our sister Bine's boyfriend—a mining engineer like him—to some colleagues in Aachen, he did not say the young man's name, which he had probably already forgotten. He said, "Here's the kid who wants to be my son-in-law." It was a test, and Andreas passed it. Our father said what he thought, loud and clear, and also what he knew: for example, that there were safety problems down in the mine because the wooden supports for the shaft, from a company executive's forest, were rotten. That got him into a lot of trouble. Still, he didn't go as far as his son would later; he also paid court to his superiors. As he wrote to our mother once: "I think Mrs. Wussow [a friend] is right after all: I'm a revolutionary, but only in secret—someone who never makes the move."

He was an exotic species in a conservative world, along with his whole family and their lifestyle. A "rare bird," as they say. Our parents' friend Ulla Hurck said that "he made the sober mining folks uneasy—he was a shock for them." In a children's story that he wrote for us, where he is recognizably the father, he is the only one not to laugh at the child who wanted a skating rink in the middle of summer. "He knew how much it hurt to be laughed at."

"If he had not been the company director at the Katharina Mines, he would certainly have been a painter," a newspaper wrote in an article about our father's exhibition at the House of the Open Door in Frillendorf in 1960, one of the many exhibitions that he organized himself as a member of the artists' society. He showed landscapes and city views, and his art, according to the newspaper critic, was "a beautiful, free expression of modern creativity."

He usually painted on vacation and signed his pictures "kip." But he didn't need a canvas to make art. In the 1960s,

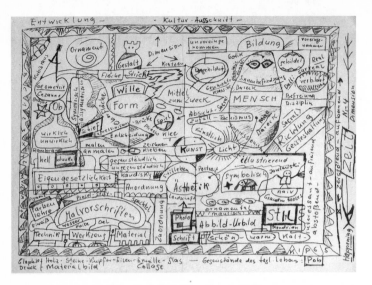

"Diagram," Gerd Kippenberger, 1965

the era of Pop Art, he made constructions from flotsam and jetsam he found on the beach, painted picture books for his grandchildren, built brightly colored wooden cities, and threw parties. He laid out gardens, first in Frillendorf and then, in his second life (for there would be another wife and more children), in Marl. There he bought an allotment, where he built hills, a frog pond, and a trellis for grapevines. He planted blackberries, raspberries, and blueberries. He named the path that the bushes were on "Blackcurrant Way" and placed his wooden figures everywhere as a special kind of scarecrow: The Passionate Lover, The Blue Angel, St. Francis of Assisi, The Market Lady with Sagging Breasts.

He wrote books about his travels, our house, the neighbors, parties, the Siegerland area, and his early years. The worse the crisis in the mining industry became, the more he clung to his private life. The stories were not invented, but he did fictionalize the truth, exaggerating, distorting, and embellishing. His brother called him a "magical realist." The world was a stage in his books, and life was a play, or more specifically, a farce, with everything more comic than it actually was. He referred to himself in the third person, as "Father"; his wife was "Mother." In one of his little books, *Hike, 1963,* about a walk he took with our mother and the two oldest children, he gave the "cast" at the beginning and ended with "The End." He was everything in this theater—director, writer, star, and cameraman—except the audience. The camera was always there. Whenever we left the house, he hung the "photey" around his neck and over a belly that slowly grew fatter with the postwar economic recovery. He had no interest in taking snapshots, though—he directed us: behind this window, on that bridge, between those columns. We sisters hated it, but Martin loved it. He later turned one of these photos, where we're standing with raised arms on the front steps of our great-grandparents' little manor house, into a work of art, a postcard with the title "Hey, hey, hey, here are the Monkeys."

Every big party was planned from beginning to end, with a written program. The guests had to sing on cue. Since his first talk as a student, he had loved to give speeches entirely improvised—"I talked myself into such a state that everyone there listened, entranced." He did not need a podium to be seen, of course, or a microphone to be heard: like all the men in his family, he had an impressive voice. It grew even stronger as he became hard of hearing, like many men in his profession—it often got so loud down in the mine that you had to scream to be heard.

To make completely sure that he would get speeches for his own birthday, he assigned them himself, along with suggested topics. Our instructions, printed in the invitation, were "Our father as he really is. Only my four daughters are qualified to speak, and they are requested to please agree on the content beforehand and on who should deliver the address." The only one of his children who could have performed the task without any difficulty was Martin, but he was in Brazil at the time. Our protests meant nothing to him—he just threatened to write the speech himself. So he got what he wanted: our father as he really was.

Afterward his cousin came up to us with a serious face and a sepulchral voice: someday we would be sorry we had given such a speech. But our father—who knew he had skin cancer and not long to live—had enjoyed himself immensely.

Not even at the very end, after seven years of fierce struggle against the cancer that finally defeated him, did he give up the reins. Our father staged his own funeral. In the weeks before his death, when he could barely hold a pen any more and his handwriting was growing more and more shaky, he wrote out his stage directions: whom we should invite (and whom we should not); where the funeral meal should under no circumstances take place; that a bagpiper should play; that he should lie in state in his miner's tunic; and that his coffin should have eight handles, one for each child and stepchild. He got everything he wanted, and speeches to his taste, too.

Indecisiveness irritated him. "I'm not the type to hesitate for a long time," he wrote as a young man, before he was our father. Once, when he heard that his semester would begin later than expected, he got on the next train, stayed with his grandmother in Siegen, and rode from one mine to the next, meeting geologists and getting new ideas. When our mother once again didn't order anything to drink at a restaurant in Munich, our father later wrote, "Either she wasn't thirsty, or she was thirsty but didn't know what to do about it." Both possibilities were equally incomprehensible to him. He liked to drink—beer, wine, liquor—this last with the guys from the mine, usually. He sometimes came home a little drunk and smelling of cigarette smoke.

Even though he was an engineer, he understood nothing about technology in everyday life. Maybe he didn't want to understand. Whenever something needed fixing, the clever neighbors had to help out; when they weren't around—if the camera broke on vacation or the film projector wasn't working on Christmas—a major marital crisis ensued. He lacked both the calm and the patience to fix things. When it was time for us to set out, whether for the day or for six weeks, he got in the car and leaned on the horn, and everyone had to be ready. It didn't matter that our mother still had meals to pack, shoelaces to tie, diapers to change, or suitcases to shut—when he was determined, he was determined, and he charged ahead deaf and blind, as he himself said, unwilling to even hear whatever the various members of the family wanted or were whining about. Otherwise, he knew he would never reach his goal. And he wanted to.

When he was diagnosed with skin cancer, he was determined to live, even if it meant having an operation every week. He managed a few years more than the doctors and the statistics had allotted him. "Onward and upward!" he scribbled in a shaky hand six months before his death, adding a stick figure climbing up a flight of stairs and sinking into an armchair. He was held up as a model patient in the hospital and even gave a lecture about how to do it: how to live your life anyway.

He always moved forward, never backward, except in his memories, which were as important to him as new experiences. He preserved these memories in little books, usually illustrated and always self-published—memories of his mother, whose name he bore (she was Gertie); of his childhood, his hometown, family celebrations; of Pastor Noa, who took his own life under the Nazis. He made the most beautiful of his books out of several hundred family letters. It's not that he lived in the past, but that for him the past was the foundation of everything that came in the present. "Remember," he told me to give me courage the night before my university exams, "you're a Kippenberger!" He meant it not as a threat or a warning, but casually and naturally: nothing bad can happen to one of us! He was as proud to be a Kippenberger as he was to be a pigheaded Siegerlander, or a miner, or a father of five (and later eight) children. "One Family One Line," Martin inscribed on our father's gravestone. This is the attitude we grew up with.

Always forward, no backtracking: that was the ironclad rule of all our walks and travels. Never walk the same road twice. On the way back, we had to seek out another path, no matter how complicated or hard it was to find, or whether we would get lost. He always ran ahead, even on vacation. How was he supposed to notice when our mother clumsily stumbled and fell in Barcelona? "The husband, three steps ahead as usual, didn't even turn around." Courteous Spaniards helped her to her feet.

He rarely found downtime, as he put it, for reading— sometimes a thriller, but usually not even that. "You called it restlessness in my blood," he wrote our mother once. She was someone who, wherever she went, looked for a place to sit and read a book, while his gaze was always directed out at the landscape or the sunset. "There's probably some truth in that. Maybe I'm only running away from myself. Sometimes life is only a kind of running away, after all."

He enjoyed life, and he loved to eat—preferably big, hearty meals. Every Saturday at our house there was thick, rich soup—split pea, lentil, vegetable—because he liked it so much. After his in-laws served him half a piece of meat and counted out the potatoes for lunch, he avoided going back. He also liked to cook, for guests and on weekends, on vacation and out camping. He cooked the same way he painted: improvising, without recipes and definitely not measuring cups. And as with his painting, writing, and celebrating, it had to be big. For him, cooking was also art, though not a pure art for art's sake—the important thing was the eating, in as large a group as possible, along with wine and conversation.

"Father Kip: Leader of the Family. Mother Kip: His wife and mother of five children." So ran their descriptions in the dramatis personae of his book *Hike, 1963*. Day-to-day matters and child rearing were her responsibility. During their years in Essen he left the house at seven in the morning, came home for lunch, lay down for fifteen minutes (during which there had to be absolute silence in the house), then drank an enormous cup of tea (he allowed himself coffee only on vacation: "it gets me too excited") and left until seven at night.

He was responsible for weekends, and sunshine. Monday through Friday our mother hauled groceries home from the co-op in two giant bags, food for a large family plus guests and the help. On Saturday our father went to the market, chitchatted with the market women, tasted the cheese, bought too much of everything (and not necessarily what we needed), and was our *maître de plaisir* for the rest of the weekend. On Sunday our mother often lay in bed with a migraine, and was finally left in peace while the rest of us took a day trip.

He was constantly getting ideas. That's when our mother got scared. Ideas meant that he would suddenly turn everything upside down, redecorate the house, maybe buy some exotic birds. Just three years after we moved into the house in Essen, when our mother had taken us children away on vacation, he wrote to her that he had "girded his loins and decided to thoroughly change some things in our house (no half measures). First the dining room. Out with the piano. We found a good place for it in the large children's room (everything with Heia's agreement). The other junk is being spread around the house too. Now the furniture will stand clean and pure in the pared-down room. Some of the pictures were already taken down off the walls—now the rest. Everything has to be rethought from its foundations."

He had found new lighting for the dining room, "five simple, clear plastic tubes in a row to emphasize the length of the table and the shape of the room." Plus it was finally bright enough: "I can't stand this gloom any longer." He was looking for a carpet to tie the room together: "Colorful, but strictly vertical stripes to emphasize the lines, you know, not scitter-scatter everywhere," he told the carpet dealer.

Maybe his family was another of his "ideas." He liked the family best when it was gathered around a long table, as multitudinous and loud as possible. He sat at the head of the table, of course. We called him "Papa," but he usually signed his letters "Your Father." And then he retreated. First he would go to the wooden loft, two comfortable rooms, that he had built above the garage in the garden and named "Father's Peace." Soon he started sleeping there, too. Then he slipped even farther away, to the apartment in Marl that our mother had bought for them to share in their old age. He seemed to grow younger: he let his muttonchops and beard grow long, adopted a Caesar haircut, traded in his old Opel Captain (the biggest family sedan available at the time) for a small, sporty Opel two-door, and took a vacation, alone for the first time, to Greece, to try to find himself among the men's-only monasteries.

He had, as he put it himself, a weakness for the romantic. And for women. As was already printed in their wedding newspaper, "From Siegerlan' / He's a ladies man / And

whoever sees him can understand / He's someone *no* girl can
withstand! / When Gerd rolls his *rrrr*'s all full of charm /
Even the coldest heart gets warm."

He met Petra Biggemann in 1968, at a union dance, and
married her in 1971. She already had two young sons, Jochen
and Claus, and a third arrived in 1973: Moritz. When he told
Martin the news, Martin immediately asked to be named the
godfather. And he was.

MOM

Born February 11, 1922, she was an Aquarius and so, in her
words, prone to creative flights of fancy but without a trace of
ambition. And incapable of logical thought: "The Aquarius
thinks in zigzags."

She studied medicine during the war, in Frankfurt,
Freiburg, and Göttingen. During vacations she had to
perform her national labor service, first in a factory and later
in a military hospital. Our parents were barely engaged when
she started imagining their future life with children, calling
him "Pappes," and enthusing about the little Hansie and little
Conrad they were going to have soon. "It can be a Barbara,
too," he would throw in. She didn't want one child—she
wanted lots of children. She couldn't wait to be a mother.

She was eight years old when her mother, Paula Leverkus,
died at thirty-four. Paula had helped take care of her husband's
factory workers as a nurse and had caught tuberculosis. Our
mother had nothing except a few vague memories of her, a few
photographs and letters; she didn't miss her mother, she would
later say, since she never knew what it was like to have one.

She was not like other mothers. She couldn't cook, except
spaghetti and noodle casseroles. She never buttered our

toast. We had to pack our own knapsacks, and when we fell she would just tell us, "Go put some iodine on it." She was definitely not one of those mothers who constantly wipe their children's snotty noses and pull up their socks. Our underwear peeked out from under our clothes. She never fretted when we started to go off on our own, and we never had to call home to say we had arrived safely; she knew we would. Bad news, she liked to say, comes anyway, and soon enough. Her child rearing methods were laissez-faire, although she could be strict and sometimes even a bit hysterical. All three of them were drama queens: father, mother, and son.

Giving presents was her passion; organization was not her strong suit. She was constantly looking for her glasses, or buying Christmas presents in summer and hiding them so well that she never found them again. Cleaning was a nightmare for her and when, after a long vacation, she finally had to do it, she gave us a few coins, if we were lucky, and sent us off to the vending machines so that she could take out her bad mood on the vacuum cleaner instead of on us. In day-to-day life, keeping house oppressed her: we didn't help out enough and were too messy. "If I was your cleaning lady, I would have given notice a long time ago," she said once.

She liked to quote the English saying "My house is clean enough to be healthy and dirty enough to be happy." For one thing, she felt that cleaning—even more than cooking—was a thankless task, the results of which were obliterated swiftly and unremarked, as though it had never happened. Secondly, she felt that "maintaining cleanliness and order, if you put too much time and care into it, works against the peace and happiness of the household." So she did what absolutely had to be done, and that was more than enough. Even the laundry, which she had to haul out to dry in the yard or on the roof, would have been enough, but then there was also shopping, helping with homework, and battling our teachers.

In the only year when all five of us children passed all of our classes and moved up a grade, our father gave her a large brooch with our names on the back as a "Maternal Order of Moving Grades." He knew she had earned it. "Tell me the truth," she said to her friend Christel Hassis once, "are we all actually idiots, since our children do so badly? I always thought we were the *crème de la crème.*"

She gave us names with an eye to our future, names that could be pronounced easily in other languages and which would go well with titles of nobility. That said, she didn't raise her daughters just to get married—we should have careers first. And driver's licenses (the only one of her children who never got one was Martin). She cared more that her first son-in-law, Lars, was "a nice boy" than whether or not he had a successful career.

She wore her hair permed—sometimes even wigs, when there wasn't enough time for visits to the hairdresser—and never left the house without lipstick and pearls. Not real pearls, of course, and she especially liked that they were fake. Thanks to her high-class background and way of carrying herself, she thought, no one would ever suspect it.

After bearing five children, she had lost her slender figure and was constantly on a diet. She liked to moan and groan that she had only to eat half a praline to gain three pounds. In fact, she had probably eaten half the box, after a day of starving herself. She usually wore big dresses, brightly colored and patterned; Marimekko was her favorite brand. Her glasses and rings were large, too, and later so were her hats. Only her shoes were flat and practical.

She could lie and read in bed for hours, or in the sun on the beach for weeks. On the bookshelves was literature that hadn't been available under the Nazis, in the early series of inexpensive paperbacks published by *rororo*: Fallada, Hemingway, C. W. Ceram, Carson McCullers, Truman Capote, Harper Lee, Roald Dahl, Siegfried Lenz, Christa Wolf, Marie Luise Kaschnitz. She devoured them. When she was finished, the book would be loaned to a friend, with a letter full of commentary. She was a critical reader: not even Goethe and Schiller were safe: "Schiller's *Don Carlos* is also utterly out-of-date. . . . What bombastic nonsense!" She started an imaginary correspondence with Goethe, among other things suggesting improvements to certain lines of verse that, in her opinion, fell short of the mark.

Then her husband met Petra Biggemann and her marriage fell apart. She died her first death then, she told a friend, and mourned the love of her life. The big, loud house soon grew even quiet and emptier: Tina left to become a midwife, and Martin spent more time in bars than at home.

For decades her main occupation had been wife and mother, and now she was a divorcée. A rarity in the late sixties, especially in her circle: I was the only child in my class whose parents were divorced. She was forced to face the fact that the society she lived in was a kind of Noah's Ark: "Entrance permitted only in pairs!" Single women were not invited anywhere because they would ruin the even number of seats at the table.

She missed her old social life. Our sister Tina took a vacation to Wales once. Our mother had been to Wales too in her day. When Tina wrote home, she asked, "How many people did you meet here?! Everyone seems to know you." People meant more to her than things, our father thought: "You can talk to people, you can write to them, they let you give them things when you have too much. The danger is just that you give away too much of yourself." She made people laugh and made herself laugh, too, until tears ran down her face, especially with her female friends.

As a child she had been raised as her brothers' equal. There was no question that she would go to a real academic high school, not some girls' school home-ec nonsense. Thirty years later, she learned that the world was not as emancipated as she had thought. But she still had her family: she never broke off contact with her in-laws or with our father. She even took care of his new sons sometimes.

Then, twice, she almost really died. After a hysterectomy she had an embolism, and shortly afterward she was diagnosed with breast cancer. She took it with gallows humor, writing to Wiltrud Roser in high style, with an allusion to Schiller no less: "Grant me my wish to be your third confederate! On Tuesday I am having my right breast removed. Who would have thought! No longer full-bosomed—now half-bosomed. Warmest wishes, Your Lore." On her New Year's card, for which Martin drew an apocalyptic picture, she printed as a motto the Goethe quote *"Allen Gewalten zum Trozt sich erhalten"* (Despite all the violent forces against us, we will overcome).

Despite everything, she flourished again in the years after her divorce. By the standards of the time, she was an old woman. When she was forty-two, the photographer in a Munich photo studio told her she had so many wrinkles that there was no point in retouching the photo; besides, it would be too expensive. Our mother put a big hat on her head and sailed out into the world. "The older my mother got," Martin later said in an interview, "the more beautiful she became. She had no womb and no breasts left but grew more and more beautiful, free, and open. More open. She got so much older, and learned that she had cancer, and then suddenly: Pow! Everything opened up.... She would say, 'Come on, kids, let's go to Paris! And no squabbling about your inheritance!'"

Having left her career almost twenty years before, she started working again, as a doctor in the Gelsenkirchen public health department, and liked it very much. For years she had not driven a car—the husband was always in the driver's seat back then—but now she bought herself a Citroen 2CV, a car that at the time was driven mostly by college students. Not that she shared all their views—free love didn't interest her in the least, she categorically opposed the pill, and she often gave lectures condemning drugs after Martin started taking them. It was just that she liked the little Deux Chevaux, and it was cheap.

What was left of the family moved out of the big house into a new duplex apartment she set up. Its great luxury: floorboard heating. No more cold feet ever again!

Martin drew the change-of-address card himself and called it "Mother Kippage and Her Children," a reference to Brecht's play *Mother Courage and Her Children.* He drew himself sprawled out in an armchair, grinning and exhausted, with long hair, and our mother in a large hat, smoking a cigarette. She had started smoking, or puffing, to be exact— she never inhaled her Lord Extras.

"Money can't buy happiness, but it sure makes the sadness easier," she told a friend after she inherited money. Until then she had lived frugally, which was how she was raised and what she was used to from the war and the early postwar years. Nothing was ever thrown away, whether it was used wrapping paper, old food, or even moldy bread; as a teenager, she wore her long-dead mother's clothes, retailored; her father wore the coats of his brother who had fallen in WWI. We children had to share everything too: clothes, knapsacks, first-day-of-school candies. Martin was lucky: as the only boy, he had lederhosen of his own. Our mother adored shopping, but, as our father wrote, "She could only get really excited about affordable things."

Change-of-address card: "Mother Kippage and Her Children" (MK, 1971)

Babs said, "It's good to know that in the end she finally took taxis, stayed in good hotels, and wasn't addicted to shopping only at clearance sales. Any extra money she took in was frittered away within the family, at the city's better restaurants." This extra income was from the "Prostitute Control Board," where she filled in for a colleague. She loved it and soon knew all the women who came for checkups every week, including a grandmother. She liked talking to them, and then she again had stories to tell us. She certainly liked the prostitutes more than the teachers she had to deal with at the public health department.

Finally, she rediscovered her Spanish blood—allegedly slightly blue as well. She had always been proud of it and did in fact look slightly Latin: tall, with black hair and long, thin fingers. As early as 1954, the first time she crossed the Pyrenees, she no sooner caught sight of the customs officials than she fell under the spell of Spain's beauty, and that of its men, especially the "bold and elegant" men who fought the bulls in the ring. She, who usually kept the peace by doing whatever our father wanted, could not get enough of the bullfight and her Spanish blood surged so powerfully that at the end of the fight she almost threw her purse into the ring like the Spanish women. Only her German frugality held her back. Of all her ancestors, her favorite was Don Antonio, a nobleman who, it was said, had been forced to immigrate to Venezuela after a duel. "He was an adventurer." That was exactly why our mother loved him. "Everything that we possess of charm and generosity, our inborn kindness, that 'certain something'—it all comes from Don Antonio," she wrote. After the divorce she learned Spanish, in Malaga and at the Berlitz school in Essen; during breaks she would step out for a coffee and chat with the bums. When she traveled to Andalusia with Babs on a cheap package holiday, "she insisted on going to flamenco and bullfights and shouted *Olé!* with the Spaniards." Martin drew her in this role once, dancing flamenco-style on the table, with *OOLEE OOLEE* next to her. It was New Year's Eve, 1974.

By then she had long since had what Virginia Woolf wanted all women to have: a room of her own where she could write. After the war, she had traded her accordion for a typewriter, on which she would write her long letters. The mailman mattered more to her than the milkman.

Before long she was composing not only letters but humorous little articles, about, for example, "our beloved dust," or Tupperware parties, "happenings," visitors, teachers. Always, frugal as she was, on scrap paper: the back of junk mail, invitations, day planners, and discarded drafts. She wrote about the comic side of our life, for the *Doctor's Paper,* the *German Sunday Magazine,* the Christian *Friendly Encounter.* "The words just flow from my pen, even if it's all just mental masturbation."

From our guestbook in Zandvoort, the Netherlands

One evening in 1974, she appeared at an event of the National Association of Writer-Doctors in Göttingen. After a Beethoven performance, poems were recited, philosophical disquisitions held on "the significance of the pause," and reflections aired on "solitude." Then our mother came onstage to present her piece: "Daddy Dummy." She knew that everything she experienced could be turned into a story, and that nothing was ever so bad that it couldn't sound hilarious on paper later.

She liked that no one could boss her around. Once, at an event for the Social Democratic Party "on the position of women in the modern world," when she expressed her own opinion and was then accused by a party member of being a traitor, she said, "That's what I want to be. I'm neither 'us' nor 'them,' I want to say what I think." She never wanted to subordinate herself to a party and its pragmatic electoral politics. "What's the use of working and struggling to emancipate myself from a husband just to dance to other men's tunes? They're probably less intelligent than he was, and I don't even love them enough to forgive them when they make me mad."

All of which is not to say that she never sought others' approval. Even her advisor's praise of her dissertation made her happy: "What author would not be delighted at such a response to his or her first work?" She was livid when a story of hers wasn't printed, and was proud when *Brigitte*, Germany's largest women's magazine, solicited a piece from her: "So now I've come far enough that *they* want something from *me*, not the other way around!"

Soon she started to dream of becoming famous. In 1968, having given herself the assignment to write a book that year, she traveled to Hamburg for the twentieth anniversary of the Lutheran *Sunday Magazine*, "to put myself out there." She drank champagne to boost her spirits and fortify her self-confidence, and met accomplished writers like Ernst von Salomon and Isabella Nadolny. She made an impression, and not only because she was one of fifteen women among the two hundred guests: "I may not be so impressive by nature, and not a famous writer, but I put a wagon wheel of a hat on my head, and it worked like it always does." A few hours later, she took the train back to reality: "At home I was met with the news that Sanni had thrown up, Bettina had fainted, and the boy had gotten into trouble." Now she didn't want any more children. "From now on I will give birth only artistically."

She also wrote about her cancer, which caused quite an uproar. That wasn't done at the time—you were supposed to "bear it stoically," as the death notice would always say.

Like our father, she planned her own funeral: compiled an address list for the guests, warned us to get the cheapest coffin and not fall for any scams, since after all it would just be burned anyway, and asked to be decked with carnations, her favorite flower.

She was at the threshold of a new life phase. Her two youngest children were about to leave home—Bine was going to be a medical assistant in Munich and I was off to university in Tübingen—and she was dividing her duplex apartment to rent out a floor. The apartment was full of contractors when the call came: the accident happened during lunch hour, while our mother was coming home from the health department. In his book *Café Central,* Martin would write about how "his mother made the transition from living mother to dead mother (a truck overloaded with EuroPallets took a curve too fast and lost some of its freight, which caused my mother's death) (so she didn't have to die a slow and painful death of cancer)." She died a week later without regaining consciousness, in 1976, at age fifty-four. She was buried in Wiesbaden, where she was born, in the Leverkus family grave.

ESSEN-FRILLENDORF

We lived in Essen-Frillendorf. After our father was made director of the mine, he moved us from Dortmund into the heart of the Ruhr, right next to mines and brickworks, where we grew up among miners and laborers.

Our parents loved Anton the pitman and his curt sayings, and laughed at Jürgen von Manger, who didn't even come from the Ruhr region (like them). The people's warmth and humor, their self-confidence, ease, and readiness to help, shaped all of us. Here you didn't make a big to-do, you just did what needed doing. People were strong characters, open and very direct, always ready to laugh at themselves. No one took themselves so terribly seriously. They drank beer, told stories, made fun of each other, and accepted people as they were, faults and all. They teased with affection.

Frillendorf was a real village, with everything that entails: candy kiosk, cemetery, public primary school, village idiot, and church. But it was a village in the middle of the city, only three streetcar stops from the center of Essen. Farmer Schmidt had his farmstead right near us, and large fields lay alongside the streets.

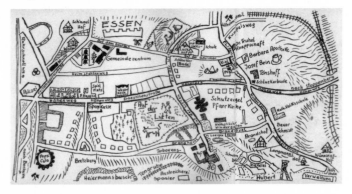

Essen-Frillendorf (Gerd Kippenberger); bottom center: Number 86, our house

A Mrs. Böhler watched over the entrance to the yard and the alley of chestnut trees that led to our house, which was at the end of a cul-de-sac. Mr. Böhler only ever appeared in the background, in his undershirt. She put her pillow in the window, rested her heavy breasts on it, and looked out at everyone, sending curses after them. There was hardly any television in those days—only three stations for a couple of hours a day—and what we had to offer was apparently more interesting to her. She shows up several times in Martin's books.

Our parents had moved often since the start of their marriage, several times in and around Dortmund during the previous few years. All five of us children were born in Dortmund and the apartments got bigger with the increasing number of children. But only now, in 1958, did they move into a house where they could really stretch out—a stage on which to perform their life. It was a paradise for us children. "A crazy house at the end of a cul-de-sac" is how the local newspaper described 86 Auf der Litten in an article about Martin when he showed his work for the first time, at eighteen years old. "The rooms and studios are stuffed full of pictures, posters, and objects. On the stairs, an outer-space hotel made of radiator parts that Martin's father put together. The chaos is welcoming, clean, and cozy. And when the sunlight plays across the garden with its naive stone sculptures of horses and cowboys, it is almost possible to believe in an ideal world again."

Or, as our mother once wrote, more soberly, "We lived in a huge house with countless rooms and just as many side rooms, nooks, and crannies. It was a nightmare for cleaning ladies—almost every time a candidate interviewed, she turned around and left. A paradise, but with its flaws: it never warmed up past sixty-three degrees, because the old heating system couldn't manage anything higher; mice would run around in the bedrooms every now and then."

There were always children running around, with bows untied and underpants slipping down—no one watched or tended them when they were playing. Life consisted of homework and playing and nothing else: no hockey practice, no saxophone lessons, no carriage rides through the city. There were a good dozen other children besides us who were always there in the yard to play. It was a life lived in public, in company. You didn't retreat into your room when you wanted to play; you went outside.

Or else to the *Kinderhaus*, or kids' house. They redid the old laundry shed in the garden for us, and for the grown-ups to use for holiday celebrations. In fact, in our family everybody had their own house: the ducks, the chickens, the pigeons, our father, and Martin, too. There was a wooden hut, the "Martin hermitage," tucked away in a little woods connected to the garden, but he rarely used it. What would he want with an isolated hut in the woods? He was never a recluse. He wanted to be with other people.

Behind our *Kinderhaus* was a playground with a slide, merry-go-round, swing, sandbox, and seesaw—all from a miners' kindergarten that had just closed. The mining crisis had already begun, and the feudal world was crumbling around us. A big slate blackboard hung on the fence, with a tree trunk in front of it as a bench—that was the school. We could sit behind the wheel of an old, brightly painted BMW and play driving. We used the nearby brickworks as a kiln for our little clay bowls and figurines. We could play croquet on the grass, hopscotch and double Dutch on the sidewalks. There was a big suitcase in the attic with costumes for dressing up.

The gigantic garden, as big as a park and surrounded by huge old trees and two little wild forests, was there to enjoy. Everything practical—vegetable garden, greenhouse—our

The Kippenberger family (Reiner Zimnik, 1961)

father tore down and then started to rebuild. So the garden filled up with bushes and trees, lilacs, goldenrain, tree of heaven, roses and sumacs, classical columns and billboard posts, a flagpole, a bathtub for cooling the drinks at parties and then the guests. More and more sculptures populated the garden: Genevieve the Pretty and others of less classical beauty—a cowboy and horse, and a hunter with dachshund, made by a retired miner who caused a sensation as an outsider artist. There was a large terrace, where later the Hollywood swing stood, and next to the old weeping willow was a lake where the ducks swam.

Other people had dogs and cats. If it were up to our mother, we would have had no animals at all—she didn't care about them, and they made extra work for her when she had

"St. Nicholas at the Kippenberger's" (Reiner Zimnik, 1961)

more than enough to do. But since it was up to our father—
who at least knew enough not to buy monkeys; if he had,
our mother threatened, she would leave him—we did have
animals: bantam chickens, goldfish, turtles, and two ducks,
Angelina and Antonius. Nobody in the family, our mother
wrote, had any more of a clue about animals than she did,
but "in place of actual knowledge they substituted enthusiasm.
The consequence for the turtles was a rapid death." The exotic
birds that our father bought all quickly died off, too. The only
animal tough enough to survive in our family was Little Hans,
the canary.

Our house was always full of children, full of pictures, full of
visitors. You were never alone. "House others happily" was the
pastor's parting advice for our parents at their wedding, but they
would have done so anyway. A year later, in Aachen, they had
cards printed up with our father's drawings to use for inviting
guests. In Frillendorf, the door was always open: whoever came,

invited or not, was welcome to sit down and join in.

There were nannies and au pairs, live-in maids and men who helped around the house (or didn't). Friends' and relatives' sons and daughters who needed a place to stay while at school or in a residency lived with us; so did various children stranded in Frillendorf. Petra Lützkendorf, the artist, brought her son Pippus to stay with us for a couple of weeks. The "Belgian fleas" spent their holidays there too: two siblings, a brother and sister, whose mother was in a psychiatric ward and whose professor father had his head in the clouds, so they were left to hop and leap over our tables, benches, and armoires at will, grabbing onto anything and everything. Pedro, the fat waiter from Martin's regular bar, lived under our roof for a while, too, since he had no place of his own. For a long while, in fact, until our mother finally threw him out.

Sigga came to stay with us from Iceland, Chantal from Belgium, and Genevieve from French Switzerland. Carolyn came from Wales for what should have been a couple of weeks, but she stayed a whole year. She was short and fat and uncomplicated, and the family chaos didn't bother her at all. We all loved Carolyn and later went to visit her in Ffestiniog; Martin stayed with her a few times.

Pelle, the student from Norway who wanted to work for a couple of weeks in Essen, was our mother's favorite. Dear, cheerful Pelle, who was training for the Olympics.

They all came and went. Only Heia and Köckel were always there: our neighbors. Without them we would have sunk into chaos, and our lives would not have functioned. Köckel fired up the old coal heater in the basement every morning and helped out whenever anything needed fixing. Energetic Heia kept things running smoothly, looked after the little ones, and kept her cool, even when her hand got caught in the blender. She roasted the meatballs and fried the potato pancakes that our mother didn't know how to cook for us, and that we used for eating contests (Bine won: she ate twelve). The kitchen was our favorite place, because, among other reasons, it was the only warm room in the whole huge house. We ate there, talked there, drew, fought, baked cookies, and did our homework, and Martin monkeyed around and imitated people.

Our father called us "the Piranha family": wherever there was something to eat, we threw ourselves at it, afraid that otherwise we would find nothing left. There were never enough treats; actually, there were sweets only when visitors brought them. But with seven family members, houseguests, and grandparents, it was almost always someone's birthday: the only day in the year when the child was in charge of who was invited, what game to play, and what food to eat. Other holidays we celebrated included Father's Day, Mother's Day, Children's Day (which our parents had introduced specially for us), the Mother-Isn't-Home Party, Confirmation Day (in "special house style"), May Day, and Summer.

Our parents were in their element as hosts: relaxed, happy, and generous. And they enjoyed themselves at least as much as their guests. "They didn't go around serving their guests," one cousin said. "They were ahead of their time that way." They just put a big pot of soup on the stove for people to serve themselves, and a hundred eggs next to the stove for them to cook on their own. After a meal our mother sometimes even pressed aprons into the hands of the astonished men so that they would help with the dishes.

On December 6, St. Nicholas came to our house in person in his fur hat and loden coat and with his golden book. For advent it was the trombone choir, and at Christmas we hosted our whole extended family, who came back again for Easter. Several hundred eggs would be painted, Father would haul

"The Kippenberger Children's Carnival," with our father as clown
(Reiner Zimnik, 1961)

them into the garden by the bucketful, and many of them would be found only weeks later, or never.

Every year there were two Carnivals, one for the children and one for the grownups. Our parents would dress as Caesar and Cleopatra, or Zeus and Helen of Troy; our mother especially liked dressing up in slutty costumes: "cheap and trashy with all my heart." "They kissed each other, loved each other, stayed in love, tragedies ensued," our father wrote. "It took three years before some people surmounted the moral crisis of our first Carnival celebration in Aachen." There was often a theme for the party, usually from a play or movie: "Greek Seeking Greekess," "Suzie Wong," "Guys and Dolls."

Even for the summer party, people dressed in costume and danced until dawn. The massive buffet was set up on a market stall—pickled eggs, cucumbers, peasant bread—and we children got to drink whatever was left in all the opened cola bottles the next morning. Every party was planned, with things to watch and things to do, from a polonaise to a pantomime show to a ride in a donkey cart. "We will expect you at 4 p.m. and assume you will stay late," read the invitation to the advent party of 1962, where more than a hundred guests spread out through the whole house and into the side houses, too, to "make, glue, decorate, bake, paint, dress, arrange, and photograph" under the direction of the master and mistress of the house, artists, and other friends. The church trombone choir appeared on the stairs. Guests were asked not to come empty-handed: "We also plan to collect clothes, toys, groceries, etc. for the elderly and needy in our community and for packages to send to the East."

Our mother said once, "No one should ever say they don't have time for Christmas preparations. I would say that they don't have the heart, or the imagination." For weeks leading up to the holiday, presents were wrapped, cookies baked, gifts put together; on the day after Christmas our mother would lie in bed, sick with exhaustion. "You love to overdo it," our father told her. "Conserving your energy is not your strong suit."

By New Year's, everybody was worn out—except our father and Martin. Our father tried his best to keep us up, he wrote, but "Mother always gets tired and then there's nothing to be done. Father is offended that no one appreciates his fireworks. Everyone's yawning or snoring." Only Martin went along with him to the neighbors next door, "since he likes dancing so much, and he's right, it's fun."

Even when they were away from home our parents threw parties, for example in Munich at the house of our uncle Hanns, the youngest of our father's three brothers. "Five Minutes Each" was the name of this party: only artist friends were invited, and "everyone is allowed to put on their own

"Easter with the Kippenbergers" (Reiner Zimnik, 1961)

show, if they want, and if they don't want to, they don't have to." One couple played guitars, a poet read, a sculptor brought out his sculptures, an illustrator told stories. The rest danced or contented themselves with being the audience.

The parties were always raucous, even when only the family members were there. In fact, those were often the loudest. No one went around on eggshells at the Kippenbergers'. "Uncle Otto made fun of Uncle Albrecht and father defended him. Then Leo was teased and Albrecht started defending him. In any case, it was all very lively." Too lively for some people. At one legendary Christmas party, when the whole extended family had come over for turkey (three turkeys, to be precise), one uncle's posh fiancée left the house in tears after a dirty joke and never returned to her intended again. Every party was a test of fortitude.

On weekends, we usually took day trips. We were dragged everywhere, to exhibitions, to Castle Benrath, to the Weseler

Forest, and to the Münster area, with its moated castles and the poet Annette von Droste-Hülshoff's Rüschhaus, which we visited again and again. Martin sought her out again later; for his 1997 sculpture exhibition, he set up a subway entrance next to the poet's sculpture.

Every year on St. Martin's Day, November 11, we traveled to Cappenberg to visit the Jansens, who also had five children. They had a big house with a fireplace and a dollhouse, and there was a lamplit procession with a real St. Martin on a real horse, which our Martin was allowed to ride, too. He was so proud of his namesake and this privilege that he was happy to share his bag of candy later. On All Saints Day we were allowed to go to the carnival in Soest with the Jansens: first came pea soup with the Sachses, then everyone got a roll of coins and could go crazy with it, and when we got lost we would be whistled back with the special family code-melody.

"St. Martin's Day Procession at the Kippenbergers'" (Reiner Zimnik, 1961)

On Pentecost we went to Siegen, to the little manor house
where our gay great-uncle lived with his Silesian housekeeper;
in early summer, it was off to Drachenfels, where the first thing
we did was have our picture taken in a photography studio—
draped on and around a donkey, or behind a cardboard cutout
of an airplane, with our arms hanging loose over the side. We
children had never been on a real plane. Then it was time
for a donkey ride or a hike on foot up the mountain, where
we stopped into a hiker's restaurant and were shoved into a
corner, since families with lots of children were considered
antisocial at the time.

All of our activities and celebrations were recorded—in
pictures, home movies, photos, and words—by our mother, our
father, and our artist friends. Petra Haselhorst-Lützkendorf,
Karin Walther, Ernst and Annemarie Graupner, Elisabeth
and Bernhard Kraus, Reiner Zimnik, Luis Delefant, Wiltrud
Roser and her sister Hildegund von Debschitz, Janosch, and
so on. Our life was turned into art. We were embroidered,
painted, sewn, woven—all hanging on our own walls. It wasn't
a matter of good likenesses, only of the idea: like Wiltrud
Roser, many of the artists didn't know us in person at all when
they received the assignment.

We look beautiful, harmonious, and cheerful in all of these
family pictures except one: the large group portrait painted
by Ilse Häfner-Mode, a small, lively woman with a pageboy
haircut and a pipe in her mouth. We had to spend hours in
her Düsseldorf studio—as tiny a room as she was a person,
though it nevertheless also served as her apartment—sitting
and standing as her models with the puppets and figurines
that populated her house. We never looked so sad in our lives.
The painting is as melancholy as all her other pictures. She
was an expressionist who had studied in Berlin in the twenties,
and a Jewish woman who had been in a concentration camp,

but that was never spoken of, only whispered. Later, after our mother's death, there was never any conflict between us siblings about our inheritance except over this one piece: Martin, who had been sent to study painting with her as a boy, absolutely wanted it at all costs.

Contemporary art wasn't something our parents bought anonymously from unknown artists—they wanted to meet the artists in person. They became friends with most of them, and most of them came to visit us. Janosch was over once as well: still young at the time, not yet famous, he bewitched us children with his magical art and sold our parents "two large oil paintings, one to Father because Mother liked it so much, and one to Mother because she wanted something to give Father for his birthday." He also made a little illustrated book, *From the Life of a Miner,* clearly based on our father.

Like many of the other artists, Janosch lived in Munich. Munich and Düsseldorf were the cities our parents visited to see exhibitions, go to plays and restaurants, see friends and relatives, and shop for art and crafts, loden coats, jewelry, pottery, furniture, and presents.

Our large house filled up. In our living room were Arne Jacobsen's "Swan" and "Egg," Braun's "Snow White's Coffin," and plastic stools from Milan that you could spin around. No wall units, no matching living room sets: individual pieces were mixed together. Our parents wanted to be surrounded by beautiful things, and what was modern was beautiful: Olivetti typewriters, Georg Jensen silverware. They were confident in their tastes, and they were right to be: things they bought at the time as avant-garde are now shown in museums as classics.

The heavy Biedermeier furniture they inherited was exiled to a room of its own that was actually never used, except when a great many people were visiting. "So fancy we are!" our father wrote. "Or at least: So uncomfortable our chairs are!" Still, our parents were thoroughly bourgeois. We all had to wear pigtails until our confirmation, except for Babs, the oldest (this was one of our father's ideas); we all had to be home in the evening precisely on time. Our mother was not conceited but she could not stand stupidity, and she also knew the limits of her own tolerance. One of her favorite movies was *Guess Who's Coming to Dinner?*, in which Spencer Tracy and Katharine Hepburn play a liberal couple who are anything but pleased when their daughter brings a black man home.

We always prayed before going to sleep and said grace before meals. "Come Lord Jesus, be our guest, / And let these gifts to us be blest"—here we clasped our hands—"*Bon appetit!* Let's all eat!" Then we threw ourselves on the food. The god we believed in was not a threatening, punishing god but a protector. Our mother believed in guardian angels, she had favorite saints (St. Anthony, finder of lost things, and St. Barbara, protector of miners), and she named her son after St. Martin, who shared what he had. Our parents' religion was a rather worldly kind: political, artistic, and, above all, social. In 1961 they founded a youth group in Frillendorf, "in a battle against Pastor B.'s pious club"; our mother helped care for the needy; our father, as a presbyter, had influence in the parish. Later he gave up his office, over an artistic argument with the church: the paraments (hangings for the pulpit, altar, and lectern) that the pastor had commissioned from one artist were opposed by the other presbyters, and "Father cannot bear intolerance." It was said of Pastor Wullenkord that he wanted to be a musician but was the son of missionaries; at Martin's baptism, in Dortmund, he spoke "more about Mozart and Goethe than about our dear Lord."

Every Christmas Eve morning, we were sent around the community to visit the old people. Our mother was glad to be rid of us during the final preparations, and the old people were glad to have someone to talk to. They told the same stories every year, mostly about their time as refugees in 1945. Every year, old Mr. Jäger told us what it was like when he and his wife had fled from East Prussia, now Poland, to Frillendorf on a horse cart. Every year, old Mrs. Haupt baked us New Year's cookies and delighted us with her humor. When her health took a turn for the worse, at over ninety years old, and she lay on the sofa moaning, "Ah! Ah! Ah!" Finally she yelled at herself, "Say *B* for once, for God's sake!"

Eventually, the house was emptier, quieter too—we were no longer children—and in 1971 we left Frillendorf and moved to a new building in Bergerhausen. Everything there was middle-class, green, and boring. "Whoever, like us, has felt true joy / Can never be unhappy again," our mother wrote in a letter to a friend. The Ruhr District as we knew it came to an end as well. "Have you been to Essen?" asked the Dannon blueberry yogurt container that Martin reproduced in *Through Puberty to Success*. "Today there is only one coal mine operating in Essen, and the derricks are almost all gone. Essen's biggest business today is retail. Essen is the Ruhr's number one shopping city. Come take a shopping trip to Essen today!"

THE KIPPENBERGER MUSEUM

Our parents were hungry when the war ended—hungry for art, too. They went to the movies, to the theater, to exhibitions, including the very first documenta. Martin later told and retold the story about our grandfather wheeling him to the show in a stroller in 1955.

"Kippenberger knew perfectly well, ever since he was a child, that pictures, as the *surrounding* for sometimes worn-out feelings, can have an immensely positive effect," Martin wrote about himself in *Café Central*. Pictures, our parents thought, make a house a home. In their wedding newspaper, our father said he wanted "pictures in all sizes and price points." Once, when they were spending a week in Munich in a hotel near the train station, they unpacked their things, stowed their suitcases, and realized that "something was missing." The pictures. The figurines. The books. "They healed the wound by using the shelf to display pictures, statues, and a tiny library." By the end of the week, the soulless hotel room looked like their own apartment.

Decades later, when our mother was very sick in the hospital, she complained, "If only it wasn't so bare in this room! No pictures, everything so insistently hygienic, all washable with disinfectants. Would a picture really mean a risk of infection? Or anything else that could give you something to look at and think constructive thoughts about?"

Our father called one of his first books—typed, illustrated, and properly bound—*The Kippenberger Museum*. Print run: one copy. The reader is led through the young couple's miniscule apartment, ten by twelve feet, as though it were an actual museum, with the sink and coffee pot and and furniture and other objects described as works of art.

Our house in Essen was as large as a villa but absolutely without ornamentation and frills—the ideal "white cube." It didn't stay white for long, though. Soon even the outside walls had paintings on them, when our father followed an artist friend's sketches and painted portraits of her figures on the walls. "The Kippenberger Museum," one of the artist friends wrote on the drawing he'd made of the pictures on our Frillendorf wall, including a picture that showed the family from behind. The walls of the high, open staircase in the middle of the house were crammed with pictures hanging right next to each other, salon style. "Images hung on the walls from the baseboard to the ceiling in our house," Martin would later say in an interview with Daniel Baumann. "Works by Beckmann, Corinth, Heckel, the German expressionists, Marino Marini, Picasso, and a lot of kitsch, too. I was faced with art on all fronts, end to end." There was Barlach, too, and Chagall, and Grosz—many artists our parents had not been allowed to see in their own youth. Still, the contemporary art in our living room was decoration more than provocation, and often more crafts than art.

HOLIDAYS

Every year our parents went on a four or five week vacation by themselves, without us. The first time, in 1953, when Martin was six months old, they took the train to Italy and stayed in a hotel. Later it was always by car, with a tent and a cooking stove. Only in the beginning did our mother hold out hope that he would take pity on her and opt for comfortable accommodations: "I'm no pioneer. I get cold too easily." But he preferred what he called the "straw sack" to normal sheets and a normal bed.

They devoured Europe. The war was over and now they could travel from the Arctic Circle to the Algarve, the west coast of Ireland to Helsinki, from Paris to Prague, the Norwegian fjords to the Hungarian plains. They drove and drove, every day somewhere else. On one trip they saw Utrecht, Amsterdam, Antwerp, Ghent, Bruges, Paris, Chartres, the Loire, Carcassone, Perpignan, Barcelona, Avignon, Bern, Freiburg, and Baden-Baden; another trip covered all of Great Britain. No sooner were they back than they sent out printed invitations for a matinee at the House of the Open

Door (a kind of village center in Frillendorf) and showed four hundred slides, together with our father's paintings, to the accompaniment of "new record purchases," such as sea shanties or Welsh miners' songs.

In Sweden they went swimming in the morning and dancing in the evening. Other people always assumed they were English, or Belgian, or even American; anything but German: they were nothing at all like the caricatures they knew from the movies. When they returned from a trip to the south and were met by a grumpy German customs official, it was like a slap in the face "after four weeks accustomed to the wonderful laissez-faire" elsewhere.

There were nannies and au pairs and neighbors and aunts to take care of us children, and we were well taken care of. When our parents came home, they spread out around the dining room everything they'd brought back, and they told us all their stories in the living room. Every trip resulted in material: for stories, for paintings, for writings. It was clear that, as our father remarked once, "they focused on people" when they traveled. The people they visited or met were more important to them than any churches and monasteries.

On school holidays we always went with our mother to Holland for as long as the vacation lasted. We had a vacation home in Zandvoort an Zee—nothing special, a modern apartment in a big apartment block with bunk beds and big windows through which you could see the ocean. After the basic furnishings were taken care of, "more pictures and more friends came with every succeeding visit: everything that makes a home homey." Petra, the artist whose portraits already decorated the outside of our Frillendorf house, painted the cupboards and the walls. We only had to cross the street and we were at the beach, where we spent the greater part of every day; when it rained, we took the train to Haarlem or

Amsterdam, to go shopping or go to the Frans Hals Museum or Rijksmuseum.

Holland was paradise for all of us. "In Zandvoort I never despaired," Martin wrote in his book *Through Puberty to Success.* Our father called Holland his third homeland. In Holland you could buy pudding in bottles and French fries from stands. Our mother once wrote her friend Christel, while we were there recovering from Christmas, that "We spend our time sleeping—til 10 a.m., with no energetic husband slash father to hustle us out of bed—and eating and reading. Now and then we play some games too": concentration, rummy, and mau-mau. She could read as much as she wanted and didn't have to cook: every night we got dinner in a big pot from the French fry stand.

Our mother settled in for six weeks at the seaside with us, our friends, and her friends; our father came on weekends in a generous mood, entertaining us with trips to the pannekuchen house, the tourist attractions in Volendam and Madurodam, or the Alkmaar cheese market. In Holland we could ride motorized scooters and jump on trampolines—children were welcome everywhere, and there were big playgrounds built for them. When we got older, we went to the flea markets and mingled with the "beatniks" on the beach.

Alone at home, our father enjoyed a bachelor's freedom. He had Heia cook for him and said "Bottoms up!" in the garden with the neighbors, feasting on cold duck, peaches in champagne, and beer. He went to the movies or the Cranger fair, hung out with friends and read thrillers. He got the playground under control with Köckel, put together his slide show, wrote talks, and redecorated the house. "There was time, time to think and time to do things."

When we drove back, we could smell, by Oberhausen at the latest, that we were almost home. Then school started up again, "the nasty thing," as our father wrote. "The boy won't do his reading, Bettina puts up a fight, and Barbara gets sick. Sometimes the other way around."

MARTIN'S CHILDHOOD

Still no boy. When Bettina was born, eleven months after Barbara, our grandfather came to the hospital, but this time he didn't bring flowers.

Then, finally, Martin arrived: on February 25, 1953, in the middle of the week. "Father," wrote the man himself,

> had just started his first job as a supervisor. He was roughly shaken awake shortly before 3 a.m. Mother jumped out of bed and her water broke as usual. The taxi came, we hurried downstairs, and Father lost his house key.
> Dr. Busse stood waiting at the hospital gate. Well, what have we here, he announced. Father told the doctor that his shift still started at 6:00. — At 4:45, the longed-for male heir appeared, with the powerful collaboration of Dr. Busse. Father showed up for his shift on time.

"We've got a boy!" Grandfather said with pride. He was the godfather, along with Martin's other grandfather. Everyone else in the family took the news more calmly. Still, mother was especially happy. She had grown up among boys, an only sister with three brothers; the one she was closest to had fallen in Stalingrad.

Our father made Martin's birth announcements himself. Our mother, to thank the doctor for not presenting her with a bill (since she was a fellow physician), gave him a poem she had written especially for him.

He was baptized Martin, but at first his only name was "Fatso." Our mother also called him "Terrier," "Mister," and "Master," but usually he was just "*Kerl*," "guy." Or "Kerly Man."

He was always something special, always different from the other boys. More imaginative, more anxious. "Seeing a mask and screaming are one and the same thing for the boy," our father wrote once. "His fear of rigid faces cannot be overcome. For months before and after Carnival, he dreams about it. We can't take him into the city for the Rose Monday parade [at Carnival] for that reason." All of big sister Babs's efforts to explain masks to him were in vain. At the same time, he loved to celebrate Carnival, dress up, and dance in the Kinderhaus. "Kerl," our father said, "dances like a young god."

Some of the other boys were afraid of him. Not physically—he was on the weak side, with "bad posture due to lack of exercise," as the doctors attested. But they were afraid of his ideas, the same way children are afraid of Grimm's fairy tales: fascinated by their fear. Tobias von Geiso, a friend the same age as Martin, says Martin's ideas were "incredible and uncanny," provocative, they made him tingle. For example, "to piss and shit in our dollhouse's chamber pot. He was always ready with something I couldn't understand." He seemed older than he was to Tobias; Tobias had the feeling of not being up to his level.

He was never short of ideas. That's why he was always invited along with me to younger children's birthday parties: to help play games. He was always good with small children. As a teenager he went to Düsseldorf on weekends to babysit. "He's great at it," our mother wrote to a friend, "Antonia says 'Martin' again and again all week." Martin's best friend was a girl, Ute Böhler, who went to school with him and lived next door. (Ute was the quiet—and, later, depressed—daughter of the same Mrs. Böhler who shows up over and over again in Martin's books as the epitome of Frillendorf.) He got along better with girls. He didn't have to act the big man with them.

He cried often, including at his confirmation—moved to tears by his own speech. The same thing had happened to our father at Babs's confirmation, which Martin had missed because he was in boarding school; our mother had described it to him: "A man isn't necessarily a weakling if he cries with emotion in an especially solemn and impressive moment."

Martin liked to annoy other people, but he himself "started to cry at the least little thing," as our mother complained. "I don't know what's going on inside that boy. He's got a long way to go." Martin is never crying in his childhood photographs, though. He grins, beams, makes faces, strikes poses. Later, though, he always remembered himself as the one who was harassed and defenseless.

He was never a good boy. We had to be home at six, and Martin was the only one who would be late, showing up whistling a happy tune half an hour late. He did what he wanted and did it emphatically, without thinking about the consequences. He could be good-natured but could just as easily be fresh—if he didn't feel like shaking a visitor's hand, he didn't do it. "He wanted to shock," says Ulla Hurck, our parents' friend. "He would look at people and see how far he could go. He did that with everyone. And we were taken in a lot of the time. I always had the feeling that he was thinking, 'God, are they stupid? Don't they realize why I'm doing this?'"

MARTIN, OUR ARTIST

He always asked for art supplies—for his birthday, for Easter, for Christmas. As soon as he could hold a pencil, he drew and painted, glued and stapled. "Nonstop," our mother wrote, "since he was never without ideas." At nine, he drew Adolf Hitler as a pitiable figure, like the one in Munch's *Scream*. At family gatherings he would pull out his pencil and draw portraits of the people there. He sold one of these pictures for ten marks.

He received what he longed for all his life: attention and recognition. Our father praised "his beautiful drawings," especially the one "of Father sitting with his thriller, you can hardly believe how good it is." Encouraged by him, Martin drew his way through the art history course that hung on our walls. But he didn't copy the pictures—he copied the styles. "Sometimes like this, sometimes like that—I imitated every style," he later told the Swiss curator Daniel Baumann. After doing so, he came to the conclusion that "it wasn't so incredible, what they'd done." Klee and Chagall failed his test; Kokoschka passed. He needed conflict with others, friction, from the beginning. When he was ten he hung a photo of one of Picasso's bull plates on an imaginary wall, drew a window next to it, and glued colorful curtains over the window.

SCHOOL

"I wasn't born to go to school," he later said. He was born to make art, and that's what he insisted on again and again, but to no avail: he passed his first test in 1959 (like every other child who could reach his arm over his head to the opposite ear) and was admitted to the Frillendorf Protestant State Primary

School. There he did what he always did: goof around. He stuck out his little leg and tripped the teacher on his first day of school. He preferred looking out the window to looking at the blackboard; what happened outside seemed to him like a movie, and he recounted it like a movie when he came home. The world seemed strange to him, strange and exciting. In *Café Central,* he describes a seaside scene from his childhood: "I still remember sitting on the edge of a grotto with my little dirty diving gear, watching the fresh fish through the diving mask clouded over with my breath, and they looked back at me the same way, and suddenly I had the impression that their eyes were actually the eyes of the sea itself."

He couldn't sit still. Rather than listen to the teacher, he filled his notebooks and textbooks with drawings and caricatures. Homework was torture for everyone involved. "Martin, pay attention!" our mother would warn, and plead, and threaten, with growing despair. "Martin, just read this!" But Martin didn't want to read. He wanted to look, listen, play, be amazed. The official diagnosis: dyslexia. "He hates books," our father wrote when Martin was thirteen. "Letters of the alphabet and sentences rub him the wrong way; he prefers picture books." But we didn't have picture books—comics weren't allowed in our house (which is not to say we never read them). And there were certainly lots of other pictures: on the walls, and on television, since eventually we, too, had a TV. *Lassie, Flipper, Fury, Bonanza, The Little Rascals,* and *I Dream of Jeannie* were our picture books. Later, on vacations, we acted out scenes with the characters, Martin out in front and our father behind the Super-8 camera.

Maybe, too, like our father, Martin just didn't have the time or patience to read. Deciphering a word letter by letter just took too long when you could take in a picture in one glance. Spoken, not written, language was his element. Even as a child he was an actor and entertainer, telling stories and doing imitations. Whoever laughed he had on his side. Miss Linden, a teacher, called him "Harlequin," but from her it wasn't a compliment.

So he used school in his own way, as a stage, a studio. A struggle began that would last his whole life: he would always be on battle footing with institutions, whether art schools, hospitals, or museums. He had something against fixed walls, narrow limits, hierarchy, and authority. He wanted to make decisions himself. He had no fear of people in power, so he got on their nerves, and they got on his case in return. He called one of his series of sculptures, all self-portraits, *Martin, into the Corner, You Should Be Ashamed of Yourself.*

His first report card could hardly have been much worse. "Participation in Class: Acceptable." Out sick this semester: twenty-three days. Scholastic results overall: "M. has made an acceptable beginning." The next semester didn't look any better. "M. will have trouble in his second year," the headmistress wrote. Only in drawing and handicrafts did he get a "Good." Everything else was "Satisfactory" or "Acceptable" except spelling, which was "Poor" (and by the third year would be "Unsatisfactory"). The drawings he filled his notebooks with didn't count for anything—his teachers cared only about the spelling mistakes. After his third year he was held back ("for health reasons," according to the report card, since his teacher had been urging our parents for a long time to send Martin to boarding school).

"If he brought home report cards as good as Mr. Kaiser and Miss Linden were trying to help him get, he would be in good shape": this was the report in St. Nicholas's golden book about whether the eight-year-old Martin had been a good boy that year. "But since he is lazy, he doesn't give anyone the pleasure of pleasing them. Like Bettina, he needs a slap on the backside now and then. Otherwise he is a good boy, he watches the workmen and gardeners working, visits the studio, and has lots of friends."

HINTERZARTEN

In October 1962, at nine and a half, Martin was sent to the Black Forest, to the "state-licensed educational home" of Tetenshof, in Hinterzarten/Titisee. He wasn't the first in the family to go to boarding school: after Babs had failed her high school entrance exam, she was sent to Bensheim, from which she would eventually be able to return to the Essen schools as a transfer student. Eventually she studied law. Tina followed Martin to boarding school the following year, as a preventative measure and to spare her the possible humiliation of failing. She stayed two years.

In Martin's estate—among kitschy postcards from Florence, childhood drawings, letters from all periods of his life, cards he received for confirmation, photographs, and tickets—there was a brochure from the Tetenshof of those days. Children frolicked, fresh-faced, pious, and in harmony with nature, between the Black Forest cabin and the Alpine pasture, the girls with blond ponytails and the boys in lederhosen shorts with a front flap (like the ones Martin himself always used to wear). Happy children among happy cows, playing ball or shoveling hay, making pastoral music on recorders and guitars, washing up (caption: "Preparing for the Inspection of the Ears"). A letter from the housemistress that Martin reprinted in *Through Puberty to Success.* said: "We still have the courage to swim against the tide of the times: no television, newspapers, cheap tabloids, sensationalism, etc., of the kind that our children are exposed to every day in city schools and public advertising. Only good books, hikes, modest celebrations that the pupils organize themselves, making music, and closeness to nature."

The boarding school included whole mountain meadows and real agricultural projects. "Inhibited children grow free and happy once again!" the brochure promised. "The work duty of 45 minutes a day is a great help toward socialization and fitting in. We have researched it as a positive factor in healing." Parents, aunts, cousins, grandmas, grandpas, and anyone else who might take it into their heads "to visit the 'poor child' away at boarding school, to take him out and spoil him," are explicitly brought back in line: just don't! Tetensdorf is not a hotel, and every visit ruins the schedule and discipline of another child. "You have no idea how much it disrupts the classroom." Such visits "are what make the child homesick, and prevent the creation of feelings of home here, which are necessary for the stay to be a success." Half the children are from broken homes, the housemistress wrote to our mother, who had apparently written asking to visit. Visits that fly by are therefore not welcome—they only cause tension. Apparently not all the parents obeyed these demands. One time, Martin wrote in a letter, a father landed on the home's meadow with a hang glider. "He wanted to see his son again, for once."

Decades later, Martin would tell Diedrich Diederichsen how he had once stood howling and crying all alone on a hill. His classmates had told on him because he had "jerked off again, until the bed shook."

Day-to-day life was strictly regimented. After the children woke up, beds were aired, teeth brushed, and shoes polished. Then came porridge for breakfast and, afterward, silent prayer. Respect, gratitude, and obedience were among the stated educational goals. "The Word of God is the foundation and guiding light of the house." Everything was so pious that the

children had to call the women who ran the school "Mother."
When Martin came home for vacations, he had a repertoire
of prayers he could say and religious songs he could sing.
Even our mother understood that all that silent prayer would
"gradually drive him up the wall."

Letters from home kept him up to date. Our mother told
her "dear boy" about Babs's confirmation in full detail, "so
that it will be almost like you were there to see it yourself." In
November 1963 our father wrote, "It's a shame you couldn't be
here, so here is a report about everything we've been doing in
the past few weeks!" Ten typed pages telling him all about what
he'd missed. There was a party for the Graupners, an artist
couple, where nowhere near all the invited guests showed up,
"only" a hundred. It started at the opening at the Schaumann
Gallery, "where Father gave a speech and everyone clapped.
It put everyone into a good mood, which was mutually
contagious, so they were enthusiastic about the paintings and
fought over who would get to buy which." Afterward everyone
came back to our studio, where our mother was waiting, "so
she only heard Father's beautiful speech secondhand. That's
too bad." One of the guests was another painter, whom they
had never heard of—"an abstract painter, wearing a shawl
instead of the tie that you would expect. Ah, artists." Our
father had set up a canvas in the studio, and every artist there
had to paint on it in oil: "They had no choice." It was, as
Thomas Wachweger would later call it, *Zwangsbeglückung*—
mandatory cheer—followed by eating, drinking, and dancing.

Then came descriptions of the All Saints fair in Soest and
St. Martin's Day at the Jensens'. He sent a carbon copy of the
same letter to Tina at boarding school, and she was furious:

Well I must say, you have a nice life! On Sunday you
go to the fair. Who has to go for a nature walk? I do!

Who goes to St. Martin's Day procession on Monday?
You!
Who has to go beddy-bye? Me!
Soon it'll go a step too far.

Everyone at home longed for Martin to return. "My dear little Kerl," our mother wrote him, "Bine and Sanni are already counting how many bedtimes they have until you're back." When he came home for the first time, at Easter break, the whole family went to meet him at the station.

He doesn't seem to have had a bad time at Tetenshof. "Martin is happily back in the whirl of things here," Mrs. Tetens wrote to Essen after the 1963 Easter vacation. "Our Kerl was glad to go back again after the holiday," our mother said in the summer of 1964, "and stuck to his opinion even though both his older sisters tried by any means possible to talk him out of it, those rascals! He is happy and in good spirits, he's not causing problems, not a crybaby anymore, and he's fitting in well." His proletariat sickness, too, seemed to have been cured by the Black Forest: in Martin's medical report of 1963, Nurse Walli attests to his "fresh, healthy appearance, bad posture, no other findings."

The most important thing, though, was that Martin had found a supporter in Tetenshof: Dr. Hans Groh, his homeroom teacher, "who has already worked wonders with our Kerl." Suddenly there was a "Very Good" on his report card, in drawing and handicrafts. For conduct, diligence, and participation he got an A–/B+. Only spelling remained merely "Satisfactory." In 1964, our mother told Martin about a letter she had received from Dr. Groh: "He wrote me to say that you're a good boy and that he's glad he can keep you for another year because he likes you so much. Make him happy by studying hard and not goofing around so much, ok?" One year later, the teacher sent our mother another letter, which Martin would later reprint in one of his first catalogs, *Mr. Kippenberger*, next to a collage he made in 1962, presumably at Tetenshof.

Groh wrote Martin a recommendation for the Odenwald School and hoped that

> I managed to pack in everything that could help Martin. He is in good spirits and looks forward to sharing a room with his cousin. If his temperament and disposition stay the same, you won't need to worry about anything. Martin has managed some good grades recently, too, so he is starting to be prouder of himself. The serious inhibitions in his artistic effort have disappeared without a trace, so that sometimes he even seems to me too mature in his pictures. Since I don't know his models—probably pictures, calendars, and books he has at home—and since I don't want to ask about them, for obvious reasons, I don't know what aspects are his own creation and what is only imitation. But if the pictures are really outgrowths of Martin himself, then it seems to me his path in life is already decided.

Martin didn't only draw, he also wrote, in fact nonstop: letters to parents, sisters, neighbors, au pairs, grandparents, aunts, friends. He wrote them on his personal stationery, which Petra, one of our parents' artist friends, had designed for him, with an illustration of Martin running with books under his arm. More often than not he drew his own pictures on the page, too—pictures of the village, pictures of skiing, self-portraits. He personalized every envelope by making a little drawing, and even the sender's name was turned into an artwork: a little house with his name as the roof. The kippenbergerization of the world had begun.

Our mother was the same way. She couldn't draw at all (just like her daughters), not even a stick figure, but she glued. All the presents she wrapped for weeks before Christmas—for friends in the East, godchildren, relatives—were decorated with little pictures: flowers, angels, and whatever else she ran across and cut out. The man at the post office drove her crazy about it: "That is NOT ALLOWED (he says). Why not??? (I ask). RULES. What rules?" She called him Fussbudget but bewitched him with words and homemade pear jelly (which no one in the family liked anyway) until he accepted the packages after all.

Martin never wrote a word about Inspections of the Ears or work duty in his letters—maybe because he knew that the people in charge of the school read them. He just wrote about slide shows and movies, games of cowboys and Indians or Lego, plays and soccer games ("We won 1-0 for us"); he wrote about another child's birthday, where he put on eight layers of clothes, one on top of another, and looked as fat as our neighbor Mrs. Böhler. In a school play, he was cast as a deaf grandmother: "I sure looked funny. Totally like Frillendorfer trash." Even if he didn't read much himself, the children were read Greek myths; in summer there was gym class in the forest, and skiing every day in the winter. "Wolf-Dieter made a real plank-salad. In real words: he broke his skis." Martin sent his skiing certificate (second prize) home so that Mother could keep it safe. One time Mr. Tetens, the housemaster, brought ice cream for everyone, as much as they wanted. "And to finish he gave orders: 'Clean the plate with your tongue!' We all cheered and started licking away like pigs."

Along with his experiences, he wrote made-up stories and illustrated them with drawings. He gave our mother an elephant story for her birthday—very dramatic, with Martin himself appearing as a character—to be continued in a week. "With five colorfull pictures and three sentimentil drawings."

He also told the story of the Kennedy assassination as a cops and robbers story and illustrated it with a coffin. He kept this letter to the end of his life and reprinted it in *Through Puberty to Success*:

> He was shot 3 times in the head. He was broght right away to the hospital. He died. The shotts came from the villa. Oswald did it. Everybody was sad. Later a nightclub owner shott im. He's in jail. – The End.
> That's what it aproximatly said in the paper.
> Your, Kerl.

"The spelling was still extremely strange, to tell you the truth," our mother said, "but the style of his letters was often amazing."

He wasn't just writing letters—he was writing them for an audience and hoping for good reviews. "I'm always very happy when someone says: 'That letter was very good.'" At the end of the letters, after "God Bless," there was usually a P.S. with his requests: for example, Babs's brown parka and the red one from Zandvoort, and three cakes and a visit from Grandma for his birthday, plus, "dear Mommy, send me sweets becuase I dont have any sweets and I have to just look wile the others eat theres."

But studying was still not his thing. Once when he was sick in bed, he decided he wanted to learn English but "I always fall asleep and dream about ice cream and marcipan." "He's a treasure," our mother said, "even if he's not a treasure who's ready for middle school."

HONNEROTH

In April 1965, Martin graduated from Tetenshof, which only went up to fifth grade. For the next three years he went to Honneroth, a boarding school near Altenkirchen in the Westerwald. The contrast could not have been greater. Honneroth had just opened, and the children lived not in the idyllic Black Forest but in what was practically a construction site. Running water was still being installed, and barracks were only gradually being replaced with real buildings. And the children were expected to do serious work to help out. There were "Work Days" instead of classes over and over again: planting trees and flowers, building huts. Afternoons were given over to "practical work," in other words, pulling weeds. "Martin took good part again in the practical work," the housemaster praised. Martin saw it otherwise: "During the practical work I sometimes have the feeling that I'm only working for Mr. Hoffmann. I've been working on the new school building for days. We clean and sweep and wipe, but always for the Hoffmanns."

Any student who talked back was "sent to jail," which meant working after school or running laps around the dining hall before class while the other students had breakfast. Our sister Bine was jealous—she would have liked to do that. She was with Martin at Honneroth for a year, one of ten girls with the seventy boys. It was an adventure for her. But she was never allowed to do laps for punishment: in the end, she was always excused from punishment because she was too nice and had too sunny a disposition. Not Martin. He got "jail" all the time (for example, when he made himself a little soup with the immersion heater) and was always being slapped. As our mother wrote: since "the missus" apparently looks funny when she's mad, "our Kerl has to laugh and then he gets even more punishment, which he doesn't seem to mind. That's how you're victimized when you have a sense of comedy."

He himself told Wiltrud Roser, "I'd really like to write a book this summer, if I can. About evil."

There was no Dr. Groh in Altenkirchen, no one who supported Martin or expected anything from him. The new housemaster's evaluation comes across as rather unfriendly: at Easter in 1966, Herr Hoffmann wrote ("not for the pupil's eyes") that "we have unfortunately not made much progress in the battle against Martin's disorderliness. He is still receiving demerits for failure to keep his notebooks clean and proper, and he continues to strew his things through all the rooms in the home." His chaos would cost him: anyone who left something lying around in the hall was penalized a dime. "Martin has to turn in the most dimes. Perhaps the parents could help by not giving Martin quite as many toys to bring along as they have done. It is also hardly possible for us to protect the sometimes very valuable toys from being used by the other students, and then Martin is often sad when this or that nice toy is damaged." But, he conceded, "In spite of Martin's disorderliness it's impossible not to like the boy for his original and cheerful sense of humor."

Martin called Honneroth "my horrorschool." "It stinks, it's so boring," he wrote to Sebastian Roser, and he looked forward to finally seeing his friend again, "doing stupid things and taking people in." Boredom tormented him constantly, and any change of scene was welcome, even in the form of Chancellor Kiesinger. Martin's report of the politician's visit in 1967 is very dramatic: a helicopter landing, lots of pushing and jostling, Martin rushing to the car and managing to shake hands with him "as he ran by." On the other hand, a visit to the circus was "Garbage. A miserable circus. The acrobats fell into the nets 3x in a row, the clowns were totally unfunny and stupid." What got on his nerves the most were the teachers who laughed anyway.

His confirmation class "makes me throw up." The best thing about it was that he could go into the city, check out shops, eat French fries and ice cream, and go to the fair. Sunday services were absolutely the only chance to get away from school. He spent the money for the church on candy. Many of the students were picked up by their parents for weekends at home, but Martin and Bine came home only on vacations. Every now and then they went to stay with Aunt Margit and Uncle Jost and their sons Micky and Pit in Siegen. When he was twelve, Martin wrote that he had smoked with Pit over the weekend, played on ditch-diggers outside, read Mickey Mouse comic books, and bought a bag of danishes that "we scarfed down with great pleasure." Then TV. One time they almost burned down our great-uncle's manor house in Weidenau.

The time of Greek myths and Christian songs was over. Painting and drawing were the only things he enjoyed. He asked for Janosch's address, and Zimnik's, and Otto Eglau's in Berlin, Clemens Pasch's in Düsseldorf—all our parents' artist friends. "What I need are skeches, beginings, scrap paper, desines. For the walls of my room and also to copy." He asked Wiltrud Roser for old sketches "even if they're just scribbles. I need models."

He griped about the boarding-school food: the horrible gruel, the "fish with old potatoes and mustard sauce: Yuck!" Even the noodle salad managed to taste bad. The thirteen-year-old Martin had only good things to say about the art teacher: "She is pretty, with long hair, beautiful legs, and a thin figure." He also pimped out his older sisters (who were not at the boarding school, needless to say), with the result that, as our mother wrote, the sisters held him in much greater esteem:

"He goes about it in real style. Brings photos of Barbara and Bettina to the older boys who seem acceptable to him; his ideas are practically genius. He recently sprayed water all over one of these boys, intending to offer him a photo of his sister to make up for it. And in fact the reparations were accepted with obvious pleasure."

In one of his letters, Martin drew himself, as he so often did, with a crew cut, big ears, and a broad smile: "Me, in a good mood."

He wrote nonstop even when there was nothing to write about, spinning his spiderweb in all directions in order to stay connected to the world. His favorite time for writing these letters was during Latin class, which he found almost unbearably boring. They read differently than the Tetenshof letters, maybe because they did not have to pass through a censor, maybe because he was older, and maybe because he was having such a bad time at this school. After a visit from our mother, she wrote, "he poured out tears when we said goodbye that went right to my heart."

He felt abandoned. "One Saturday," Hoffmann the housemaster wrote, "he had expected to be picked up by relatives and had already put on his Sunday suit for the occasion, but when they did not come, my wife suggested he change back. Martin refused these instructions and went around the rest of the day and evening in his Sunday suit."

Martin certainly got enough attention—he made sure of it by being so fresh. He got his coddling in a different way: even though his health was "thoroughly satisfactory," the housemaster wrote, "he gets himself mothered by the nurse: a prescription, or applying a band-aid." He demanded love. "St. Nicholas approaches!" he wrote in one letter, like a threat. "Write me!" was the demand underlying all his letters. "Write me already like I write to you. Pappa too please." Once he drew the whole long journey of a letter, from dropping it in the mailbox down its long route to him, where he awaited it with arms raised in delight. "Since I still havent gotten any letters or packages, I feel forced to write to you. This is already my third letter."

No matter how many letters he did get, they were never enough.

Was it really true that he—the troublemaker, the back-talker—received so much less mail at boarding school than darling Bine? Probably not, but that's how it felt to him.

In June 1966, when he was thirteen, he wrote a despairing letter that he later reprinted in *Through Puberty to Success*:

Dear Daddy, dear Mom!!
   12:31 a.m.!!
I got a postcard from you yesterday, it said "I look forward to your letter, hopefully I'm not waiting in vain." Three guesses who has been waiting for the mail here. It's been four weeks already since I've heard a peep from you. But dear little Sabina, sweet darling Sabinie gets one package after another. Every time, Mr. Hoffmann says Kippenberger Sabine has mail, nothing for you Martin I'm afraid! Try to guess how disappointed I am every time. Every time I think "tomorrow I'll get something from home!" But then it's again nothing. Finaly a card comes and I think "now I'll hear a little about what's going on at home." But no, another disapointment. But Bine, dear sweet Bine, you have a nice story to tell her, yes indeed. I'm bad, I don't get any mail. Doesn't matter. Packages are too expensive anyway. So it's better to do it "Ladies first!" and that means Bine. I don't get any news about how you're all doing, what's new in

the garden or the house? Even the weather!!!!! None of that matters, he doesn't get to hear those things only Bine. I have no one who writes to me anymore. No friend in the world.

Four weeks ago I heard from you i.e. Tina on the phone and I said you should send me and Bine a little package. But I guess you have to ask 1000x in letters first. I don't know, sometimes you only think about Bine and forgett me. Yes, yes, that's what I have to think every day. I think about you the whole time. And you? "Yes well it doesn't matter." Bine told me today that we got a Holliwood swing but Kerl doesn't need to know that. Bine gets a letter, not Kerl, Bine gets a package, not Kerl, Bine gets a second package, nothing for Kerl. I'm supposed to just sit here all by myself. So I hope you now know what I'm thinking about.

At the bottom, he drew a furious face with a telephone: "Call me please. Write me!! And send a package! If you don't I'll run away! But I probly will anyway. Your dumb Martin." In the margin, he scribbled a request to send him Aunt Ev's and great-aunt Lissy's addresses: "If you write me already I'll write back otherwise I'd rather write someone else!!!" Finally he added in the margin in small letters: "I'm gonna kick the bucket on Sunday if I havent heard anything from you by then. And if you tell me that you don't only write to darling Bine! I don't get any mail from anyone. I'm all alone here."

That same summer, he took a camping trip to Scandinavia with our parents, Tina, and Babs. In the book our father wrote about the trip, Martin is a lively child, longing to see only two things: French fry stands and toy stores. When he goes swimming he doesn't want to come out of the water, and when a lifeguard holds out a cigar box full of swimming badges he can't resist. "He is always interested in badges." He didn't let himself be led around on the vacation: "Martin demanded a plan." He took the guidebook in hand and looked for campsites "with all the amenities." When they stayed in a bed and breakfast, he entered his profession as "Student" in the guest book.

The following year, he left Honneroth. The report card was covered with "Satisfactory" and "Poor." Art: "Very Good."

The only person who didn't worry in the least about Martin's future was Martin. He knew he was an artist. At fifteen, our mother said, "he was filled with boundless optimism and saw himself already raking in the millions, he wouldn't work for less!"

ADOLESCENCE

"Honneroth," our mother summed up, "was more of a step backward for [the children] than forward. Our Kerl had a nice long nap for three years and now I'm trying to get his totally somnolent brain back into gear." When it came to school, she wouldn't succeed. He attended a private high school in Essen, where they paid just as little attention to their students as at Honneroth. After failing to pass sixth grade for a second time, he had to leave the school without graduating.

The only school he liked and did well at was Aenne Blömecke's dance school. Chubby Miss Blömecke fell prey to his charm and dancing ability, though she did occasionally admonish him, "Mr. Kippenberger, not so much shaking your behind back and forth, please." For the ball at the end of the year, he had our mother dress him up: velvet suit, tailored white shirt, giant black bow tie. "He looked like Franz Liszt, The Early Years."

At ten, along with pencils (black and colored), erasers, drawing paper, and an easel, he asked for a camera ("since Father has one too"), plus a wristwatch, long pants, and a tie. He carried the camera like our father did, proudly hanging down over his belly like a part of his clothing. "He is more vain than all four girls put together," our mother noted down when he asked for more clothes and a fancy Schmincke paint box for the next holiday.

He knew that an artist needs appropriately artistic clothes, just as an actor needs a wardrobe. So he always decked himself out for his appearances. Before embarking on his first long trip (a couple of weeks in South America at age sixteen, working his way there and back as a cabin boy), he equipped himself in Hamburg with two Hawaiian shirts, sunglasses, polo shirt, straw hat, belt, and pipe. At home, our mother loaned him her Indian shawl of brightly colored silk—out of pity, she said: "He has such a sense for beauty, color, and form, and what is he allowed to wear? Practically nothing decorative with bright, happy colors."

It turned out, though, that men's fashion was changing more quickly in those years than our mother was comfortable with. "He looks like Rasputin," she wrote when Martin was seventeen, the same year that she saw him as young Liszt. She continued, writing to her friend Wiltrud Roser:

That center part, that sheep's-wool overcoat (old Finnish military surplus, not to say *very* old, and with bullet holes in various places! or holes of some kind). He wears it night and day now, he got it for Christmas from Gerd, he said it was what he wanted most of all and we had no idea how filthy the thing was since he bought it in a store with a good reputation. Now it's even filthier, and it takes a certain social courage to show myself in public as the mother of a son in clothes and a haircut like that. Gerd's parents have already disowned him in their thoughts, totally written him off. No lack of complaints from that side too, but what can you do. Now I'll go make some dinner, since there's nothing else I can do!

He liked to wear a long bedouin robe, long hennaed hair, bright orange overalls, and red toenails. Martin's friend Hanno Huth said that Martin "was a *Gesamtkunstwerk* [a total, multimedia work of art]. He not only was loud, he looked loud too."

Now he was starting to perform the *Gesamtkunstwerk* in public, too. He had his own domain at home—a large room cut off from the rest of the house—but he was hardly ever there. Instead he was out at the Youth Cultural Center, nicknamed the KZ,* where kids met up, played go, and smoked a little pot; or at the Pop-In, a disco; and most of all at the Podium, a tiny basement bar that was the first of the many "locals" he would have in his life. He spent every evening there, literally every single evening. It opened at seven, and by six thirty at the latest Martin would be sitting on the little wall in front. Martin would later think of Manni, the owner, with his "predilection for Western-style behavior," as akin to Michel Würthle, the proprietor of the Paris Bar in Berlin.

Helge Schneider describes the Podium in his autobiography as "the only drug and jazz bar to go to" in the city. There was everything there, and lots of it: pot, LSD, and "Dutch capsules," a kind of Ecstasy, with the appropriate live music to match. Among others who played

---

* This is an outrageous nickname for the "Kulturzentrum," because "KZ" is the common abbreviation for the Nazi concentration camps ("Konzentrationslager").

there were Withüser and Westrup, "two German marijuana-folk-bards from the seventies," as the German newspaper *taz* later described them; "German dope music," another critic wrote. "Have a Joint, My Friend" was the title of one of their songs, from the album *Trips & Träume* (*Trips & Dreams*). Helge Schneider also describes seeing "a strange band" at the Podium, with "the woman playing the drums naked while the man blew into his bamboo tube. It was Limpe/Fuchs, a so-called 'free jazz formation.'" The musicians from Kraftwerk played there, too.

Essen, "the shopping city," "the Ruhr's white-collar city," had a flourishing music scene, with one of the most important pop-music venues in the country, the Gruga Hall. Everyone played there: the Beatles, the Rolling Stones, Eric Clapton, Nat King Cole, Joan Baez, Louis Armstrong, and German acts like Heintje and Willy Brandt. The rock and pop festivals there were famous nationwide, and people came from all over to see Pink Floyd, Fleetwood Mac, or Frank Zappa, to smoke their first joint, to lose their virginity. Martin saw *Hair* and *Fiddler on the Roof* there and pushed his way ahead to meet the actors at the stage door. One of the two short-lived conceptual bands he founded later, in Berlin, was called the Grugas. He painted a picture of the Gruga Hall, too, called *From Zappa to Abba*.

Martin was one of the youngest patrons of the Podium—in truth he was too young to be allowed in, but he wouldn't let that stop him. Besides, he was so entertaining. No matter what he was drinking or smoking, his friend Hanno Huth says, he had "as much of a need to communicate as ever." He also had "the all-important thing," or "the admission ticket," in Huth's words: long hair. Helge Schneider, in his autobiography, describes feelings that Martin must have shared: "Now I feel totally *groovy*, I'm a hippie. I dance by myself and throw my head back and forth, my long hair needs to fly out, far, far out!"

Martin's first public exhibition was at the Podium: *Esso S,* an oilcan made out of wood; *For the Rhine Fishermen;* and a little crab in a box of Lord cigarettes (*Krebs* in German means both "crab" and "cancer"), which he called *Oh Lord, what have you done to me.*

He had long since discovered women, and he fucked them, banged them, screwed them, nailed them—he never ran out of words for it, or of girls either, it seems. Our mother was amazed: didn't he have horrible, sweaty feet? He was obsessed with sex and apparently had it in the disco itself, at friends' houses, at whorehouses. One time, after breaking up with a girlfriend who was older than him (as they so often were in those days), he stood grinning in front of our mother and said, "You have your son back, chaste as Joseph!" "I always wished that originality was rewarded more at school," she commented. "Then our children would do a lot better."

Our mother was by no means always amused by his drifting life. They had serious fights about it all the time. Every other week he would be screaming into her face that he wanted to run away from home, but he never did it and never would. Instead, he brought home a girlfriend who had run away from her home. "There they stood at the door, St. Martin the Protector and a delicate blonde little thing, trembling like an aspen leaf, wrapped in a maxi coat." She had gotten into a fight with her mother because her mother had opened a letter from Martin addressed to her, which started with a collage that the mother found obscene, "and what Kerl wrote after the collage was even more obscene (what wouldn't a boy in puberty write who feels enlightened? Thanks a lot, Oswald Kolle!)" *

Martin held his first "happening" in the garden of our house, on a Sunday, with a hundred and fifty people invited.

---

* Oswalt Kolle was a German popularizer of information about sex; his works played a cultural role more or less analogous to *The Joy of Sex.*

"'This afternoon a few people and a great band will be coming by,' Martin announced. What came was an invasion," our mother wrote. "They camped out in little groups on the grass, like happy cows, chewing the cud and staring into space. Cows chew cud but what were they chewing? Impossible to find out and impossible to guess." From a distance (in bed with a migraine), she observed how the visitors lazily said hello to each other; to her, they all looked the same. Our father was in his element and made soup from leftovers and whatever was around ("we never had more grateful guests"). The music was loud; the neighbors complained, and the police showed up; finally a real band performed, inside the house. "At ten at night, our son told them they had to go now, his 'mommy' (he really said 'mommy' and no one thought it was ridiculous, they thought it was sweet and nice, those hippies) was sick and needed to rest. Then they went home, quiet and well behaved, or went wherever, in any case they left."

The proceedings were not always as well behaved as our mother described here. One time, when the family was away, Martin's "strange friends" (as our mother called them) showed up, all tripping on LSD. "The earth opened up at our feet, the ceiling came down and rose back up, we couldn't talk," says Hanno Huth. When a few older musicians who were even higher came by, Martin gave them a special performance: he went upstairs, shaved off part of his hair in front, pulled on a striped bathrobe with a hood, and came back downstairs with a large, marmalade-smeared knife in one hand and a candle in the other, making horrible faces. It was like a scene from a horror movie. The people there really flipped out. At that moment, Hanno Huth decided that "this was a guy you want as your friend, not your enemy."

People Martin's age both admired him and hated him for daring to do the things they were too timid to try. For having such a big mouth and so many girls, and taking hard drugs, and cutting school.

For his sixteenth birthday, Martin got a letter from our grandfather, who was also his godfather. The retired bank manager explained that you can aspire to be free and independent only on a solid foundation:

> Special talent alone is not sufficient. The effort to one day raise oneself above indolent mediocrity is inextricably bound with diligence and hard work, first and foremost with expanding one's knowledge and abilities into as many areas as possible. . . . Your parents responsible for everything, and you living idly from their efforts? You know yourself that that is not right. You bear the responsibility for your own self and no one can take that responsibility away from you. . . . I cannot personally judge your abilities in drawing and painting. The predisposition toward it is in any case inherited, and comes at no charge, for which I hope you are grateful. But it is no less certain that it is not enough to build a life upon.

Discipline, order, and hygiene ("of body and soul") are what it means to grow up, he wrote. "You must fight with all your strength to subdue yourself and any temptations that come at you from without."

And since he hadn't graduated high school, Martin should at least learn a respectable trade. So, under pressure from our parents, he applied to the Böhmer shoe store, which rejected him as an apprentice window-dresser ("and may we suggest a graphic career for you, given your drawing abilities"), and to the Boecker clothes store, which hired him as a decorator in 1970. He entertained the family with his imitations of the end-of-summer sale, but he didn't find the course of vocational study nearly as entertaining. He cut classes, didn't go to work, promised and promised to do better in the future but then did whatever he wanted. "But at the same time, he's a total softie," our mother wrote. "When he saw how I was in real despair yesterday, he almost started crying himself and gave his word that he would finish vocational school." In the end, Martin proved to be incompatible with women's outerwear, and shortly after this touching scene he quit anyway.

He was more interested in getting out and seeing the world. He traveled to Wales for the first time at fifteen, to visit our former au pair. At sixteen he took a ship to Brazil, sharing a cabin with a friend. It wasn't a pleasure cruise—they worked on board, with Martin as cabin boy. "That meant I could have some of whatever the captain was having: chicken, sausage, potatoes, the best cuts." After work, at night, he plunged into the swimming pool. "I hope he won't go to any negro whorehouses or other dens of iniquity," our mother wrote when he left. "I don't even want to think about the dangers lurking in every corner, but they do need to leave home sometime." She was right to be worried—in Brazil he did in fact go to a "negro whorehouse" and had his money stolen there, too. But she'd known for a long time by then that you couldn't stop Martin from doing what he wanted.

Most of his trips produced more bad news than happy postcards: from England, for example, the telegram "Money stolen." He was seventeen. Our mother wanted to send him more money but then changed her mind and sent these words instead: "Work, maybe a harvest-time job, be patient. Mother." It was hard for her to be firm with him, and she consoled herself "by buying a dress, on clearance, 25 marks." The girls he borrowed money from in England came to Zandvoort to get it back from our mother, and they liked it there so much that they stayed and had a little holiday with us. When Martin finally came back to Zandvoort, he kept Wiltrud Roser up all night telling her about what had happened, furiously repeating over and over again, "Work, child!" He could not comprehend how his own mother could leave him in the lurch like that.

Most of the time, though, no matter how annoyed she was, she gave in in the end. Once, when she went to the airport to meet him, furious about something he had done, he just came up to her with outspread arms: *Mommy, you're here, my darling mommy!* "What was I supposed to do?" She took him in her arms and laughed. He attacked her with her own weapons. ("From my darling mother my cheerful disposition and fondness for telling stories.") Whenever he needed money, he had only to make her laugh. Even when she was lying in the hospital, sick with cancer, he entertained her and her friends.

The low point came in 1971, the year our father remarried and we moved out of our house in Frillendorf. Martin ended up in the hospital with drug poisoning. He had, our mother wrote, "taken LSD on three consecutive days and various other things too. Then he collapsed." The psychologist told her "what I knew myself, that he is insanely sensitive."

Discharged from the hospital, he went back "to his drug den" that same night. So he was sent to Norway, to our dear friend Pelle, with the hope that the trip would cure him. Instead, as he put it, he shared with a girl "his free time, conversations, and her gonorrhea." He traveled on, but tourism bored him: he didn't care about the midnight sun; Stavanger seemed just like Recklinghausen in the Ruhr; the airport looked like barracks on a golf course. He fought off boredom by working in a photo shop and took pictures himself of whatever there was to see: birch trees, fjords, wood, more wood. Finally he left for Stockholm, a wild city. A poem came out of it later: "In Stockholm I took speed / Cigarettes I didn't need." He bummed around.

Eventually the German embassy sent us a telegram saying that he was begging at their doorstep for his parents to please send money. Our father went and fetched him home.

Martin turned eighteen. That year, the first newspaper article about him appeared, in *NRZ,* the local paper. It described him, his art, and his friends Birgit and Willi, with whom he had mounted a group show at the Podium. A photograph shows the three of them with their artworks, in our garden, with the caption "And Venus has a hole in her head" (referring to a sculpture in our garden).

Martin works "on the side" as a decorator, while Birgit and Willi are studying graphic arts at the Folkwang School. They live day-to-day—which doesn't mean that they're beatniks. "Beatniks," Martin protests, "are the people in the city who play their bongos and guitars, and usually just stare into space." No, they're not dropouts, these three. They want to "live life to the fullest" (that phrase is their magic formula) and then turn their experiences into art together. Without needing to follow a career, if possible.

Martin already had two movie projects in mind: one to restore the honor of the typical German, and a grotesque *Easy Rider*-style movie. "It's enough for us when we see that we've made progress every day and are always learning something new," Martin told the reporter.

Our mother wrote to a friend, "We've made it through three bad years, which was almost too much for the boy. He loved and respected his father very much, and his world collapsed [when his father left]. He took refuge in drugs, even morphine, and by late 1971 I had truly given up hope. But then the miracle happened and he pulled himself together."

CHAPTER TWO

HAMBURG

It's a commune and that means communication.

— MK

Martin didn't choose Hamburg at all—our mother and our uncle Erich did.

"The only thing that helps with Martin is prayer," our mother once wrote. She said she felt like "a chicken that had hatched a duck, and now is clucking anxiously on the shore while the duck happily paddles around in the pond." Martin himself never worried that he hadn't finished high school, that he'd ditched his job, that he took drugs. He knew he was an artist!

But this time, in 1971, when our mother took him to the hospital in Essen—maybe he really had taken too much, maybe it was just a particularly histrionic acid trip, maybe our mother simply didn't know what else to do—he ended up in a large hall in the men's ward where most of the patients were old, coughing miners. He felt pushed aside and abandoned. In any case, he told Hans Meister it was a traumatic experience. Meister was one of the founding members of Release, the "Association for the Struggle against the Narcotics Threat": the first self-help group that aimed, with the support of the Hamburg city government, to wean addicts from hard drugs by using softer ones. Martin described Hans Meister in a letter to our mother: "Hans, formerly an assistant window-dresser, four years morphine, shot heroin, founder, married, to Vaveka the Swede, two kids, responsible for drug advice, repairs, interviews, makes music and sound pieces." Our mother had begged her brother Erich, a banker in Hamburg, for help with Martin, and he had found out about Release. They signed Martin up and he agreed to go.

Via Hamburg, Martin ended up at Otterndorf (near Bremerhaven), where the Association had a commune in the countryside. It was a huge farmhouse with a converted barn where Martin, as he wrote to our sister Tina, "could relax after that whole screw-bang-nail-fuck-do it-screw it thing in Stockholm." There he could do what he wanted to do: make art.

Martin played the drums and danced, and at Release you could drum on pots and pans for three days straight if that's what you needed to do. He jumped over a dike naked, long hair flying, and used the photo for a poster fifteen years later ("The Battle against Bedsores"). Most of all, he painted. There was a studio for radio plays and music in Otterndorf, and the artist Hermann Prigann had a space "where they painted like crazy," Hans Meister recalled. Martin even dyed his underwear "in every color," which was the fashion at the time, and he learned how to enlarge photographs and sew on a sewing machine.

He had a remarkable talent for making himself at home immediately wherever he was. As soon as he got to Otterndorf he felt better: "accepted, not abandoned," as Meister put it. "He realized he wasn't crazy, he had just had visions on acid that he couldn't explain." There, sympathy was based on mutual understanding. He had a new family. That's what the commune was: a kind of extended family, with fixed rules and a daily schedule, including cooking and eating meals together. For the first and last time in his life, Martin stuck to a healthy diet. He was so enthusiastic that he even thought the macrobiotic food tasted good.

"It's a commune and that means communication," he wrote euphorically to our mother after two weeks. "It's going brilliantly! The day before yesterday I built myself a bed as well as a table and much more! My pad is slowly getting homey." The table stood by the window with a view of the landscape, cows, and clotheslines. Eighteen people lived there, and Martin described every one in his letter:

> Wastel, 6 yrs old, going to school. Anna, 3, wants to be Winnetou!* Holm, 25, nine years on heroin, been here two months, they got him out of the insane asylum, officially labeled "a serious threat to public safety," very nice and totally normal and very smart!!! Uwe, 23, five years on heroin! Just done with withdrawl, still gets seizures, colapses a lot! And finally: Martin, 18, going to AofA (Academy of Fine Arts) in the fall! Me!!

He added his requests in a P.S., just as he had done from boarding school: "I need sheets, lots of stamps, pocket money, Plaka paints from my room, and my big phone book!"

He had pulled it off: been accepted to study art at the Hamburg Academy of Art without a diploma, with only a portfolio and talent (something possible only after the changes of the sixties). He would have to take a preliminary class first, and then he could enroll in the summer of 1972.

Martin stayed with Release in Otterndorf for six months, maybe as long as nine months, then moved to central Hamburg. There was always something happening there; visitors from everywhere showed up constantly, and he met Gil Funccius, a graphic artist ten years older than him who had just moved

---

* The Native American hero in several of Karl May's enormously popular Western novels.

from Berlin to Hamburg "to do something social." But she soon found the group at Release too alternative and their constant discussions too self-flagellating, so she spent most of her time with "Kippi," as everyone called him back then, "because that was the most fun. Kippi knew how to go out, how to get out of obligations, too." As Martin would later write in *Through Puberty to Success,* Gil "was the very only one at Release who allowed herself not to suggest me on the message board in the kitchen that had topics to discuss at night sitting in a circle in the attic after two joints ('Tell us about your problems!')."

A lot of people were always roaming around, just like the hippies in our Frillendorf garden. Then again, there were repeated conflicts at Release, "highs and lows that everyone always has to discuss!" as Martin wrote to our mother.

> Because we're living in a collective, that's exactly why we're criticized more, and I'm trying to figure out the reasons for lots of things! In the past few days I've gone into myself amazingly sharply. Over the weekend I saw the core of the problems in my brain, and it was almost too much for me! Sometimes I'm afraid I'll flip out!

Martin was always on the move, "always had to put on some show or another": set up a tea-room, swim across the Alster River, change apartments.

Our father was enthusiastic, in any case. "That's great, everything you guys are doing!" he wrote to Martin in Otterndorf in the summer of 1971. "I wish I could join in, building and woodworking and painting and all that. That's what I've always done. When I was just 18 like you, I painted the insides of all the barracks in bright colors." Did they have pillows and a sewing machine in Otterndorf? "The ladies could sew something like that very well." He would get Martin some brightly colored fabric on clearance. Maybe they could start a whole production line.

Later, when Martin was working on his idea for a tea-room, in 1972, our father gushed: "That idea might have come from me, if it hadn't come from you!" He went on and on about Japanese ladles and started thinking about the tea service, never mind that they didn't have much money: "teacups are not the same as coffee cups, you know." By the next letter, he was furnishing the tea-room with armchairs, lamps, books, underground books, and magnifying glasses, and hanging pictures on the wall: they had to be "soft," like the tea. "Modern landscapes maybe. Better yet: Faces. Faces are expressive and even intellectual, so to speak. — But then something poetic, something that tells a story. Narrative has almost disappeared from painting since the Blue Rider."*

ONE OF YOU — AMONG YOU — WITH YOU

"Maaaaartin!"

Martin doesn't hear. He is racing around the garden, jumping high up in the air and having fun, almost tumbling and falling on his face. He wants to play, not listen to anybody. This Martin is tall, dark, and shaggy—a dog like a teddy bear. Ina Barfuss and Thomas Wachweger had named their giant schnauzer Martin "because it's a name you can say both forcefully and affectionately."

The garden is enormous. After the fall of the Wall in 1989,

---

* The Blue Rider (*Der Blaue Reiter*) was a Munich group of expressionist artists including Kandinsky, Jawlensky, Franz Marc, Gabriele Münter, and Paul Klee, active 1911–1914.

the artist couple moved from Berlin out to Brandenburg, into an old village inn, to retreat and recover from their excessive lifestyle. They had come to Berlin in the first place because of the other Martin: when my brother had moved from Hamburg to Berlin, he convinced them to come along, not go to New York as they had planned. He said the show was on in Berlin now. Where he was. The fact was, he didn't want to go to Berlin alone.

Thomas Wachweger knew what was what the first time he saw Martin—or rather, heard him. ("He couldn't stand me either at first," Martin later wrote in a catalog.) It was in the cafeteria of the Hamburg Academy of Art in Lerchenfeld. Even when it was full, everyone could always hear Martin— he led the conversations and was always surrounded by people. "His big mouth was his greatest weapon," Gil Funccius says, "his entree." For him, the cafeteria and the Ganz on Grindel Lane were stage, living room, and workspace in one. "Have some fun, drink some beer, meet some people": that is how his friend, fellow student, and housemate Jochen Krüger described the course of study. The academy was small and easy to get a handle on; students often met in the cafeteria for breakfast in the morning and boozed there at night too. Their meal program included beer.

"Where do you go to school? At U of Cafeteria?" was a favorite saying at the time. But it was only half true. He once got a letter from the Lübeck district court addressed to "Mr. Martin Kippenberger, Worker," and he kept the envelope until the end of his life. He was, in fact, a hard worker to the very end. He gave one of his pictures the title *Work Until Everything's Cleared Up.*

When Ina Barfuss remembers Martin, she hears four slaps so hard they sound like fireworks. They were in the same class, taught by the Vienna artist Rudolf Hausner, who painted only his so-called Adam pictures and almost never showed his face at the academy: "he would swing by once a semester, deliver some Viennese nonsense, and disappear again." He had an assistant, nicknamed Plato because of his bald head, who also didn't like showing up to class. On this particular day he was hours late, but Martin wanted to show him some work and discuss it anyway. Martin wasn't just there for fun: he really did want to learn something there, especially different techniques (lithography, etching, bookbinding—he took the most varied courses he could). So the assistant received a few thunderous slaps from his student: "Left, right, left, right, *I've been waiting for you!* It was like a movie," Barfuss recalled.

Martin "always wanted to prove that he could really do something, despite everything: *You might say I'm a do-nothing, a good-for-nothing, but I'll show you!*" He called one of his first large series of self-portraits, using photographs of himself from each year of his life to make a collection of postage stamps to mark his twenty-first birthday, *One of You – Among You – With You*: explicitly staking his claim to belong.

Ina Barfuss and Thomas Wachweger were a couple of years older than Martin. They had begun their studies in the sixties and were more experienced; they had already had some success and—this was very important to Martin—knew Sigmar Polke. They were kindred spirits: Thomas's parents were also divorced, and he had also hated school and suffered from being sent away to boarding school. "He's smart," Wachweger's father, a judge, said of Martin. "Smarter than you." In Thomas's view, Martin had above all "an extreme emotional intelligence: he could feel what was inside another person right away, and immediately imitate it."

Thomas and Ina were what they still are (and something relatively rare at the time): a stable couple. Like a little family. Other people found it bourgeois and "square," and some tried to break up their relationship, but not Martin. He sometimes told Thomas that he envied him for not having to look for a woman anymore. Martin changed girlfriends more often than sheets, which wasn't a big deal since a lot of other people were doing the same thing, but he also went to the movies and saw *Dr. Zhivago* over and over again: Wachweger says Martin was in love with Lara.

Martin forced himself on them, or at least that's how they saw it at first: that he was pushy. But then they became friends after all. They went out to bars together. Sometimes he would drop by every day, and if they weren't home he would leave a message, card, or letter. He ate at their house at least once a week and always wanted stuffed cabbage—nothing else was allowed. He usually brought someone else along with him, for instance, our father: "to show him that it is in fact possible to survive as an artist."

Together with Thomas, Ina, and Achim Duchow, he met Sigmar Polke: in Martin's view *the* great artist of the seventies. Martin often traveled from Hamburg to Düsseldorf to visit Polke and lived in the country with him in 1974: "it was very funny, lots of hippies, music, drugs, and dark beer." When Polke became a professor in Hamburg, Martin stuck by his side and once even went with Polke, Ina, Thomas, and Duchow to Berlin for a week. Polke gave him an assignment: "Take photos of drunk people." Martin later made a poster out of one picture, showing Martin with a camera in front of his belly and his pants pulled down, and Polke in the background with his pants unbuttoned. A lot of people resented Martin for working his way into the star's inner circle like that.

But at that time they still went around together—"they were unstoppable," Gil Funccius said. Beer and words flowed in torrents; Polke's sharp tongue impressed Martin. Martin's admiration for Polke's humor, irony, confidence, and artistic impudence and lack of inhibition never wavered, though he did, like many people, come to find Polke as a person more and more difficult, even vicious. Near the end of his life, some six months before he died, Martin told a friend that Hamburg in general and Polke in particular had ruined him by giving him the idea of turning his own life into art, "throwing one's physical, bodily existence onto the scales. We had to, back then, at the price of destroying ourselves." But by then, in 1996, Martin felt it was too late to change course.

ALL YOU EVER DO IT MOVE, CHILD!

Thomas Wachweger and Ina Barfuss were happy when Martin came over to visit, but they certainly never wanted to live with him. "He was too dictatorial. Everyone else had to be subordinate."

In his first years in Hamburg, he constantly moved apartments—whenever he had finally finished renovating one place, he moved on to the next. "All you ever do is move, child!" our mother wrote to him. His answer:

> To find your own milieu you need to gather a lot of different life experiences. Every apartment—every roommate—is a step in that proccess. — Whenever you realize that theres no more room to move, no way to develop, you have to move out. Every change is a new beginning, and it all ends up being a development. Progress. People don't only invest financially, its more important psychologically— thats what I'm after.

At some point he ended up in a shared apartment at Zippelhaus 3, across from the Speicherstadt warehouse district. Today the hundred-year-old office building with its magnificent art nouveau facade has been splendidly restored, and it houses "Kandinsky—Market Leading Merchandise," but at the time it was a dilapidated repurposed industrial building housing nothing but art students. "It's important for me to come into as much contact as I can with people who can take me somewhere with them, who can carry me away.... Human contacts in a limited space are advantageous, since I only need to go to the next room or the next floor and already the relationship or whatever I'm involved in takes another step forward." The good thing about the Zippelhaus apartment, for him, was that everyone there was so different, doing something different: "painting, photography, writing, filmmaking. Everyone shares their technical knowledge with everyone else."

His best friend there was Jochen Krüger, or "Joey," an art student from Bremerhaven. He was skeptical when Martin introduced himself, "with his red leather pants, red hair, and a red Coca-Cola can in front of his face." Jochen was no groupie of the type Martin was already collecting: he had no interest in laying himself at Martin's feet. He was a stubbornly independent artist, if anything rather aloof, with a dry, north-German sense of humor—just what Martin liked about him. He was one of the first artists whose work Martin showed.

Martin brought to his Zippelhaus room a professional art cabinet with drawers for graphic work, all his colored pencils, and a Rolodex where he noted down, in neat, beautiful handwriting, the addresses of all the attractive women he met. And there were many, especially tall blondes. Almost every morning, when Joey was having breakfast in the common room, "another naked young woman came gamboling out of Martin's room."

Life in the building took its easygoing course; everyone who lived there was tolerant. Noodle casserole was more or less the only thing Martin could cook, and he wasn't into washing dishes or cleaning rooms. Once, lying hungover in bed, he himself was taken aback by the chaos and mess, "which had once again reached one of its most extreme states." His room looked gruesome, our father reported after visiting him there. "And he pays 380 marks a month rent plus 50 for the telephone," our mother wrote angrily. Visits from our uncle Erich, who was supposed to keep an eye on him and who gave him the money he needed to live and work, got Martin to straighten up the place and to draw "day and night" so that he would have something to show when Erich asked "So, what have you been doing?"

The only real disruption in this idyllic student life came from without. The Schleyer kidnapping* had whipped the mood in Germany into a frenzy, and someone thought that a terrorist or terrorist-sympathizer was hidden in the house. "There was a raid," Martin said years later in an interview. "They stormed whole buildings. They showed up at the door wearing bulletproof vests, knock knock knock, I go to the door thinking the mailman's early today, you know, my sense of time, go to the door naked and open it and wham I'm up against the wall." He was in shock—the idea of being locked up in prison, of no longer being his own master, was Martin's greatest fear. So he behaved well, well enough not to cause any trouble with the police, in any case.

He drew a lot in that apartment, very precise drawings with colored pencils, working all night long for months at a time. "A perfectionist," Jochen Krüger called him—a worker. What did he draw? Himself ("I sit for portraits of myself—big freehand pencil drawings"), friends, and family.

---

* Hanns-Martin Schleyer, a former Nazi and an influential businessman in postwar West Germany, was kidnapped by the far-left Red Army Faction (RAF) and later killed, at the height of the RAF's 1977 terror campaign, known as German Autumn.

He made the wedding announcement for our sister Bettina, a double portrait of her and her husband Lars, and our father congratulated him on it: "You are definitely on the right path, not least because in everything you draw or paint you work out something that has to do with you." His style was realistic. Krüger had no patience for such fussy things, but when he told Martin about an exhibition of Blinky Palermo's in Bremerhaven, it was Martin's turn to be dismissive: "Four chalk lines in the corner, OK, OK, that's art?!"

Soon, however, drawing was not enough for Martin: it took too much time and resulted in only one picture, when he wanted to be visible, to be seen, to be everywhere. So he started copying. "He couldn't walk past a Xerox machine without sitting his naked ass on it," Ina Barfuss and Thomas Wachweger wrote. The photocopier was a brand new technology at the time and a toy that artists loved to play with. He made hundreds of address labels that he stuck up everywhere, designed postage stamps, left behind lighters with sayings of his and Jochen Krüger's in bars. He also took a lot of pictures with the new camera he had asked for as a present from the family, and one of his favorite occupations was to sit in a photo booth, alone or with other people, make funny faces, and have his picture taken. The medium fit well with his natural tempo: hundreds of pictures, just like that.

He wanted to put himself out there and get himself known, by any means necessary. "Mr. Kippenberger, since you were kind enough to leave your card in each of the three garbage bags that you placed at the emergency exit of the garage between the dates of Friday 1/11 and Sunday 1/13, we are happily in a position to convey to you our heartfelt thanks for your filthy mess," wrote the proprietors of a parking garage around the corner from Zippelhaus. "If it ever crosses your mind to leave your garbage bags in or in front of the garage again, we will pursue legal action against you." Martin would later reprint the 1974 letter in one of his books.

Warnings were always turning up: from the tax office, from the printer's. Money was always tight; his bank account was constantly overdrawn. He looked for jobs and had a special talent for "finding jobs where he didn't have to work himself to death," as Jochen Krüger recalls. He painted three hundred windows for a health insurance company, licked envelopes, set up chairs, and signed up when the labor office needed "2 Men, strong" to load trucks for seven marks an hour. Once he got a job as a bookkeeper "even though he couldn't even read his own bank statement," Jochen Krüger said. "And he charmed the ladies so much that he wasn't fired right away." Our mother, from a safe distance, was especially impressed by this job and the fact that, as he reported, he washed, shaved, and shined his shoes for it every day. ("Next thing you know I'll have to make him black satin sleeve protectors!") Sometimes he said yes to two jobs at the same time, so he could call in sick to one and make twice as much money.

Our mother wrote him long letters that were a mix of worrying, warnings, and declarations of love. They often got on his nerves. She reminded him to send a thank-you letter to his grandma ("if you don't do it now you never will") or to show up for his military service exam (even if he would never be called up, given the drug use in his past, he shouldn't get on the authorities' bad side). "Stop smoking," she warned in a letter, and included a newspaper clipping ("Did you know that every year in West Germany approximately 20,000 legs— so-called 'smoker's legs'—have to be amputated as a result of excessive nicotine use?" or "Did you know that constant exposure to loud thumping music can lead to permanent hearing loss?"). "Please go to the oral vaccination between Jan. 21 and Jan. 26, you're not vaccinated for anything." "You're a boundless egomaniac, darling, there's no one else in the world besides you who is worth your notice, including your little mother, who has spoiled you for far too long," and then underneath: "Kisses, kisses, your little mother."

She was always "terribly worried" about the "boy of my heart," as she called him in her letters. "Or maybe I should say boy of my hurt?" she wrote once, when it was going particularly badly with his teeth and he needed to have several extracted. She was also, naturally, annoyed when he called her up in the middle of the night yet again, or brought a new girlfriend along every time he visited Essen. In his early Hamburg years, his visits brought her to despair—hanging around, sleeping late, suddenly disappearing and just as suddenly showing up again, "blind drunk for a change and getting on my last nerve." It was a badly needed break for everyone whenever she gave him a trip to Berlin, "where he could stay with one of his countless girlfriends." Afterward, at Christmas, he would be a friendly, happy kid again.

THE GOOD COUNTERPART

Meanwhile, Martin had fallen in love, with a pretty, brash, strong, lively, and capricious woman named Inka Hocke: his first long-term relationship. According to Gil Funccius, Inka "was a calming influence"; she also "had a giant apartment she had lived in forever, while we were constantly moving." "Prewar building 4th floor nice neighborhood," as Martin summarized. They had met at a costume party at the art academy. Inka was there with her friend Meheret, an Ethiopian woman whom Martin married in 1975 so that she could stay in the country (they divorced two years later). He looked bold that night, in his leather pants, loden coat, cowboy boots, and henna-red hair. He was twenty-one, and she four years older. "Red curly hair—covered with freckles all over her body— ex-married—8 yr old daughter—good mother—part time model—not histerical—balanced + quiet—good counterpart- not pretensious, doesnt want to conquer the world" was the description he gave to friends in Berlin.

He didn't have her address, but right after the party he asked all the neighbors where the woman with the red curly hair and the child lived. He showed up while she was ironing. They talked for hours and went on a walk, and "it was actually very thrilling." It was his birthday that day, as she found out later. The next day a package came in the mail, with every sentence she had spoken written down on paper. She was won over.

From then on he was always there.

He got along wonderfully with Inka's daughter, Mimi— "they were on the same level" and they played cards and squabbled with each other. The three of them "made a family." They painted Easter eggs, cooked noodles, played Battleship. He liked that Inka made him get a haircut or take a bath; outside he was wild and crazy Kippi with a big mouth, but in private he could feel sorry for himself "and he would be pitied and taken into someone's arms. He could be a little boy." He could be childishly jealous as an artist, too: he couldn't stand it when someone else was more successful than he was. "He was always proving himself, always going full throttle," Inka says. When they went out, he would introduce her as "my girlfriend who has absolutely no interest in art."

When she told him that she didn't like his long red hair and mentioned that she liked the actor Helmut Berger, "he turned himself into Helmut Berger within two days. He was changing all the time anyway, and always looked different." He had an antique mirror behind the door in his Zippelhaus apartment, he wrote in a letter, "something I inherited, and what I see in it changes all the time and every now and then gets quite seriously on my nerves." At night he told Inka bedtime stories; during the break he went to Zandvoort with her, to show her where we had spent our school holidays; he took her to Marl to meet our father and told her that our mother had been so strict with him that she had often pinched him on the arm. When they were apart, he wrote her "moving, very loving letters." They often went for a drive in the country on weekends, "with daughter + kit + caboodle + ex-husband + holding hands," as he wrote to a friend. Even if their day trips weren't quite as idyllic as he made them out to be, Inka's home was a safe place for him. "As soon as he went out, it was a different world."

And that world was his stage. One time he went to a concert in the Market Hall with Ina Barfuss and Thomas Wachweger: a father, mother, and two sons were playing "terrible music. They acted like they were satirizing someone but they were the joke. Then Martin jumped onto the stage, danced the boogie-woogie (with the mother as well), and saved the night. The whole audience, three hundred people, went wild." When the musicians handed out autographed photographs afterward, Martin naturally signed his name too.

He was with Inka for three years, although they never officially lived together. "I go back and forth from my place to hers," he wrote to friends, "usually I work at my place and sleep there." Inka gave him the key to her apartment only when he was going to Florence and already knew that he was moving on. Inka said she had already known as much: "Martin's a wanderer." To console her, he gave her a trip to New York as a farewell present.

He himself took a major trip in 1974, to Mexico. When he died, he still had the souvenirs in his possession: sugar packets and moist towelettes from the plane, tomato-can labels with pretty girls on them, stickers showing Mexican women in folkloric costumes, a big pile of postcards, a thick plastic plaque that he must have pried loose from the airplane ("Please. Lock. Door."), and pages on local foods and drinks torn out of his guidebook: "The Mexican eating customs are a mix of pre-Columbian and Spanish traditions. The cuisine is full of flavor and dishes that are very spicy are called 'hot' even if they are served cold...." "Don't throw this away" is not only written on one of his early works from Berlin (a silkscreen print, called "colander prints" in German, that he made with a kitchen colander—"It can still be used for noodle casseroles," he added), it was clearly one of his life mottos.

He booked the trip at a student travel agency, the cheapest possible. But in Mexico City, "the trip's home base and starting point for side trips," he lived as he so often would later: "comfortably. Work space, bedroom, private bath, maid who cooks meals, straightens up, and does the laundry." He did it by borrowing money from Ralph Drochner, a friend from Essen who happened to be in Mexico at the time. He never paid it back, and Ralph was left with nothing by the end of Martin's trip.

In terms of art, Martin found the trip disappointing. "Historical museums are the only thing interesting here. Modern art hasn't really arrived yet. They crown the one modern artist they have like a king over and over again: Diego Rivera, who painted the struggling masses, liberation, and social issues in large format. The content may be right but the style is like Nazi sculptures." Despite speaking no Spanish, he got by, cracking jokes, making faces, and dancing: "Everyone likes that." Whenever anyone grumbled about his taking their photograph, he grumbled back at them in German for as long as he needed to until they stopped.

WE LIVED WHATEVER LIFE HAD TO OFFER

In December 1975, Martin moved in with Gil Funccius, his old friend from Release. Gil and her boyfriend, Tony Petersen, lived on Feldbrunnenstrasse, and a third roommate had just moved out. "The apartment is totally art nouveau (window, furniture, doors), parquet floors, 15-foot ceilings. One giant room 400 sqft & one 190 sqft. The big one will be my studio, the small one my bedroom." Just because he moved so often doesn't mean that he didn't care about where he lived: he always wanted it nice. "Kippi always hustled the best room," Gil says.

The situation went well, even if Gil's boyfriend didn't always like it. There were no big arguments: "Kippi was always very bossy, but since he could also be so adorable people forgave him." They would sit in the kitchen all afternoon long and talk for hours. "She gave me a boost and I gave her a boost," Martin wrote later.

Gil says, "Kippi brought people home, I brought people home, Tony brought people home." As was common in shared apartments, the doors were always open. Even while Martin was in the bathtub there would be guests around, drinking and talking with him and each other. If a door wasn't open, Martin just opened it, and if he found two people in bed together, all the better—Martin especially liked starting a conversation in those circumstances. At night it was time to tour the bars: the favorites were the Ganz or the Marktstube, the Madhouse for dancing, and by midnight at the latest, Hamburg's red-light district, the Reeperbahn. "We lived what life had to offer," Gil later said. "People lived without being settled." It was a time of not yet being grown up, of playing, of experimenting. Everything wasn't so serious, including art. Gil remembers it as a happy time.

In the big apartment in the old building on Feldbrunnen-strasse, Martin worked on his pictures, was photographed, and offered, as he put it, "the simplest ideas and my face as a model for record covers." He was an ideal model for Gil because "he always knew exactly what I wanted," she said; he was delighted to act out in front of the camera, striking the most varied poses. Here Martin did for the first time what he had been groping toward in our house in Essen-Frillendorf, and what he would later elevate to an official policy at Kippenberger's Office in Berlin: he turned his home into an exhibition space, an art space. Two shows took place there, both in 1977: *Chimerical Pictures,* with Ina Barfuss, Hajo Bötel, Anna Oppermann, Thomas Wachweger, and Jochen Krüger, and then *al Vostro servizio* (At Your Service), with Achim Duchow and Krüger again. They were two big parties; "Kippi invited everybody," Gil Funccius later said, "and I invited everybody, too." The drinks weren't free, though—Martin sold them. "He was always very practical about such things."

Hamburg was the right city at the right time for Martin, in the view of Gisela Stelly-Augstein, wife of the founding editor of *Der Spiegel* and a filmmaker and author herself. It was a port city, a "transit city": "Something really got started for him there. He was seeking something, and he found it, and then he really put it into practice in Berlin." She and Martin met each other near the end of his time in Hamburg. She remembers him at their first meeting as like an angel, with his long blond hair, but the occasion was earthly enough: the opening of a trendy new restaurant. Martin had come with his friend Peter Preller, an interior designer from Pöseldorf and Martin's first patron. "He arranged for a steady income for Martin," according to Martin's friend Hanno Huth.

Preller, as introverted as Martin was extroverted, was also dyslexic (as Martin was happy to learn), and Martin, this strange, loose, and spontaneous being, made an enormous impression on him. Martin was up for anything, stood outside of dogmas and norms, provoked people, and was always at the center of wherever he was. When it all got to be too much for Preller, he simply retreated for a time. Martin was no less fascinated by this successful man who took him to restaurants he could never have afforded, introduced him to people like Rudolf Augstein and Jil Sander at teas served by butlers, had a dressing room of his own filled with the finest shoes and shirts. Gisela Stelly-Augstein thinks that the relationship between the gay aesthete and his father also fascinated Martin. Preller's father worked in timber, and Preller had a dust allergy, so he had an asthma attack whenever he came near his father. "This psychodrama moved him deeply." Martin called their relationship a "dust complex" in *Through Puberty to Success* which was dedicated to his own father: "For Papa (mother complex), from whom I inherited my father complex."

On the evening Stelly-Augstein met Martin, Peter Preller introduced him to her as "very gifted," although she didn't know why. Martin had not yet started painting seriously. She met him as "someone wild and restless, seeking creative expression on all levels."

The next time she saw him it was as a fallen angel. He called her one night and wanted to meet her in a bar. That was impossible, since she had a small child, but he needed to see her, he said, so he went out to her neighborhood and when he showed up at her door, quite late, he was a mess: he had gotten into a brawl, had a cut under his eye, and had shaved off his hair. There was for it but to bandage him up. "He wanted to be under someone's wing, wanted a mother to take him in."

This destructive and self-destructive side of Martin, Gisela Stelly-Augstein says, "was the other side of the coin."

Once, after two weeks on Ibiza, he wrote, "Got myself some suntan, booze, and beatings."

They continued to use the formal pronoun with each other for a long time: "it went with his romantic ideas."* He asked if she would be opposed to his being her admirer: would that look wrong? He would write her letters, give her presents, visit her, make a little installation for her out of toys and cheap department-store kitsch.

Love and Adventure was the name of her movie, whose lead actress Martin had discovered at a flea market. He himself insisted on playing a policeman with a German shepherd. Filming with him was a lot of fun, and he entertained the whole crew over meals. Later he often visited from Berlin, sometimes overnight, and when he did "he was totally different than out in the wild world. He still talked nonstop, but he didn't have anything he was trying to prove." Her husband and Martin never exactly got along. It was Rudolf Augstein who uttered the sentence that Martin was all too happy to quote later: "Kippi can't even make himself a sandwich."

UNO DI VOI, UN TEDESCO IN FIRENZE

Martin was done with Hamburg. He went to Berlin more and more often, stopped going to class, and "just decided in 1976 to be a professional artist," according to Daniel Baumann, the curator of his major Geneva "Respective" covering the years "1997–1976."

---

* In German (like French), there are two forms of the word "you": the informal *du*, used among close friends and family or when speaking to children, and the formal *Sie*, used in public situations or with less intimate friends and colleagues. Among younger Germans, it is common to use *du* relatively quickly; here, MK maintains an old-fashioned, courtly tone.

But before he moved to Berlin, there was one more stop he had to make. In 1976 the family celebrated Christmas together at Tina's house in Chiemsee—three months after our mother had died and a month after the birth of our first niece, Lisa. Martin came with Inka and her daughter. From there he took the train to Florence.

Clearly, as a German Romantic, he had to go to Italy at some point—the home of noodles and art, of love and cinema. He wanted to stay in the Villa Romana, a German artists' residency in Florence, but they didn't accept him.

At first, Martin felt homesick and alone in Florence, and maybe abandoned as well, since our mother had died. Toward the end she had been optimistic about his future—if he was in good spirits then so was she. "He is really satisfied with himself now and I think happy too. In terms of quality, I think what he's doing is very good." Six months before her death, when she thought she had discovered a new lump in her remaining breast, she wrote to him, "I so want to live long enough to see the great artist you are becoming. But it's out of my hands."

Florence did not welcome Martin with open arms; quite the contrary. It didn't help that he didn't speak the language. "It's Monday today," he wrote in a letter, "which means *Der Stern* and *Der Spiegel* on the stands at the train station—overjoyed—something in German. I read more intensively now that I'm in Italy." Our father wrote an admonishing letter, surprised that Martin hadn't learned any Italian yet, but still wished him good luck during his stay. "In my life I myself always put more weight on work than on luck though."

The prospect of having no one to talk to but himself horrified Martin. "Searching for nothing (in particular)—looking around—drinking—keep searching, don't know for what," he wrote to our father shortly after he arrived. He found it annoying to have no schedule, no guiding thread.

In frustration he went "shopping, shopping, shopping. It's so sh---y to be alone." The Italians called him "Adolfi" since "I apparently look like Adolfi, the way they imagine Adolfi to look down here."

He would never again write as many letters as he did then. It was a mountain of letters, already practically conceptual art: one on vellum, another on postcards glued together to make a sewing pattern; one letter was three feet long. Every day he waited desperately for the mail, like an addict. He didn't like silence; peace and quiet had nothing to offer him. He wrote to Gil Funccius that he was grateful just to hear a dog bark. The card game mau-mau, his lifelong passion, was what he longed for the most: his "fantasy. Like in Mexico, when I had the shitters, when all I dreamed of was a clean toilet, a loden coat, and noodle casserole."

Florence was too much for him at first—too beautiful, too chic, too old. "Let's just say: It made me insecure." But he stuck it out and asserted himself. "I've gotten past the worst of it now": after a long, demoralizing search, he found a room in a villa away from the crowds of tourists, "very magnificent architecture: hall, foyer, another hall, with a sun porch (giant), massive wood furniture, doors, windows, guest room. Feels like a room, not an in-an-out booth." Many of the pension's guests had lived there for months, even years, and at last Martin had people to play cards with: "I love being able to cheat." He added, "The upper crust of German artists used to come and go here before the war." The writer Oriana Fallaci had lived there too, and "I read her book *Letter to an Unborn Child* in bed, everything in the book happened in that room. Live theater." There were landscapes and ancestral portraits hanging in the hallways, picturesque views out the windows (the square, the roofs, the houses, the mountains), the Boboli Gardens around the corner, and an aristocratic landlady over eighty years old.

Despite his initial disappointments, Martin turned Florence into his "happy hunting ground." First he went looking for a local bar and found the café where he would have breakfast every morning and take his many visitors. He met his landlady there: the Principessa del Mare. The café was across the street from the Palazzo Pitti and was run by two brothers, whom he soon painted. One brother always stood on the left behind the counter, the other on the right; they spoke English and a few words of German and tried to teach Martin some Italian. They also translated for him what the other regulars were saying: the sourpuss, the park warden, the former consul, the head of the Boy Scouts (no one knew if that's what he really was), all talking about kidnappings, the Communist Party, and everything else. What especially fascinated Martin was how the Italians talked with their hands and their eyes, and how fast they ordered, drank, paid, and left. And came back. "If you stay in the café you can see almost everyone come back every half hour, or at least every hour."

Martin stopped by the Villa Romana regularly, even if he hadn't been invited to stay there—it was right across from his pension. He liked the atmosphere there better than the scholarship-holders' art, though. Anna Oppermann was his favorite: "We're both from Hamburg and that's a tremendous bond." She was later one of the artists he showed on Feldbrunnenstrasse in Hamburg, in his *Chimerical Pictures* exhibition. She showed her work there as a favor to him, and he was duly grateful. She "looked a little like a witch in a gingerbread house" and "she protected me from inappropriate remarks in the Via [*sic*] Romana."

What he really wanted in Italy was to star in a movie, "but no one discovered me," even though he looked, as he himself liked to say, "like Helmut Berger in his good years." So instead he made the big move and bought turpentine and paint. "My head is giving off puffs of smoke and seeing good things," he wrote. He had been spoiled by photography, which let him shoot dozens of pictures in a few minutes, and was a little afraid of painting, but then he bought his canvases (twenty by twenty-four inches, "a transportable size—I made sure of that") and an 6'2" easel, the same height as him. He painted copies of postcards, newspaper clippings, and his own photographs and experiences. He painted his room, his ice cream parlor, his drinking buddies, the backside of the lion monument on the street where he lived, a cop-killer, his work table, the Palazzo Pitti porter, the cobbler's shop window, baked Florentines, bangers and mash, "the fixed stare unconsciously looking up at the ceiling," a retired Nazi, Tuscany, "two glowing cigarettes," a "Sicilian criminal," "3 fireflies on their way home," tourists on the bus, and his birthday cake that Gil had sent him from Hamburg in the form of a photograph. Eighty-four black-and-white paintings in three months, usually one in the morning and one in the afternoon, with his inviolable midday nap in between. They were left out to dry in the kitchen, the bedroom, and the hall. As he later put it, he painted like a musician who plays a gig every day.

He was excited about his (as he himself put it) megalomania: "My brain mass swings back and forth a little— it hums + you can hear the pure tones," he wrote to his friend Herbert Meese in Essen. "I mean things come together in my head and are already ready—not to be modest, amazing ideas.... Everything is really going to blow up!"

His project was to paint a stack of paintings as tall as he was, but he stopped a few inches short. He left the empty canvases and his towel behind in Florence. He called the series *Uno di voi, un tedesco in Firenze* (One of You, a German in Florence).

"To assert yourself," our father had written to Martin just before his tenth birthday, "means being able to influence your own life, to do some of what you want to do, what matters to you. To assert yourself also means, though, not blabbing along after whatever other people say." Behaving well may not count for much: "It's much more important to know what you're doing and why you're doing it." Florence was the turning point for Martin. He had lived abroad for the first time and would often do so again, though never again for such a long time alone. For the first time, he had really thrown himself into painting, and after nine months he returned to Hamburg as an artist, with work to exhibit too: *Adventure pictures in 6x audiovisual show, drawings, souvenirs.* For the group show he organized in October 1977 with Achim Duchow and Jochen Krüger—*On the Occasion of a Journey to Italy: There and Back*—his first ever catalog was published: *al Vostro servizio.* Print run: one hundred copies.

"I am a seeker," Martin was already saying back then, and "variety and experience" were what he sought. It was time to move on, even if he would return to Hamburg often to see friends old and new (such as Albert Oehlen and Werner Büttner, who moved from Berlin to Hamburg just when Martin was going in the other direction) and to show his work in exhibitions in the Artist House, at Fettstrasse 7a, in the World Bookstore, or in Ascan Crone's gallery. Now, though, he wanted to take the money he had inherited after our mother's death and invest it in his future in Berlin. "He gave himself two years," Jochen Krüger said, "to make his career."

The Hamburg Academy of Fine Art later claimed him as a graduate. But "as an independent artist your diploma is: to be an independent artist. Slips of paper don't mean anything," Martin had once written to our mother. "I dont have an employer like other people, or a union—someone to represent my interests. I'm on my own." In Florence he experienced for the first time what it means to be an independent artist.

Lore Leverkus and Gerd Kippenberger (in miner's tunic) on their wedding day, 1948

The Kippenbergers in Essen-Frillendorf, 1961: Bettina, Martin, Susanne, Lore, Barbara, Gerd, Sabine (l. to r.)

Martin in the *Kinderhaus* in Frillendorf

Trip to the Drachenfels: Father, Sabine, Susanne, Martin, Pippus (son of the artist Petra Lützkendorf), Mother, and two au pairs (l. to r.)

Polonaise at a summer party on the Frillendorf lawn

On the front steps of our great-grandparents' manor house in Siegen-Weidenau: Martin, Barbara, Sabine, Susanne, Bettina (bottom to top). Photo by our father, which Martin turn into a postcard in 1985: "Hey, hey, hey, here are the Monkeys."

Martin and Susanne in Amsterdam, 1964

Lore Kippenberger in the mid-1970s

Martin with his friends Birgit and Willi, in the Frillendorf yard, with the artworks they had exhibited in the Podium

Martin and our father, passport photo booth, mid-1970s. Martin used this photo as the title image of his *Homesick Highway 90* catalog

Martin with Inka Hocke, ca. 1975

Striking Poses, Feldbrunnenstrasse, Hamburg

Martin during the 1978 World Cup soccer tournament, in Kippenberger's Office, Berlin

Self-portrait from Florence, 1977

< *Uno di voi, un tedesco in Firenze*: When no one wanted to buy the series of black and white paintings in a uniform size (20" x 24") from Florence, Martin gave them to his friend Michel Würthle in exchange for lifetime free food and drink for himself and a guest at the Paris Bar in Berlin.

Tabea Blumenschein and Martin on Ulrike Ottinger's table

Martin in East Berlin, with a camera around his neck as always

"Photographed Glued Shellacked Flooring from One Week Intimate Life with the Skoda Family and Circle of Friends (1300 pieces)" (caption by Martin)

In front of S.O.36

Ratten-Jenny inside the Punk Club, Blockschock, in Berlin-Kreuzberg, 1987

"Disco-King Rolf Eden congratulates Basement-Emperor
Kippenberger on closing S.O.36" (caption by Martin)

Dialogue with the Youth: Martin in the hospital after being beaten up by Ratten-
Jenny's friends, 1979

The poster for Martin's 25th birthday was put up all over Berlin. The halo of words reads: "Squanderer – Long-time-painter – Ringleader – Host – Bringer – Introducer – Voyeur – Poser." The caption: " 1/4 Century Kippenberger / as one of you, among you, with you."

"Farewell to the Youth Bonus!" Catalog for Martin's 30th birthday. In front of the family house in Frillendorf with the four sisters in the background

CHAPTER THREE
BERLIN

Being young, being where it's at.

—MK

"This is what happened. The Russians did build a death barrier. Everyone wants to get out but they can't because there's barbed wire everywhere. And soldiers behind it. Everywhere there are watch towers with soldiers inside and they look out with binoculars to see if anyones coming. If they see anyone or any group of people they have to shoot. If they dont they are enemies of the state and are seriously punished. The highway from Hamburg to Berlin is also a border between the two zones."

At nine, two years after the Wall was built, Martin described the border and illustrated his story with a drawing of barbed wire. Now, in 1977 at age twenty-four, he was crossing that border fairly often. With one leg firmly planted in Hamburg, the other was already in West Berlin. "Everything looks kind of hopeless in Hamburg," he wrote while he was still living there. "People here repress their uncertainty too much by being cautious." There were too few friends and "communication partners" for his taste. "Part of it may be that my development involves drastic changes of direction that take me out of one circle and throw me too quickly into another."

He was ready for a wild city that was up to his own energy level. "I will do a lot and learn a lot with whatever I can do," he wrote before one of these visits. When he was lucky, Peter

Preller paid for a plane flight, sparing him the slow train connections and the border patrol's chicanery.

INTIMATE LIFE WITH THE SKODA FAMILY
AND CIRCLE OF FRIENDS

Martin quickly made himself at home in Berlin, found all the bars that you needed to know about, and connected with a family. In 1974 or 1975, on Ibiza, he had met Claudia Skoda, the designer (*"chic in Strick"* as he described her, "chic in knits"), with her army of followers. They met at Anita's Bar, "with lots of beautiful people standing around the table." Everyone went out to the beach to work on their tans, but Martin stayed behind, bone white, with hennaed hair and gaps in his teeth. He was the only one, Claudia Skoda later recalled, "who was totally dressed," in jeans, a shirt, and dress shoes, and he talked and talked "without a break," a Bacardi in one hand and a cigarette in the other. When he wasn't talking, he was taking pictures and shooting home movies.

One of the beautiful people from Anita's Bar was a design student and model named Jenny Capitain, who would later become a fashion editor. "Don't I know you from the antisocial scene in Berlin?" she asked him. It was the beginning of a lifelong friendship. Martin always admired her, calling her his "permanent fiancée."

And so he became, as he put it, a "friend of the house" at the *Fabrikneu* (Factory-New) in the Kreuzberg district of Berlin. Three couples split the rent of five hundred marks a month for the 3,750 square foot loft on Zossener Strasse: Claudia and Jürgen Skoda, Jenny Capitain and Klaus Krüger (a drummer who played with Tangerine Dream and Iggy Pop), and Angelik Riemer (an artist) and Reinhard Bock (a teacher). It was a community under one roof, at its best an extended family, with home cooking every day. "He was in the middle of things," Skoda said. "He always put himself into situations in progress." In October 1976, he built the knitwear designer a stage that he himself wanted to use too, for speeches, dancing, and slideshows. It was a photo-collage runway, his first Berlin project, and he had high hopes.

Photographed Glued Shellacked Flooring from One Week Intimate Life with the Skoda Family and Circle of Friends was his title for the twelve by one hundred and fifty foot work, shellacked with synthetic resin. He used in the piece thirteen hundred photographs that he had shot and developed himself, as Andy Warhol and Sigmar Polke had done before and Nan Goldin would do later.

The collage can be seen as a whirlwind tour of Berlin, almost like a movie: back courtyards in the Kreuzberg, Charlottenburg Park, shop windows in the city, pool halls, the Wall with its watchtowers, public toilet stalls with graffiti ("Smash the red mob!"), Woolworth's, housing developments, city highways; you ride through the streets in a double-decker bus, past beautiful women and children, dogs and dog signs ("We have to stay outside"), past Leo's Manger with its Charlottenburg pilsner, Africola, and Kassler pork chops for sale. Martin captured on film men's bathrooms, French fry stands, and ads for Milka chocolate ("I'm insanely soft!") along with life in the Fabrikneu: in the kitchen, over breakfast, in bed, with everything from the toothbrush cup to the record player. He shows up, too, looking a little like James Dean, mugging with Angelik Riemer's small son, dancing in front of the mirror, and making disrespectful faces in a gallery of modern art.

They used the runway for fashion shows and sometimes even fashion dances, with Jenny Capitain modeling, Martin filming, Klaus Krüger taking care of the music, and Ulrike Ottinger, the filmmaker, taking photographs. "Armies of fashionistas crowd into Claudia Skoda's studio on Zossener Strasse," the *Berliner Morgenpost* wrote in fall 1977:

> Latecomers get only a tiny little space on the floor. In a hot atmosphere with cosmopolitan flair, garishly made-up models move to the disco sounds. The designing trio of Claudia Skoda, Hella Utesch, and Tabea Blumenschein has come up with a myriad of ideas: There were loose-knit superwide sweaters over skintight skirts, and shining satin pants (wide tops, narrow cuffs) with pop sweaters. Whether it's suits, coats with an Indian look, or glittery knits over naked skin, you won't find anything more original in New York or Paris.

But just as the extended Skoda family looked strange on the streets of Berlin in Martin's photographs, so too the critic for the *Tagesspiegel* found it difficult to reconcile the show inside with the reality outside: "The ambitiously floral-patterned models are fascinating like pop stars from Andy Warhol movies: after the show, visitors to the Fabrikneu studio have to take a deep breath before they can face gray, everyday life again."

NO WAR ANY MORE BUT NO PEACE EITHER

Berlin was still a shabby city, not as scrubbed-clean as Hamburg. The parks were more overgrown than cultivated; the many coal stoves, in both halves of the city, made the air thick with dirt. It was a cheap city, too, a subsidized outpost of the Western democracies where alcohol and even postage stamps cost less than everywhere else. If you could get along with not much (coal heating, toilet in the hall), you could live on almost nothing. A lot of the shops in Kreuzberg stood empty; if you wanted to rent an office you could do it at any time and then move out a few months later. Many contractors, laborers, and shopkeepers had gone bankrupt in the slowdown after the Wall was built, and lots of young families had moved to the concrete housing projects on the edge of the city, or left for the West.

Berlin was a city that showed its wounds. They gaped everywhere on the streets; even in the middle of the city, there were plots of land with nothing but bombed-out ruins, still not rebuilt, and buildings were pockmarked with bullet holes. "No war any more but no peace either," it says in Martin's catalog for *Truth Is Work*.

Ulrike Ottinger, who had lived for a while in Paris and then in Konstanz, was so enraptured with this Berlin, so full of history and so different from everywhere she knew in West Germany, that she decided to shoot her films there instead of in New York as planned. In his review in *Der Spiegel* of Ottinger's movie *Portrait of an Alcoholic Woman* (a.k.a. *Ticket of No Return*), in which Martin and Tabea Blumenschein have small parts, Wolf Donner enthused about the "attractive *tristesse*" of Berlin, which reminded him of New York. He loved the "touching cross between Zille* and Las Vegas... The city of Berlin has never been shown on film as lovably and horrifyingly as in this movie."

The absurdity of the world was before Martin's eyes every day (he would later portray it in the book *Psychobuildings*, filled with his photographs of failed or otherwise mistreated

---

* Heinrich Zille (1858–1929), illustrator famous for his depictions of Berlin's working-class life, prostitutes, beggars, etc.

buildings, and add to it with "nonsense construction plans" like the "METRO-*Net*," a system of subway entrances without subways scattered around the world). Berlin was a city of dead-end streets, bridges to nowhere, and streets ending suddenly at the Wall—which should have been, as Beuys had said and Martin loved to quote, three inches higher, for aesthetic reasons.

Berlin was different. There was no closing time at the bars and no military service required of the residents—two more good reasons to move there. "It's inconceivable, what [being called up] would have meant, if I'd had to go," wrote Helge Schneider, who was in the same situation as Martin but who stayed in Mülheim and so lived in fear of the mailman for eight years. After spending years simply ignoring official, registered-mail requests to report for military examinations, as well as parental warnings, Martin could relax.

Many people who lived in the West Berlin of those days, surrounded by the Wall, remember it as an idyllic, subsidized biosphere. One of them, Annette Humpe, told Jürgen Teipel that "for me West Germany was a bourgeois mish-mash. Berlin was already all sealed up, which was a good defense against the idiotic West Germans." Attila Corbaci, from Vienna, experienced Berlin as a "blossoming ghetto": he had come to Berlin to be an actor but ended up using his talents as a waiter in the Exile, a restaurant founded by Austrians and frequented by foreign artists. "Berlin is full of people who are alive, but it's not too full," the American sculptor George Rickey remarked; he was one of the artists lured to Berlin by the DAAD (German Academic Exchange Service) Artist Program. "There are not many big cities left that are good for walking around. Berlin is one of them."

It was a time out of time, to a certain extent: after the ideological conflicts of the '68 generation and before the violent battles of the squatter scene, a relatively calm phase during which so much seemed possible. Especially in the Kreuzberg, where the Turks were opening their first grocery stores and where punks, freaks, skinheads, and artists lived in the ruins. In 1977, when Martin finally moved to Berlin, Rainer Fetting, Helmut Middendorf, Salomé, and Bernd Zimmer opened their gallery on Moritzplatz; a year later, Martin opened "Kippenberger's Office" and took over S.O.36. The German Autumn of left-wing terrorism, which Max Hetzler (later Martin's gallerist in Stuttgart, where the Baader-Meinhof group died in Stammheim prison) described as "very emotionally loaded," had relatively little effect in Berlin.

So were the late seventies in Berlin really the good old days? "It was a great time," the musician Sven-Åke Johansson said; excessive, playful, and "carefree," in gallerist Bruno Brunnet's words. "There was no AIDS; there was no tomorrow, only the night, that you could spend in Kreuzberg getting hammered for eight marks."

There was enormous freedom under the protective shadow of the Wall, and it was easy to cross boundaries. The artists didn't live in separate ghettos—with sculptors here, musicians there, and fashion designers somewhere else—but shared a common stage, as at Fabrikneu. It was a time of "genius dilettantes," as they were called in Berlin at the time: people who did whatever they wanted, not only what they were good at. It was the time of the *Gesamtkunstwerk*. Salomé and Fetting, for example, two of the painters from the Moritzplatz gallery, designed clothes and also modeled for Skoda; Ulrike Ottinger cast amateurs in her movies alongside the professionals, including Martin and several people from his circle. Her movie *Portrait of an Alcoholic Woman* (a.k.a. *Ticket of No Return*), which was a great success, included several scenes shot in Fabrikneu. Tabea Blumenschein, Ottinger's life partner and the star of many of her movies, also sang, designed clothes, posters, and book covers, and directed her own movie, *The Dollar Princess,* which Martin wrote the music for and then showed at S.O.36.

Martin, too, was in love with the beautiful actress and drinker. Were they a couple? "Oh, you know," Ulrike Ottinger said, "a couple? It was a different time." They had fun together—at a photo session in her Charlottenburg apartment, for example, where they danced to rock and roll in the studio on a giant table that also served as the dining table. "A lot of people got carried away with Kippi, with his charisma and verve," the drummer Klaus Krüger said.

It wasn't only different kinds of artists who mixed in Berlin: the boundaries between groups were more permeable then, too. Martin and his friends drank their way through the bars alongside the Wall—two bars on every corner, with tapestries of flowers and German shepherds on the wall. Martin played mau-mau, stared as the truck drivers gulped down fried eggs by the dozen, and shot photos he would later use in magazines, in catalogs, and on posters. He always had his camera with him. At this time it was much more important to him than a paintbrush, since there was so much to take pictures of, whether gravestones in the dog cemetery or German shepherds on the barroom wall.

However wild and electric it was, Martin's West Berlin was at the same time totally manageable and familiar. The artists' city was more like a village, consisting of Kreuzberg, Charlottenburg, and the stretch in between. "There were really only a few places you could go," the artist Uli Strothjohann said—the Exile, Einstein, Fofi's, the Paris Bar, Axbax, Zwiebelfisch, Gabi's Bar, the Kingdom of Saxony, the Jungle—"so you ran into each other all the time." Martin called this stretch of bars his "beaten path."

Like many others, he lived and worked in the area around Oranienplatz. The Moritzplatz with its gallery and Oranienstrasse with S.O.36 were nearby, and you ran into people over dinner at the Exile, where the poet and owner Oswald Wiener held court, read the paper, and exuded charm and poison, while his wife, Ingrid, an artist herself, stood at the stove and cooked. Bernd Zimmer, the artist, worked there as an assistant cook; Bruno Brunnet, later a gallerist, was a waiter; Dieter Roth and Joseph Beuys and Arnulf Rainer showed you what it meant to be a real artist; Fassbinder hung out there with his clique, as did Peter Stein with his own troupe (the Schaubühne theater was not far away). Alongside the young artists, you could run into their teachers: Koberling, Hödecke, and Lüpertz. The Exile was one of the few places in Berlin where you could eat well and get an espresso. "It was cozy there" in the little wood-paneled inn, says Achim Schächtele. "Everyone was surprised to see how good life could be."

DANCE HALL AND GARAGE:
KIPPENBERGER'S OFFICE

At some point Martin had had enough of life in the Fabrikneu. He wanted to be a head of household, not just a friend of the house. So, right after meeting Jenny Capitain's sister Gisela over a game of mau-mau, he asked her if she wanted to move with him into their own factory. They started looking around Kreuzberg, and the third place they saw was Max Taut's beautiful 1920s building on Segitzdamm, ready to occupy. A week later they had a lease for a whole floor, three thousand square feet "for a studio and a gallery." The rent was a big splurge for the time, fourteen hundred marks a month and another three hundred for the high heating costs. They divided the floor and the other side went to Hella Utesch (a restorer of old paintings and a fashion designer, whose "Berlin-West Leather Combine" Martin became "general sales rep" for) and Klaus Krüger (who was on the road with Iggy Pop most of the time anyway).

Martin called the place an "Office" since Andy Warhol had already taken "Factory." "I was already well known then, and could use my own name. But not as an art dealer: as something abnormal. I was really a very controversial figure in those days." Kippenberger's Office was sparsely furnished—most of the space was used for shows. Gisela and Martin each had a little cell to sleep in; Martin's bed, actually only a mattress, had a bedspread with "Without Masses Rubble" written on it. There was a small kitchen and a round Bauhaus table with a couple of Bauhaus chairs in the main room, where they ate breakfast at noon when Gisela came home from her job as an elementary school teacher in Schöneberg. Finally, a platform with a Bauhaus writing desk and an executive armchair.

Gisela Capitain remembers life with Martin as "very relaxed." They shared the housework equally: "Martin also did some shopping, and cooked breakfast, other than that we each had our own daily schedule." Of course she had to help out at the Office, folding copies of Martin's zine *sehr gut, very good,* typing up price lists, and putting up stickers in the bathrooms of local bars. At night they went out.

On May 20, 1978, at "19.30 (academic time)," the opening took place: on the program were "Aschamatta, Balkan folklore, beer, pictures, young people, and Angie with candles." The Balkan folklore was provided by Gisela Capitain's Turkish schoolgirls; Angie was a stripper although, as it turned out, she didn't want to dance at the opening. There were pretzel sticks and beer, Klaus Krüger played the drums, and Ina Barfuss and

Thomas Wachweger showed slides of their trips with Martin and Sigmar Polke.

The Office was basically a private club, according to Sven-Åke Johansson, who performed there as a musician. Martin arranged readings with Michel Würthle and Oswald Wiener, showed slides of everyday life in Berlin with his Moritzplatz colleagues Middendorf and Fetting, and screened Super-8 movies he'd brought back from New York, with accompanying music by Lydia Lunch. There were other, smaller events, too. For the 1978 soccer World Cup, which Germany would win, Martin set up two TV sets in the hall, hauled crates of Radeberger beer from the East (something not usually done at the time), laid out artificial grass on the floor, and hung team photos and newspaper headlines on the wall behind it. "Well then lads!" He had himself photographed against this backdrop with a sad expression on his face and holding a big cardboard sign: "Helmut. My Phone Number: 614 79 28." He went around the city with a patch of artificial grass and a soccer ball, posing passersby on the grass with the ball under their arms and photographing them. During the actual games, Fetting and Middendorf came by to watch, Klaus Krüger showed up, and Martin even invited his landlord, who came in gray overalls and shook hands with Martin for a picture. Might come in handy, a picture like that.

In short, the provocations which were the Office's real raison d'etre. Werner Lange wrote in the *Tagesspiegel* that

"Kippenberger's Office," on the seventh floor of a 1920s high-rise, is used as a storeroom, roller-skating rink, editorial headquarters, dance hall, and garage for mopeds, an all-purpose room so to speak, and the sharp young Mr Kippenberger is there as the all-around multipurpose manager. Now, to fill the long dreary walls of the hall with some life, he has turned it into a gallery too.

Martin did not use the Office as a painting studio, but he made it available to his artist friends at irregular intervals. Hans Bötel, for example, or Meuser with his colorful plastic panels ("Mommy take me out of the mine, I can't stand all that black anymore"), or Jochen Krüger from Hamburg with his sayings ("Hurry up, people! The concrete is coming at 12").

After two years, at the end of March 1980, Kippenberger's Office had to close. The money had run out. Hellmuth Costard, the filmmaker, took over the space and received a two hundred thousand marks as a subsidy for his movie *Kippenberger's Commentary,* which was eventually shown on German public television as *Humorlife.* Costard was supposed to pay Martin five thousand marks for the title, but he probably never did.

MONEY PLAYS NO ROLEX

He was just waiting, Johann-Karl Schmidt said—waiting for the chance to waste money on himself: "The inheritance was a great stroke of luck for him: it gave him the means to start squandering himself in Berlin." Finally he could do what he wanted, unchecked and uninhibited and with no regard to the cost. He didn't have to fritter away his time on furniture-moving jobs or beg people to buy his art supplies for him; he could hire expensive bands at S.O.36, furnish Kippenberger's Office the way he wanted, go out to eat every day (and drink, too), make his own records and produce other people's, make books, hire sign painters, shoot movies and photographs at will, risk flops, and plaster bar walls with his stickers and posters. He could stretch out and make himself known.

Our mother had died in September 1976 and it took a while before he received the inheritance (several hundred thousand marks). She had her doubts when it came to Martin's relationship with money—even as a child, his monthly allowance was spent by the first of the month, usually on candy. "Martin, he has very long hair, but money with him is rather rare," a friend of mine wrote about his teenage years, when he was constantly borrowing from friends and chance acquaintances without ever paying anything back. Our mother usually took care of it when his creditors came knocking on her door. As a last resort, he would sit on the street and beg. Money was always an issue between mother and son: he never had enough, he always (in her view) spent too much, and he inevitably charmed her into giving him more anyway.

After her death, an uncle of ours wanted Martin to receive his inheritance in installments, but in the end Martin got it all at once, and spent it all at once too. "The mother's suspicion was proven right," he would write ten years later in *Café Central,* "the darling boy couldn't handle money. And that's how it still is today: he has simply no relationship to money."

But he did invest the inheritance well, in the end—as Henri Nannen once said, "You have to throw money out the window, then it'll walk back in through the door downstairs." True, it took a long time before it started walking back in, but eventually it did, especially after his death.

His only investment that was a real mistake, and which he himself was very upset about, was Hella Utesch's Kreuzberg leather workshop, next door to Kippenberger's Office. Years later, Martin would describe the

seven employees, the Berlin-West Leather Combine, with Hopi weaves and massive purchases of leather. But the girls there only did yoga all the time instead of working. And the clothes cost 2,800 marks, absolutely no one wanted them, they didn't even fit well. Later they were sold off at a sale price of 220 marks, not even enough to cover the cost of the leather never mind the manufacture. The whole thing really ate up money.

All the money that Martin poured into Hopi weaves was thanks to our maternal great-great-grandfather. In his early years he had told a friend, "Sträßer, I'm going to get rich." And he did. Carl Friedrich Wilhelm Leverkus (1804-1889), a pharmacist's son from Wermelskirche in the Bergisches Land, founded a clan of eleven children and forty-two grandchildren, and also a thriving business. After studying chemistry and passing his apothecary exam ("1st Class"), he went to Paris, over his parents' objections, to gain practical experience. He earned a living manufacturing flashbulb powder and selling it to the Paris theaters, among other things. In 1830 he wrote to his brother Wilhelm: "Either I'll become a manufacturer and not be a pharmacist any more, or I'll do both at the same time, or I'll end up as nothing."

He followed the first path and manufactured artificial ultramarine dye, something he had learned to do in France. (The blue powder, which up until then had had to be expensively extracted from the semiprecious lapis lazuli, had been used as far back as ancient Egypt, where it decorated graves.) "A magnificent color," the mayor of Wermelskirchen enthused. It could also be used as a bleach: anything yellowish, whether fabric, paper, or sugar, could be whitened with the help of this pigment.

Business boomed, and soon the factory in out-of-the-way Wermelskirchen was too small. He moved the business to the Rhine, bought meadows and fields from the peasants, and soon owned a large property with railroad and shipping connections. It had only one aesthetic flaw: who could run a modern big business in a place called Wiesdorf ("Meadowville")? So Carl Leverkus simply made up an address—the fields and meadows would now be called Leverkusen. Everything else followed: food co-op, casino, businesses, bowling alley, apartment buildings, spa, school, fire department. His son established another fire station and a choir and organized card-playing evenings and hikes in the nearby mountains, because otherwise, a colleague later said, the young people would be living in a place with no civic variety and would "inevitably fall into depression." Seventy years later, the city's name was officially ratified, after debates about whether Leverkusen should be named Wuppermünde after all.

By then, the Leverkus family no longer played an important role in Leverkusen. The boom had been followed by a slump, due to too much competition, and so several companies combined into United Ultramarine, most of which was eventually sold off to Bayer, a Wuppertal company that wanted to expand into Leverkusen. Our mother's brothers took what was left of the business after WWII—not much— and managed it well in the fifties, making good money.

Martin inherited more than some cash from our great-great-grandfather. He had his entrepreneurial talent, too, and the decisiveness to be his own boss. He may not have named a whole city after himself, but he did leave his mark on many cities, including Cologne and Berlin. In his zine *sehr gut, very good,* which he "premiered" at S.O.36, he gave his title as "Boss." Martin never had a factory, but he had the seventh floor of a factory in Berlin. The poster for Kippenberger's Office said "Please make use of our entire range of services: agency, consulting, pictures," with illustrations of a painter's palette, brushes, cash, and checks. Later he painted the "Cost

Peaks" and "Profit Peaks" pictures: he was familiar with both, which was one reason he started painting larger canvases as time went on—he could sell them for more. He made no secret of the business side of art; he made it one of his themes.

"I'm very interested in leadership," Jeff Koons wrote in the issue of the art journal *Parkett* that he designed with Martin in 1989. "I like the seduction of making a sale." Martin, who saw himself as this successful American artist's German counterpart, could have said the same. He was head of sales and head of marketing in one: everyone knew him, lots of people were afraid of him or hated him, but no one had to tell him that a bad reputation is a whole lot better than no reputation at all. In an interview with Jutta Koether, he called his gallerists "middlemen": he was the one in charge of his own business and he never liked to put it entirely in their hands, no matter how much use he made of their infrastructure. With charm and a flood of words he sold the customers works—often works that didn't actually exist yet. And he scared off customers, by savagely attacking them and their taste, as forcefully as he had acquired them in the first place.

The Kippenberger business grew more and more complicated as his activities multiplied and the productions and people involved grew more and more intertwined. "But Martin always had his business under control," said Michael Krebber, Martin's assistant for a year. "He had unbelievably good management skills, his timing was always spot on, and he never had problems delivering on time." His American gallerists were especially intrigued that Martin, despite boozing it up night and day, was so punctual, hard-working, disciplined, and reliable—exactly how you would imagine a German businessman.

One reason he had no problem delivering on time was that he had countless helpers, some of them official but most of them unofficial, including small children and old grandmothers. He knew how to delegate and command, how to exploit others' talents for his own benefit; he was constantly giving orders and assignments and making requests. Just as he had demanded paints, sweets, and jean jackets in his letters from boarding school, he wrote postcards to Hanno Huth, who had moved to Berlin before him: "Hanno durrling, Rmember to get the set (Saxo) in Kreuzberg and German shepherd cards too if they have them. Kippy." Or: "Hanno Bayybee, Send some photies. Kippy."

He needed to keep his business in order because he was living in high style: while his friends lived on five hundred marks a week, he would spend five hundred a day, or a thousand in a single night. "Lots of people think Martin was swimming in money," according to his Düsseldorf friend Meuser. "That's not true at all. It's just that he spread it around." One of Martin's *Picture Titles for Artists to Borrow* was: *It's sad you always have to leave me so soon, money.* He wanted to make money with his art—a lot of money. Our parents had told him when he was young that that was precisely what you couldn't do, and he wanted to prove them wrong. At the same time, he wasn't the slightest bit interested in money as such. Martin took one of the earliest checks he ever got (30 marks for a piece he had sold to Reinhard Bock in Berlin in 1975), cut the outline of a palette out of it, and painted it: "Gotta clown. Waddeveridcosstss. Leonardo Luxury."

At times he had everything, at other times nothing—for Martin, money was always there to spend and show off with, never to hoard. The grandson of a banker who always made us take the present he had just given us and put it in a steel safe before his eyes, he never saved for the future. He lived in the here and now. "No account number, no phone number" read one of his rubber stamps. Phones and credit cards were too virtual for him: he liked his life live. He always paid from a thick wad of cash he had in his jacket pocket—he wanted to be free to go anywhere at any time, on the spur of the moment, and free to leave again too. Once, when asked why he didn't have a credit card, he answered: "I'm on the run."

He never invested in real estate, either. Not a few of his fellow artists eventually owned estates or castles, but he never wanted to. Five-star hotels, on the other hand—in later years he often made that a condition of his accepting an exhibition invitation. For all their comforts, though, it was not so much a matter of luxury for him—he could barely enjoy any luxury in the tiny amount of time he actually spent in the rooms—it was about status. The expense that his hosts went to was a sign of respect, and Martin thought he deserved the best.

Which is not to say that Martin couldn't also be frugal. However much he poured himself into work, he was always economical with resources. Martin was known for reusing things many times over, especially photos from his childhood, like the one that showed him deep in the act of painting—he reprinted that one in several catalogs and on postcards. Poems showed up onstage, in a book, and then again as the title for a picture or exhibition; he took a conversation between Joachim Lottmann and Michael Krebber from his book *Café Central*, reprinted the first half again in his *Peter 2* catalog and the second half in *Journey to Jerusalem*, and used excerpts, translated into Serbo-Croation, yet again in his *Crtezi* catalog. If something went over well, like his lamppost sculptures or the *Peter* exhibition, he would make a few more—just as long as they weren't exactly the same, because that would be boring.

His way of using leftover things was even more pronounced. As a postwar child, and as a conceptual artist who saw everything as material and his work as an ever-expanding spiderweb of connections, Martin never threw anything away. Sketches for the Peter sculptures ended up in the art cabinet of the Petra exhibit, and material that didn't make its way into the *Truth Is Work* catalog was printed on the slips of paper cut off of the edge of printed pages, resulting in the minibook *Introduction to Thinking.* When the printer of *Michael,* an accordion-fold book in homage to Krebber, mistakenly printed the color illustrations in black and white, Martin turned it into a second accordion-fold book that he called *Micky.*

Sometimes his efforts to save everything had something "touchingly helpless" about them, according to his assistant Johannes Wohnseifer. After the Pope visited Cologne, and the whole stadium's turf had been covered with chipboard to protect it for future soccer games, Martin looked into what they were going to do with the wood. It was due to be thrown away so he arranged to get it at no cost. He used it in some of his works, such as the "Tabletops blessed by the Pope" in his Kafka installation, but transporting and storing the giant, heavy boards was so expensive that he ended up spending many times more than what he saved.

Meuser said that he always knew exactly when Martin ran out of money: "he would be on edge and in a terrible mood," and his jokes were no longer funny, just cutting. It was no joke for Martin to be out of money, even if he made fun of himself for ending up in that situation ("We don't have problems with the Deutsche Bank, because we spend our money before entering"). It was demoralizing. "You can see the lady at the bank counter not bother with you and make a dumb joke about you just because you're out of money." "Thats why I dont go into banks, I sign things for other people and let them go in. Its too existential for me what goes on there." Meuser did go with Martin into a bank once, where the teller told him: "Mr. Kippenberger, I have already explained to you that you can't get any more money." Martin thought for a moment and responded: "I don't see it that way at all!"

He himself never refused anyone anything. Michel Würthle wrote on his portrait of Martin as a cowboy: "You can have his last peso but you can't have his melancholy-module." That quality only made it worse for Martin when his friends refused him. At one point in the early eighties, he had hopelessly overdrawn advances from the Hetzler Gallery in Stuttgart, and when Bärbel Grässlin came to Cologne to visit Martin, Hetzler made his overly kind gallery partner promise not to give Martin another penny: "Enough is enough, the account has run dry, now he has to learn to manage his money!" When she invited Martin over to eat, the question naturally came up: "Do you have a little pocket money I could have?" She later recalled that she said: "'I am under strict orders, I can't.' He held that against me his whole life, practically to the very end: that I left him in the lurch. That's how he saw it—leaving him in the lurch. He brought it up again and again."

Since Martin almost never had as much money as he wanted to spend, he became a master of the barter system. He had a restaurant in almost every city where he could eat and drink for free; in Zurich he traded artworks for custom-made shoes, in Graz it was for a grand piano, in Düsseldorf for dental work. He also, of course, traded art for art, ending up with an impressive collection.

He was not practically inclined—and was only too happy to leave this side of his work to friends, students, assistants, and gallerists, keeping them on their toes with his perpetual requests—but he was pragmatic. In Hamburg, when he didn't have the money for a catalog—and he always wanted a catalog—he bought a doormat and a bicycle seat from a gas station on the way to the gallery and built multiples from them. In Copenhagen, when there was no money for a party in honor of his receiving the Köpcke Prize, he made a couple of drawings and used the proceeds for the festivities.

He had already tried out his business acumen as a boy: when he'd spent all his allowance on the first day, again, he sat on the sidewalk during school vacations and sold his drawings. "I've always been involved with wheeling and dealing," he said, and he had to be, since he never received official subsidies in the form of scholarships or the like and won prizes only toward the end of his life. When he had exhibits, his projects almost always went over the respective institution's budget. When he came back from Florence with his giant stack of paintings, he sent (or rather "Mattin Kipmberga" sent) "Dear Madame Stelly" an offer: 490 marks a piece, "for you, 465," with discounts for bulk purchases—a dozen, small selection, a third of the set, half the set, large selection, or the "Complete Program" of eighty-four adventure paintings for 20,580 marks ("for you, 17,640"). "I hope these prices do not have a depressing effect on you," he added. In fact, he sold her no more than four pictures and gave a couple away as Secret Santa presents on Feldbrunnenstrasse.

Martin was always caught in the same cycle. Since he wanted to produce so much art, realize all his ideas, and put together so many exhibitions, catalogs, posters, parties, and postcards, he needed huge sums of money. But since art was his only way to earn that money, he always had to make more and more to finance his countless projects. "It's no fun at all to make art when you have no money," he said, and added in the same breath that it was also no fun when you had too much money—he was afraid of becoming rich, well-fed, and sluggish. "Its a kind of engine, this never having enough. Its probably from nature somewhere, and we have to work to live, you know? And when you suddenly do have money... me, I'd get lazy, and when I'm lazy, and dont work, right away I get drunk." His motto was "Envy and greed, that's what I need."*

Still, he did have a few simple but effective tricks for dealing with his perpetual shortage of cash: pinball, gambling, and mau-mau. In his lowest periods, that's how he made money for food. He played mau-mau to excess, with anyone and everyone, sometimes for days and nights on end. In Tokyo he taught a distinguished Japanese lady how to play; on an airplane flight to San Francisco he passed the time playing mau-mau with the artist Rosemarie Trockel and won seventeen drawings from her. Martin always wanted to win and usually did (and if he didn't, look out: you had to keep playing with him until he came out ahead, no matter how long it took). No one was ever as much in practice as Martin, and no one cheated as much as he did, either.

Since winnings from the game were debts of honor, he went all out to collect, whether it was money (sometimes a lot of money, since the stakes got higher as the night went on), or a mining lamp from his brother-in-law Andreas, or the red wine that Gisela Capitain had to buy him after their first meeting at the Exile, or the MRI of his own brain that he won off a radiologist's son and used as the cover of one of his catalogs (*We Always Thought Kippenberger Was Great*), or the Kelly Family poster his nephew Benjamin had to get him.

What Martin bet was almost always his art, but every now and then he lost money, too. He once owed three thousand marks to Bärbel Grässlin's life partner, the musician Rüdiger Carl. Then Martin made him an offer: cash or some fun, a trip to Tokyo or San Francisco (Martin had invitations to both cities for openings). Carl decided in favor of some fun, in America,

---

* In German, *Neid und Gier, das ist mein Bier*—literally, "Envy and greed, that's my beer."

and Martin was relaxed and in good spirits after the success of his exhibition at the San Francisco Museum of Modern Art:

> He always had it in him to just get into a mood, so that you'd think: You dumbass. This time he took care of me like an angel. He'd decided to make things as nice for me as he could have possibly wanted if he were in my place. How easy he could make everything, with his refined sense of luxury and glamour! But that trip had everything, he even brought the ladies with big boobs to the hotel. I can't remember any time in my life that someone took care of me so sweetly, sensitively, tactfully, and good-naturedly. Without crowding in on me—it's not like he was all buddy-buddy all the time. But not all lordly either: *I own America, let me show it to you,* that sort of thing.

Taking care of other people, spoiling them, was Martin's specialty. He would hang an especially beautiful tie on his Vienna friend Martin Prinzhorn's doorknob or bring his Cologne friend Hubert Kiecol a particularly accurate Serge Gainsbourg doll because he knew Kiecol was a fan. When Brigitta Rohrbach visited him in Florence and her most valuable possessions, three cameras, were immediately stolen from her car, he went to a nearby toy store and bought her a child's camera. "He treated me like royalty," the American artist Christine Hahn said about her visit to Berlin. Martin introduced her to everybody, took her to all the restaurants and museums, the New National Gallery and the Bauhaus Archive, and explained every work to her precisely, "like a perfect little art history course." When he wasn't free, he asked Gisela Capitain to show her East Berlin. His attentions gave her a new sense of confidence.

161

Especially with women, Martin was very generous, showering them with attentions and bouquets of flowers. When they sent him packing, though, he could just as easily shower them with nasty remarks in public.

He gave away countless pictures, often with a dedication and sometimes made especially for the recipient. A lot of the time, though, his giving was also a taking. When he invited someone out to a bar, that meant he had someone to talk to and an audience—he didn't have to be alone and he also got ideas that he could immediately appropriate. When he invited a friend on a trip, he got both company and a chauffeur. When he invited the photographer Andrea Stappert to Spain for Christmas, hotel costs included "so you can't say no," he got someone who could photograph the trip. And when he invited Johannes Wohnseifer to Greece for an exhibition and a week's vacation, he knew that he was bringing not just another artist but an assistant he could send on errands.

He wanted to be a St. Martin, sharing his cloak: "Everyone needs a nice warm corner of the world. We're all looking for that. If I'm political at all then I'm a socialist: here's some cash, there's some cash, here's some food." When he had enough money, he wanted to take people out to eat every night and buy art without restraint. He sometimes seemed like a Robin Hood, giving to those who had little—he never passed a beggar on the street without giving him something—while ripping off the rich. Martin thought the owner of the Daxer art space in Munich was an idiot, for example, and so always stayed at the Four Seasons at his expense, left him with his girlfriend's phone bill (3,000 marks), and ordered the most expensive materials for his catalog there: deckle-edged paper, glossy photographs, silver dust jacket.

Then again, Martin never followed rules, not even his own, so he liked to spend poor gallerists' money just as much.

One day, without any warning, Jes Petersen in Berlin got a bill for stickers Martin had ordered for his series of events *Through Puberty to Success*. When Martin designed the poster for the new multiples store that the young Cologne gallerists Daniel Buchholz and Esther Schipper were opening—and he absolutely insisted on doing it—it was supposed to be as cheap as possible since the gallerists were broke, but every idea Martin had made it more and more expensive.

THE ARMORY SHOW

In November 1979, Kippenberger's Office put on its most important operation: the group show *1st Extraordinary Event in Image and Sound on the Theme of Our Time: Misery*. Ina Barfuss, Werner Büttner, Walter Dahn, Georg Herold, Kippenberger, Jochen Krüger, Meuser, Albert Oehlen, Markus Oehlen, Brigitta Rohrbach, and Thomas Wachweger took part and Mania D., Luxus ("Luxury"), White Russia, Mittagspause ("Lunch Break"), and Syph provided the music at the glittering opening, which cost ten marks admission. "Various punk groups played that night for up to two hundred people at times, most of them paying customers," Werner Büttner wrote. "Everyone was in a good mood. There was only one incident: a phone got torn out of the wall, and someone who was obviously innocent got ruffled up a bit over it by the master of the house."

The critic from the *Berlin Morgenpost* noted that "Only two of the people showing work are professional artists; the rest are cooks, waiters, or plumbers." Not for long. To Jutta Koether, the Misery show was the Armory Show of its time for young German artists, especially painters: "Almost everyone whose name we know today debuted there," she wrote in the journal *Artscribe*. The show's title, *"Elend"* in German, didn't take any thought—Martin found it in the newspaper:

Elendt Painting Ltd., 1 Berlin 26, 58 Brodersenstrasse, Object: Display of paintings and tapestries of all types as well as dealing in paints, lacquers, wallpaper, floor coverings of all sorts... Painter Uwe Elendt, owner and manager.

The show soon gave rise to two sequels. The first, *Extraordinary Event in Image and Sound: Action Piss-Crutch—Secret Servicing the Neighbors,* took place on April 3, 1980, in the Hamburg Artists House. Then came *Fingers for Germany*, in Immendorff's studio in Düsseldorf in the fall, with the concert in a bar called Ratinger Hof. Martin was a regular there too. Carmel Knoebel, wife of the artist Imi Knoebel, had undertaken an artistically inspired "demolition" and radically redesigned the bar from scratch in 1977. Markus Oehlen, who had studied at the Düsseldorf Academy right around the corner, played there with his band, Mittagspause, and Joseph Beuys's class met there.

s.o.36

What Ratinger Hof was in Düsseldorf, S.O.36 was in Berlin. The place itself couldn't have been uglier: a long tunnel lit with cold fluorescent lights and furnished with heaped-up fridges, bar tables, and beer cans, otherwise an empty space just waiting to get filled. That, as Martin explained later, "was the decisive thing about the club: the challenge of the black space. People didn't just want to hear great music or be shown an interesting exhibit, not at all, really the most important thing for everyone there was to cross this black space, they wanted just to get across it through the hall to the stage where there was light, no matter what we had there!"

He didn't found the club, as is often said—he just took it over and made it his own. Achim Schächtele and two buddies had started it; the name was taken from the postal code, since Schächtele, from the Neukölln district (and one of the few native Berliners on the scene at the time), had worked for the post office himself, at the telephone exchange. He had also imported leather jackets from London. He was actually looking for a movie theater. There used to be one in the Oranienstrasse space that became S.O.36 and then a penny arcade, but when he found it, there were just rats. Schächtele and his friends cleaned the place up and built walls for bathrooms out of stone from buildings the city was tearing down in the area ("demolition redevelopment," as it was known at the time). The club opened on August 13, 1978, the seventeenth anniversary of the building of the Berlin Wall, with eleven punk bands and free butter cream pie.

Martin was a regular from the beginning. He seemed like a hard worker to Schächtele when he came rattling up on his moped with a cap on his head that reminded some people of Tyrol and others of the East German leader Erich Honecker (it also served as a protective helmet in S.O.36, where beer cans were always flying through the air). "I thought he was a worker, straight from his shift," Schächtele later said. "I didn't understand him at all at first. I thought *That's someone like us*." Not for long. Martin never liked being just a spectator, so he jumped onstage, tore the mike out of the musician's hand, sang, shrieked, covered himself with shaving cream, threw salt shakers. The bouncers wanted to throw Martin out, but already the short, compact, straightforward Schächtele did what he would so often do again: step in, protect Martin, and let him do what he wanted.

Martin wanted a stage for himself and his events that was more public, and more extreme, than Kippenberger's Office. He also wanted to throw himself a big birthday party. So he besieged Achim Schächtele, hung around Schächtele's apartment, "and never got off our backs. He slept under the table. We thought: What is he doing here, he has a nice place of his own! We didn't even have a bath."

Only after Schächtele was out of commission for a few weeks due to hepatitis, which kept the club closed and desperately in need of money, did Martin prevail. He bought out one of the club's owners who was looking to sell and celebrated his twenty-fifth birthday (a year late) for two straight days at the club, with a printed program and an accompanying book, of course—*1/4 Century Kippenberger, From Impression to Expression*. The book was printed by Verlag Pikasso's Erben (Picasso's Heirs Press) in Berlin/ Paris, another of Martin's fronts, and consisted of empty pages and childhood photos you could glue in: Martin as clown, little Martin with a hat on his head and a beer bottle in his hand, young Martin's drawings (a can opener; John Lennon and Yoko Ono), Martin as hippie in a bedouin coat in Essen-Frillendorf, Martin with long hair, Martin holding a coffee machine up high in his hand, Martin as Turkish cleaning lady, Martin in front of the Berlin Wall.

An English New Wave group played at the party and Tabea Blumenschein's movie *The Dollar Princess* was premiered with Martin's music, along with "Kippenberger Junior: Video, Normal 8, Triple Sound and Light Show, Dancing, Fun" and our father's "Kippenberger Senior: Aboveground/ Belowground and Zandvoort an Zee (Double Projection)." Posters announcing the show were hung throughout the city, which showed Martin being hugged by a bum and beaming idiotically, with words radiating out from his face like sunbeams: "Squanderer—Longtime painter—Ringleader—Host—Bringer—Introducer—Voyeur—Poser."

And so it kept going at S.O.36. Martin was always there, greeting the visitors, who danced, pissed (sometimes against the paintings), and of course made music. Along with German groups like Mittagspause, PVC, and DIN A Testbild, bands from around the world played there; a man named Zensor (German for "censor") went around with a tray selling records you couldn't get anywhere else; there was TV (Muhammad Ali's boxing match), photography (Jim Rakete taking pictures, for instance), fighting, drinking, punching, and painting. Middendorf, with Fetting, painted a sunset onto the wall that was gone two weeks later and projected movies of sunsets to go with it, movies he had shot from the window of Kippenberger's Office. Bernd Zimmer's *Subway, m 1/10 sec., in front of the Warsaw Bridge* was shown for one day only. Gerhard Rühm came by, Martin presented his zine *sehr gut, very good* and movies he had found at a flea market, and Martin, Ina Barfuss, and Thomas Wachweger showed "Buonas Dias" (a pun on "hello" in Spanish and "Dias," the German word for slides), "but after fifteen minutes no one was paying any attention," Helmut Middendorf said. "No one took things all that seriously."

In *Through Puberty to Success* Martin reprinted an English article called "Want to Be Your Dachshund" that described a night there:

> Iggy Pop staggered into West Berlin's Klub S.O.36 recently to see the Warm Jets who were with the drummer from Tangerine Dream and Anglo-saxophonist Bob Summer.
>
> During the last number a guy called Kipper Bergen started goose-stepping round the stage in a

Tyrolean goatherder's outfit.

Deutschland's Andy Warhol as Bergen is known in certain artistic quarters, was attempting to exorcise his nation's Hitler guilt complex by parodying the Third Reich's European adventures. After this little overcompensation he decided to strip to the sensuous rhythms of The Warm Jets who saw someone push Bergen into a bemused audience.

Unpreturbed Mr. Bergen clambered back on stage and pleaded to be beaten up. Paul Ballance, being the obliging rock singer he is, duly whipped the man's naked buttocks. At which point the Ig exited rapidly.

YES SIR, I CAN BOOGIE

"On Sunday we heard a music piece by Joseph Hiden," Martin wrote from boarding school at age nine. "It was loud at the begining and then soft later. I liked it alot."

"I have no sense of music," he said thirty years later.

He couldn't even play the recorder, though he did learn how to plonk on the piano. "Flohwalzer"* was about the only piece any of us could play; when our sister Tina broke her arm and was happy because that meant she didn't have to go to her piano lessons, the experiment in music instruction for the Kippenberger children came to an end. If there was anything, there was singing—not well, but loud—especially at Christmastime, on birthdays, and in church. From our parents' point of view, music was there to be danced to.

"He was absolutely clueless about music," according to Jim Rakete, the Berlin photographer who became famous as a Neue Deutsche Welle (German New Wave) producer.

---

* Comparable to "Heart and Soul" in the U.S.

"But his chutzpah in going at it, and the way he acted like a wild animal onstage!" It's precisely because he was clueless that Martin drummed, sang, and produced and staged music. He called it his "principle of embarrassment, the do-it-even-more system. Don't be ashamed of doing something stupid, do something else really stupid."

Martin and his friends were not the first. Above all, there were the Dadaists, the great artistic revolutionaries who also did everything: painting, literature, sculpture, music, dance. They were angry and loud, funny and spontaneous, absurdist and deeply political, and no other twentieth-century movement had as much in common with what Martin and company were doing. Its guiding principle was to overstep boundaries; its preeminent form was collage. They turned the banal into their most important material, they worked in groups, they played with language, and they turned every exhibition into a statement, a concept.

"Music is nice / How should it go? / The louder / The better," Martin wrote in *Through Puberty to Success* He could throw himself into music more playfully than into any other medium, and used music to let off steam, all live. He went wild on the strings of his air guitars, flailed away on the drums at the Ratinger Hof with childish delight, sang the words to Joseph Beuys's *Yeah Yeah Yeah Yeah Yeah No No No No No* in a deep voice—in a way, the title was the motto of Martin's life. He had three versions of the song, in fact: one for grown-ups, one for children, and one universal version.

He certainly didn't invent punk, or bring it to Berlin, as is sometimes said. Punk had been there a long time. But Martin gave it a platform at S.O.36 and jumped up onstage with it. What did punk mean to him? "Nothing," according to Albert Oehlen. Or not as music: what interested him was the attitude. "That you do what you want," said Gisela Capitain. That you break all the rules and cross all the boundaries, especially the bounds of good taste. What he liked was the intensity of the shows, how wild and anarchic the punks were, and that the music was chaotic and didn't last long. "We play waste-sound," Martin said about his own band, Luxus, consisting of him and Achim Schächtele, the filmmaker Eric Mitchell, and the artist Christine Hahn, who also played so-called "art rock" at S.O.36 as the drummer of her artist band, Static. Luxus declared war on the common image of the artist as shabby ascetic. The band existed for only one record and was never intended to last any longer.

Records were as much a part of artistic production as invitations, posters, and catalogs. As Albert Oehlen wrote in the catalog for *Truth Is Work*, "To the obnoxious question 'Mr. Oehlen, you've made a record but you can't sing at all, why did you do it?' there is only one answer: 'I can make a record anyway.'"

The music scene at the time was more brash, bold, and free than the art scene. It was also a part of life and of what it meant to be alive, not shut away in museum basements. That may be another reason Martin liked music so much: he fit in better in that world, the world of pop stars and rock stars, than in the serious, dignified art world of his day. Working in a group, being surrounded by groupies, the fast pace, the loud shows, the divalike behavior, what we call "star quality" in general: it was all natural and accepted in the music world. "Martin onstage was always bigger than whatever he was onstage for," Jim Rakete says. "There was something so sleek about him, something—it wasn't just being brash—it was something subversive and deeply intelligent." With his unbelievable self-confidence, unchecked energy, and cocky slogans, "it was like he knew the world," Sven-Åke Johansson said. It is also significant that Martin's most important critics, and the ones most well-disposed to him, came from the music scene: Diedrich Diederichsen and Jutta Koether, who both worked for *Spex* magazine. The art critics preferred to ignore him or tear him down.

They also seemed less than pleased with the close relationship between the music and art worlds. In 1988, one writer for the American magazine *Art News* seemed quite irritated by the fact the German contemporary art struck him as similar to rock and roll: he found so many allusions to music in their works that it seemed to him the music was the soundtrack to the art. He said that the expressive Moritzplatz painters "burst onto the scene simultaneously, like a new sound," but regretted that all he could see were boy bands: "One might say that up until now, new German art has not produced even one female lead singer."

"When you're young," in Sven-Åke Johansson's view, "you need a band. You can't go it alone." So the artists the Stuttgart gallerist Max Hetzler took on in 1980-81 were called "the Hetzler Boys" and preferred to appear as a group, with Martin as the leader. The Hetzler Boys also did make actual music: singing together became a regular part of their art-opening and dinner-party ritual. "Glühwürmchen" (The Glow-Worm) by Paul Lincke was an old standby; "Glück auf," the old miner's song named after the old-fashioned miner's greeting, came out around midnight; "Ding-a-ling-a-ling, Here Comes the Eggman" was Martin's theme song.* Later, when Martin had students in Kassel, part of the lesson plan was to make them sing in public at the Christmas market: practicing performance art, practicing the embarrassment principle.

Music, for Martin, was another way to express himself and communicate—an especially good way, given his extreme

---

* "Der Eiermann," a hit in Germany for Klaus & Klaus.

emotionality and physicality. Martin's wife Elfie Semotan said he "was not someone you had a philosophical discussion with. He never really talked about things at all, he just did them. Martin was proof of the idea that you don't think with your head, you think with your whole body."

As a 21-year-old student in Hamburg, when he got his first stereo system, "50-watt speakers and an amplifier with a radio, headphones, and record player," he was thrilled: "All right man, let's go!! The stereo moves me, lets me dance, changes my mood for the better, and promotes my creativity." He would dance, write, and draw to Pink Floyd, David Bowie, and the Rolling Stones, and he always cleaned the house accompanied by "musick" (as he liked to spell it). "I'll probably never be an intellectual." For as long as he lived, he would always paint to music, and even years after painting a picture he would know "exactly what music was playing" when he painted it.

It was his music that horrified friends like Oehlen and Diederichsen. Not only did Martin have no clue about music, he had no taste, as he himself knew. According to the gallerist Friedrich Petzel, Martin's taste in music was horrendous— Petzel had to listen to "If You Don't Know Me by Now" by Simply Red for weeks on end while putting together the multiples installation in Gisela Capitain's Cologne gallery, "eight beats for six weeks." Martin's American assistant Jory Felice said that "he could get excited by terrible pop music": Wilson Philips ("Hold On"), the Traveling Wilburys ("Handle With Care")—"emotional kitsch." Martin called people like himself "crooner addicts," hooked on songs like "My Way," "Bang-Bang," and "Yuppi Du," all songs that he himself sang on his *Greatest Hits* record. He loved Lee Marvin, whose hit "(Ah-eeee was born under a) Wandering Star" was probably the only song Martin knew by heart, as he once admitted. In Albert Oehlen's words, he had "a woman's taste" in music, not least because he could listen to his favorite songs a hundred times in a row, "which men normally can't do." He played Leonard Cohen to excess and would listen to the soundtrack to *The Bodyguard* over and over again in his studio in the Black Forest, singing along with Whitney Houston.

He played boogie-woogie as well as punk at S.O.36— "I'm open to anything"—and in L.A. he had Jory Felice advise him about rap. In fact, at one point he had an idea that he needed to learn about classical music, had Valeria Heisenberg put together a list for him, and bought a shopping bag full of classical CDs. He just probably never listened to them.

Whether he was writing, singing, dancing, or "making paintee paintee," it was all the same to Martin—all art. His art. The connecting thread was his self, the artist who saw himself as his medium. "Music," in Jim Rakete's words, "was a T-shirt with his face printed on it." The only thing that mattered was whether it all fit together and "added up to a proper Kippenberger or not."

Better Too Much Than Too Little was the title of a 2003 exhibition at Berlin's NGBK (Neue Gesellschaft für bildende Kunst) about that legendary time in Berlin, when music was *the* mode of expression and, as Thomas Graetz wrote in the catalog, the run-down world of painting got a shot in the arm from punk. "Painters would hang out at the S.O.36 club in Berlin and, starting in 1978, let the punk groups who played there infect them, so that, spurred on, they could bring impetuous equivalents into the world with their brushes and colors. Even [the older director of the Berlinische Galerie] Eberhard Rothers enthused about their works at the time: rage, lust, verve, zest, beat, rock, vitality!"

Even though that applies especially to the Moritzplatz painters, not exactly to Martin and his friends, uninterested in being wild painters, the fact remains that music was simply *there,* everywhere, always, and left its mark on most young painters of the time more than visual art did. And the boundaries were fluid. In one of Markus Oehlen's performances with Mittagspause at S.O.36, he took a canister of cleaning powder he found backstage, poured it over his drum kit, stood on a ladder, and started scrubbing. His brother Albert sang and put out records and ran—still runs today—his own record label, Leiterwagen (Handcart). Martin invited the Berlin Philharmonic to his events at Café Einstein as well as the teenage punk rocker Ben Becker and his band, the Canary Birds.

Martin never cared about music as such and rarely went to big concerts; what interested him was always the ensemble, the interaction. For instance, the combination of sound and image that he loved in movies—he practiced it in his studio and liked to make music a part of fashion shows or art openings—or the tension between artist and audience. Friction, resistance, communication: that was his art. Jutta Koether said, "Music for him was always a lubricant."

He found kindred spirits in Sven-Åke Johansson and Rüdiger Carl, free-jazz musicians with whom he would collaborate and stay friends until his death. They also crossed boundaries, broke rules, and refused to stick to the laws of harmony and rhythm; instead they made noise, tried to find new forms and structures, and looked to see "what would happen if we moved this thing here or shook that there," in Johansson's words. Like Martin, the Danish Johansson made use of everyday objects—traffic signs, corrugated cardboard, wind turbines—and made all of West Berlin sing. His favorite instrument was a phone book, and he could produce entirely new sounds by flipping the pages, throwing it, hitting it, drumming on it, and tearing it. Not to the audience's undiluted pleasure: as Johansson said, there were riots when they "put on intellectual free music at a punk bar."

"Some rocker pulled the plug out of the RIAS* broadcast van," Rüdiger Carl said, not that the reporter was much happier when it was plugged back in:

> Some kid stoned out of his mind kept climbing up onstage and plucking around on the cello, then the RIAS lady who was sitting in the van with headphones on came out and said what is this shit, it's unbearable, and meanwhile this idiot kept going. Then one of the gang of bouncers tapped him on the shoulder from behind and hit him in the head, and while he lay on the floor the bouncer took his feet and dragged him through the whole bar like some wild animal he'd shot and threw him out in the street. That was how people did things back then.

Before it was over, more people were thrown out and took revenge by overturning the broadcast van. Afterward, the show was put out as a record, with a painting by Martin on the cover.

"Hey, can you only play like that," Martin asked the free-jazzmen after one of their concerts, "or the right way too?" And so, in 1984, their dance band was born: Night and Day, a swing orchestra founded by Johansson and Carl together with Alexander von Schlippenbach and Jay Oliver to provide music at one of Martin's openings with Albert Oehlen and Werner Büttner at the Folkwang Museum in Essen. Night and Day went on to accompany Hetzler Boys openings and play at all sorts of other art events in Europe for ten years. The radical avant-garde musicians were delighted to do exactly what they didn't want to do—American standards, "songs

---

* *Rundfunk im amerikanischen Sektor* (American Sector Broadcasting), a West Berlin radio and TV station.

everyone knows," as Carl put it, "Broadway and stuff"—but as a concept, and as part of the do-it-on-purpose system, not to mention earning some money too.

Night and Day recorded a studio album but it was too trite for the head of EMI records, so they put it out themselves, with a cover designed by Martin, of course. The band name was given as the Golden Kot Quartet (Golden Crap Quartet), and photos showed Martin on the drums, Albert Oehlen on piano, Hubert Kiecol on bass, and Günther Förg on saxophone. Neither names nor pictures of the real band members appeared anywhere. "There were serious reviews" and the critics were amazed at how well the four artists could play their instruments.

When there were no art openings where Night and Day could play, Martin ran around after the band anyway: "suddenly he'd be standing there with polished shoes and two girls," Rüdiger Carl said. He may have been clueless about music, but "he had it in his bones," according to Carl.

"The impressive thing about his dancing," Albert Oehlen said, "was the musicality of his body language. It came from within." Martin damaged his body terribly with cigarettes, drugs, alcohol, and lack of sleep; he never exercised, and he depicted his body as a shapeless lump in numerous self-portraits—but he was sleek and graceful from head to toe when he danced. He proudly showed off his calves in Austria once: muscles he had not from skiing but from dancing. "I'm clueless about music," he said, "but I love to dance. Arm in arm, cheek to cheek, it's heavenly, you don't even need to go home and go to bed together."

His body was the one musical instrument he ever mastered. Jory Felice, Martin's American assistant, said he was "shocked" the first time he saw Martin dance.

Especially in the seventies and early eighties, almost every night ended at the disco: the Madhouse in Hamburg, the Jungle in Berlin, the Bear's Den in St. Georgen. It was the era of buttons that said "Fuck art—let's dance!"

At a time when artists tended to be macho, with men standing at the bar and women sitting at the tables, dancing was "one of the few times that the men's world and the women's world came together. We all liked it very much," the gallerist Tanja Grunert said. For Martin, it was a chance to be happy for a moment. He was never alone when he danced—he always had a woman in his arms. His relations with the opposite sex were rarely as harmonious as they were then.

He almost always danced in a pair, arm in arm, not solo and freestyle, and his specialty was classic music: boogie-woogie, foxtrot, waltz, samba, and rock and roll. With them he did what he always did as an artist: take something that was already there and kippenbergerize it. A young gallerist, Sophia Ungers, described how in a piece called "The Dance of the Kippenberger," which he assigned her to write. She said he took the rules not as orders but as suggestions, and always varied them: "transforming, defamiliarizing, and appropriating" them. Now wild, now elegant, dancing for him was a form of expression using legs, arms, torso, and face instead of words—a form of communication. "When I dance, people start to think," he said once.

"If you gave yourself over to his style," according to Gisela Capitain, who danced often and especially well with him, "it was always fun and entertaining." The artist Angelika Margull says that in Berlin the women would line up when he arrived at the Jungle or shoved the tables aside in the Exile. "He went all out, no man could keep up with him." She herself—a very tall woman, and somewhat shy, in her own words—felt "so carried away. He gave you the feeling that you were doing the right thing, that he was so loving and tender at that moment."

"That's when he was sober," the photographer Jutta Henglein commented. "When he was drunk, it was horrible, he threw you into the air."

"Dancing," in Albert Oehlen's words, "was a show." No matter how full the disco was, he always managed to clear the floor with his dance partner before long. He wanted to shine, and if he ended up in only second place, as he did once at a *Spex* dance contest, he was insulted. Here too, of course, he polarized people: some admired the intensity of his performance and his physical presence, others saw it as provocation.

And if it was a show, it was an utterly natural one, not rehearsed. His absolute naturalness and lack of inhibition or restraint were on display when he danced, Sophia Ungers says. He didn't need a real stage or a big audience—he could just as easily dance around the empty Café Central at night with the cleaning lady. At his wedding, Martin danced with his young niece Elena while sitting down—moving from chair to chair—and when he danced with his even younger daughter, Helena, on a table in Rotterdam, it looked like a duel, or like something choreographed without a choreographer. When the artist Rosemarie Trockel watched Helena or our father dance, she said, she recognized Martin: "They dance exactly the same way: knowing that 'I can do that!' The same excess is there, the lack of restraint, the sense for movement."

DIALOGUE WITH THE YOUTH

Martin was dancing on the volcano's edge in Berlin, Achim Schächtele says, and at S.O.36 it erupted. The mix of audiences was explosive. As Helmut Middendorf said, "all the artists, all the music people, and all the no-future people," gays, addicts, and punks, were there at once, and every so often the mixture exploded. "Beer Too Expensive, Rockers Beat 400 People," the newspaper report ran: "Because the beer was too expensive for them, 2.50 marks, 35 punk rockers with painted faces stormed a Berlin discotheque, attacked the 400 patrons with clubs, and stole 4,500 marks from the cash register."

The most famous fistfight didn't take place at S.O.36 at all, however. It was at Nollendorfplatz, instigated by Ratten-Jenny (a famous Berlin punk, nicknamed "Rat" because she kept rats as pets) and her gang. They were not just pissed off about the price of beer, but also, in gallerist Bruno Brunnet's words, "mad at Martin for having bought his way into S.O.36" and for using punk for his own purposes, while at the same time regularly going to chic restaurants like Fofi's and the Paris Bar. They didn't like that he did everything you weren't supposed to do: wear a suit and Tyrolean hat, cut his hair short, use the formal "*Sie*" with people, throw money around. He didn't play by their rules.

Jutta Henglein, the photographer, described Ratten-Jenny as a "bird-brained Berlin brat—a punk girl with no sense of humor . . . a crazy, disgusting drug addict." Her gang ambushed Martin at Nollendorfplatz and he was badly injured, especially in the head, but even as he lay bleeding on the ground he couldn't keep his mouth shut: "Your mothers should have made you finish high school."

When Martin wasn't feeling well—for example, when he'd had too much to drink—he suffered from what Jutta Henglein called "distorted reality." "He was horrible to people when he was wasted, he picked fights, but then Achim always smoothed things over. Achim was like his bodyguard." But Achim wasn't there that night. "Take care that no one beats you up / Or else it's better not to go out alone" went one of Martin's poems two years later. Martin must have felt terrible that day, his friends say, especially since he could usually defuse the situations he got himself into, even much more dangerous situations, on his own, with charm and by making fun of himself. "You couldn't have a real argument with him," the publisher of Merve Verlag, Peter Gente, said. "Sooner or later he would always come out with a joke, an ironic comment."

No sooner did Martin arrive at the hospital—one of the worst in the city—than he picked up the phone, still drunk, and started calling people to come see him. By the following day, Polaroids of his mistreated head were being handed around at Café Einstein. Jutta Henglein was one of the people he called, so that she could take pictures of him. "It was bad," he could have lost an eye or suffered brain damage. She thinks that he staged the whole to-do about it afterward to save face. "He was absolutely driven to cross lines, plumb depths, and then he was surprised when something happened."

Later he struck back, but with his own weapons: art, language, and humor. He called the self-portrait of his beaten, bandaged head *Dialogue with the Youth* and made it part of a trilogy called *Berlin by Night.* The other two pictures show a swaying man (*Big Apartment, Never Home*) and a rat with an overturned glass (*Codename Hildegard*). His nose would be crooked for the rest of his life, and the scar never went away; nor did the feeling that he was no longer welcome in Berlin.

There have been so many stories told and written about S.O.36 that you would think the club was open for years. In fact, it was less than a year, and only six months with Martin as co-owner. "It went by in a flash," Achim Schächtele said, but so intensely that it wasn't only Max Hetzler who said that six months of S.O.36 "felt like ten years."

It closed on June 30, 1979. Either the police shut it down, or there was no more money, or everyone just felt done with it. In any case, Martin staged the grand finale: "Keller-Kaiser

Kippenberger" (Basement-Emperor Kippenberger) accepted congratulations on camera from Rolf Eden, the disco king of the Ku'damm, and Valie Export and Ingrid Wiener, among others, appeared for the last show, as did a real llama, which as it happened refused to go onstage.

Martin was later both proud and amused to hear that S.O.36—the ugliest space in the world—had been turned into a protected landmark. He chalked it up as a success and as proof that content matters more than form: that you can make something out of anything.

Martin was interviewed for television in his office once, and the bewildered journalist asked Martin what he thought he was doing: what is an artist doing if he doesn't make art, or at least none you can see and hang on your wall? "Being young," Martin answered, "being young, being where it's at. Everywhere it's at. What it has to do with art? Dunno."

PUT YOUR EYE IN YOUR MOUTH

Really, you read books? I don't.
—MK

And suddenly he was gone. In 1980, without knowing a word of French, he left for Paris: to become a writer, he said. He did everything an aspiring writer along the Seine is supposed to do—found himself a garret room in an old Marais hotel and a café to sit in, like Hemingway and Fitzgerald, Sartre and de Beauvoir. Now all he had to do was write.

"It didn't work out at all," Martin said fifteen years later. "Four or five good poems came out and that was it. My career as poet and litterateur came to an end and I went back to Berlin."

There was no way it could have worked out. How could someone who had never in his life read a novel suddenly write one? A dyslexic who wrote only with difficulty and in block letters, someone used to hurtling around Berlin, someone whose motto was "Think today, done tomorrow": how could he expect to stay in one place for six months and do nothing but sit in silence and write?

Maybe it was never supposed to work out, like the plan to go to Florence to become an actor. Max Hetzler, Martin's gallerist later, thought that this project too was meant in advance to fail so that Martin could work the failure into his art and his artist's biography. Maybe escaping into the life of a writer was part of a concept of the Total Artist as someone who crosses all boundaries, or who fails. A poser. In any case, Martin could travel to Berlin to open a show and write "Currently he resides in Paris"; could print little sayings ("I'm going to Paris." "Bah you pig.") and have Serge de Paris recite these "poemicles" at Café Einstein. Of course he published them, too: in the INP-catalog ("Ist-Nicht-Peinlich" or "Is-Not-Embarrassing"). He wasn't embarrassed; he never let anything go to waste.

But even if Martin was never a real writer, he was a man of letters. He simply preferred short forms (his exhibition and painting titles became catchphrases) and speaking rather than writing his literature: for him, it was a performance art, life as a play. His New York gallerist Roland Augustine felt that way when Martin showed up with his students at the gallery and told him, "OK, now take them out to lunch!" "It was a strange kind of drama that you became part of," Augustine said. Martin did in fact have a literary gift; it just worked better on the stage of daily life than between the covers of a novel. He was better suited to be a character in a novel than a novelist. The critic Renate Puvogel wrote that "his method, of freely and recklessly mixing fragments, quotations, and unprocessed material from art and real life together with invention and personal experience, suggests that he took the life around him itself as a mixture of reality and fiction."

PRINTED & UNPRINTED PAPER

Of course he didn't need to write a novel to make books, which he did to excess, like everything else in his art. He wanted to trump Dieter Roth and overtake our father and produce a bookshelf-foot or two more than Kirchner, and he did it: the catalogue raisonné lists 149 titles, from *al Vostro servizio* in 1977 to *No Drawing No Cry,* planned before his death in 1997 and published in 2000 (the third in his series of drawings on hotel stationery—with all but one of the pages blank). He averaged roughly seven and a half books a year, even if some were not exactly tomes (the smallest, *Introduction to Thinking,* measures four by three inches) and many were co-productions with other artists. When Walther König emptied out the big shop window of his Cologne bookstore and filled it with Martin's books the night after Martin died, people couldn't believe their eyes. "Martin always wanted that," according to the photographer Andrea Stappert, "a whole window at König's. It was like documenta."

For Martin, who was so often shut out of the official German art business, books were an especially important way of staying visible and making himself known. "I use every means I can to make something that will last, that will speak for itself. Because I think that before I get the other kinds of 'recognition,' like 'hanging in a museum,' I'd need to see the museum directors hanging in a museum. And that won't happen."

His books were a part of his artistic production and very much like his painting and sculpture in their variety and scope. His strategies were the same as well: repetition, variation, exaggeration, and misleading or withholding from the reader. He designed a book called *Untouched & Unprinted Paper* for the New York nonprofit bookstore Printed Matter, which consisted of a stack of blank paper wrapped in brown packing paper in a slipcase.

Almost every book of Martin's looked different, and every one went against the grain in one way or another. For example, *Women,* published by Merve Verlag in 1980. This small Berlin publishing house, run with great consistency and humor by Peter Gente and Heidi Paris, publishes all its books paperback, in the same small format and with a uniform cover design. There, among all the highly theoretical structuralist and post-structuralist texts, was Martin's volume of nothing but pictures of no more and no less than what it said on the cover: women. Female strangers, friends, colleagues, and our mother, too, laughing in Martin's arms. The only words in the whole book were the author, title, and publisher on the front cover and the publisher's colophon on the back.

Martin preferred to let other people do the writing whenever possible, just as he preferred to let other people do the painting. After a rest cure at Knokke, the Belgian seaside resort, he sent Annette Grotkasten, the book designer in Hamburg who had worked on his *Truth is Work* catalog, there to spend five days retracing his footsteps so that she could write up how he had probably experienced the place. *1984: How It Really Was, Using the Example of Knokke,* dedicated to his friend Werner Büttner, looks like the little yellow books in the well-known Reclam classics series but was actually published by the Bärbel Grässlin Gallery. In 1987, the text went unchanged into Martin's book *Café Central: Sketch for a Study of a Figure in a Novel,* in which the character from a novel is, of course, Martin himself, though he mostly left the writing to his assistant at the time, Michael Krebber. The book opens with a "Hellish Prelude with Tape Recorder," which involved setting Krebber loose to answer questions from Joachim Lottmann ("Stupid questions, right answers"). The rest of the book consists of text dictated to Krebber or sent to him in the form of letters. *Café Central* was published by Werner Büttner's Meterverlag press and illustrated with humorous drawings from the estate of Albert and Markus Oehlen's father.

The network of friends who provided texts for his books and catalogs grew ever tighter and more stable: Diedrich Diederichsen, Jutta Koether, Roberto Ohrt, Werner Büttner, Martin Prinzhorn. Martin felt that they understood him and could express what he meant. He used his writer friends, too: Oswald Wiener, Rainald Goetz, Walter Grond. One time he printed an entire play by the Austrian playwright Wolfgang Bauer in a catalog, which Bauer then performed at one of the openings. Anything someone else could do better, Martin didn't have to do himself, he simply assimilated the other person's work into his own oeuvre. The exception: he never asked real art critics to write for him. He said he couldn't stand "art-history German."

He played with the myth of the artist and the artist's authorship (who is an artist? what does he actually do?) in countless ways. For *Women,* Martin left it up to the printer to decide the order of the pictures. In a used bookstore in Paris he found copies of a book called *Les mémoires d'un Cordon Bleu* and bought up every copy, numbered and signed the shrink-wrapped books, and lo and behold, another genuine Kippenberger. The majority of his books were, if not self-published, at least self-financed, at least in part. He had two real publishers: Rainer Pretzell in the early years in Berlin and, later, Walther König in Cologne.

THERE HE GOES AGAIN, THAT BOOKWORM

As a dyslexic child, Martin had hated reading books. This was incomprehensible to our mother, and certainly unacceptable, so she sent Martin with our father to the Baedecker bookstore, where her friend Ulla Hurck worked. They came out with a bag of books about the medieval German hero Klaus Störtebeker. At home Martin pretended to read them, but it was much too difficult and boring—he only turned the pages, though very convincingly, since he wanted to receive praise and he knew there'd be praise for reading. That is how he tells the story twenty years later in *Café Central.*

As an adult, he continued to show how well he could perform with books. "Smart Is Where It's At" he wrote on the cover of the tenth anniversary publication for Merve publishers, whose demanding list (Virilio, Baudrillard, and so on) was read by everyone who wanted to prove their intellectual chops. Not Martin: he ordered "3 ft. light reading + serious lit. = 981.10 marks," according to the receipt from the Bittner Bookstore in Cologne that he reprinted in a little booklet he included as an insert in a special issue of the art journal *Parkett*. In their obituary for Martin in *Spex,* Cosima von Bonin and Michael Krebber said that Martin bought the books at Bittner in order to carry them home past his regular café so that the people sitting there would think, "There he goes again, that bookworm."

He *couldn't* read, because he needed the empty space in his head so that he could stay open to everything he encountered, "could organize his free filtering process himself," as he put it in *Café Central.* He needed emptiness so that he could fill up himself. Martin Prinzhorn believed that since he didn't read any books, "he had the brain of an elephant." He needed space to breathe, in his head no less than in his apartments, where he hated knick-knacks and clutter. "I couldn't work like that. I need an empty desk and a clear head," he wrote during his Hamburg period to a friend who had a lot of junk. "My 4 walls are white and they'll stay that way."

Life, not fine literature, is what interested Martin. On the rare occasions he did read a book, it was a biography: *Nora,* about James Joyce's wife, for the sex and because it was the story of a woman who had cleared away obstructions for her artist husband, or Pepys's juicy diary, or a biography of Romy Schneider, the German actress he loved for being so beautiful, vivacious, and happy, and at the same time so melancholy and broken. He recommended *Overdose,* about John Belushi, to Michael Krebber, along with Kurt Raab's biography of Fassbinder—he thought it was great that Fassbinder's former close collaborator would dare to write something so bad about the master so soon after his death.

Martin didn't read, he turned the pages. Newspapers, magazines, and catalogs were important sources for him of reality, art, and the zeitgeist; they stimulated and challenged him. And he listened. "As a dyslexic," the artist Rosemarie Trockel said from personal experience, "you have a different coding system: you can pick things up relatively quickly, you have your own ways of learning things." Anyway, why should he read when other people did it for him. Friends like Albert Oehlen, Werner Büttner, Michael Krebber, Roberto Ohrt, Martin Prinzhorn, or whoever else was around told him about what they'd read, and—just as he always preferred to paint or draw from photos or postcards instead of from nature— he thought retellings were often more interesting than the originals. For example, he sent people to the Jewish Museum in Frankfurt with the most enthusiastic recommendations, saying it was the most interesting museum in the city, even though he had never set foot inside himself. "I always hear what people say, what people have seen or heard, and I store it up."

He once had Michael Krebber ("MK1") draw up a list of twenty important books; Martin ("MK2") then printed it in *Café Central*: Knut Hamsun, *Hunger*; Musil, *Three Women*; Huysmans, *Against Nature*; Huysmans, *La-Bas*; Kafka, *Amerika*; Gogol, *Taras Bulba*; Goncharov, *Oblomov*; Baudelaire, *Paris Spleen*; Baudelaire, *My Heart Laid Bare*; Rigaud, *Suicide*; Vache, *War Letters*; Carroll, *Alice in Wonderland*; Vischer, *Auch Einer*; de Laclos, *Dangerous Liaisons*; Lermontov, *A Hero of Our Time*; Babel, *Red Cavalry*; Proust, *Swann's Way*; Diderot, *Rameau's Nephew*; Macarenko, *Road to Life*. (The list has only nineteen books.) Krebber had to buy them all for Martin and bring them to Teneriffe, and it seems that Martin did in fact glance through them. Some of the titles appeared later as titles for artworks, for instance, a *Rameau's Nephew* sculpture: a cardboard book box from the Roggendorf moving company with wallpaper glued to the inside that shows a little man sitting on a park bench and eating, with a few pigeons at his feet, and the words *"Ne me regarde pas manger"* (Don't watch me eating). He reprinted all of Vischer's *Auch Einer* in one of his catalogs and turned Franz Kafka's *Amerika* into the gigantic installation *The Happy End of Franz Kafka's "Amerika."* He originally intended it to be a book "that you keep by your side and turn to for strength, like a Bible," but instead he used his sculptural means to give Kafka's unfinished novel a happy ending.

TALKING INSTEAD OF WRITING

Talking is what he most loved to do, as he had already said in the late seventies in Berlin: "I like it more than painting—it goes faster." "Kippenberger's whole existence," according to the Austrian writer Walter Grond, "is an excessive speech." For Martin, art was always communication, a way to convey himself, and so conversation (or the monologue it often mutated into), talking, telling jokes, and telling stories were the literary forms that suited him best: the most immediate and spontaneous forms of communication, ad lib art. "Kippenberger conducted his relationship with the discursive while entirely avoiding writing," Diedrich Diederichsen said. That is mostly true, although from childhood on, Martin used letter-writing as an artistic form of sharing information, telling stories, and finding himself. While in Hamburg, he admitted to a friend he regularly sent letters to that writing actually wasn't his way, "because for me there are other paths of communication," such as taking the subway or walking around. So he mostly stopped writing letters as his artistic production increased; he came to prefer postcards, where it was enough to write a little and the picture was, of course, part of the message.

He was an excessive talker, but he talked, Rosemarie Trockel recalls, "in short form, like in comic books.... It was speech-bubble-German. He talked like a comedian." In his slogans and jokes he brought things to a point in just a few words, a quality that many people admired and some feared. That is why he so enjoyed reading the tabloid *Bild*: along with all the soccer scores, he found the craziest stories, written in telegraphic style with snappy headlines. He did criticize *Bild*'s racism, "but other than that, what's in there is tops."

Many of the titles of his paintings, books, and exhibitions

were as pointed as the *Bild*'s headlines, for instance the series *War Bad*, which he made during the heyday of the peace movement. "The whole moral rearmament was never put into words so sharply," Martin's friend Meuser said. Martin had already asked Meuser to come to Stuttgart, in 1981, before an opening, "to slap together some titles," and earlier still had written some of his "poemicles" in France with him. Meuser had also grown up in Essen; they spoke the same language and "had a similar vocabulary—it was like home." While they were slapping together titles, the artists sometimes had to be careful not to fall off their chairs from laughing so hard.

Germany, Its Waters; Cold on Canvas; Tina Onassis's Favorite Aunt on Her Way Home; Ashtrays for Singles; Nothing Heard, Nothing Hurt; I'm Going to Pieces, Are You Coming Too; Turn It Then Toss It; Steel Helmets in the Early Afternoon; What on Earth is Happening on Sunday? (a silly rhyme in German, *Was ist bloß am Sonntag los?*). Those are some of his picture titles. His exhibition titles have their own poetry: *Helmut Newton for the Poor; Buying America & Selling El Salvador; The Battle against Bedsores; Sand in the Vaseline; Peter: The Russian Position; Nada Arugula; Give Me a Summer Hole (Under the Volcano Part II); How in Times of War Do I Cope with Broken Bones and Futurism; 14 Million for a Howdy-Do; Clotheslines Backwardsround; Capri by Night.*

Many of his titles and mottoes became catchphrases ("Dialogue with the Youth," "Farewell to the Youth Bonus," "Taking the Law into Your Own Hands Through False Purchases"), and others were used by curators again for group shows later: *Dear Painter, Paint For Me; From Impression to Expression; Deep Looks; Do I Really Exist.*

Being unread, or you might say un-miseducated, turned out to be an advantage for him. "Words come to him like a stray dog rolls up to you on the street," the *Schwabian News* wrote in 1982 on the occasion of his show at the Rottweil Forum, "and from this accidental encounter he makes a little picture." Sometimes, Niklas Maak wrote much later in the *FAZ*, you even had the impression that Martin threw together his pictures quite quickly, almost reluctantly, just to have something to give a good title to. And sometimes he even skipped the painting step altogether: in 1986 he published a book called *241 Picture Titles for Artists to Borrow*. One of the titles is: *With Nothing in Hand, There's Nothing That Can Go Up in Smoke*. Also in 1986 he put out a portfolio of posters called *TU* ("Title Unnecessary").

Indeed, the titles had a life of their own—they never explained the pictures they went with and often the two didn't go together at all. The relationship between picture and title was like that between an exhibition and its catalog: they stand alongside each other, complete, undermine, and counteract each other, but do not simply explain or illustrate anything. At its best, the result is what Martin admired in certain films, like *The Graduate* with its music by Simon and Garfunkel, which Martin thought of as one of the first music videos, or *Doctor Zhivago*, which he saw countless times. "You don't just take in the image—and not just the sound—but both together." One time, on Brussels Hotel Amigo stationery, he drew garden furniture and gardening tools with their measurements and wrote underneath: "If only that goddamn manicuring would stop."

He often put the text right into the picture, messing up the picture in the process: he stuck large stickers on paintings ("I Love Nicaragua," "I Love No Waiting," "I Love Collagen," . . .), stapled sayings and quotes to photographs, sprayed silicon onto canvases to make squirts of letters, often reducing the language so much that only initials remained: *H.H.Y.F.* ("Heil Hitler You Fetishists"), *S.h.y.* ("Siberia hates

191

you"), *T. M. H. F. G. W.* ("The Modern House Of Good Will"). Sometimes Martin himself forgot after a few years what the initials stood for.

"Wrong I write wrong things, never mind, I'm dyslixic," he explained to a prospective girlfriend in his first letter to her. He always treasured spelling mistakes and other errors and used them as creative, poetic possibilities. If it's wrong, then do it right and make it really wrong. "The coffe, capucino, and its big brother Americano empty us out: Sure theyre German but we're not used to drinking and handling so much coffe, capucino, and its big brother Americano. How do they do it?" The text is from "Address to the Brainless," a talk Martin and Albert Oehlen gave at the Viennese Academy of Applied Art and later printed with a postscript: "Original grammatical mistakes copyrite Kippenberger-Oehlen."

Annoying readers and viewers until they could no longer tell which mistakes were actual errors and which were made intentionally was something Martin loved to do. He acted this out in many of his books, but also in his other languages: painting, sculpture, or photography (his photos were often grainy, blurry, or out of focus).

"Isn't misunderstanding what someone says the most acceptable misunderstanding in communication?" Martin asks in *Café Central* while describing the origin of his *Peter* sculptures: a Spanish carpenter had totally misunderstood Michael Krebber's instructions. Both artists were so excited by the results that they started building in errors themselves. Martin had similar luck later in Andalusia: he asked a Spanish farmer to bring him one live chicken at twelve o'clock, and the farmer showed up with twelve dead chickens at one o'clock.

No small part of his literature was created live, in conversations at the bar or the dinner table. It was a fleeting art that would nonetheless be preserved in other people's stories. The Swiss artist David Weiss called it "literature in situ": Weiss was at a dinner party given by a gallerist in Zurich when Martin stood up and gave thumbnail portraits of everyone at the table, many of whom he had never met. *Through Puberty to Success* contains several such portraits, for example, "Hans-Peter Feldmann, antique toy dealer, lives sauna-style." Sometimes it was enough for him to give someone a name, and almost everyone was misnamed, as though they were characters in Martin's personal play. Hans-Jürgen Müller, the proselytizing contemporary art dealer, was rebaptized Hans-Jesus Müller; Reiner Opoku, Dokoupil's assistant, became Okudoku; Birgit Küng, a very thin gallerist from Zurich, was "the Swiss pretzel stick"; Martin's own assistant Johannes Wohnseifer was called Didi at the beginning because Martin thought he could be Diedrich Diederichsen's little brother. Wohnseifer saw Martin's turning the other person into his own creation as an "educational process"; once the process was complete, Wohnseifer was Johannes again.

Martin's ad lib performances, when he stood up at a meal or in a bar and told an age-old joke, were like solo pieces. He loved these jokes for the fact that they told stories, sometimes whole life stories, in the shortest possible form, quick and dry and surprising—then Martin's joke was to take these jokes and drain all the humor out of them, destroying their concision and dragging them out for half an hour, or longer. In the words of Michel Würthle, "That's something you rarely see: this mix of dry humor and Maghrebi embellishment."

In one of these jokes, a man leaves a doctor's office and steps out onto the sidewalk in the shopping district "and the way he described it was magnificent," Johannes Wohnseifer said. "Every planter of flowers, every bike rack." Martin could keep it going for hours, having the poor man think: "What do I have? Do I have lobster? Do I have cod? Do I have salmon?"

If he was telling the joke in Kassel, it was the Kassel shopping district, down to the last detail. "It still makes me laugh today," Wohnseifer says. Finally, Martin had the man go back to the doctor and ask him what he has: "You have cancer [the same word as *crab* in German]." "Other people got tired of the joke, but Martin made me laugh till my sides hurt. When he saw it he kept ratcheting it up until I sometimes had to beg him to stop!"

Martin said once that he could stop painting but he could never stop talking.

Another time, he said that what he really needed were people to write down whatever he said in passing. Some people did; Martin did have a few Boswells. But many people today are sorry that no one kept a tape recorder running. He rarely gave interviews to journalists, for the same reason that he never let art historians write his catalog texts: he was afraid to be misunderstood or pigeonholed. But he did give a few interviews to non-journalists, often artists themselves, which served, as he told the fanzine *Artfan*, to "let him formulate something," as his earlier letter-writing had. He considered publishing one of them, the interview with Jutta Koether, as an experimental novel.

GERMAN LANGUAGE GOOD LANGUAGE

Martin loved the German language, and whenever he was abroad he bought *Bild* (which you could find in every village in Europe) and *Der Spiegel*. He didn't speak any other language except English, though he often acted like he did, or just talked with his hands. Not being able to do something, or being able to do it only badly, had its own appeal, as he showed at his exhibition at the Centre Pompidou in Paris. Instead of being embarrassed by his limited linguistic ability, he gave an on-camera interview with his curator Roberto Ohrt that could not have been more comical: to answer Ohrt's questions he simply read passages from his own book with a serious face in fake-French. Which sounded more like Dutch.

"German language good language," he said. "You can play with it, always take it in a new direction." He did with it what he did with everything: whatever he wanted. He freed it from conventional rules, treated it as a living thing, and saw words as pictures or just took them literally as words. When Michael Krebber said, "Art is an allotment garden," Martin built a little artwork out of a garden fence; when he made "Hunger" sculptures, he drilled holes in the styrofoam figures' bellies. He loved discovering words he'd never heard, like the English word "spoiler" for the thing on the back of a car. As Albert Oehlen said, "he invented his own language. He gave things names, but not made-up names, just words that he thought fit better. He turned this word around, used that one ironically, a third sounded like a certain word but was actually different." Jutta Koether called it Martin's personal "jive."

His habit of compressing language meant that people often couldn't understand what he was saying. He took the shortest path between two thoughts, even if that meant others wouldn't know exactly what lay between them. His jive left a lot of gaps. For example, he wrote on a menu in Burgenland during a meal, "Mommy's birthdaywishhappy with insalata seed & sweetbird." In other words, the noodle casserole our mother used to make that he always requested for his birthday as a child, with a corn salad, called *Vogerlsalat* in Austrian (roughly, birder's salad), made with sweet pumpkin seed oil.

The more he drank, the more cryptic he became, until he finally went under in his own secret language, as Roberto Ohrt called it. At the same time, Martin couldn't understand that other people couldn't understand him: "I'm not talking funny at all." That was one reason he insisted that Martin Prinzhorn write about him: Prinzhorn, a linguist, "took the dyslexic aspect into consideration," as he put it. "Martin was very conscious that dyslexia gave him a different approach." As a dyslexic, Martin not only mixed up letters when he wrote, he also combined different thoughts in an extremely idiosyncratic way, free-associated, thought in leaps and jumps, and "started his sentences in one place and ended up somewhere completely different," according to Isabelle Graw, editor of the art journal *Texte zur Kunst* (Texts on Art). "They were never complete sentences. He talked very fast, swallowed a lot of words, spoke in keywords and bullet points—it was totally brilliant and funny, and very unique." She called his way of talking "wild" while Martin called described it, in his "22nd papertiger not afraid of repetition" like this: "Even if you can't understand what this shit is saying, you know what it means."

American artists seem to have had an easier time with Martin's language: since they didn't understand German anyway (or Martin's English, which sounded like German), they didn't try to understand his Kippenberger-German either. They watched him tell jokes simply as a "stand-up comic's performance," according to Christopher Wool, who said he almost died laughing at the 109th telling of some nonsensical joke despite not understanding a word of it. "His sense of humor could be very abstract." Martin told Jutta Koether that in telling jokes what matters is the form, "how you put it together, how you tell it." The American artist Stephen Prina said, "It was as if Samuel Beckett was telling a joke. When Martin started telling his turtle joke, we thought, Here it comes again. How will it sound this time? We gave ourselves over to the poetry of it."

Even as a fourteen-year-old Martin wanted to write a

book, "about evil no less." He never totally gave up his Parisian dream of being a writer. "Predestination says I'll write the VERY GREAT book," he said. "But I know I can't write it alone, so I'll do it with art people who know how."

He never did, but he did write what he called a long poem, shortly before his death, and recited it at the opening of his major exhibition at the Modern and Contemporary Art Museum in Geneva:

People de la Muse
a typical Artist poem

PEOPLE WHO KEEP YOU WAITING
YEARNERS FOR THE ALWAYS-AVANT-
    GARDE
WHINING BOOKSELLERS
"I HAVE ALL YOUR BOOKS" BOASTERS
CIRRHOSIS OF THE LIVER IS NO EXCUSE
    FOR BAD ART
NOT BORN AN ARTIST
LIFETIME TENURED PROFESSORS
Artist of his generation
Collect small & paint big yourself
Collector with 2 1/2 PICTURES INSTEAD OF
    ONE
CHARITY EVENTS
EXCELLENT ARTIST RESTAURANTS
Sensitive furniture-moving for art
Art-lovers who hate letting you finish what you're
    saying
WANDERESSES WALKING IN TIME ON
    THE WIDE PATH
ARTISTWIDOWTERROR

POSTHUMOUS ARTIST COUPLES
NO CATALOG CHEAPSKATE-PETERS
BECAUSE OF MISER-FATHERS
ARTISTS WHO PUBLICLY ADMIRE OTHER
    GALLERISTS
UNIVERSALLY-CONSTANTLY-CRITICAL
    NON-MUSEUM-GOERS
$10 SPONSORS AND $18500 VOLUNTEER
    WORKERS
BUILT MUSEUMS AS AVAILABLE SPACE
    FOR ARCHITECTS & EMPLOYEES
ARTISTS WITHOUT A CORRECT SENSE
    OF SELF-PRESENTATION
IMPOTENT QUEER FISH WITH OR
    WITHOUT POCKET MONEY
ART BUSKERS
DISCOVERERS WHO BUY EVERYTHING
NONDISCOVERIES FLEEING THEREFROM
SHE BIDS IT UP, HE KNOCKS IT DOWN
INTERESTED PARTIES WHO'LL DROP BY
    AGAIN NEXT WEEK
YOUNG GERMAN ART BUYERS IN N.Y.
PEOPLE WHO WOULD RATHER SAY NO
    THAN FAIL
ART WARM
Painted-on gray
PLASTIC GRANDMOTHERS
Attempts at exposing without revealing
DRAWING MOMENTARY FORM
    THROUGH TIME
Chatting up conservative preserves qua art savvy

SUPPOSEDLY INTELLECTUAL HUMOR

Retouched "I KNOW THAT ALREADY" attitude
ECO-PRO & CONTRA-LONGLIFE
   INCINERATORS
Operetta = megapicture
RESPECTABLE PERFORMANCE = lots of
   moss
Re-cabling not de-naveling
SQUARE-CIRCLE-SCRIBBLE-STONESAW-
   FRACTION

"LET'S GO WEST" CURATORS
"LET'S GO SOUTH" CURATORS
Enfant-terrible-critics for everything
WINE LABEL ARTISTS
Reserving 3 pictures (worse than not buying)
Theory-heavy contemporary art

CIAO MEGA ART BABY!

THROUGH PUBERTY TO SUCCESS

"We were trying things out," the director Ulrike Ottinger said about her time in Berlin. "We were preparing ourselves, Martin was gathering his energies, preparing—it was the period when chaos swirled inside you, before it congealed and formed, and something came out." Berlin was probably the most intense time of his life. "He was like a sponge, sucking everything up." Helmut Middendorf said that the photographs and newspaper clippings that would serve as models for Martin's paintings for years to come hung in the bathrooms at Kippenberger's Office.

But eventually it was time to give the sponge a good squeeze. It was 1981, shortly before Martin left Berlin for good; he was already halfway to southern Germany in spirit. The period of being a genius-dilettante and do-it-yourself gallerist was over: paintings were being snatched out of the hands of the Moritzplatz painters, as well as the Mülheim Freedom painters in Cologne and the painters from Italy. "1980 was a rupture in Germany," the critic Manfred Hermes wrote. "Painting had just recently seemed empty, invalid, and irrelevant, then suddenly 'to paint again' was an unavoidable slogan among contemporary artists. It was, to be sure, a specific kind of painting that ruled the day: large pictures, figurative, often coarse and with an aura of emotional directness." The Moritzplatz painters had their breakthrough in 1980 with their exhibition at the Haus am Waldsee, a turning point for the whole art scene in Germany. To the arts editor of the *Tagesspiegel* in Berlin, it was "like a warm spring rain after a long drought."

Martin were in contact with the Moritzplatz painters and went to all of their openings, which were more than openings—they were huge parties. But he himself had "imposed" on himself "a prohibition against painting."

Baselitz later said that painting had never been dead, "but it was not allowed. I knew what we weren't supposed to do— but of course I didn't know what we were supposed to do."

Martin also knew what he wasn't going to do: dash up to an empty canvas and go to work, cheerfully slathering away with his brush. He had produced very little in Berlin, for example *Lovey-dovey, Here's My Super Breakfast* (a painting later used as the album cover for Johansson's S.O.36 show), a German shepherd painting called *Here, Asta, Lick Me*, and *But Ducks Don't Need Cotton Socks, Their Feet Always Stay Cool and Fresh in the Water.*

How can you paint when you're not supposed to paint any more?

Martin's answer: Get someone else to paint for you. Huge pieces, done in style. Martin didn't sign up just anybody, he used the best of the best, "the star among stars," as he would later write: Werner, the movie-poster painter he had met through his friend Hanno Huth, the movie producer ("they liked each other right off"). "In the Ufa film studios," Martin wrote about his representative,

> he started doing ladies and gentlemen like Greta Garbo and Hans Albers (50 mark tip) in the size they deserved. He was off and running, by the square meter. In the postwar years, the ruined Ku-damm consisted primarily of advertising pictures from the master's hand. 56 now, he is clearly the holder of two European records: extended outdoor exhibitions, from the Ku-damm to Bielefeld, and the second record in size: he did a St. Nicholas of more than 2150 sq ft.... After painting Bud Spencers and Hanna Schygullas, he did Kippenbergers, who forbid himself to paint some time ago.

Martin gave Werner the assignment to make twelve oil paintings, six by nine feet each, from Polaroids, many of them featuring Martin. Martin may not have set his hand to any of the painting, but he showed them in the Realism Studio of the NGBK, a left-wing collective headed by Otto Schily (later Germany's minister of the interior). Martin called the show *Dear Painter, Paint For Me.*

It was a thunderbolt, a dialectical master stroke: for Diedrich Diederichsen, it was "a pointedly non-naive conceptual work that at the same time expressed the greatest enthusiasm for naiveté, simplification, and sentimentality. What underlay it was the deepest, but also the most cheerful, mistrust of the artist-subject." Martin had done it: had his cake and eaten it too.

This first major exhibition, like so many of his later ones, came about because of his own efforts: he just decided he wanted it. While many people in Berlin considered him nothing more than a discotheque type, he put on a gray, slightly tight suit, tucked his book *1/4 Century Kippenberger* under his arm, walked into the Realism Studio on Hardengergstrasse, and said that he wanted to "do some exhibition." The curator, Barbara Straka, was among those in the NGBK who were looking for new forms of political art beyond socialist realism, and she liked what she saw: "the ironization of reality by means of everyday banalities transformed into art; defamiliarizing them by combining them into (apparently) context-free montages of text and image." The show turned out to be a surprise for Straka herself: "He didn't have us visit his studio first and didn't let on what he was doing." She didn't know that in fact he had no studio—not even an apartment of his own.

There had never been such a conceptual project at the Realism Studio, not to mention one with so much humor. For the first time (according to Martin), he sold a large painting—and right at the moment when his inheritance was entirely used up.

The thunderbolt then turned into a real lightning storm: several weeks of Kippenberger showing what he was capable of, right before he left the city for good. Kippenberger as painter, employer, author, performer, musician, conceptual artist, and monopolizer.

"Through Puberty to Success" was the overarching title for the series of events. "The whole thing was thoroughly orchestrated," Barbara Straka said, "in a way that hadn't existed at the time." It started on Martin's twenty-sixth birthday, February 25, with a book presentation in the Paris

Bar for the book *Through Puberty to Success*. It was a kind of balance sheet of his life and travels to that point—a collage of pictures and texts, bursting with ideas. The events continued on March 1 in Wanne-Eickel in the Ruhr, at the Our Fritz Mine (Martin's printed program made no mention of the fact that this was where and when our father was celebrating his sixtieth birthday), then came the opening of *Dear Painter, Paint For Me* at the NGBK on March 6 at 7:00, and a few hours later *Kippenberger in the Noodle Casserole Yes Please!* opened at the Petersen Gallery nearby. On March 11, at the Munich group exhibition *Rundschau Deutschland* (roughly, "Germany Today"), he showed his VW bus among all his colleagues' paintings—to the great annoyance of the event's organizer, who actually set up concrete bollards to stop it. Achim Schächtele, Martin's chauffeur on this occasion, got a dozen students to lift the bus up over the barrier so that Martin could stand on its roof as planned and give his speech. Finally, the crowning event: live shows at Café Einstein on March 24 and 25.

There were not many galleries in Berlin at the time, and very few with reputations that extended beyond the region: Rudolf Springer had one (where Martin always wanted to get a show but never did), and there was René Block, who gave a platform to Beuys and the Fluxus movement. But Martin had found a kindred spirit in Jes Petersen, who showed *Kippenberger in the Noodle Casserole Yes Please!* "Anarchist like a hedonist / Avantgarde like a Satanist / With a giant silhouette / Giant hat on his giant head / That was Jes as a gallerist" (so went the 2006 eulogy to Petersen by a friend). Petersen was seventeen years older than Martin, a farmer's son from Schleswig-Holstein in the north who had refused to do what he was supposed to do: follow in his father's footsteps on the farm. Instead he discovered modernism; preferred reading Kafka, Musil, Henry Miller, and Hans Henny Jahnn to tilling the soil; corresponded with Picasso, Raul Hausmann, André Breton, Allen Ginsberg, and Gerhard Rühm; traveled around; and became a publisher, author, and exhibition organizer who, in Thomas Kapielski's words, "showed the right things early, in the seventies and eighties." Like Martin, Petersen had a marked interest in crossing the lines between literature and art, and a predilection for Austrians like Konrad Bayer and Gerhard Rühm. Petersen was an extravagant, excessive man, always with too little money and too many debts; after the fall of the Wall, he ended up in jail for dealing cocaine.

Petersen had never believed, in any case, that you could make money with art. But even when he was diabetic and obese and could move only with difficulty in his little Charlottenburg triangle (apartment, gallery, and his local bar, the Zwiebelfisch), "you could still smell his enthusiasm," as the artist Georg Herold said. He was an autodidact who put on shows in his gallery on Pestalozzistrasse out of passion, "perversely going his own way," in Angelika Margull's words. He didn't show what promised to be a success—he showed what he liked. Martin would have two more exhibitions with him: *From New Style to Free Style** a year later, with Barfuss and Wachweger, and *Clotheslines Backwardsround* with Georg Herold in 1985, long after he had put Berlin behind him.

Martin put on a variety show at Café Einstein: a "One-Time-Only World Premiere" co-produced with the composer Gerhard Lampersberg (twenty-five years older than Martin) called "Whatever May Be / Berlin Stays Free / Jimmy Carter." With another book (print run: four hundred copies).

It was not Martin's first appearance at the Einstein. Back

---

* The title riffs on the German word "Jugendstil" (literally "New Style"), the movement corresponding to Art Nouveau.

in 1979, the young Matthias Matussek had already written in the daily evening paper *Abend* about Martin's *Slaves of Tourism*, an evening showing slides with Achim Schächtele of their tour of America:

> He's struck again: Together with "Akim from '44," the clever avant-gardist has pulled off what artists with serious reputations can only envy him for, and packed Café Einstein full to bursting. . . . People have once again coughed up their six marks, enjoyed a stifling, conspiratorial atmosphere, with candlelight to create an outpost of enlightened consciousness amid the late-capitalist decadence, and waited in suspense for what would come next. For no one knew what the title *Slaves of Tourism* was supposed to mean.
>
> All at once the candles were blown out and the electric lights turned off, and the title melody from *Once Upon a Time in the West*, on the harmonica, rumbled out of the loudspeakers.
>
> In walk Kippenberger and friend, in cowboy hats and heavy leather down to their boots. They use their flashlights to clear a path to a bed that had been set up for them, get undressed, relax with the beer they'd brought with them, and start running a prepared movie.
>
> A film strip with lots of red stripes, a hectic collage pace, a totally dated experimental-film attitude with content that's not up to snuff: oversized snatches of asphalt cracks in Manhattan sidewalks and the gorges of the Grand Canyon. The only organizing principle seemed to be Kippenberger himself.... What audience was this show actually meant for?

The people in charge of Café Einstein were apparently happier with the event than Matussek: immediately afterward, they hired Achim Schächtele (unemployed since S.O.36 had closed) to run their cultural events program.

KIPPENBERGER OUT OF BERLIN!

"Anyone as out as Tuscany and me / Shouldnt wear leather pants anymore," runs a poem of Martin's from July 1981. "Kippenberger Out Of Berlin!": the phrase had already started appearing in bar bathrooms all over town—put up by Martin himself. Now it was time to put the demand into action.

"Berlin," said the artist Angelika Margull, "was like a pressure cooker. At some point you had to get out." Precisely what had made the city so attractive—the combination of wildness and manageability—grew hard to take after a couple of years. At some point, Martin wondered why the Jungle was still, after years and years, the only disco in town—"To me that's the sign of a scene circling round and round on the same little spot." Gallerists had been clamoring for pictures from the Moritzplatz painters since the success of the Haus am Waldsee show, and the underground was turning bourgeois— the Selbsthilfegalerie (Self-Help Gallery) they had founded in 1977 closed in 1981. Middendorf thinks that the movement's success was one reason Martin left Berlin: "It was hard to go up against it."

Martin was in the middle of the scene but at the same time shut out of it. He had "contributed a lot of his own special qualities to the liveliness and confidence of the group of artists," according to the curator Johann-Karl Schmidt. "He was the motor for many of the artistic activities—even if an outboard motor." In Kippenberger's Office, he showed mostly other artists. Barbara Straka saw him as "an exotic species in the Berlin scene." In 1982, a major show, *Zeitgeist*, opened in the Gropius building. Christos Joachimides and Norman Rosenthal had invited all his friends to show work—Ina Barfuss, Thomas Wachweger, Albert Oehlen, Werner Büttner—but not Martin, who embodied and shaped the zeitgeist more than almost anyone. Martin had already photographed the sign for dogs—"We have to stay outside"— and built it into the platform he had constructed for Claudia Skoda. It was something he would often experience himself.

The mood in the city grew more aggressive, too, with more and more violent clashes between squatters and the police, whole streets blocked off, the Kreuzberg in flames. After closing Kippenberger's Office in 1980, Martin no longer had a fixed residence in Berlin. He stayed a few months with Angelika Margull, painting a little, and this was the period when he went to Paris. He then moved to Charlottenburg to stay with Uschi Welter, the costume designer. As he wrote in *Through Puberty to Success*:

> Uschi has a built-in closet with a mirror that I dance and run back and forth in front of and every now and then I think about if what I have in my head is really right; when she's there I ask her—and then she answers. After that I wander around through the room or take my afternoon nap . . . on the bottom shelf of her china cabinet there's the necessary ingredients to make spaghetti, if I feel bad.

On top of everything else, Martin needed money—desperately. In the summer of 1981, the tax office threatened to kick down his apartment door (that is, Uschi Welter's apartment door) to collect the 1,080 marks he owed in back taxes; a year later,

Deutsche Bank cut off his credit because he had overdrawn his account by 6,734.75 marks. All his Berlin activities—exhibitions, catalogs, stickers, concerts, the Office—had cost money, a lot of money, but brought in nothing.

He brought in a little playing mau-mau and pinball, but he couldn't live off that. And there was no way he wanted to go back to the kind of unskilled part-time jobs he had had as a student in Hamburg. He had to make money, and since art was the only thing he could do, he had to produce art he could sell.

The decisive impetus to really start painting came from his friend Meuser, the Düsseldorf sculptor. Martin later called it a turning point. Meuser said to him at the Paris Bar, "'Kippenberger, the way you talk—you should just start painting pictures exactly the way you tell stories.' And then I was off. Somehow that was a clear argument." But not many people understood Martin as well as Meuser did. Martin's painting would give rise to lots of misunderstandings in the years ahead.

Once again, Martin moved to Italy to really start painting; he also needed to find somewhere else to start selling his work and decided to return from Italy to Stuttgart and the Black Forest, not to Berlin. Berlin lacked not only major galleries but also buyers with disposable income—a lot of young people had come to Berlin, and the old people had stayed, but the middle-class, middle-aged adults had largely left for West Germany. It was time to leave town. Martin's excessive lifestyle was also getting too boring, and too dangerous. Christel Buschmann, the director who gave him a small part in her movie *Gibby West Germany*, still remembers the exact moment when she was sitting with him at the window of the Paris Bar and he said, "I'm either going to the loony bin or to the Black Forest."

PARIS BAR

Berlin no longer interested him, but there was still the Paris Bar and its owner, Michel Würthle. The Paris Bar was home base on the highway of Martin's life—the "psychological port from which he set sail," as Meuser called it. Martin knew that whenever he went, there would always be someone there for him, morning, noon, and night, seven days a week. Spoerri's snare-picture assemblage would still be hanging from the ceiling, the same waiters would be there, oysters and blood sausage would still be on the menu. He knew he would run into someone—friends, enemies, strangers, Dieter Roth, Otto Sander, Bruno Brunnet, Lüpertz, Koberling, maybe Fassbinder, too. The food and drink were free for him and a guest: back before Martin could sell his art, he made a deal with Michel Würthle to trade the black and white paintings from Florence that no one else wanted for lifetime free food. Now the pictures were hanging in a corner of Paris Bar near the bathroom.

He could act at home at the restaurant on Kantstrasse— he was allowed to climb on the tables, pull down his pants, tell his endless jokes, drink, and insult people. The owner did it, too. They danced together until dawn, and then "the hour of turning into an animal" struck, as Heiner Müller called it.

When Michel Würthle and his partner, Reinald Nohal, took over the Paris Bar in 1979, it was already a French-style bistro with an artist clientele. Then the two Austrians gave it their own special touch, drawing on their memories of Café Hawelka in Vienna. Michel embodied the combination of cultures, with his worldly Parisian elegance and sharp Viennese humor; his real name was Michael, but he preferred to speak French with his waiters. Despite having lived in Paris for years, Michel came across less as a Frenchman than as an

"First Meeting at the Exile" (Michel Würthle)

actor playing a Frenchman, with the way he smoked, the way he dressed, and the way he performed at his bar. The Italians, too, had taught him important things about style and *la bella figura*: "That was bananas for me, in Rome, to see someone keeping a spare pair of silk socks in his Ferrari but no money for gas."

"Michel Würthle: Foreigner (Au), unrecognized vocal talent at a given hour, e.g. to give just two representative examples: 'Humanity is the hit, that's it' and '(What's up here with) Doodle-ee-doo.' Can smoke through his nose while performing." This is Martin's description of Michel in *Through Puberty to Success.*

Michel's grandfather ran a well-known gallery in Vienna. Michel had gone to the arts and crafts school in Cologne at sixteen, studied with Kokoschka at the Salzburg Summer Academy ("I liked him, he was so well dressed, a dandy in flannel slacks"), and ended up at the Art Academy in Vienna, where he found the stench of academia so repulsive that he spent the whole time going to the movies. He could find a lot to copy there, too.

He was ten years older than Martin and had come to Berlin in 1970. They met each other at the Exile, the Viennese bar and in Kreuzberg that Michel ran with Oswald Wiener. In Berlin, the environment was not so Catholic and conservative, but another form of cultural barbarism ruled the day: the culinary kind. As a result, Ingrid and Oswald Wiener and Michel Würthle opened the Exile with artists like Dieter Roth, Günter Brus, and Richard Hamilton helping to decorate it.

Wiener and Roth carried out the principle of provocation, the same way Martin liked to. "Nothing but tests," Michel said. "The ceremony consisted of the most unpleasant shit-talk you can imagine, using the most ordinary expressions, and the examinee's role was to not show any shock." He later described his first meeting with Martin as "a kind of sniffing each other out, Mexican dogfight style. Later I already felt that he really loved me." Wilhelm Schürmann said that Martin "trusted [Michel] with every bone in his body"; Michel was his best friend, stage partner, drinking buddy, and travel companion. "All night long Martin could only look at Michel," said Johannes Wohnseifer, Martin's assistant. In Wohnseifer's view, one thing Martin admired about him might have been his stamina: every evening Michel would be standing ramrod straight at the door of the Paris Bar, greeting the guests, even if he had spent the whole night before pulling down his pants with Martin and dancing on the tables and sometimes falling

MI HERMANO KIPPENBERGER

YOU CAN HAVE
HIS LAST PESO
BUT YOU CAN'T HAVE SEIN
MELANCHOLIEMODUL.

"Portrait of Martin Kippenberger" (Michel Würthle)

off of them, too. Martin liked this extreme "combination of insanity and professionalism," as Michel's wife Catherine described it: "the ambiguity, the irony and performance." Catherine said Michel was "ready at every moment to give you the most stately Viennese kiss on the hand and let fly with a fart at the same time."

When Martin was in Berlin, he was at the Paris Bar almost all day—morning, afternoon, evening, and all night too, even if he had a room at the Kempinski (a hotel he liked chiefly

because of its location, around the corner from the Paris Bar).
He didn't even have breakfast in the hotel. Instead he went to
the Paris right after waking up and sat down with the staff,
who ate breakfast at 10:30. He talked and joked with them,
drew and pondered, and had them tell him stories. Their life
stories. Michel said, "He had the waiters in the palm of his
hand. They loved him, they had fun together, he could do
anything with them."

The legendary Herr Breslauer, with his artful combover,
won Martin's special admiration: "Employed as a conveyor of
meals and drinks in one and the same bar on Kantstr. since
before I was born," as Martin described him in *Through
Puberty to Success.*

All over the world, old-school maître d's like Herr
Breslauer were recognized by Martin as kindred souls. They
had attitude, pride, and style; they never curried favor or
demeaned themselves; and they always used the formal *Sie,*
even with regular guests, at a time when using the informal
du was almost mandatory. They were not students, temps,
or wannabe artists, but professionals in the world of service,
as skilled and masterful in their career as Martin was in his,
to the point where they made it look easy. In their uniforms
they were born performers who knew they were playing a role
and at the same time were fully themselves. And so Martin
always treated them as his equals, with respect, and as artists
in their own discipline. Many waiters remember Martin as
kind, funny, and not arrogant in the least. What they had in
common, in the view of Attila Corbaci, a waiter at the Exile
in Berlin when he met Martin and later the owner of Café
Engländer in Vienna, was that they were born to be what they
were: like art, "gastronomy is something you can't learn at
school. You either have it or you don't."

Martin later said that he only used the medium of

painting "to tell stories or make a copy of myself." He used the Paris Bar as his stage, or his museum, where he could show his own works and later a part of his collection. In 1991, on the night the large Metropolis exhibition opened at the Martin Gropius Building—all the important contemporary artists were represented, all except Martin—he rehung paintings throughout the entire bar. In a spectacular action, he put up an entire exhibition of his own with the help of friends and students in one night. "It was magnificent," Helmut Middendorf said. "He knew that after the Metropolis opening everyone, absolutely everyone who was anyone in the art world, would come to the Paris Bar. It was the best contribution to the show." "The most alive and lively," according to Fischli and Weiss, the Swiss artists, not least because Martin's exhibition showed many young artists, especially female artists, whom he found interesting: Louise Lawler, Laurie Simmons, Zoe Leonard, Andrea Fraser, and others. Of course many more people saw Martin's show than the Metropolis show, since it hung on the walls of the bar for years. Yellowed with age and lived-in like a real home, the Paris Bar now had as many pictures on the wall as we once had on the walls of our house in Frillendorf—some of them actually the same pictures.

Martin continued to come by the Paris Bar, out of love for Michel, even when he started to think Berlin was horrible and no longer felt as much at home, even in his old favorite bar. After the fall of the Wall, there were Bonn politicians, Berlin hairdressers, and tourists among the artists; the place lost some of its exclusivity since it now had competitors in the city. During the nineties, Martin preferred to visit Michel at his house in Greece instead of at the Paris Bar.

CHAPTER FOUR

STUTTGART AND THE BLACK FOREST

Invest in oil!
— MK

"Berlin needs a new paint job," Martin declared in a postcard to Berlin from Stuttgart. "Arrived safe and sound." Redoing the past was never Martin's way—he would rather move somewhere new, where the paint was still wet, as it were, even to provincial Swabia if the opportunity arose. Max Hetzler said, "Stuttgart was good for him."

One day, Martin showed up at Hetzler's front door to unload an entire VW bus full of art. He had said on the phone that he had painted some pictures he wanted to show the gallerist and Hetzler had said OK, thinking Martin would come by with a few photographs, maybe one or two paintings as examples. He hadn't expected a load of freight like this.

But Martin always worked "for the moment." Whatever he had, he wanted to show without delay: paint today, exhibit tomorrow. He had driven to Siena with thirty blank canvases and had come back a couple of weeks later with thirty paintings. He had called his old friend Achim Schächtele from Italy and told him he needed to come down, and so Achim did, getting a week's vacation in Martin's bed and breakfast, painting another few paintings for him, and then driving him back to Germany. Martin sat in the back of the van on a little chair, crammed in among finished paintings, stretchers, and barrels of oil paint that he proudly explained he had gotten dirt cheap. Hetzler wasn't the only gallerist Martin had called, but he was the only one who didn't say no right off the bat.

They had met in Berlin two years before, while Martin was still an artist without any art, without a studio, and without a home. Hetzler had visited him during his grand tour with the older, established Stuttgart gallerist Hans-Jürgen Müller. The IXth International Art Congress and Deutscher Künstlerbund (German Artist Association) exhibition was due to take place in Stuttgart in 1979, a major event that yielded lavish grants and support for related activities as well, so Hetzler and Müller were traveling through Europe to collect contemporary art for their exhibit, "Europa '79." They had hit if off with Martin and spent their nights going around Berlin with him, but he didn't end up in their show. If you don't have any paintings, you can't show any paintings.

Now it was different. His show *A Secret of Mr. A. Onassis's Success* opened on September 18, 1981. The paintings hung close together on the walls of Hetzler's gallery, all the same size (twenty by twenty-four inches) and in a series, like the Florence paintings, but this time in color:

Series A: Guitars Not Named Gudrun
Series B: The Prevented Flannel Rags
Combo F: From Fussyfred to Heartybrink
Combo G: Capri by Night
Assortment I: The Hermann Family
Assortment I 2: New Conservatism
Assortment I 3: Funny, Funny
Set: Known from Movies, Radio, Television, and
     Police Call Columns

The motifs included a refrigerator (*What Saves Every Shared Apartment*), a torso (*AOK*, which is also the abbreviation for the cheapest German health insurance), pasta tongs (*My Friend Udo*), and a stupid joke (*Older Lady Cleaning the House*). This time, he hadn't gotten other people to paint for him—or only as rare exceptions—even if the invitation said "Paintings by Hans Siebert After Models by Kippenberger," whether to confuse the public or confuse the punks. (He was afraid, he told a friend, that the punks might come from Berlin and destroy his exhibition.) The truth was he had painted the pictures himself, with the "courage for garbage" he always demanded of himself. He was helped only with hanging the pictures, and with the titles, by his friend Meuser from Düsseldorf.

He had done it: found a commercial gallerist and thus a home in the art market, along with a whole artist-family. Hetzler also represented Albert and Markus Oehlen, Werner Büttner, Günther Förg, Hubert Kiecol, and Meuser. Many of them were already Martin's friends, and he would soon meet the others through the gallery. For the first time, Martin was taken seriously as an artist, not just seen as a character on the Berlin scene; for the first time, the public was not just being entertained by Martin, they were buying his work, too. "Invest in oil!" the invitations cried. "Starting at a couple hundred marks, choose for yourself!"

In Stuttgart he acquired a circle of collectors, who would remain faithful friends and supporters from then to the end of his life (if their finances held out that long): the Grässlin family in the Black Forest, Uli Knecht in Stuttgart, Helmut Seiler from Augsburg (who slept in a sleeping bag in the gallery, since he had no money to spare for a hotel), and Wilhelm Schürmann, visiting from the Rhineland. The Essen collector Helmut Metzger bought work as well, as did

Hans-Jürgen Müller, who had just changed camps and was now a collector instead of a gallerist.

The pictures were cheap, but that was not the only reason people bought them. Max Hetzler says today, "They bought them out of real pleasure. Here was an artist you could reach out and touch—someone you could go out with at night. Martin really was an amazingly entertaining person, who got people excited and intrigued with him. Back then he didn't snub people so much either. It was a very friendly atmosphere, no aggression, no pressure, no competition." Everyone knew each other in the small Stuttgart art world. "It was very relaxed," according to the photographer Wilhelm Schürmann, "people didn't feel pushed to act glamorous."

So the collectors followed Martin's advice and invested in oil, which is not to say they saw the paintings as financial investments—no one at the time could have predicted that art was about to increase in value so dramatically. They bought the pieces because they were funny and different. "We had never seen pictures like that," Uli Knecht said; he was excited by "their vulgarity, their shock value."

These were precisely the reasons others didn't buy. Rudolf Zwirner, an art dealer from Cologne who was successful with American artists, among others, tells the story of meeting a major collector at Martin's show who was complaining about missed opportunities: "If only we'd met ten years ago! We could have bought a great collection—Warhols, Rauschenbergs, Lichtensteins, Jasper Johns, all the big stuff." That's water under the bridge, Zwirner said, but here we are today with the chance to start something now—with Kippenberger. The collector just laughed at him. "Oh, I mean real art! That's not painting."

What Martin liked about Stuttgart was the small circle he found there and the chance to begin something new far away from Berlin. Stuttgart had the advantages of the periphery—it was easier to get established there than in Cologne, for example—without being entirely provincial. There was, after all, the Neue Staatsgalerie, the Ketterer auction house (whose auctions drew the whole art world twice a year), and Hans-Jürgen Müller's gallery, opened in 1958, where he had shown the international avant-garde (Frank Stella, Yves Klein, Cy Twombly) quite early on. "The pictures cost $100 each," Müller recalled, "and still had no buyers." Of course he did sell some pieces—unlike the Berliners, people in Swabia had money—as well as advising the Essen collector Helmut Metzger and the Grässlin family in Sankt Georgen.

Müller had meanwhile given up his gallery and was just starting to assemble what would soon be a major collection of art from the 1980s, shown in 1985 in a Darmstadt museum as an exhibition called *Deep Looks*. (One of Martin's pictures from his stay in southern Germany is titled *Small Apartment, Deep Looks*; another is *Big Apartment, Never Home*.) Müller was a hard-drinking enthusiast for modern art with a real sense of mission; he would soon turn his missionary zeal toward ecology and culture. At the time, he was in a relationship with Ursula Schurr, who had a gallery in the same building as Hetzler. He met Bärbel Grässlin through her before she joined Hetzler.

Then there were Tanja Grunert and Achim Kubinski: younger, wilder gallerists. In 1981, Martin sent out invitations to a *Dialogue with the Youth* show at their gallery; when the youth didn't actually show up, everyone just went out to lunch. Still, Martin ended up with a nice invitation he could show people: a photograph of his bandaged head after his beating at the hands of Berlin's youth. Later, he would paint a version, too. In general, his invitations and posters were always more than merely informative announcements: they constituted an independent branch of his graphic work. Martin also sometimes made what he called "belated posters," if he wasn't able to pull one together before an opening (for the *Farewell to the Youth Bonus II* show with Albert Oehlen in Thomas Borgmann's gallery, for example).

THE SAHARA PROGRAM AND
ANTI-SAHARA PROGRAM

After the opening at Hetzler's gallery, Martin took a break that could hardly have been more radical: he retreated to a small town in the Black Forest. After the excesses of his life in Hamburg and Berlin, he spent a winter living a family life and drying out. He called it his Sahara Program.

Martin titled a 1990 catalog *Homesick Highway*, and it is hard to imagine a more concise description of the life he led between the two extremes: constantly on the road at top speed, constantly settling down in another different city. Jutta Koether wrote in the catalog, "If you want to understand Kippenberger, you have to understand him as an artist who always makes use of a skewed, backward perspective. He stays in one place, for a time, lives life to the fullest there, then abandons it just as quickly." He always intended to stay in a given place, as he assured Koether in 1991: "I never managed to do it, but the intention was always there and still is." To stay was always a possibility that turned out to be an impossibility after all; Martin's craving for a home could only be satisfied temporarily.

Martin made a series of drawings with the floor plans of all his apartments and rooms—taking stock of his *Moves 1957-1988*, as the catalog was subtitled—and called the series *Input-Output*. For Martin, the cliché of being happily married with two kids was a terrifying vision of comfortable domesticity that would have meant the end of his life as a creative artist. He was always angry at fellow artists who made things too easy for themselves—accepting professorships, moving out to a castle in the country, working in only one style or on only one theme once it had proven to be successful—though of course it was stressful to lead the restless life that he led. "Insanely stressful."

He was at home with people, not in particular places.

Martin sought out rest stops along his highway, places he could refuel for a night or a few days, sometimes even enjoying a domestic life for a few weeks without it smothering him. These were friends who he knew would take him in, with whom he would not have to constantly produce. He had portable families everywhere and he could show up without warning, be welcomed like a prodigal son, be spoiled and not need to take responsibility for anything—he could worry only about art, a good time, and women. When his tank was full he could disappear again at any time, driving on down the highway of his life.

He often moved in with someone else rather than looking for a place his own. On one poster, he called himself "Occupant"; Grässlin's granddaughter complained he was more like a squatter, since he made every house his own, the same way he reshaped, overran, and appropriated his bars or his cities.

The Grässlins were his most important host family. Martin called them "his alleged family" in the 1994 catalog for their large Kippenberger collection, collected since 1981. In the Black Forest idyll of Sankt Georgen, he found what had long since disappeared from Essen: a mother, a home, and a large family that collected art. His move to the Black Forest was a return to his childhood. Sankt Georgen was even near the boarding school he had attended as a boy. On New Years Day 1982, he visited the school with Karola Grässlin and did what he had always dreamed of doing: went to lunch at the Golden Eagle and spent the night. Of course, he was no longer a child. He allowed himself the Anti-Sahara Program on holidays, but it turned out to be impossible to get a drink in the evening, either in the inn or in the village, and they ended up clambering up a steep mountain in deep snow in search of a nightcap, with Karola in gold pumps. He told Karola how strict it had been at boarding school, and that whenever he misbehaved he had had to go running through the woods and around the lake. He could not remember anything good about his time there.

The Grässlins were big, loud, tightly knit, and firmly rooted. The composition of the family was a familiar one for Martin—three sisters and one brother, and Martin made five—but in this family, Martin was the oldest! Bärbel Grässlin worked for Max Hetzler but was still so influenced by the bourgeois world of her youth that Martin was "a shock" for her: he always seemed more than just one year older than she was, since "he already had such a totally different life behind him." Thomas Grässlin was in a nearby town, studying to take over as his father's successor in the family business; he was an artistic advisor for the Rottweil Forum and was a driving force behind extending the art collection in a more contemporary direction. Sabine was studying haute cuisine near Lake Constance and came back to Sankt Georgen on weekends; her young daughter Katharina, nicknamed the Scream Monster, stayed with Sabine's mother. Finally, Karola, the youngest, was just finishing high school. It was a clan with which Martin could eat, drink, party, dance, fight, and play mau-mau. He could make fun of them and interest them in his projects.

They were one thing he wasn't: rich. Their father, Dieter Grässlin, had run a very successful company that made electric timers and had started the family art collection, concentrating on Arte Povera and Art Informel. He was Baroque in both personality and physical appearance, and bought art "like a feudal prince," acquiring pictures by the dozen, according to the gallerist Hans-Jürgen Müller. He had died suddenly in 1976 (the same year as our mother), and his children had just started focusing on the artists of their own generation, including Martin and the Oehlen brothers, Büttner, Förg, Kiecol, and Meuser, and later Franz West, Michael Krebber, and others.

　After Dieter's death, his widow, Anna, became the head of the family. She was a strong woman, her hair in a flawless wave, whom Martin was only too happy to let mother him. "He was really very vulnerable," she would later say. "Strangers could find him shocking. He knew how to behave himself, he had manners, he just didn't always put them into practice." He always treated her with great respect—"he never said a single nasty word to me"—however mean and cruel he could be to her daughters. "Anna was always the greatest," Martin's assistant Johannes Wohnseifer later said. "He would never let anyone criticize her." He liked her nonchalance, her kind-hearted discipline, and her humor. Never once in all the years he visited and spent the night there did he do what had so gotten on our mother's nerves: bring home another of his ever-changing girlfriends. "It would never have crossed his mind," Anna Grässlin said. She could say things like "I'd never be Kippi's little floozy!" and he would quote them in public and in his catalogs with great delight. In general he loved the family's unique language, how they said *jetset* instead of *jetzt* (now)—"jetset it's dinnertime" or "jetset we're talking," for example—or *Ha ja* instead of *Ja* for "yes" (he turned *Ha ja* into a painting). Martin brought Anna matchboxes from all over the world, and she did a lot for him, but she never turned into another member of his entourage—she always maintained a certain skepticism. On one occasion, when the art shipper delivered the EuroPallets that her children had paid a fortune for as Martin's sculptures, Anna "almost flipped out, practically fainted. I couldn't understand it at all."

The first time Martin arrived in Sankt Georgen it was evening. Anna was sitting in front of the TV quietly knitting with her daughters Sabine and Karola. Even if Karola never picked up her knitting needles again, Martin liked this initial glimpse of wholesome family life and its atmosphere of security. After a test-residence at the Grässlins' house, he came back as soon as the Stuttgart gallery opening was over and moved into an apartment of his own that the family had made available to him. At twelve on the dot he walked through the deep Black Forest snow to lunch at the rustically furnished house—noodle casseroles that surely tasted better than our mother's. This family knew how to cook.

He always played little jokes on the grandmother of the family and sang a song that made her laugh every time: "Ding-a-ling-a-ling, Here Comes the Eggman." He gave her one of his egg paintings, a self-portrait, which she hung over the sofa with its throw pillows and armrest-covers in her Black Forest living room. She had formerly worked as a maid, and Martin praised her ironing artistry to the skies, to other artists too: he told Meuser that he absolutely had to have Grandma iron one of his shirts someday. He could also discuss pasta for hours with "Eggman's Grandma," as he called her in the Grässlin catalog—his favorite food and her absolutely least favorite, "that Italian stuff."

The family rituals and dramas fascinated him, of course. For example, Grandma, who lived downstairs, came to dinner every night with her own plate and her own butter, bread, and sausage. Every night, the same scenario unfolded, "like in *Dinner For One*," Thomas Grässlin said, "the same every night." The last knife and fork were barely laid down on the table when Grandma whipped away all the plates; every night Anna said, "Mama, don't worry, we'll take care of it"; and every few weeks a fight broke out over it between mother and daughter. And of course Martin had to do something with Grandma's hobby, latch-hook, so he did bath mats. He showed latch-hooked bath mats as multiples in 1990 at Bärbel Grässlin's Frankfurt gallery: *A Handful of Forgotten Pigeons*, with yin-yang, New Age, and Goethe City designs. Grandma hadn't made all of them—Martin dragged everyone he could to Sankt Georgen to work on them, children as well as old people, all co-ordinated by Sabine Grässlin.

"Dear Berlin Filmikin!" Martin wrote to his friend Uschi Welter on November 26, 1981, from "St. Georg City," "I've polished off the hustle and bustle with var. slipups in the snow + now i'm sitting dry as the Sahara in the hotel Garni Kammerer cafe + waiting til the shops reopen. Hours: 8:30-12:30, 4:00-6:30."

Café Kammerer was his local during the day, where he regularly met with Karola Grässlin, his girlfriend at the time. She cut school a lot: "It just didn't interest me at all any more." It was more fun with Martin, and she learned more, too: "He laid out the whole art scene for me. I thought it was super interesting, everything he knew." At Café Kammerer he unpacked the shopping bags full of stuff she had bought at the only department store in town—absurdities of life that he would turn back into art, such as little gummi animals or an eraser with "Absolute Hardship Case" printed on it (he had himself photographed with the eraser stuck in his mouth). It was Karola, one time when she and Martin were enjoying themselves at a bar and two women stared at them, who turned around and said: "Envy and greed, that's what I need." Martin liked the phrase so much he immediately turned it into a painting.

Saturdays at Café Kammerer he always sat at the table with the regulars, the same way he played dice with the locals at the Klimperkasten, a lumberjack bar. In no time everyone in Sankt Georgen knew him—he had chatted with everyone, told his little jokes, and was known as an odd duck. Martin said once that he had had the same experience over and over again: in the most isolated places, people would react to him as though he were E.T., would be horrified at first, but then would affectionately take him under their wings. That was why, he thought, there were so many bars where he never had to pay.

Then again, the reverse was also true: after his Kreuzberg nightlife, the village and structured family life with lunch and dinner on the table at the same time every day were as alien to him as American suburbia was to E.T. Even in his own childhood, he had never lived like that. Karola even complained to her mother once that the Grässlins' life was too sheltered, which Martin right away turned into a painting: *Mommy, You Never Showed Me Misery.*

* * *

A week after the first postcard reached Uschi Welter in Charlottenburg, the second one came, with a picture of a Black Forest girl and a Black Forest cake (with recipe) and the message "7th day Sahara Program—150 canvases & easel arrived." For the next few weeks, hopped up on nothing but coffee, apple juice, and Mother Grässlin's cooking, Martin painted in his attic apartment like a man possessed. Visitors like Uschi came every now and then, and Martin took long walks with them. At night he went to the bar or went dancing at the Bear's Den with Karola, putting on shows à la John Travolta on the wooden dance floor with everyone else standing around the edges, watching in wonder. That was another advantage of the provinces: you could shine even brighter there.

He left sometimes, most often to attend art openings, and when he came back he brought Karola heaps of records, all groups she had never heard of: the Lounge Lizards, Kraftwerk, Deutsch-Amerikanische Freundschaft, punk music that had never made it to Sankt Georgen. He "broke open" Thomas Grässlin's taste in music, as he said himself, introducing the dedicated jazz fan to Palais Schaumburg and Laurie Anderson and encouraging him to be more playful, in everything. Karola copied the records Martin brought onto tapes so that he would have something to listen to in the studio. By that point, he was really in full swing, making three or four paintings a day and prepping the next day's canvases at night. Karola later said: "That was the great thing for me, to see for the first time how work like that is made."

He packed it all up for Christmas, while the Anti-Sahara Program took effect for a few days, and hauled all his work to the Grässlin family's house. He took their art off the walls and hung his own paintings around the whole living room, floorboards to ceiling, some with the paint still wet. Mother Grässlin was not amused—first of all, it was Christmastime; secondly, nothing like that, so real and concrete, had ever been hung in her house before. Then the family spent Christmas Eve arranging Martin's paintings into series, big and small, while Frank Sinatra records played and Karola, at Martin's insistence, wore a Black Forest folk costume. The whole holiday season that year smelled of oil paint instead of pine tree and roast goose. In return, each of them got a picture as a present: Thomas's was *Buying Feels Great, Paying Feels Terrible*; Karola's was *I Too Wanted to Be the First*; Sabine's was a photo of a gravestone at the dog cemetery, *Our Little Bimbo. Remembered Always, With Love.* In Martin's opinion, the best Christmas present anyone got was Thomas's new slot-car racetrack. Martin played with it the whole time.

FIFTEEN LEGS, STILL ALONE

The Sahara Program and Anti-Sahara Program / Life is hard and unfair was the title of Martin's show at the Rottweil Art Forum that opened on February 28, 1982, three days after his twenty-ninth birthday (and its accompanying Anti-Sahara Program). The invitation showed a humpty-dumpty eggman who had fallen off a wall; the poster showed a cheeky, confident Martin in the Black Forest snow, sitting in a Beuys felt suit on the Erich Hauser sculpture the Grässlins had placed in front of their company office. He occupied art the way he occupied houses.

Hauser, the big fish in that small pond, didn't think it was funny. He smelled competition. Martin was the first artist in the new generation to show at the Forum, which Hauser had launched. The distaste was mutual. "There was a storm in the air," Anna Grässlin said, and it hadn't helped that Martin had unashamedly lain down on Hauser's sofa and made out with Karola. Mrs. Hauser had had a hysterical attack. The great Joseph Beuys, on the other hand, found Martin's rudeness funny and simply did to Martin what Martin did to everything: he appropriated the appropriator and turned a Kippenberger into a Beuys, stamping and signing a series of Martin's posters.

The opening was packed with two hundred visitors. The artist supplied the beer himself. Martin gave several speeches at the same time, getting other people to read for him; Michel Würthle, who had come from Berlin, called everyone together for a group portrait, but the press photographer didn't think that was his job, "so the likewise attending Papa Kippenberger took it with his pocket camera. That only sometimes worked—'The thing fell into the toilet.'" The critics were confused by the number of different styles and pictures, but they recommended the show.

On view were his six-part series of Black Forest motifs (Sankt Georgen's City Hall Square, the Grässlins' windmill), called *Fifteen Legs, Still Alone,** and his most famous series to date, *Well Known Through Film, Radio, Television, and Police Call Columns.* The latter had grown from fourteen to twenty-one pictures by that point, mostly portraits—of Helmut Schmidt and his wife (*Let the Weeds Grow*), Yasser Arafat (*Arafat Is Sick of Shaving*),** a beaming Ronald Reagan with a mouse in a bloody puddle on the collar of his suit, a Francis Bacon–style self-portrait with a spattered face (*Little Asshole Kippi*). The Grässlins bought the whole series. The show also included *Berlin by Night*, the three small pictures that summarized Martin's years of excess in Berlin. They were all grubby little pictures in his usual twenty by twenty-four inch format, copied from photographs, painted as garishly and badly as possible, and jammed up next to each other in a single row around the gallery.

The catalog (*Mr. Kippenberger*) ended up a bit too nice, too tasteful, for Martin, but otherwise he was happy with the exhibition and proud to be able to bring our father to see it. He introduced his two families to each other the way he wanted to.

---

* A rhyme in German: "*Fünfzehn Beine, trotzdem alleine.*"
* * Another rhyme: "*Arafat hat das Rasieren satt.*"

Martin's Black Forest mission was accomplished and the Sahara Program completed. "Suddenly he felt pulled away again," as Mother Grässlin said. He couldn't have stood it any longer in the idyllic small town where everything closed early, so he left the desert behind and moved on to the next oasis.

FAVORITE THEME: MISERY

"Suddenly, there was Kippi," the men's clothier Uli Knecht says. He no longer remembers where, when, and how he met Martin for the first time, just that there he was and he wouldn't stop being there. Martin lived in Stuttgart for only six months (he had often visited before), but it felt like years to many people. He lived in the converted basement apartment of the building where Hetzler's gallery was, on Schwabstrasse, and he was with Hetzler "day and night."

But he worked at Uli Knecht's place. Knecht emptied out his garage (actually a warehouse for his business) and Martin set up a studio there, in the middle of the city right next to Knecht's store and under his office. From there you could easily get to everything on foot—most importantly, Martin's two locals: a Spanish restaurant and an Italian restaurant, Come Prima, one of the few places allowed to stay open late in Stuttgart. He quickly befriended the owner, and even at 3 a.m. Martin could drink, talk, smoke, and do anything he wanted at Come Prima.

After having had to get by with not much money for such a long time, Martin could finally spend freely, buying things for himself and taking friends out. At the time, Uli Knecht was for men what Jil Sander was for women, except he didn't design his elegant clothing himself, he imported it from Italy: Armani, Brioni, Cerrutti, in an era when most Germans couldn't spell the words. Knecht bought Martin's work "fresh from the studio, as it came out the door," and gave him in return coupons for free clothes, which Martin then gave away. Some as gifts to ladies of the night—"and then he was the boss"; some to me and his other sisters.

Martin "had a good home base" in Uli Knecht's store, Knecht later said. "The store was always full of pretty girls and things going on and something to look at. First he'd check out the girls downstairs in the store, and if they said no he'd come up to the office. He always gravitated toward whoever listened to him the most, whoever was nicest to him." He especially liked hanging out with the ladies who worked in Knecht's front office. He brought his record player, played them Paul McCartney songs, and chatted them up.

Martin picked up additional coupons at the office and used them downstairs in the store to shop some more. Horse-leather Alden shoes from America, for example: "they cost five hundred marks, such sturdy, classic shoes, handmade, it was a real status symbol at the time." He took them back to the studio and covered them with paint—this mix of chic and sloppy would become his trademark. Knecht admitted that Martin had good fashion sense, "but after all, he'd had time to look around." He spent hours trying on clothes, going in and out of the changing rooms: "All the girls had to stand at attention and serve him. After six suits I said, OK, Martin, take that one and we're done." The Swabian clientele were annoyed—they weren't used to such impudent behavior, and "people didn't talk as openly back then as they do now." So Martin would be sent away, or better yet, tempted away: "suggest something else fun for him to do and you could get rid of him." Then it was time for lunch, then back to the office to tell stories about his nightlife, the women he'd met, and the people he'd told off, and then out to the bars when the office closed, and on into the night. "You couldn't say 'OK, time to go home' at eleven; that was a pathetic night—it wasn't a night at all. That's when he was just getting started. And there were seven days in his week."

Whenever it did get to be too much, or when Uli Knecht, his faithful drinking buddy, wasn't in the mood for once, Martin took a short trip to Ludwigsburg to see Knecht and his wife and fill up his tank on the comforts of home. "There he could spoil himself" in a beautiful bathroom; he used the softest hand towels and was given the thick Jil Sander bathrobe, which meant a lot to him. He relaxed, watched TV, ate good home cooking, and let himself be pampered.

If a Stuttgart night ended early after all, Martin went back to the garage and painted some more. His next shows were approaching fast: *Fmoking, Frinking, and Felling* at studio f in Ulm (the pictures for the selling, or Felling, in that show were already getting larger—three by four feet) and the group show *You Have to Cross Seven Bridges* at the Coach House in Berlin.

But even at Hetzler, exhibiting work was never enough for Martin. Art for him was always more than just hanging pictures on the wall. "He identified himself with the work so strongly," Hetzler said, "that he saw himself as part of the gallery, not just as an artist. He always wanted to be involved with organizing things." Thus he went to the art fair in Basel for the first time in the summer of 1982, calling himself "Mattin Kippenberger" on the invitation. He was not there to take a quick look at the show but to be there the whole time. He hung the World Cup soccer results up on the wall of his booth and had a TV there, too, but as Pakesch, the Viennese gallerist, said, "watching the game was not as important as talking about it." Max Hetzler and Martin struck him as being "welded together—they showed up everywhere together and each admired the other equally: for Martin it was Max's self-assurance, for Max it was Martin's big mouth." They popped up at Pakesch's booth, too, and told him they wanted to work with him. Martin said Pakesch's booth was all wrong. Later that summer, on the way to a fasting cure in Carinthia in southern Austria, they came to visit him in Vienna and confirmed their collaboration, which was to last ten years.

Martin's efforts weren't only aimed at promoting himself: "he was a catalyst," Hetzler said. He considered himself the "bandleader" of the Hetzler Boys, the group of artists just coalescing and already practicing what Albert Oehlen called "extreme artist-behavior." They gave the public what it wanted (and what it soon enough began to be afraid of): the artist as wild man. When they were together in a group, every evening was a happening.

After all, they were "The New Painters," as an article in the magazine *Twen* was titled in May 1982:

Stuttgart, Hetzler Gallery, Friday Night. The opening of an exhibition of batik pictures by Markus Oehlen, in one of the two most important galleries of new art, with Maenz in Cologne. Kippenberger arrives late, but to great effect, and greets the suspiciously prominent opening-night guests in a suspiciously tailor-made gray suit. Everyone speaks softly; Kippenberger talks loud and acts exactly like it is an opening for his show.

He tells embarrassing jokes in a barracks voice, makes a deal with a dentist to trade his picture *Plaque* * for a new crown on his upper teeth that were smashed up by Berlin punks last year. At the same time, the artist—who knows exactly what his reputation is worth—stares into the dentist's wife's eyes with a

---

* The film on teeth, not a sign or nameplate, which is a different word in German.

masculine look. Kippenberger knows how to sell himself. And since he's started painting pictures, he knows how to sell them too. Out of the roughly 250 pictures from last season, in standard 20 x 24 inch size, more than 200 have changed ownership by now.

Up to now, Kippenberger, with his various activities connected to art, has been seen as an eccentric self-promoter, something like the village idiot of the art scene. Is that behind him now? He says: "I've checked that off my list. Now it's time to give people something tangible. Before, I entertained people; now they get entertainment they can lay their hands on. And this entertainment costs twelve hundred per picture. The prices will go up in June. It's that simple."

There was a short interview at the end of the article:

TWEN: Do you even know how to paint?
K: Yes.
TWEN: Do you have a favorite theme?
K: Misery.
TWEN: How do you paint?
K: It varies.
TWEN: Do you have a favorite style of painting?
K: Stop-painting, keep-going-painting, just no cock-and-pussy-painting.

These were Martin's own ways of stilling the "hunger for paintings" that the critic Wolfgang Max Faust attributed to him in this period.

Martin's collaboration with Albert Oehlen, his most important artist friend and the one he most admired, also began in 1982. Together, they showed their painting-filled

Orgone Box by Night at the Hetzler Gallery, *Door by Night* at a gynecologist's office in Tübingen, and *Capri by Night* at Tanja Grunert's garage gallery. Grunert had opened her Stuttgart gallery in 1980 in the same building as Hetzler's gallery, but she had since moved to a garage "23 feet high, 50 feet long": the ideal site for the Ford Capri painted in orange-brown paint mixed with oatmeal flakes. The opening took place at eleven at night and in the dark, since there was no electricity (the gallerist hadn't paid her bill), so the car doors were all open and every possible light source was on, from headlights to cigarette lighter. Shoved into the back of the trunk were paintings by Martin. Thirty or forty people came to the opening, "peanuts compared to today" in Tanja Grunert's words, and none of them bought anything. There were cheap cans of beer and steaming dry -ice, everyone was drunk, and one Stuttgart artist felt so outraged by the work that he picked up a fire extinguisher and started spraying the art and the artist. "Martin himself was already a real live provocation," in Tanja Grunert's view. "Many people were jealous of the fact that he just stood up and made his statements."

Martin was starting to get invited to group shows as well. Zdenek Felix, the head curator of the Folkwang Museum in Essen, accepted Martin, Oehlen, and Büttner along with other artists from Cologne and Berlin for his "Contemporary Painting in Germany" show. After the opening, in Bologna, the three artists jumped up on the table with Hetzler, as usual, and pulled down their pants. The outraged Italians called the police, and the *carabinieri* had to be calmed down. That didn't stop Felix from inviting them to their first major group show, *Truth is Work*, in 1984.

Stuttgart was over. Cologne was calling. But first came another of Martin's interludes: he worked for three months as a guest of the Folkwang Museum in Essen-Werden—"a home game," he called it, and he was particularly delighted that he, the Essen dropout, was housed in an old school. At the end of the three months, members of the Folkwang Art Circle could visit him in his brightly lit studio, ask him questions, and look at his pictures before they were sent to Ulm for his next show, *Fmoking, Frinking, and Felling.*

Karola Grässlin had moved with him to Essen. After a drive at top speed down the autobahn, with Martin sticking his tongue out at everyone who was driving too slowly for his liking, they stopped into a typical Ruhr District bar. Karola had graduated by then, and Martin kept hammering into her head that she had to move away from the Black Forest immediately. When she said that she couldn't cut her ties that fast, he said yes, she should do it instantly, otherwise she would never make the leap. In the end she actually did go to Stuttgart to study art history, for which "Martin was largely responsible."

Martin sent the Grässlins one of his pictures from Essen along with a postcard that he would later include in the 1994 catalog of their Kippenberger collection. As the caption in the catalog, he wrote: "Postcard M.K. to his alleged family (Homesick)."

CHAPTER FIVE

COLOGNE YEARS: BEGINNINGS

All roads led to Cologne. From Stuttgart, Hamburg, and Berlin, Kiecol, Oehlen, Büttner, and Förg all came to live, show work, or at least visit often. Georg Herold, who had studied in Hamburg and worked in Berlin, was there already: "The whole rumpus was happening down on the Rhine." There were collectors—ones who didn't only look but also bought—and critics, gallerists (first and foremost Zwirner, Werner, and Maenz), art stars of the earlier generation (Beuys, Polke, Richter, Immendorff, Graubner, Rückriem, Palermo), Cologne eminences like Astrid Klein and Jürgen Klauke, and the younger generations long since hot on their heels. Like the Moritzplatz painters in Berlin, the young artists of the Mülheimer Freiheit movement (sometimes known in English as the "New Wild Ones") satisfied their hunger for pictures with "effervescent productivity" (*Der Spiegel*). Dokoupil, Dahn, Bömmels, Adamski, Kever, and Naschberger were already stars, and they had a head start over Martin: they had started to paint seriously in the late seventies, while Martin was still in Berlin running S.O.36 and his Office. Cologne was hip.

One decisive factor in Cologne's pull was Kunstmarkt, the art fair Rudolf Zwirner and Hein Stünke had founded in 1967. It was a small affair at first, with only eighteen galleries represented, but "after all, that was all there was of the German avant-garde at the time," Zwirner says today. "The market was very, very limited: few dealers, few artists, and even fewer collectors." In gallerist Hans-Jürgen Müller's words, "For us, a collector was someone who owned five pictures. Even the banks hadn't started to collect seriously." A few days before the start of the first Kunstmarkt, a colleague called Müller and told him he should bring a chess set—otherwise, they would be bored to death at their booths. It didn't turn out that way.

The success took them by surprise at first but soon became the norm. The first Art Basel fair took place in 1970; ARCO in Madrid was in 1981; London, Berlin, and Miami followed. Cologne quickly became what Germany had never had up until then: an art capital. "Until then," Müller said, "foreign dealers and collectors had to travel around the whole country to buy—Cologne, Düsseldorf, Stuttgart, Hannover, Munich.... Now everything was in one place on the Rhine."

Like many gallerists (such as Michael Werner), Müller moved to Cologne in the rush of this success. The artists, he said, had forced him to. He did good business there—the Rhineland was affluent, with many collectors, and he sold as much in a month as he had sold in a year in Stuttgart. But with the success came pressure. "Cologne was tough, like New York," the gallerist realized. For Müller, the city came up short on intellectual or sensual life: "In culinary terms, Cologne was barbaric." And as for wine, "You had to bring it up from southern Germany yourself." In 1973, Müller moved back to southern Germany.

Along with the Kunstmarkt, there was another revolution attracting artists to Cologne: the Ludwig collection, on loan to the Wallraf-Richartz Museum starting in 1969. Not even in America was there so much American pop art to be seen in one place: Lichtenstein, Warhol, Rosenquist. When I talked to Rudolf Zwirner, he held the heavy catalog from the time up over his head and said, "Look at that! It's like a bible. Try to imagine, it's the late sixties and the venerable Wallraf-

Richartz Museum is putting garbage like that on the walls! Every museum curator in the world was shocked. You can't overestimate the difference that made."

According to Zwirner, up until that point the museums were showing only abstract art: "They were only interested in restitution, in art that atoned for the past. Everything they showed had to be [what the Nazis had vilified as] 'degenerate art,' or, if it was modern, then École de Paris, Henry Moore, nothing offensive. Abstract art was a guarantee that you wouldn't have to engage with German history." So no Neue Sachlichkeit, no Dadaism, no surrealism: "Anything representational at all, and the official collectors were not interested—and stuff like Kippenberger did later, politically/ sociologically/otherly critical, was even worse. The scene couldn't have been more conformist: abstraction was the only style in the world. In that context," says the dealer who played a major role in building up the collection, "Ludwig and his stuff was a shock."

This view was shared by Johann-Karl Schmidt, the curator who would invite Martin to give his first solo show in a German museum (Darmstadt, in 1986). He arrived in the Rhineland from Florence in 1970, an art historian "with the baggage of a completely classical, academic way of looking at things." He first heard the names Andy Warhol and Robert Rauschenberg in Cologne, and he was surprised not only by what the Ludwig collection contained but also by how it was shown: "It was the most contemporary mode that existed in museum practice. The museum didn't address itself to just a narrow, bourgeois, self-improving class of viewer, it threw everything open—it set out not to preserve, but to experiment. You didn't have to go down on your knees in respectful silence before the Great Art, you were taking part in the present moment of the culture."

The temporary loan was made permanent in 1976 and the collection became a museum; ten years later, it would move to a new building of its own near the cathedral and the main train station. By then, the collection and its museum practice no longer seemed so revolutionary—a new avant-garde, a German avant-garde, had taken root in the city. It was in order to see their work, which was not in the Ludwig collection, that American curators, artists, and gallerists flocked to the Rhine.

Meanwhile, the hip art-city had gotten even hipper, the art market even more lucrative, the artists younger, the pictures bigger, and the public greedier. "At some point," in Max Hetzler's words, "it was clear that you had to go to Cologne."

Martin moved there at the end of 1982. He had visited the region many times already: his friends and fellow Hetzler-artists Markus Oehlen and Meuser lived in nearby Düsseldorf; Martin had visited Hans-Peter Feldmann there, a maverick artist he held in high esteem; one of his most famous self-portraits, from the *Dear Painter, Paint For Me* series, shows him in front of the Düsseldorf club Ratinger Hof, arm in arm with a fat man. Earlier still were the visits to Sigmar Polke's farmhouse. He had also had a girlfriend in Düsseldorf, Brigitta Rohrbach.

But Düsseldorf was not for Martin: it was too chic, too smooth, too academic. The art scene was deeply under the influence of the Academy, with its hierarchies and traditions. Our great-grandmother had studied there; the über-father Joseph Beuys taught there; the Bechers and later their students were about to cause a sensation there with their cool, forbidding, mostly uninhabited photographs. "Düsseldorf," in the words of the Berlin gallerist Bruno Brunnet, "was the High Mass of dogmatism."

Cologne, by contrast, was free of the dust of the Academy; it was also, for Martin, virgin territory, a land you could conquer. Before long he was the "King of Cologne," in the words of Thomas Borgmann, an art dealer who had long been based there: "He was so funny, loud, and quick-witted. The people who had been established there a long time benefited greatly; he really brought new life into the whole scene." As in the other cities where he lived, Martin put his stamp on this one with exhibitions, posters, and "hotel improvement actions"; with talking, going to bars, having affairs, and birthday celebrations; with his omnipresence. The king gathered his court around him in the bars, a regime devoted to art. "Martin dashed through Cologne full of excitement," Jörg-Uwe Albig wrote in *Art* magazine in 1985, "hounding gallerists, tracking down raw material, recruiting assistants." The only star in Cologne whose status was arguably higher was Polke, who ruled the city in the opposite way: by making himself scarce.

Martin stayed in Cologne longer than anywhere else—more than a decade, though not in the same place the whole time. As always, he constantly changed apartments and studios: Friesenplatz, Lindenstrasse, Hildeboldplatz, Hansaring, Eifelstrasse, Jülicher Strasse. Cologne was also his home base for trips out into the world, a few weeks here, a few months there: Vienna and the Burgenland, Syros and Brazil, Sevilla and Madrid, Nice and Los Angeles. Cologne was the opposite of Berlin: not an island, but a hub. You could get to Holland, Belgium, or France in an hour.

Even long after he left Cologne, he remained "the Cologne artist." This city was the organizing center of his life; his gallerist, Gisela Capitain, was there, along with his office, his assistant, his collectors, his storage room, and his hotel room. His friends lived there, and later his daughter and her mother.

The wide world lay right outside Cologne but the city

itself was a village, despite its million inhabitants—more manageable and contained than Berlin. Bars, galleries, museums, bookstores, cafés: in this metropolis with a Roman foundation, medieval street plan, and narrow alleys, everything was within walking distance (or, if necessary, a quick taxi ride away). Jochen Siemens, a journalist, wrote in *Tempo*, a trendy magazine for young people, "You can spit across Ehrenstrasse, one of the Cologne boulevards, it's so narrow. All the buildings in Cologne are dull and dirt-colored, like the striking-surface of a matchbox. The people of Cologne stand in front of them and talk. In no other city in the world is there so much talking as in Cologne; people here talk even when they are by themselves on the street." They weren't alone often, though: you had only to cross the street and you would have already bumped into five people you knew, not only residents of Cologne, but art-lovers from all over the world.

TEN MINUTES IN A CIRCLE

The central meeting point, where sooner or later you ran into everyone no matter what artistic camp they belonged to—the village pub, as it were—was Walther König's bookstore. Martin called it his "bar" even though no drinks were served there. It was in the heart of the city, on the so-called Bermuda Triangle adjoining Ehrenstrasse, just steps away from galleries, studios, paint stores, the Bittner Bookstore, Café Broadway, and the Italian stand-up restaurant Ezio.

The regulars gathered at the table in the middle of the narrow bookstore, packed with new books, catalogs from all over the world, and catalogs of the house press. "Every morning the Cologne artists crept around the table in single file," Siemens wrote in *Tempo*. "The 'König roundabout' is an unofficial requirement for anyone who wants to stay up to date in Cologne. The important thing is who walks in front of you and who walks behind you."

Martin said, "Ten minutes in the circle and I knew whatever I needed to know in Cologne." He came by every day, on his way to or from Hetzler, Capitain, Zwirner, or Nagel, or the Broadway, or the paint store. He sent his students and assistants there too, to browse and buy books. Circling around the table saved him lots of trips to museums: nowhere else could you get more current information about what was happening in art; the bookstore itself was like a museum, showing not only pictures but also the artists' books.

Martin bought books at König by the bagful, spending thousands of marks there. Being a regular, he took books on credit, wrote up his own IOUs on the pad lying next to the cash register, and sometimes paid with drawings. He often sat down at the big table on the second floor as though he were at home. "At König's it feels like at a bar, and if you have nothing better to do you can always say I have a good idea for a book, so what about printing it here?" Then Martin and König would sit down for an hour or two and work out everything that needed to be worked out for a new book.

Chop-chop! That was their speed. Walther König was another wild man, possessed by art and stubborn as a mule; no wonder Martin liked him so much. He was everywhere and nowhere, often perched at his tiny little table in the gallery, where he could talk on the phone, write, observe the whole store, send employees scurrying, and advise customers on the other side of the room all at the same time. Martin maintained a kind of respectful dislike of König's brother Kasper, the curator, but with Walther there was a relationship of mutual friendship and respect. They used the formal *Sie* with each other until the end.

BREAKTHROUGH

Cologne's having been so badly destroyed during the war, and so hideously rebuilt afterward, was no disadvantage, in the view of the critic Wolfgang Max Faust. In fact, he felt that this was one of the crucial reasons why the city became such a center for art. The postwar architecture was so boring, Faust wrote in the journal *Artscribe* in 1986, that all of one's attention was channeled onto the people there. For him, that was the main feature of the Cologne art scene: "It's about people, about communication and relationships. It's about debate, argument, competition." A city of talking, playing games, and having arguments; a liberal, laissez-faire city, a little slovenly even, marked by cliques and Carnival and the Catholic church, whose magnum opus, the Cathedral, had been worked on for centuries and never finished—a city made for Martin. Heinrich Böll described this city of his heart as having a "Neapolitan flair."

When Martin moved to Cologne, the city was feeling a new sense of optimism. *Spex: The Magazine for Pop Culture* (a kind of German version of early *Rolling Stone*) had set up its offices there and was turning lots of music fans into enthusiasts of contemporary art. Paul Maenz was successfully promoting the new Mülheimer Freiheit artists as well as painters from Italy, including Chia, Clemente, Cucchi, and Paladino. Benedikt Taschen had just founded his publishing house, which revolutionized art-book publishing; his 1991 monograph on Martin contributed greatly to Martin's growing popularity among the cognoscenti. The young publisher had so much success, and thus so much money, that he would later become one of Martin's biggest collectors, along with the art dealer Thomas Borgmann and the doctor and Proust specialist Reiner Speck, also in Cologne.

Cologne was where Martin's career really got started. "Cologne was the breakthrough for every artist," Max Hetzler said. Martin turned thirty in February 1983, shortly after his move to Cologne, and marked the occasion with a catalog called *Farewell to the Youth Bonus*. Our father had always said that you have to make it by the time you're thirty; Martin himself said, in his 1991 *Artfan* interview, that by the time you're thirty your years of development are over: "You need to have figured yourself out enough so that you can make your mark at 30." At thirty, Martin also put the name "Kippi" officially behind him. Or tried to, "but no one wanted to listen."

THE HETZLER BOYS

"Martin was in the vanguard," Max Hetzler said. "He led the way. Wherever he was, you couldn't miss him." Hetzler followed Martin to Cologne in 1983, with Bärbel Grässlin, and opened a new gallery in Dokoupil's former studio, on Kamekestrasse. Gisela Capitain left Berlin and gave up her teaching job to join them, and then in 1986 she started her own adjunct gallery of Hetzler artists' drawings. Tanja Grunert and Achim Schächtele moved from Stuttgart, Hans-Jürgen Müller moved back to the area for a short interlude (into Paul Maenz's former space), and Monika Sprüth opened her own gallery.

Martin's move from periphery to center was much more than a change of address. "It wasn't all lovey-dovey like in Stuttgart," Hetzler recalled. "For the first time, artists and galleries saw themselves as each other's competitors. You had to assert yourself, define yourself, stand out." Especially, in Hetzler's case, against Monika Sprüth, who represented many women artists, and Paul Maenz, who had been running a gallery in Cologne since 1970. Martin couldn't stand Maenz and what a friend of Martin's called his "affected, eety-peteety gayness," but he respected Michael Werner, who had moved to Cologne from Berlin in 1969 and whose gallery, where he showed Baselitz, Lüpertz, Immendorff, Polke, and Penck, was a model for Hetzler and his boys.

The Hetzler group consisted of Albert and Markus Oehlen, Günther Förg, Werner Büttner, Hubert Kiecol, Reinhard Mucha, Meuser, Georg Herold, and Martin. They did not represent a single school or have a style or even a medium in common: Meuser, Mucha, Herold, and Kiecol were primarily sculptors; Förg was a photographer in the early years; the others made paintings, drawings, and collages. What linked them was their attitude, their way of thinking, their themes, humor, language, age, and gender. They provoked and polarized and were as hard to handle as their art. Hetzler again: "They were artists who took extreme positions and brought a sharp intelligence to bear." They admired and criticized each other, took each other's places, and motivated and competed against each other. As Albert Oehlen said later, "We were a group without a name, without an agenda. We spurred each other on, and every one wanted to wow everyone else."

Most of them worked independently, but their joint appearances at openings, or in bars and restaurants, reinforced their cohesion—both within the group and in how they were seen from the outside. The Hetzler Boys almost always appeared as a group in the early eighties: talking, singing, provoking, and stripping. The main thing was to be loud. "With Hetzler," Oehlen later said, "we made asses of ourselves and made everyone hate us. We climbed on the tables and pulled down our pants—extreme artist-behavior. It was also extremely exhausting." They ruled Cologne and excluded, practically exiled, others; their judgments were merciless. And according to Andreas Schulze, one of Monika Sprüth's artists and thus from the enemy camp, as it were, Martin "was the boss. He always had the biggest mouth, and the others followed him."

As a group consisting solely of boys, they forced women aside, and their macho slogans and comments didn't help their popularity. Hetzler supposedly said that women weren't meant to be artists, maybe gallery assistants at best. The Hetzler Boys ordered women over forty to lay their sagging breasts on the table and grabbed the breasts or crotches of younger women. They tolerated very few women of any age at their table, and when one did join them, other women attacked her for it afterward.

In Cologne, as elsewhere, Martin did not limit himself to producing works of art; he worked on how the art was presented, the framework and the sideshows. "Martin was tremendously committed to the gallery's artists," Max Hetzler said. The Vienna gallerist Peter Pakesch thinks Martin did an enormous amount for the Hetzler Gallery's success in his double role "as clown and strategist.... Max without Martin's strategy would have been unimaginable in the early years." In Jutta Koether's view, Martin "was the one who brought the movement to life so that it became known outside Cologne."

Martin may have been the catalyst, but he was once again seen as primarily a catalyst for others: "No one took him seriously as an artist at the time," according to Pakesch. "His organizational and PR skills were valued—the fact that he never stopped moving, that he was involved in everything—but the others were seen as the real, good, serious artists." Büttner, for instance, who "gave the impression of being the chief thinker" in the group (in the words of Wilhelm

Schürmann, the collector and photographer), "or Albert, who was considered the best painter." Joachim Lottmann described him as a character, not an artist:

> Kippi dances wildly over the plates and glasses, does the crazy-shuttle, bites a wineglass to pieces, swings from the chandelier, drops to the floor like a rock, unbuttons his pants, waggles his tongue like Gene Simmons from Kiss, babbles and blathers away, mutters and mumbles—he is the absolute epitome of the bold and reckless anarchist in the bourgeois wine-tasting gallerists' imagination.

As a result, the curator Kasper König invited Büttner and Oehlen to show in his major exhibition of contemporary German art—*From Here,* a two-month show in late 1984 at the Düsseldorf Convention Center—along with many of Martin's other friends (Barfuss, Wachweger, Kiecol, Förg, Markus Oehlen) and enemies (Salomé, Dokoupil, Dahn). But not Martin. König saw Martin's art as "party-basement painting."* When Büttner and Oehlen protested, Martin was given two pages in the catalog as a compromise, but no space in the show itself. He put his answer on a poster, turning the show's title, *From Here,* into *For All I Care* (*"Von hier aus"* into *"Von mir aus"*; *hier* and *mir* rhyme).

Then again, sometimes the reverse happened and the other artists were tainted with a kind of guilt by association. Albert Oehlen said, "We lost favor with some people too—art-lovers, gallerists, museum people—when we supported Kippenberger. He was unserious. They said, 'Do you want to

---

* German houses at the time often had a "party basement," where otherwise upstanding citizens could go a little wild. König is being very sarcastic about Martin's petit-bourgeois pretentions to acting out.

go with the monkey house or with us?' I said I'd rather stay with the monkey house, thank you—or rather, that *that* was real art. Not the stuff you think is art."

MAKE YOUR OWN LIFE

Cologne was paradise for Martin: a city full of artists. He had only to step outside to trip over one, and he was constantly stepping outside. Life in Cologne was one long process of going somewhere with someone—from the bar to the bookstore, from the bookstore to the gallery, "and then meanwhile I'd thought of something else," so over to the café to talk to someone.

"There's nothing Martin liked more than other artists," Max Hetzler said. "He needed the discussions and debates with them—it inspired him, it made him happy. They understood him." In the gallerist Burkhard Riemschneider's view, "He had a very strong artist's ethic: *We Artists.* A bad artist was still a lot better than someone who wasn't an artist at all." A bad artist was someone he could still rub the wrong way, make fun of, create some friction. He rarely spent time with people who were not part of the art scene.

"There was no such thing as not working, for Martin," said Peter Pakesch. Sitting around in a bar wasn't rest and recuperation after a hard day's work in the studio, it was an exchange with others and a performance in front of an audience: annoying them, entertaining them, developing new ideas, striking (or refusing to strike) a certain pose, concocting schemes, planning exhibitions, making sketches, and of course making sure he won the women's hearts.

One time, when the American artist Stephen Prina had spent the night at the Hotel Chelsea in Cologne and saw

Martin coming down to breakfast the next morning, his only thought was, "Oh no! Here comes work! It was never relaxed with Martin, he always demanded your full attention." Many people found the intensity exciting but also insanely stressful. After an hour with Martin, Attila Corbaci said, he needed a break: "It took so much energy to talk with him. He did everything so intensely! Like it was his last day on earth."

For everyone in Cologne, "going out was like going to work," the critic Isabelle Graw said. The conversations were always about art: who thought who was good or bad, who was showing where, who had bought what by whom for how much. It wasn't just chitchat, "it was about something real." But it was also about the best arguments or punch-lines, the best jokes, who could give the best explanation of Marcel Broodthaers's work. Often it was more of a fight than an exchange of ideas, and in fact it occasionally did come to literal blows among the artists. "There was a very special intensity there, which didn't exist anywhere else," in Graw's view. "It was extremely ferocious. People didn't act nice with each other and didn't want to. No one ever said they were having problems, or lovesick, or anything like that. It was about status, your rank as an artist, power relations. No empathy. There was an extreme reaction in the early eighties against the bleeding-heart culture of the seventies."

An exhibit that traveled through the United States in 2006, devoted to this phenomenon of the tightly knit artist community, was titled after a quote of Martin's: *Make Your Own Life.* Against the backdrop of today's global art market, the exhibit portrayed the Cologne of the time as a more intimate space, where artists could discover and present themselves. The community spirit in Cologne, even with all the rivalry between various gallerists and artists, seemed especially unique and enticing to the Americans who came to Cologne in such great numbers in the eighties and early nineties. In New York it was every man for himself; in L.A., people lived hours away from each other. Twenty years later, that Cologne seems almost mythical. Even the exhibit's curator sees this show, with its romantic picture of a vanished Cologne, as "a symptom of a real loss of community within an art world that is ever more professionalized, spectacularized, and deracinated from local specificity."

A VIRTUOSO AT GIVING OFFENSE

Martin Prinzhorn used to come to Cologne from Vienna for at least a week every two months while he was in graduate school. "I was insanely fond of Cologne, with its unbelievably fun pub crawls and a totally different culture, talking and arguing at the Hammerstein every day. At the time I found this whole Rhineland conversation culture very liberating."

The Hammerstein was typical of the eighties scene: cool furniture, an open kitchen with everything prepared fresh, long breakfasts, and food available all day long (a rarity at the time). Most importantly, you could run into everyone there before the different camps scattered to their respective bars: Mülheimer Freiheit artists like Dokoupil and Dahn, older masters like Lüpertz and Immendorff, Rosemarie Trockel and Monika Sprüth, and the whole Hetzler group. Martin first met several of his future friends at the Hammerstein, including Reiner Opoku and Andrea Stappert. The Hammerstein gave him what he needed: friends, enemies, and a large audience.

Enemies were important for Martin. Once, after a party at Martin Prinzhorn's Thomasburg castle with only friends, Martin complained, "So boring I could throw up. This one knows that one, admires that other one. Where are the people we can attack or take the piss out of, have a little fun? Where are they? We need them."

Martin always discovered people's weak spots and went right for them—"beat people over the head with them," as his student Tobias Rehberger says. "This had pedagogical value, to some extent, since your weak points were, after all, your weak points, things you should part with. But of course people's weak points are often precisely the things they can't do anything about." Whether it was sagging breasts or being cross-eyed, Martin would call attention to it and make sure everyone in the café noticed. If the person was embarrassed or ashamed about it, then they really got an earful. "You were not allowed to have any shame—there was no such thing."

Martin saw it as his highest duty to say out loud what everyone was thinking. He never said anything behind a fat woman's back about her weight, like so many other people do; instead, when he left a disco with her, he would ask, "Should we walk down the hill or just roll?" (This actually happened; the woman in question cried about it for a whole day.) He said everything to everyone's face, whoever or whatever they were. Even someone who found Martin extremely unpleasant and felt attacked by him, the Cologne artist Andreas Schulze, admitted that "He was never fake. He didn't lie." Martin hated the hypocrisy and pretended innocence of the art world, where enemies acted like friends and gave each other little kisses on the cheek. That is another reason he liked the company of "regular people": bartenders, waiters, children. However kitschy it might sound, he saw them as true and genuine in a way that he felt was lacking in the art world.

With his ruthless honesty, Martin was "a virtuoso at giving offense," as Werner Büttner called him. The truth hurt, and it should, just like art. Martin's girlfriend Kazu Huggler experienced many such moments: "There are things he said

252

that stay with you. Today we can laugh about them, because they were so true." Inga Humpe had the same experience: Martin told her that what she and her band Neonbabies were doing in Berlin was "department-store punk." As angry as the singer was, she secretly thought, "Shit, he's right. We were middle-class punks."

However hateful it may have sounded, what Martin said was never meant to be mean, at least not from his point of view. On the contrary. He only wanted the best for the person he said it to. The truth was a provocation, "a prod to think deeper about something," in Attila Corbaci's words. "It prompted you to be creative. He was only demanding of others what he demanded of himself: improve the quality of what you're doing."

But even if he loved to say nasty things to other people, that didn't mean other people could do the same to him. He was very sensitive. In any case, few other people dared to. Even Martin's friends were afraid of him, afraid he would take them apart. His New York gallerist Janelle Reiring said, "It was a little terrifying to know that you couldn't put anything over on him. Sometimes you really want to present yourself the way you wish you were, after all. But he never let you get away with that."

He wasn't afraid to say what he thought. "I have a camouflage battle suit," Martin wrote in 1981, "which is as much as to say: I am a free person."

I'M NOT A BRAWLER BUT I AM
A RATHER UNPLEASANT PERSON

A gay friend of Martin's, This Brunner, only laughed at Martin's gay jokes; for him they were funny, affectionate teasing. Similarly, Reiner Opoku, the son of an African father and German mother, liked Martin's black jokes. Martin thought he had a right to tell them since, after all, he had married a black woman back in Hamburg.

The provocations were always a test: Can you take it? Are you up to being around me? Do you really love me? He had to make sure that no one thought he was a straightforward person. Of course no one would have anyway. Martin rarely made instant friends; most people felt repelled by him before they felt drawn to him. But what other people experienced as attacks, Martin's friend Meuser saw as a kind of greeting: "Hello, so who are you?" "Slanders too are only meant in jest," Martin wrote in his book *Joints I*.

There were no such tirades or insults in smaller groups or one-on-one interactions. Being alone with Martin was "extraordinarily pleasant," according to Rüdiger Carl, the musician:

you were just talking with him, telling stories, not for someone to write down but just because he wanted to hear your stories, for example, things Charlie Parker and people like that used to do. Before artists got so famous, Pollock and so on, the most exciting things going on were in music and he was always curious to hear about that. About beautiful singers too. He was never full of himself. It was only when other people were around that he ramped it up and wanted to be an uncontrollable genius.

In any case, even though Martin went after so many of the people around him, it only rarely came to physical fights. "He gave off a kind of energy," said Elisabeth Fiedler, a friend from Graz, "that made people walk away. No one started a fight with him." In the view of the Swiss artists Fischli and Weiss, Martin "was charming and winning. That's why he could take his obnoxiousness so far." Martin also didn't spare himself;

Fiedler thought the jokes Martin told about himself and his lifestyle were particularly harsh. "There was a certain despair about it."

There was probably another reason why situations didn't come to blows: Martin could be fierce and loud, and he did have firm principles, but he was never fanatical, dogmatic, or ideological. Thomas Grässlin later said that he had learned from Martin how to have an attitude but always keep it playful. Martin wanted others to play along, to defend themselves. He couldn't stand it when they started crying.

Of course, there were times when his charm left him: when he was in too much despair or had had too much to drink. And sometimes he certainly did mean the things he said as personally as it sounded.

Like a child, Martin needed all the attention in the room on himself, and if his listeners weren't listening—if they talked or even coughed while he was telling one of his jokes, for example—he would start over from the beginning. "With me, inattentiveness gets a scolding." "Doesn't listen, only talks himself" was his self-description in a short text called "Kippenberger and Cafés."

This need to force things on people was also, in another sense, a selfless quality, as Albert Oehlen saw it. "What he was trying to do was keep this big entertainment system running. Even when he demanded that everyone listen to him, which was often rough, his goal was to keep the big fun-machine going." Isabelle Graw says, "I think he felt obligated to make sure that people were having a good time, that the entertainment never stopped. That was another reason he always took over and seized the floor: he couldn't stand the emptiness, the silence."

Be that as it may, he wasn't so selfless that he never demanded contributions from others: a song, a joke, or a story that had to be told upon his command. "You couldn't just sit there," Andrea Stappert said. "Martin didn't like when people simply consumed him, when they thought Martin was taking them out and they didn't have to do anything in return."

In 1982, the magazine *Twen* asked Martin if his bad reputation bothered him. "At some point," Martin answered, "I realized that I had one and I couldn't do anything about it. So I cultivated it. People need someone they can see as an enemy, so I was someone they could see as an enemy. One of my main functions! Really there aren't many definitions of the enemy out there, like 'The police are bad, we're good!' So here's one: 'Kippenberger bad!'" Martin worked as hard on his "bad boy" image as he did on his "bad paintings." If he couldn't be taken seriously as an artist, at least he would get noticed.

He could be different when he wanted to be. Rosemarie Trockel, with whom Martin was "more or less" together in 1983, says that around her he was always "incredibly loving and nice, always extremely civilized. I absolutely cannot complain." Once, after coming home very late at night again, Trockel found him lying curled up with her old sick dog on the kitchen floor. Martin knew how much the dog meant to her, and Martin said that since the dog wasn't strong enough to come to him, he went to the dog instead.

Trockel, who saw herself at the time as extremely shy and polite, liked the fact that Martin could be so different at openings, dinner parties, bars—so confrontational, so "wild, unashamed, audacious. He could be an absolute monster." She didn't always like it when he laid into other people, "but that was a part of him, this nasty sting that went after blood. With Martin you took the bad with the good. You couldn't choose one side of the whole package, you also had to take the other." Trockel also saw something self-destructive in Martin's mercilessness: "When you have this sting, it's directed at yourself, too. Anyone who can see through other people like that sees himself in a clear light, too."

In the interview with the magazine *Artfan*, Martin said in reference to his art, "I only want love. But too much love and you get scared. So one thing you do is test people, the other is throw a few beams so that you don't get too much love."

MORNINGS HE RECEIVES VISITORS
AT THE BROADWAY

"Not a week goes by in which Martin isn't written up in the Cologne *Express*, for a case of pulled-down pants, little anti-Semitic provocations, or at least excessive dance moves," the 1988 Cologne issue of the travel magazine *Merian* reported:

> Mornings he receives visitors at the Broadway, one of the cool trendy cafés. He sits at the end of the mirrored catwalk, starting the day off right with a Cuba Libre, and giving you a friendly laugh across his beer belly. "I don't have time to wait eight years until I'm hanging in the Ludwig Museum," he says.

The Broadway was more cramped, simpler, and more alternative than the Hammerstein—"a smoky little hovel," as the *New York Times* described it with a certain irritation. There, Martin conducted his "research," as he called it: he always sat looking out at the street, to see right away who was coming in, or might come in, so that he could catch them. He always had a big table at which he could gather people around him, and he sat there for days and weeks on end. The work he did there was concrete. Ideas were born, and printing and exhibition arrangements were made. Often he sat there with F. C. Gundlach, the Hamburg photographer, collector, and gallerist who supported Martin.

THEN YOU NEVER GOT RID OF HIM

> What does the cow do
> Moo
> What do you do
> Ado
>   —MK*

For a couple of years in the mid-eighties, at the height of the art boom, Martin had an even more exclusive living room: Franz Keller's restaurant. The owner, from a well known Baden family of gastronomes and vintners, was a pioneer of new German cuisine who eventually cooked his way to two Michelin stars. He was drawn to the Rhine after a falling-out with his father. Having also considered Hamburg, Frankfurt, and Düsseldorf, he decided on Cologne, "the weirdest."

But Martin didn't go to Keller's restaurant for the fine cuisine. He preferred to sit at the staff table in the back, where he played mau-mau with the waiters and cooks and ate what they ate (plain fare, usually stew). That worked for Keller, too: "there were the fewest other guests there, so I had the best chance of keeping him under control." The words flew back and forth between the kitchen and Martin's table, and when the restaurant started to empty out, if not sooner, "the real debauchery started."

During the opulent eighties, a lot of art dinners took place at Franz Keller's restaurant. The success of the contemporary

---

* The last line is literally "Make trouble" and the rhyme is more childlike in German: *"Was macht die Kuh / Muh / Was machst du / Mühe."*

artists resulted in a new flood of guests at the openings, and since there were more and more artists and galleries, there were more and more openings—"a shot in the arm for the whole business," in the words of longtime Cologne gallerist Paul Maenz. Even if someone was not invited to the meal after the opening, they could be sure of meeting everyone, even the stars, in the bars of the city afterward. Reiner Opoku says the openings then "were more fun than today. The art trade has since become a highly professionalized business, almost an industry. Everything very meticulous, but it's lost a bit of its soul. Nowadays if you smoke, or have a drink at lunch, people look at you funny." At the time, you were suspect if you didn't.

Martin got his food for free at Keller's, and whenever the bill ran up too high, he had to give Keller a picture. Keller didn't necessarily get the one he wanted, only the one that Martin "prescribed" for him—the same thing Martin did with many of his collectors. One time he made a giant screen especially for the restaurant, with the Hunger Family on it. To keep the proprietor up to date—since Keller couldn't go to openings himself, of course—Martin brought him his catalogs: "Here, read something good!"

Along with the artists and gallerists, Keller's restaurant was full of people with money, from bordello owners to a chocolate manufacturer, Imhoff, who had himself chauffeured from the factory every day at 6:30, polished off his meal, and dashed out the door at 7:45 to make it home in time for the nightly news. It was never boring. Martin "thought it was fun to observe these people, these moneybags." When he went too far, got too crazy, insulted the other patrons too harshly, or pestered the waiters too much, Keller threw him out, "but it didn't matter, he just came back in through the back door." By the next day, all was forgotten.

Sometimes they crawled the pubs all night and then Martin went straight to his studio. Other times Keller put him in a taxi or took him home at 3 a.m., then there he was in front of Keller's door at 6:30 a.m. "You have to go to the market anyway!" Martin told Keller. There was a bar there, too.

SUNDAY IS THE EMBODIMENT OF THE
MIRROR IMAGE OF MARTIN KIPPENBERGER

Everyone who knew Martin speaks of his unbelievable energy with amazement. He could stay up drinking all night and then show up at nine the next morning with new ideas and plans and projects. His lust for life, for people, for art, was probably the most important source of his energy. Once, when he was asked what he thought his great talent was, he answered, "That I have a happy nature. And that I'm curious." The gallerist Tim Neuger said, "Martin could have a good time getting his hair cut." He took such childlike pleasure in his own jokes, Andrea Stappert said, "in whatever struck him as strange or funny. He could laugh at his own ideas. You could see it in his face when something he was about to say had already made him happy." Defiance and contrariness, his student Tobias Rehberger thought, were sources of energy for Martin, too—"and an incredible will." Finally, let us not forget, there was his midday nap, and alcohol. His energy could not be portioned out. He never dared to try to put the brakes on, Georg Herold said: "It would have been like pulling the plug on him."

He was always afraid of the moment when the lights went out. He knew that that was when he would encounter his other side. As he wrote in *Café Central*, "Sunday is the embodiment of the mirror image of Martin Kippenberger, whether on Ehrenstrasse or the Rambla." On Sundays the city was dead, and places especially lively during the week seemed especially dead.

"Many people confuse vitality with robust strength," the Frankfurt artist Thomas Bayrle says. "But Martin was extremely sensitive and fragile." Whenever he saw Martin alone in the halls of the Städelschule art academy in Frankfurt, he says, Martin seemed deeply melancholy: "If the security system of communication isn't there, you are thrown back on yourself, on the wretchedness of life."

"Maybe no artist has ever needed so many collaborators to represent existential loneliness as Kippenberger," the critic Rudolf Schmitz wrote in the context of Kippenberger's Kafka piece. Martin always gathered crowds of people around him, offering them food, drink, work, and entertainment. "The way he organized his life so that he would never have to be alone," Rüdiger Carl thought, "was extremely cunning and involved lots of subtle little strategies. He couldn't just apply direct pressure: *If you leave now I won't look at you for a year.* That would be too weak. He always had to come up with a way to turn the situation the way he needed it to go."

He would call up Gisela Capitain at five in the morning to ask what she was doing; 8 a.m. would find him in front of Eleni Koroneou's door in search of beer and coddling. He promised Sabine Grässlin pictures in twenty-five percent increments if she would stay out, a quarter of a picture for each hour she stayed with him. He once phoned Günter Lorenz, a manager at BMW, in his Amsterdam hotel room at 4 a.m, after everyone else had gone to bed, to request some "artist-coddling": Lorenz had to go to Martin's hotel and keep him company at the bar until dawn.

The worst was being alone at the end of a night in a group, after one companion after another had disappeared. If Martin didn't have a girlfriend at the time, or a one night stand, he would ask (or force) a female friend to lie in bed with him "like a little brother and sister," as one of them said. He would even ask a female curator he didn't know if he could sleep in her hotel room with her, totally chaste.

"Martin was hyper," his New York gallerist Janelle Reiling said, "hyperactive, hyperintelligent, hypersensitive." Just as he could never not work, and never not communicate, he could never not perceive. There was no off switch; he was always at a boil. Even when he finally did go to sleep, he didn't get any rest. "I'm so tired in the morning," he told Jutta Koether, "because I dream so much. I have a whole day's work behind me as soon as I wake up!"

Sometimes Martin didn't go to bed at all, but straight from the bar to the studio. There he could withstand the solitude—he needed it there. He didn't drink there, either.

The proprietor of his regular bar in the Burgenland called him "a truly special person." One of a kind. His Graz friend Elisabeth Fiedler said that was why he was so excited when his assistant Johannes Wohnseifer found a painting of an Indian chief for Martin that looked just like him: "He had the feeling *I'm not alone.* Who understood him? No one understood him. This solitude had something desperate about it." He suffered from loneliness but at the same time valued the fact that there was no one else like him. Peter Altenberg, the Viennese coffeehouse writer whose works Martin so admired, once said, "It is sad to be an exception, but much sadder not to be."

TRUTH IS WORK

At the start of his time in Cologne, for the first time in years, Martin rented a proper apartment of his own. It was big and old and beautiful, directly on Friesenplatz; Rudolf Zwirner's

former wife had lived there, Gisela Capitain lived there with
Martin for a while, and Max Hetzler would live there after
Martin. Cologne really was like a village. He could paint there,
and he did—lots of big paintings. He always had another
exhibition to produce work for.

In June 1983, Martin showed *Marks of an Innocent Man*
with Zwirner, which was something of a coronation. Zwirner
was one of the pioneers of the Cologne art scene who,
first as an art dealer and then as a gallerist, had sold works
by many famous modern artists and brought the younger,
contemporary artists along in tow. He showed very different
artists on the different open floors of his gallery: "I might
be showing Richter, Warhol, Kippenberger, and Picabia at
the same time, i.e. works ranging from ten thousand marks
to a hundred thousand dollars. When people insisted on an
expensive painting, I said 'Why not take something more
contemporary too?'"

Also in 1983, Martin showed work for the first time with
Erhard Klein in Bonn: an exhibition with Albert Oehlen
called *Women in My Father's Life*. Klein was Polke's and Beuys's
gallerist, and Martin would later have other shows with him,
with titles like *What Is Your Favorite Minority—Who Do You
Envy the Most*. Klein was always up for something unusual,
was very interested in artists and their projects, and took great
care with artist's books, as a librarian himself. He was a good
drinking buddy as well.

But the biggest event in these early years was *Truth Is
Work*, a group show at the Folkwang Museum in Essen, with
"Mattin" (as he called himself), Albert Oehlen, and Werner
Büttner. The 1984 opening is one of the legendary events
of the time, with Martin doing handstands in the bathroom
and pouring a plate of spaghetti over his head (all of it
documented in photographs) while the band Night and Day

established itself as the go-to dance orchestra for art openings. The most important thing was the catalog, which Roberto Ohrt would later call "the incunabulum of the eighties": "It reduced to a minimum the conventional function of a catalog, with its demoralizing reduction of the artist to providing the illustrations in need of commentary." Albert Oehlen said that he and Büttner prepared the catalog largely on their own in Hamburg, as a kind of collage: "Martin was too impatient for that. We spent weeks cutting and gluing. He came by for a few days and dropped off his cuttings, added them in, it was good like that. Anyway, he also took our material very much to heart and created a lot from the text. Several phrases appeared later as his picture titles."

Zdenek Felix, the director of exhibitions of the Folkwang Museum, used the show to make up for what he had missed out on before. His earlier exhibit *Ten New German Artists*, from 1982, had omitted precisely these three, and now he wanted to give them their own platform. "It turned out that the New Wild Ones didn't last—their fast painting ran out of steam fast too. It was harmless. These three were doing something different: they were more radical, tackling taboo subjects like the Nazi legacy, but they weren't crusading do-gooders. They were just interested in showing social and political life as it was."

Felix believed that these three complemented each other well, and in fact they formed a sort of core or mini-group within the Hetzler group. Büttner and Oehlen knew each other from Berlin and had moved to Hamburg in the late seventies, just when Martin moved in the opposite direction. "We were as extreme and excessive as Martin," Oehlen later said when asked about what they had had in common. "We were euphorics."

Büttner said: "We were a classic pack of dogs, career-wise." He dated Inka Hocke after she and Martin broke up, and he eventually married her. "We were a fighting team, and we acted according to the motto 'Success is the best revenge!'" They talked about new movies, about artists and books, and told stories about their adventures, "but we never really talked seriously, about our love lives or death. It was all about who was quicker with the bright ideas. We were three quick-draw cowboys with big mouths. When we were together, no one else had a chance." Their politically incorrect humor, Büttner says, "prepared the way for Harald Schmidt." One crude performance with the title *Herr Doctor, Herr Doctor, I Think I Have Three Balls,* was infamous—the men pulled down their pants and stood on tables while the women in the room had to go up and feel their balls. Büttner says, "We were a reaction to the terrible seventies, when everything was so normal and black and white. They wanted to be cool and untouchable."

The Essen exhibit prompted two different reactions: artists liked it, while several critics were outraged and even thought the curator should be fired. "I had compared the three of them to Goya," Felix later said, "that really made their blood boil." Due to the negative reaction and fearing a scandal, the curator had Martin remove one of his pictures (of a blonde with a startled look holding a gigantic, floppy, garden hose–like penis in her two hands) "as a precaution. I was afraid the whole exhibition could be shut down." Martin took it off the wall but left empty the place where it had hung.

VIENNA

"Six weeks ago we went to an opening in N.Y. Big city, it was too boring there. So we decided to go to Vienna, we'd always wanted to anyway." This is how Martin and Albert Oehlen explained their presence in Vienna in their "Address to the Brainless."

Vienna was a big city too, of course—but not too big or too fashionable, and with a culture of hospitality that New York lacked. Since the two places most important to Martin, Oswald & Kalb and the Old Vienna Café, were on the same street, Martin's Vienna was on a very manageable scale.

Unlike New Yorkers, the Viennese spoke Martin's language and understood his jokes. The first time the Berlin gallerist Rudolf Springer met Martin, in the late seventies in Berlin, he thought Martin was Austrian though he no longer recalls why; it couldn't have been because of Martin's accent, which was unmistakably from the Ruhr and which Martin especially emphasized, for example by pronouncing his name "Mattin." It was probably more his clothes, his style. "In the mass of badly dressed Berliners, he was always the best dressed man in the room—except for the Viennese," in the words of Attila Corbaci, who worked at the Exile at the time. The Viennese wore English suits and custom-made shoes, even in the Kreuzberg. Most likely of all, it was his way of talking that made Martin seem so Austrian: the ambiguity and irony, the performance, the provocative clowning, the characteristic mix of black humor and melancholy, being charming and giving the finger at the same time.

Sabine Achtleitner, from Graz (Austria's second-largest city), says, "The Germans take a word literally, as what it is. But with us Austrians it's often meant differently from what it literally says. Martin was a real master of this enigmatic style. What he said to people often had a very nasty surface message, but I never thought it was nasty, it was...critical. He said it full of humor, wittily." Martin often felt that humor was lacking in Germany.

Thanks to Michel Würthle "and the whole Austrian

gang" in Berlin—Oswald and Ingrid Wiener, Reinald Nohal, Lampersberg, Attila Corbaci, the owners of Café Einstein—Martin "got very familiar with that Austrian way of using language, that clowning: I learned a lot." Austria was everywhere in the Berlin of those days—in the restaurants and also in the Kreuzberg backyard of Martin's publisher Rainer Pretzell, who had a special love for Austrian literature and looked after its playful practitioners (he also published Friederike Mayröcker, Elfriede Czurda, and H.C. Artmann). Martin must have also liked that so many Austrian writers and artists crossed the boundaries of their own media and were active in numerous areas.

And then the language: that slightly old-fashioned, sometimes almost archaic German with something poetic about it, something of a sound-painting. Even the street names—Naschmarkt, Himmelpfortgasse (Heaven's Gate Lane), Morellenfeldgasse (Field of Morels Lane)—and names of dishes: Paradeiserl, Melange, Schmarrn. . . The language was like the people. Vienna was earthier and more primitive than New York, filled with catastrophic drunkards and surly characters. Helmut Qualtinger was one of the latter, an actor who later reproduced Martin's and Oehlen's "Address to the Brainless" in a filmed performance.

Whatever the language, Martin always talked in his own characteristic style: voluble, quick, and direct. Even in Austria, that rubbed some people the wrong way, while others admired it. "He was full-on shameless," said Peter Pakesch, his Vienna gallerist, "and at the same time played up his Germanness very cleverly, so that people could see it for the caricature it was."

When Martin went to Vienna in the early eighties, it was a city, like Berlin, where the war seemed to have just ended. There was no Berlin Wall around Vienna but it was so far out on the edge of Western Europe, just a few miles from the Iron

Curtain, that it also seemed like a city that time had forgotten. Peter Pakesch says that the Vienna of twenty-five years ago, when he opened his gallery, still had an air of *The Third Man* about it. You could see, smell, and taste history everywhere. "To make matters worse," Oehlen and Martin said in their "Address to the Brainless," "it's really very dirty here. Can't someone clean up the birdshit from Bäckerstrasse and not dump it right back on Lugeck Square?"

In Vienna, the art scene was undergoing a breakthrough much like the one in Cologne, with artists like Peter Weibel, Franz West, Herbert Brandl, and Heimo Zobernig leading the way. In 1981—the same year that Martin showed with Max Heztler in Stuttgart for the first time—Peter Pakesch opened his gallery on Ballgasse in Vienna, showing work by Hermann Nitsch, arguably the wildest of the Actionists. Pakesch soon shifted his focus to the younger generation, showing work by Büttner, "Mattin" Kippenberger, and the Oehlens two years later in a show called *Swords into Faucets*.

Martin Prinzhorn later said that the show "was a great success. A blockbuster." The four artists were glad not to be conflated with the New Wild Ones of the Mülheimer Freiheit movement for a change, unlike in Germany, where the violent style of painting was so prominent. At least in artistic terms, they wanted nothing to do with that movement. Martin may have belonged to the same generation, the curators of his Kafka show would write years later, "but Kippenberger is a savage in a manner all his own."

Martin "thoroughly orchestrated" the opening of the *Swords into Faucets* show, according to Peter Pakesch: "The drinking lasted a whole week." It mostly took place at Kurt Kalb's, who threw large dinner parties. "He must have spent mountains of money."

Oswald & Kalb was for Vienna what the Paris Bar was for

West Berlin. Evelyn Oswald, an art historian, and Kurt Kalb, an art dealer, had opened the restaurant on Bäckerstrasse in 1979; Kalb ran his gallery there too. "They whitewashed the vaulted ceilings and furnished it simply," it said in the *Frankfurter Allgemeine Zeitung*, "combining an attention to cozy comfort with laconic modernism." There were numerous soccer trophies on display, from the restaurant's soccer team: they employed only Yugoslavian waiters, so Croatian players from the national team played for the restaurant against the other restaurants' teams. Oswald & Kalb were invariably the league champions.

When Kurt Kalb was given the "Gold Order of Merit for Service to the City of Vienna," in 2006, the journalist Eva Deissen praised both his sense for authentic, non-kitschy art and his gastronomical activities, which revolutionized the city's restaurant scene. "With his legendary generosity, he made life possible for many artists." Pakesch called Kalb "a crucial social nerve center and a source of money too. He sold art, he had connections." The Vienna Actionists often had just a few shillings for the streetcar, but they showed up in the city center and Kalb served them. The food there was to Martin's taste, too. His posthumous papers include an old menu listing all the traditional specialties of the house: chopped calf's liver, house-cured meat with horseradish, boiled beef, homemade blood sausage with sauerkraut, and Styrian caraway cutlets with parsley potatoes.

Prinzhorn says that Martin went to Oswald & Kalb "every night, to rumble around at top volume and live out the cliché of the German. The Viennese are a people who are on the one hand incredibly frightened by such things, but on the other hand totally fascinated. Kurt Kalb used Martin, too, as an instrument of terror to shake up the city's certainty." With great success.

Kalb, along with Pakesch, was the most important figure for Martin during his early period in Vienna, according to the photographer Didi Sattmann: Kalb "believed in Martin and understood him." What did Kalb like? "Martin the entertainer, the jolly drinking buddy, the bad boy," Peter Pakesch surmises. They were also both friends with Michel Würthle. In "Address to the Brainless," Martin himself said what he liked about Vienna: "Aunt Maridi's good food at Oswald & Kalb and the table of regulars that we try to avoid." Of course "he sat at the regulars' table often enough," according to Peter Pakesch. But it was very Viennese—there were insiders' rituals there that had developed over decades. The regulars would close ranks and fiercely defend their territory. There were people who were Martin's type—the Graz gallerist Bleich-Rossi, Kalb himself, the Attersee artists, journalists like Eva Deissen—but also politicians (especially from the Austrian Socialist Party, and even Sinnowatz, the chancellor at the time, and Fischer, the current president), notorious figures like Udo Proksch, and the various ladies who went with them. It was a place where the various classes of society mingled, where even a neo-Nazi politician like Jörg Haider would try to gain entry until it was made clear, relatively quickly, that it wasn't going to happen.

Eventually Kalb had to give up the restaurant—his generosity grew to be too expensive for him to sustain. Peter Pakesch describes how Kalb used to "close the doors at one and from then on everything was free. The guests got calf's liver out of the kitchen themselves and helped themselves at the bar, Evelyn Oswald ran over to the gallery for the record player, and everyone danced until the wee hours." He sold the restaurant to the waiters, "but Kurti couldn't leave well enough alone" and he became part owner of the Old Vienna Café across the street. The Old Vienna was known for the posters that covered the walls right up to the ceiling, "so Martin started to make posters like crazy until he'd managed to have the walls of the Old Vienna entirely covered with his own posters."

When Kalb gave up his restaurant, Martin lost his free-food privileges. As compensation, Kalb gave him a pair of custom-made shoes, which was fine with him.

Martin had his first solo show at Peter Pakesch's gallery in 1984: *Shock Out Is the Name of the Game*. The poster showed him doing a handstand in the toilet. Martin had found a family and home-base in Vienna as well—Pakesch showed most of the members of the Hetzler group (Büttner, Oehlen, Herold, Kiecol, Mucha, and Meuser) as well as Austrian artists Martin befriended in Vienna, such as West and Zobernig, and like-minded Americans, such as Mike Kelley, John Baldessari, Stephen Prina, and Christopher Wool.

It wasn't friendship at first sight between Pakesch and Martin. They met in 1982, at an exhibition of German painting at the Basel Kunsthalle that included most of the artists from the Mülheimer Freiheit and Moritzplatz groups, and Albert Oehlen, but not Martin. Later, Martin would call one of his catalogs for a show at Pakesch's gallery in Vienna *Are the Discos As Stupid As I Think They Are, Or Am I the Stupid One*. Pakesch says, "He leveled his protest at everyone in the restaurant after the show in Basel." In an homage to Martin after Martin's death, Pakesch wrote: "His attacks were often very witty, but you could feel the deep sadness of someone who felt himself to be in the right but not acknowledged." At the time in Basel, though, Martin only "incredibly pissed [Pakesch] off. I didn't understand how someone could go on and on like that. He turned the whole opening into the Martin Show."

They got to know each other better a few months later, at the Art Fair in Basel. Martin told him his booth was weird (Pakesch was showing, among other things, a bicycle with an apple). "I said 'Max, who's that guy with the chubby cheeks?'" Martin said later. And the way Martin used the fair as a performance stage impressed the gallerist: "I realized he was really engaging critically with it." The three men agreed to do something together and over the course of the following years they collaborated often. "And no matter what we did," Martin said, "it was allowed." He attributed to Pakesch "a truly very fine way of behaving, doesn't take everything so seriously, enough to be successful but still he can overlook it if an artist smokes a bit too much pot and talks stupid stuff and cries and so on. Then he calms him down... so, he's a nice guy, Petzi is." Things between them were not always quite as harmonious as all that—especially in the nineties, there was serious tension between them, and Pakesch started to keep his distance.

BUCKLIGE WELT

It didn't take long for Martin to find a place to retreat and paint, in the Bucklige Welt region in eastern Austria. Martin Prinzhorn, who would later write so much for and about Martin and about art in general, was studying linguistics at the University of Vienna at the time; he had inherited a castle in Bucklige Welt, more of a ruin than a castle, but in a small part of it it was possible to live, work, and occasionally throw parties—big, blowout parties with the whole clan. Martin came, as did Oehlen, Pakesch, Kiecol, Schlick, Bonin, Krebber, Diederichsen, and so on.

Dokoupil had introduced Martin to Prinzhorn during one of Prinzhorn's trips to Cologne; when Martin heard the word "Vienna," he was all ears because he knew he would be going there soon, with Albert Oehlen. When Martin and Oehlen arrived, they occupied Prinzhorn's apartment in the city right away: they didn't like it at the hotel so they dropped by for a few hours a day, played and worked, and discovered a specialty paper store nearby where they found material for their collages. Later, Martin sometimes borrowed the apartment to seduce a woman with his noodle casserole.

Eventually Martin asked Prinzhorn if he could come to the castle. Prinzhorn agreed, thinking he meant for a short visit. "Then suddenly a car pulled up with all his things. He had just been in Italy; he brought his favorite painting stool and all his things like that and set up shop." Martin lived in this idyllic hill country for a whole summer, in 1984, and often went back there from Vienna later. "At first he was totally shocked when he realized that it was an utterly isolated house, on a cliff, an hour on foot to the nearest bar. He was really depressed." But after he overcame his initial shock, he soon got used to the idyllic surroundings.

The two of them focused on their work. Prinzhorn, a few years younger than Martin, was there to write his dissertation, "so every day it was 'How many pages did you write?!' Then he bragged how many pictures he'd painted. Sometimes it was three or four a day." The next show at Pakesch's gallery was fast approaching, as was a show in New York.

Martin took long hikes with Prinzhorn and when he got too bored, Prinzhorn had to play mau-mau with him, which Prinzhorn in turn found "insanely boring, so he tried to tempt me by any means possible; there were special prizes for me, drawings." They ate noodle casseroles, traded stories of boarding school (Prinzhorn had attended one too), and even read. Since Martin "couldn't rampage around as usual" in isolation, and had spare time, his host recommended he read H.C. Artmann's complete works: Martin "enthusiastically worked his way through it." Martin also got Prinzhorn to read him works by Wolfi Bauer out loud.

Prinzhorn was more of "a literature person," he says. "When I met Martin I didn't really understand anything about art." When they were in the city together, Martin would take his friend to the museum, where he "explained things to me, he really liked doing that." He told Prinzhorn that our father had always dragged him to museums as a child and how important that had been for him. "I had the feeling that he thought his father was responsible for making him an artist."

Since Prinzhorn had to finish his thesis before his exams, he didn't want to go out drinking all the time, and Martin was "not as tyrannical as usual" with him. He let him go home at 1 a.m. without protest, whether in the city or in the country. Martin had found a bar even out in the country, of course: the White Cross, an inn run by a large family. "As always, he quickly made friends and slaves out of them—they loved him and he liked them a lot too." He proposed marriage to one daughter in public, at a firemen's festival; the other sister's husband, "poor thing, had a job where he had to be up and out the door by five in the morning, but Martin acquired him to chauffeur him around the Burgenland to discos" (Martin didn't have a driver's license). Martin hatched plans with the father, who was also the mayor—he wanted to build a gas station to expand the inn's business but Martin preferred the idea of a vacation camp, and "they had serious discussions on the topic."

The White Cross was also where, in 1991, during one of Martin's many later visits to the region, he gave a long interview over a hearty meal to an anonymous writer for the fanzine *Artfan*. The interviewer said he was amazed that Martin "did that with himself—this strain and effort, all that drinking, and then relaxing at a place like this." Martin answered, "You can only relax if you're tense, how can you relax if you're not tensed up?"

WITH ALBERT OEHLEN IN VIENNA

At some point the castle got to be too cold for Martin—and maybe, in Peter Pakesch's opinion, he was worried that Albert Oehlen was gaining too much ground on him in Vienna. So he returned to the city, where he and Oehlen were sharing an apartment.

Of all the artists Martin was friends with, Albert Oehlen was the most important for him. Their relationship was marked by competition, friendship, and great admiration. When Oehlen met Martin, he saw him as a poser:

> The preparations for his twenty-fifth birthday were underway and Berlin was holding its breath. He was quite the rebel, and at the time I thought it was just pushy. But when I realized that he's an artist, I actually liked it, this combination of braggart and artist, exactly what other people thought was shit because they thought an artist can't be like that, so ostentatious, so tacky, with that whole performance of himself. So many people think of the artist as this oddball genius sitting in his garret with his charcoal pencil, not bothering anyone. He was just the opposite.

Still, Oehlen didn't like Martin as a person until after the *Misery* show in Berlin:

> That's when I understood how he is. You just had to get the hang of it, and once you did it was fun to be around him on a personal level too, it wasn't like you constantly had to put up with him, he was really a great person. You just had to clear this little hurdle. It wasn't just bragging, he was generous with the way he

told you about his work and his discoveries and the whole adventure.

There were weeks, sometimes months, when they didn't see each other or even talk to each other: neither of them was the type to call the other and chitchat. Six months might have passed, and then Martin would call to suggest that they go on a trip, and they would be off to Italy for a week of drawing and going out to eat.

When they were together, it was with an intensity that made Martin's girlfriends jealous. They made books together, records, pictures, and exhibitions, and they worked at the same table. In this early period, Prinzhorn said, they had a symbiotic relationship that both of them profited from. There were similarities between the two (in Albert's words, "we both had fathers who were difficult in their excess of humor and their need to be part of everything") and dissimilarities too (Albert was calmer, better read, more political, more musically trained, and a more abstract painter). "For me," Martin said, "Albert also represented something different. A supplement." He may have taken Albert's art more seriously than his own, in the early years. Martin told *Artfan* that what he valued in his relationship with Albert was the exchange, the trust, the mutual respect: that they "recognized things" in the same way "and had fun with it, I'm never bored with Albert. He sees the whole panorama of your discoveries, the big picture, and he has one, too."

They lived together a few times—in Vienna, and later in Spain. "It was like we were engaged," Martin said in retrospect.

And always scheming around, what is important now, what's the right thing, or is what we just said maybe the worst ever, dumbest ever, and pow! you've gotten good practice, now you can throw it on the floor and forget about it, pow! you can work some more.... It's like Laurel and Hardy, hurling jokes at each other so fast that you could make a movie in three days.

When you're so on each other's wavelength, in the morning when you get up he needs his two hours, he just stares at the table, bores a hole in it with his eyes, and has doubts about life. I have doubts about life in the morning too, those first two hours when I'm waking up out of my dreams, I despair too: Shit, do I really have to put myself back together, build it all up, build visions, everything will have its good side too, get up and do something again. Into the void like that. As an artist you're always working into a void.... So I let him sit there for two hours first, in the living room, over breakfast, and there he is, alone, and he has his peace and quiet and then I unobtrusively go in and sit down, drink a little something, Howdy Albert, it gets better so slowly, and then you can start to talk again. Every day a new relationship . . . it was about how do you motivate yourself to live or act out your life. In fun ways, in style, finding your style, always a new one.

They lived together in Vienna for six months, constantly in cafés, exchanging ideas—"more than we could put into practice," Albert said later. "We were fruitful for each other. He was one of the very few people I could talk about my paintings with." They also had fights—Max Hetzler later said, "it wasn't as though Martin and Albert had twenty years of the most loving and close friendship. But their drive to get somewhere led to great moments."

In Vienna, each of them painted at his own end of the apartment, but there was a big table in the middle with piles of collage material on it. "We made great progress together," Oehlen says. "He made a leap in his own work, and I in my work. Everything went well, the things were totally great. You forced yourself up to a higher level—both of our collages were more daring and funnier than they would have been if we were each making them ourselves. It was a competition. It was great."

Not that they were stuck inside all the time, of course. They had readings, made books, put on events; "in Vienna it was extreme," Oehlen later said:

> Too much. We were done afterward. Vienna was brutally stressful. Especially toward the end, Martin promised an unbelievable number of things and we had to carry them out, it was insanely tough. And the girls too, everything was always a madhouse, and I was unhappy, we partied a lot out of despair, and worked, and drank. The final phase was really apocalyptic, in those last few weeks. Our paths diverged for a little while then, to be safe—and from the girls, too. We flew off in different directions, to survive.

Even for onlookers it was stressful. The two men were soon the "terrors of Vienna," as the Graz artist Jörg Schlick called them. Among their many activities was the "Officer's Club," a vodka drinking contest between German and Austrian artists at the Club am Opernring, a basement bar that Attila Corbaci ran for a little while.

"Martin was unbelievably enthusiastic and meticulous and worked incredibly hard organizing it, with posters and flyers," Corbaci later said. "He even hired a paramedic and we set up a hospital bed in the next room—there were one or two people who needed it." Anyone who wanted to watch had to pay an entrance fee. The artists stood in line, and whoever's turn it was stepped up to the table, drank, handed the bottle back, crawled under the table to the other side, and then went around to the back of the line. The Austrian team was the first to empty their ten bottles.

The pace of these actions and events was relentless. One Friday at noon there was a carriage race, followed at 7 p.m. by the "Address to the Brainless" that Peter Weibel (a vodka-drinking-contest participant) had invited them to give, then at midnight the Peter Altenberg Cup was handed out to the winner of the carriage race in Café Alt Wien, then the next day at 6 p.m. came the closing of Martin's *Shock Out Is the Name of the Game* show at Pakesch, then on Sunday morning Albert and Martin appeared onstage at the Museum of the Twentieth Century as the Alma Band with Martin as the singer (singing "freestyle," in the artist Hans Wiegand's description, "panting across the stage with the microphone in his hand").

Every event with its own poster, of course. Despite the announcement, though, the First Vienna Carriage Race took place in a deserted Prater Park—no one showed up on that cold December day, unless you count Attersee, the artist, and Didi Sattmann, the photographer whom Martin had asked to document the event. Photographs and stories and the presentation of the winner's cup were enough to create the legend. They had met up at the Old Vienna Café, gone to Stephansplatz, the cathedral square, and hired two tourist fiacres for a price everyone was happy with. Then came the race, not particularly fast—Sattmann guessed that the winner had already been decided in advance. Martin's later announcement ran as follows: "1st Place: Martin Kippenberger. 2nd Place: Albert Oehlen. 3rd Place: Not awarded due to shortage of serious participants."

"I thought it was just magnificent," Didi Sattmann says. "I had never seen anyone like that. It fascinated me that an artist could follow his path like that—so creative, so direct, so unconventional." Sattmann and his camera often accompanied Martin, who wanted to be documented as a living work of art. Sattmann photographed the drinking contest, the "Address to the Brainless," and whatever else took place, or even things that never took place, for instance Albert and Martin lying passed out from alcohol on the floor (they were actually completely sober). He did so both on his own initiative and under pressure from Martin: "You have to!" Martin had said. He liked Sattmann's pictures, "and he knew that I'd be there." He was there even when there was no fee and no newspaper that would publish his photographs, and even if he had to postpone other assignments. When Martin said "Come on, we're going to the disco to dance the boogie-woogie," Sattmann went—apparently the Austrians could dance it as eagerly and well as Martin. Or when Martin said "Come on, we're going to buy shoes," they went to a cobbler who still made shoes by hand.

Even though Martin had a certain exotic status in Austria that he lacked in Germany, he polarized the Viennese even more than Albert did. Opinions varied widely even between close friends, for example between Walter Pichler and Christian Ludwig Attensee, Vienna's two great art heroes. Pichler, representing sublime High Art and the autonomy of the work of art, disapproved of Martin, while Attersee respected Martin just as Martin respected him (poking a little fun at him too, but that was par for the course).

RENT ELECTRICITY GAS

Martin painted like a world champion in those days—1983, '84, '85. *Heil Hitler You Fetishists; Not Knowing Why but*

Knowing What For; Hysterialand; It's a Shame That Wols Is Not Alive to See This; With the Best Will in the World, I Can't See a Swastika; opinion pictures, architecture pictures, Is-Not-Embarrassing pictures, profit-peak pictures. There was one exhibition after another in 1985: at Ascan Crone in Hamburg, Van Beveren in Rotterdam, Metro Pictures in New York, Silvio Baviera in Zurich, Hetzler in Cologne, CCD Gallery in Düsseldorf, Leyendecker in Teneriffe, Heinrich Ehrhardt in Frankfurt, Bärbel Grässlin in Frankfurt, Kuhlenschmidt in Los Angeles, Petersen in Berlin, and Erhard Klein in Bonn.

Johann-Karl Schmidt, the curator, said of himself that it was in Cologne that he "learned that museums do not always have to work with eternal values, but can work with present-day ideas." When Schmidt became the head of the modern art department of the Hessian State Museum in Darmstadt in the late seventies, he wanted to create a platform for the new contemporary art movement, together with Hans-Jürgen Müller. Necessity was the mother of invention, since the Pop Art collection that a new building was being built for was on loan in Frankfurt. But by the time the building was finally finished, in 1984, the idea was not so easy to put into practice: artists like Fetting were already too expensive ("they made it unbelievably fast"), and most young artists already had solo museum shows behind them. Only Martin was unspoiled territory—no museum director had given him a show yet, because they saw him as a clown, not an artist, or because they were afraid of him and his unpredictability. "It was too awkward for me," admits Klaus Honnef, who at the time ran the State Museum in Bonn. "I had the feeling that it would blow up on me, that I couldn't control it."

The collaboration in Darmstadt went smoothly; the curator now recalls only the discussions that went into the catalog as a problem. They were both bashful: "We absolutely didn't speak the same language. I couldn't handle Martin's vitality and he couldn't handle my intellectualism. So he sat there like a good little boy, and I did too, both of us totally embarrassed." Maybe, Schmidt adds, Martin wasn't shy about him in person but about the institution: "Maybe it was uncomfortable for him to finally be accepted into the art market and to have those demands on him, or to show work in a museum with its claims of permanent value."

Rent Electricity Gas was a show of paintings and sculptures, mostly on the theme of architecture; it included many of Martin's classic works: Betty Ford Clinic, *Haus am See Sanatorium – Negative, Positive, Right-Left Reversed; Houses with Slits; If You Stand In Front of the Abyss, Don't Be Surprised If You Can Fly; Two Proletarian Inventresses on the Way to the Inventors' Congress;* the Cost Peaks and Profit Peaks, the *Hunger Family, New York Seen from the Bronx,* and EuroPallet sculptures like *Essen-Frillendorf Station, Student Housing in Riad,* and *Design for an Administrative Building for Rest Center for Mothers in Paderborn.*

"Painters are rediscovering the world," Michael Royen wrote in a review of the show in *Skyscraper:* "Kippenberger has thrown in his lot with this world. That's what he looks after."

There were no scandals; Schmidt has "no clear memory" of the opening. One reason no conflicts arose, most likely, was that Martin was given free rein to design everything himself, from the poster to the invitations to the catalog—the whole thing was supposed to be "an artist's exhibition, as authentic as possible." Martin included in the catalog not only Schmidt and Bazon Brock (a professor of aesthetics and leading thinker in the Fluxus movement) but his friends and colleagues, even with just a word or two: Hubert Kiecol, Martin Prinzhorn, Diedrich Diederichsen, Georg Herold; Wolfgang Bauer was represented with an entire play, *A Cheerful Morning at the Hair Salon,* which he also performed at an opening at the Hetzler Gallery.

Schmidt says that one should not overestimate the importance of the show. "It was hardly a milestone in Martin's biography—there wasn't a Before Darmstadt and After Darmstadt. Kippenberger was dynamic enough on his own not to need the exhibition." Still, it was his only solo show at a German museum until shortly before his death. (In 1997, eleven years after the Darmstadt show, *The Eggman and His Outriggers* opened at the Abteiberg Museum in Mönchengladbach. The museum director, Veit Loers, was a friend of his.)

For the curator, on the other hand, it was a turning point: "the exhibition was such a success that I was made director of the Stuttgart City Gallery." Which is not to say that the masses stormed the gates of the museum, not to mention the critics, who largely ignored the show. The catalog (print run: 1,500 copies) was eventually remaindered.

THE MAGICAL MISERY TOUR

The day after the Darmstadt show opened came the next event, *Give Me the Summer Downtime* at the Klein Gallery in Bonn, accompanied by three booklets and two editions. And that was just a fraction of the material Martin had brought back from Brazil. He had spent a good three months there— one of his worst trips but also one of his most fruitful. It was like a sequel to *Slaves of Tourism*, but more extreme: The Magical Misery Tour.

Martin had set out for his trip to Brazil in high style. He threw a farewell dance on December 13, 1985, in Cologne: "10 p.m. to 4 a.m." Night and Day played; Martin joined them onstage and loudly declared his love for Ursula Böckler (involved with another man at the time) in front of a large painting Hubert Kiecol had made for the occasion, which showed a ship in the waves and the caption "Kippy Come Back." Gisela Capitain said that Martin "wanted to show Cologne that he was leaving." Festivities continued the next day with a brunch at Andrea Stappert's (sixty guests), and then he was off. Hanno Huth and Curny, two childhood friends from Essen, traveled with Martin to Rio, along with Albert Oehlen, though he only stayed for ten days.

Even now, more than twenty years later, Oehlen describes the trip as though he would have preferred to escape from the very beginning. The Rio travel report by Martin and Albert in *Café Central* says: "With the first door we opened, the starting gate went up for drug abuse, insanity, prostitution, and shabba-da-shabbad under a superheated nicotine bell jar." In the blazing sun they drank Sexy Piranhas from morning till night—Martin's hands were shaking so badly that he couldn't butter his bread, and "our heads, attached to our legs, started to itch," as he described it in *Café Central*. The most dangerous thing about Brazil, the passage continues, was "the belief that everything was just like at home, only warmer." Culture shock struck them with full force.

Hanno Huth remembers the trip perfectly, especially the New Year's party it included. They rented an apartment in Copacabana on the thirteenth floor, apparently furnished in psychedelic style: a "desolate accumulation of colors, shapes, and sea-sail posters. Kippenberger had insisted on his right to claim the biggest bed, which looked like an oversized stereo system with broken knobs. (You have to bring your own Dolby.)" On New Year's Eve they went out to eat and only just managed to force their way back through the crowds of people to their apartment with a view; they rushed to the window just in time for midnight and saw "a couple million people dressed in white on the beach, sending candles on little boats into the sea, and at that moment the music started: a Viennese waltz. The Blue Danube Waltz. Tears ran down our faces." A fat black cleaning lady was in the apartment with them; she had asked if she and her family could spend New Year's with them. "When I turned around, Martin was dancing a waltz with her. It was one of the most emotional moments of my life."

Albert Oehlen, on the other hand, who was certainly adventurous enough, found the whole thing decidedly too adventurous: "too stressful, too crazy, just suicidal. I was totally overwhelmed emotionally by all the new impressions I was taking in: poverty, wealth, the samba, the girls everywhere— not prostitutes, just beautiful girls who wanted things in various degrees or sometimes didn't want anything at all. We were always on the edge; there was such a color difference (white and rich or brown and poor), and you felt it the whole time. Always. It made a huge impression on me and was a huge burden. I could barely stand it; I was so damn happy when I could leave."

"You have to hang yourself in misery" was Martin's motto: immerse yourself in the misery of the world. He said you have to "fall down the hole and feel it so you can report on desolation all the better, that's how you can be so intense." In Brazil, he definitely crossed his pain threshold. As he later said in an interview with Jutta Koether,

> I always know here come some stupid minutes, now it won't be much fun. You have to get through that too. You have to have spent three months in Brazil! Not two weeks and cross Brazil off your list and say Now I've had the girl from Ipanema and her sister too, and then it got to be too much for me and then I left and . . . talk about "poor people," "I saw poor

285

people!" That's it? That can't have been it! You have to be able to stick it out! To experience things that flip the greatest feelings of pleasure and fun into their opposite and to stay!

He did stay, first in Rio and then in Salvador, where Ursula Böckler joined him as his photography assistant, driver, and companion. When she arrived "he was already a bit unnerved by the whole thing, frightened too." He had been robbed—and no wonder, since he went around like the prototypical tourist, in shorts, sneakers, and tennis socks with a camera hanging down over his belly. They drove around together, and he was interested in the architecture: all the "Psychobuildings" he saw on the roadsides, then a sixty-foot sculpture in the middle of an intersection. Naturally he had his picture taken standing in front of it. The gas stations fascinated him too, not least because they had alcohol coming out of some of the pumps.

He bought an abandoned gas station in Salvador de Bahia (Russ Meyer had had a similar gas station in one of his movies already), named it after Martin Bormann,* and had Ursula Böckler take his picture striking a pose in his shorts between the pumps. Böckler found it easy to photograph him: "he was a good poser." She was not a professional photographer herself, just someone who liked photography, but Martin liked that about her. He did sometimes heap abuse on her, when he thought she wasn't trying hard enough: "The division of roles was clear; there was no discussion about it. Martin was like a mad professor for me, who never stopped trying to teach me how things should be."

It was hardly a dream vacation. "When he was in a good mood, it was nice," Böckler says. But he was often in a bad

---

* Hitler's close confidante and chief of staff, one of the most powerful Nazis and one with a particularly brutal reputation.

mood. Martin was determined to work even when they had just had another fight; once she took his picture in just such a moment, a series of portraits that turned out especially well. They also played a lot of mau-mau,

> because we didn't get along with each other very well. Over mau-mau, you didn't have to talk, and you could drink. And then it turned into a meaningful activity and was used for an artistic postcard action: he kept all his friends and the art people who mattered to him up-to-date with the running mau-mau scores, and Erhard Klein "finally" published them in a series of booklets [called *Finally*]. We usually had a lot of fun, with the mau-mau at least.

Martin celebrated his birthday at a dance bar and arranged to have noodle casserole onboard a boat for lunch, which moved him to tears. On the street, Martin gave "foreign aid" to young boys, namely a lecture about how selling was better than begging along with buying bags and bags of peanuts off them (and eating them too). Using nothing but hand gestures, he taught them how to bargain.

No sooner was Martin back in Europe than he called up all sorts of gallerists and said he wanted to show work. Erhard Klein, the Bonn gallerist, told him he had already committed to shows by two other young artists, Jo Schultheis and Albert Oehlen, and then by two older artists, Sigmar Polke and Imi Knoebel, at which point Martin told him: "Give me the summer downtime." That turned into the title of the show.

He certainly had something to show from the trip. With Albert he made three records—*The Alma Band: Live in Rio, White and Dumbass: Rio Clamoso*, and *The Know-How Knockers: Knocking for Jazz*—along with a book of texts and drawings called *14 Million for a Howdy-Do,* a book of poems called *No Problem,* and a collection of material called *It's Not Your Fault.* He published photographs and made multiples like *Copa and Ipa*: garish Brazilian beach towels and cheap fabric from Cologne sewn together with sleeves, which Andrea Stappert had had to cut off of Martin's expensive Uli Knecht shirts before he left for tropical Brazil. A series of paintings came out of it: *Anticipation the Wrong Way Round: I Have To Stay At Home.* His "Analyses of Things Written on T-Shirts" was later "revealed as *Picture Titles for Artists to Borrow.*" In the *Sand in the Vaseline* show in Düsseldorf, he exhibited photocollages along with pictures our father had taken on the beach in Zandvoort. He drew floor plans of the apartments he had lived in throughout his life on receipts from the Bahia Othon Palace Hotel, Salvador, and titled the series *Input-Output.* He showed silkscreens of sketches along with texts about Rio he had written with Albert, in a show called *23 Proposals in Four Shades of Gray for the Modernization of the Backstroke Swimmer* (the Backstroke Swimmer in question being the famous statue of Christ the Redeemer above Rio, with his arms outspread). He cut circles ("Everything in Brazil is round: the samba, the sun, the soccer balls") out of cardboard boxes ("This is what they make their shacks out of down there") and painted the boxes the Brazilian national colors.

"Now it all seems so conceptual, so completely thought-out," Ursula Böckler says. But the whole thing seemed much more chaotic to her at the time, when she was with Martin in Brazil. Albert Oehlen, on the other hand, thought that Martin had it all planned from the beginning, and that that was why Martin stuck it out so long in the poverty and misery:

He always had insane plans like that in mind. The older he got, the more complicated the plans were. He knew: If I go to Brazil I'll make a Martin Bormann gas station there, I'll buy a hundred washcloths and embroider this and that word on them, that'll be the connection to the book that has the photograph of the gas station, then I'll have it embroidered in gold again and include it in the record I'll have Albert press in Germany and then I'll hang the photograph of the record up in the gas station, but I should do it as a multiple, Erhard Klein'll take it, he'll give me $X for it, and if any's left over I'll make such-and-such and Ursula can take a picture of it and so-and-so will print it and that'll be my Graz show . . . All the content and meaning proliferated alongside the financing situation—it was like a three-dimensional spiderweb of financing, printing, exhibition obligations, plus this whole insanity of the content. No one could keep up with it. But the whole construction did in fact exist. Sometimes, in later years, people were tempted to wonder if all he really did was drink away all his brain cells or just tell jokes, but looking at this whole fabric, they had to realize that it was all still there.

REST CURES

It was so relaxing: to go unrecognized once a year, not to have to put on a show, not to play the wild man. At his rest cure near Innsbruck, Martin was a clown only on the wall (he had given the hotel a painting, a genuine Kippenberger for the gym room) and The Wild Man was just the name of a local inn, where he regularly went and drank water. In the clinic he sipped tea and ate dry bread, a hundred chews per bite. After a few weeks he had reacquired his usual tastes—"it resensitizes everything for you"—and he felt hungry again. He needed his hunger, in life and in art: he always said that "not-having-enough" was his motor. The only thing he indulged in during his cures was smoking like a chimney.

Martin never took vacations as such, trips to really relax. He traveled to Siena to paint, to Teneriffe to plan sculptures, to Madrid to drink, to Tokyo to shop, to Paris to write, all over the world for exhibitions. He tolerated breaks only in order to work better afterward and sustain his wild life.

The Grässlins, who were regulars at the clinic, introduced Martin to the rest cure as a kind of better, shorter version of the Anti-Sahara Program. From that point on, Martin regularly took rest cures at various places, most often in the Lanserhof near Innsbruck and sometimes with others such as Max Hetzler, Werner Büttner, or Albert Oehlen. "It was nice," Valeria Heisenberg told me about her stay at Bad Pyrmont with him. "So restful." They played mau-mau and went for walks in the woods.

"It was," said Alex Witasek, Martin's doctor, "a fairy-tale time." Martin told him in the nineties that he would never escape his role as a wild man—it was his brand. But at the Lanserhof, where no one knew or cared he was an artist, "he was sweet as a lamb, almost like a baby, sometimes even maudlin." They understood each other well, the patient and the doctor— Witasek played the cello and also liked to push himself to his limits; like Martin, he talked fast and went through life "with a wide-angle lens." Martin surely liked having a doctor who didn't just scold him. "You have to take people as they are," in Witasek's words: he thought you couldn't get anywhere with accusations and threats. The doctor gave Martin tips about how he could drink less, but he knew that Martin would never stop altogether: "He had decided that quality of life was more important than quantity." As Martin once said, "I'm the only one who can repair myself, that's something only I can do. That's why that drink is called a screwdriver."

After his rest cures, he felt ready to conquer the world. He always looked "magnificent" afterward, Gisela Capitain thought. Rosemarie Trockel said she could hardly recognize him when he came back to Cologne in the early eighties, slim and tan with short hair. Only in his last years was he unable to restore himself quite so completely. His big belly, which he used to stick out for self-portraits in underpants pulled up high, was due not to eating but to drinking; even after the cures, his hands were still red. Martin drank less at the end of his life not only out of love for his wife, Elfie Semotan, but also because his body could no longer tolerate as much.

What remained from the fairy-tale times was work. He transformed the rest cures too into art, of course: a gigantic painting of a cigarette-lighter sandwich, and then a small drawing of it in his *Little Cure Booklet,* or a painting of the *Haus am See Sanatorium – Negative, Positive, Right-Left Reversed.* Even on a cure, he could never stand not working at all: hobbies, walks, TV, miniature golf, conversations, and looking at caves in the mountains were not enough. He developed ideas, called his assistants, gave them assignments, ordered catalogs, drew, and even taught in Kassel. Roberto Ohrt wrote this about Martin's stay in Tyrol, in the catalog of the Widauer Collection:

He looked very precisely at what was around him, talked with the people in the restaurants and cafés, whether Café Central or up in the mountain villages, went out to the soccer fields or tennis courts disguised as a jolly tourist ("up the mount'n in my city shoes"), flashed victory and peace signs at the huts, made his rounds through the shops and galleries—not that there were any of the latter—reflected on the beauty of the Tyrolean women, and got along marvelously with the local farmers, as long as they didn't tell him how great his art was, because all he wanted to do was play cards with them in peace.

As always, he took whatever he found and incorporated it into his work: Tyrolean local color, Martin-style. Johann Widauer, the gallerist and collector known as "the Schwarzenegger of Innsbruck," was Martin's point of contact in the area after Martin returned home, and he arranged a lot of things for Martin while he was there, including putting him in touch with the crucifix carver he would use for numerous assignments in the years to come. The carver made Martin his crucified frogs, in natural wood and sprayed with metallic auto paint; giant oversize pills for his installations with birch forests; a bust of Richard von Weizsäcker; Martin's own head for the sculpture series *Martin, into the Corner, You Should Be Ashamed of Yourself;* pizzas for Martin to spatter (*Lousy Spread Toppings on Pollocked Student Pizza*); the Kippen Seltzers; the Open Manta dashboard; and the wooden cellphones Martin showed in Innsbruck's Café Central.

Eventually the crucified frogs would be shown in Umhausen, quite nearby, at the three-day art festival organized by Herbert Fuchs, another wild man. Martin Prinzhorn used to detour around Umhausen out of "fear of a booze-fest. You would be wasted for days."

THE GARDEN GNOME DOCUMENTA

Taking stock of his career at the end of his life, Martin could point to one unqualified hit he felt he had had as an artist: the

1987 *Peter* exhibition at Max Hetzler's gallery in Cologne. The sculpture show was the talk of the town—everyone wanted to have seen it—and since documenta was running at the time in Kassel, Martin's show had a lot of out-of-town visitors as well. Even today, this is the show that the people who knew Martin are most enthusiastic about. Gisela Capitain says, "*Peter* was a bombshell. The show divided the art world of the time even more clearly into two camps: those who admired his work and those who despised it."

"Peter" had become one of Martin's favorite nicknames: he called a collector and chocolate manufacturer named Ludwig "Chocolate Peter," called a baker "Roll Peter" or gave other people names like "Catalog Peter"; maybe he felt a bit like "Black Peter" himself (the bad card you get stuck with in various card games—in English usually called Black Maria). By the mid-1980s, Martin expanded this relatively standard German usage of "Peter" into all sorts of other meanings, applied to both things and people—"Peter" meaning "thingee" was a perfect label for what filled the *Peter* show. Meanwhile, the "salon style" of hanging paintings (crowded together on the wall, floor to ceiling—the way they were in our stairwell back in Essen-Frillendorf) is called "Petersburg Hanging" in German, after the Russian city whose Hermitage Museum uses that style. Ascan Crone hung pictures that way at his Hamburg gallery, so Martin put on an exhibition called "Hamburg Hanging" at Gisela Capitain's gallery in 1989. And the *Peter* show used "Russian Placing": Max Hetzler's gallery was stuffed full of sculptures.*

While the *Rent Electricity Gas* show had been about architecture, the focal point of the *Peter* show was the issue of

---

* The show's full title in German is *Peter: Die russische Stellung,* usually translated as "Peter: The Russian Position." *Stellung* also means the act of positioning or placing sculptures, analogous to "hanging" pictures.

furnishing a room: tables, shelves, boxes, coatracks, tea trays, or, to be more precise, objects that looked like tables, shelves, boxes, coatracks, and tea trays gone terribly wrong. There was a bookshelf titled *Wittgenstein,* a mirrored screen called *Rainer Werner Fassbinder,* a box filled with boxes (*Masterwork*), a chair on a pedestal (*Not to be the Second Winner*), a rolling trestle with briefcases (*Work Timer*), a table with assorted stuff on it (*I Have Nothing Against Depressions As Long As They Don't Come Into Fashion*), a tabletop (*Who Was It We Bought At the Table Again*), a table with a Gerhard Richter painting as its surface (*Model Interconti*—the most famous piece in the show and, because of the Richter, the most expensive), a triangular thing on rollers (*Pyramid Colonia*), and other pieces: *Simone de House Bar; When the Rain Starts Coming Through the Roof; Once a Friend, Never Just an Acquaintance Again.* Forty-five bulky, tragicomic objects in total, crammed into a gallery that started to look like a junk room. This was Martin's answer to the sculptors of his time, artists like Herold, Mucha, Rückreim, Donald Judd, and Jeff Koons, and to the large shows that were always so neat and tidy and manageable.

One visitor found this "blocking up the gallery space" to be "truly wonderful," as he wrote in a letter that Martin immediately had made into a poster: "this mix of handicraft art, storeroom, and garden-gnome documenta.... Once you've seen *Peter* there is no going back. It takes you by surprise even when you see it a second time." The gallerist Bruno Brunnet said that *Peter* "opened a door"; Jutta Koether felt that Martin had pioneered new dimensions in conceptual art by allowing in everything that had previously been excluded "and ghettoized in neo-expressionist painting": fullness, multitude, forcefulness, humor. "Of all the exhibitions that shaped my understanding of art," the gallerist Esther Schipper said, "this one was one of the most crucial." *Peter* was a hit in every sense except the commercial one.

There was no going back for Martin either. Suddenly, he was taken seriously as an artist: "it dawned on me," Peter Pakesch said, "that what Martin was doing was in a whole different league." He had earlier focused on painting and graphic work, but now he threw himself into three-dimensional media—sculpture, multiples, installations—and soon he would start his series of drawings on hotel stationery. From this point on, his path diverged from those of Albert Oehlen and Werner Büttner.

A whole round of shows followed *Peter*, and the catalog for each one used the same design: a white booklet with a picture of a sculpture on the title page. There was *Petra* at Gisela Capitain's gallery, *Peter 2* with Peter Pakesch in Vienna, *The Applause Simply Ends* at Grässlin-Ehrhardt in Frankfurt, *Sorry III* at Metro Pictures New York, *Broken Neon* (a group show) at steirischer herbst in Graz, *Pop In* at Forum Stadtpark in Graz, *Journey to Jerusalem* with Bleich-Rossi in Graz, *67 Improved Papertigers Not Afraid of Repetition* as a Julie Sylvester edition, and *Once Again Petra* the following year at the Winterthur Kunsthalle.

In the catalog dedicated to Michel Würthle, Diederichsen wrote that "not-thinking," as he called Martin's artistic method, was what determines

> how the parts are put together, where and why they are coated/not coated with whatever, where why and with what sewn, nailed, burled, knobbed, and which intentional or unintentional but respected mistakes would be painted over to what extent and in what colors, so that on the one hand the mistakes are still visible but on the other hand so is the decision to recognize the mistake as a mistake and thus need to

correct it, but also need to interrupt this correction halfway through, out of respect for the beauty the mistake gave rise to, and still leave the beginning of the correction alone, out of respect for the fact that the beauty came to pass because of a mistake, and respect for free will, and no doubt also not entirely without keeping in mind that so much respect might give off a certain beauty of its own.

Diederichsen's text came out of a long interview with Michael Krebber about the creation of the sculptures—in which Krebber himself played a large role.

A LIAISON DANGEREUSE : MKI AND MK2

Martin liked to say he had two friends, both named Michael. They were Michel Würthle and Michael Krebber. Meanwhile Krebber—and Martin too, for that matter—liked to say that he didn't believe in friendship.

Martin had long dreamed of finding an assistant who would help bear his burdens. Dokoupil had had one for a while, Reiner Opoku, whom Martin tried to lure away ("You can't seriously want to work for the worst painter in the world!"), but in vain. Martin always had someone to help him—run errands, perform various tasks, chauffeur him around, bring him material—but never someone who could do everything, truly everything for him, from making phone calls to painting pictures.

Until 1986, when Michael Krebber showed up and offered his services.

He was only a year younger than Martin and, unlike most of his assistants, had long been an artist, not just an aspiring artist. But he had done what Joseph Beuys only threatened to do: quit. In addition, Krebber (like Martin) had inherited some money and then quickly spent it all, and now he wanted to spend a year without having to worry about income. He didn't want a normal job, and he knew he wasn't cut out to be a manual laborer or work in the trades. He wanted a position. He applied first with Hubert Kiecol, but Kiecol wasn't interested—perhaps he disliked the idea of having an artist his own age working for him. Martin was number two on Krebber's list.

They had much in common: both were friends with Albert Oehlen, both admired Oswald Wiener (Krebber even more than Martin), both had lived in Cologne, Hamburg, and Berlin. And then their initials—in Martin's book *Café Central*, Krebber is called MK1 and Martin himself is MK2. Both men were outsiders in the art business, and both were passionate about art. There was nothing they were more afraid of than making "normal art."

Jutta Koether wrote in Martin's catalog *Homesick Highway* that there was never an anti-Kippenberger because Kippenberger was always his own opposite already. Now, in Michael Krebber, he had found a living opposite: someone like him in many ways but primarily by being a mirror image, exactly reversed.

Martin always looked older than he really was, while Krebber looked younger—and still does (today, at well over fifty, he looks like a tall schoolboy). Krebber read a lot, Martin read very little; Krebber did drink significant amounts but couldn't hold his liquor as well as Martin. Krebber had a dominating father, too, but one who dominated by his absence, not his presence. Krebber had studied with Lüpertz, had been Baselitz's assistant, and, like Martin, had wanted to be an actor.

297

Like Martin, Krebber worked conceptually; while Martin consistently expanded his artistic means and methods, though, Krebber preferred renunciation. Martin opened one exhibition after another, but Krebber showed absolutely nothing for long periods, refusing all invitations to present work; if Martin could paint a picture a day, Krebber contented himself with one a year. Or none at all. Martin crammed the Hetzler Gallery full of his Peter sculptures, but Krebber, the following year, had a show at the Christoph Dürr Gallery in Munich consisting of empty rooms that contained nothing but a single Broodthaers quotation. While Martin did everything all at once, Michael Krebber was more like Herman Melville's famous Bartleby the Scrivener, forever repeating the same sentence: "I would prefer not to."

Martin seemed to make everything in his life public, in the form of stories or artworks, but Krebber cloaked himself in an air of mystery. Martin's trademark was quick, voluble, aphoristic talking; Krebber cultivated a hesitant, faltering way of speaking. Nothing was embarrassing to Martin, and he would unload his opinion of you when you walked in the door, or shout across the room what he thought of you, your art, your haircut, and your wife. Krebber, on the other hand, is said to have once bitten through a glass of beer at an artist's opening so as not to have to say what he thought of the artist's work. When he did say something, he could be as merciless as Martin—maybe even more merciless, since he didn't soften his judgment with irony or humor. But it took you a moment to understand what you had just heard Krebber say, since he wore the same schoolboy smile on his face no matter how malicious the comment was.

Krebber is a "communication hound" like Martin was (the description is from the Frankfurt artist Thomas Bayrle, whom Martin substituted for at the Städelschule and whose professorship Krebber would later take over). But Krebber prefers to communicate by e-mail, whereas Martin never touched a computer, used the telephone only to quickly exchange information, and never owned a cellphone—for him, communication always had to be live, and he never felt comfortable around machines. Once, in his Hamburg period, he wrote to a friend that he had "inhibitions": whenever he was around electronic gadgets, he said, "I keep quiet."

They thought the way they talked: Martin spontaneously, directly, and instinctively; Krebber via detours, around corners, at a distance. Krebber once explained his artistic approach like this: "Actually with me up until this point there has not been a method except insofar as not having a method manifests itself as a method and I can enjoy it very much, having that as a method, because now I can work with it."

As the catalog for a 2000 show at the Brauschweig Kunstverein under the direction of Karola Grässlin says, "Michael Krebber (b. 1954, Cologne) worked on his legend before his first picture came into existence. He is surely one of the most rigorous observers of art, which has inhibited his own production of work to this day."

From a very young age, Martin, full of love for pictures and performances, threw himself into his life as an artist. But when Diedrich Diederichsen asked Krebber about the various forms of artistic life Krebber had journeyed through ("For a very long time now, you have existed as an artist who shows no work, whose ideas are taken up by others but whose name is missing, but then that changed and there were exhibitions"), Krebber answered, "The first form was of desperately trying to be an artist." Martin's light, playful, uninhibited artistic life— and his lack of inhibition about making use of other people's ideas—was foreign to Krebber. "I hesitated for years about my debut in the art world, hemming and hawing, at least that's how it seems to me," Krebber said.

While Martin, accused of being nothing but a clown, devoted a series of paintings to the figure of the fool, Krebber availed himself of the figure of the dandy, someone who likewise turns his life into art but without producing actual works of art. For example, Krebber took care to always wear something no other artist was wearing, "even if it was just a certain pair of shoes." He also gave himself a pseudonym in his early years, since he hated his real name: someone had once said to him that an artist's birthplace worked well as the artist's name, so for a while he was Mario Köln (the German spelling of "Cologne"). In the opinion of Valeria Heisenberg, who met him when she was a student in Frankfurt, Krebber "was like a fabricated character."

It was clear from the start that the relationship between MK1 and MK2 would not be an easy one.

When Krebber applied to work for Martin, they had already known each other for years. They had met in 1980, in Hamburg and Berlin, unpleasant encounters from Krebber's perspective: "When I'm asked today how I met Kippenberger, when and where, there is only one answer: I met him at such-and-such and he made me want to throw up," Krebber said in the interview Martin had him conduct with Joachim Lottmann and then used as the introduction to *Café Central* under the title "Hellish Prelude with Tape Recorder (Stupid Questions, Correct Answers)." Krebber was no less repelled by Martin's art: "At the time, I thought the Kippenberger works were bad, blunt, and insensitive. It took me five or six years to see the quality in them."

Ten years later, Krebber and his wife, Cosima von Bonin, would write in their obituary for Martin in *Spex*: "For a very long time it wasn't clear whether this was an artist you could work with, or if you had to take a stand against him or ignore him or something like that. Until at last you decided: he's good.

The stories that made us suspicious were the stories about him showing off, acting swanky, throwing Rolex watches around."

Martin included work by Krebber in his early exhibition in Hamburg, *Action Piss-Crutch*, without asking Krebber first, and even dedicated the catalog of *Truth Is Work* to Krebber—a challenge, to a large extent, at a time when no one really knew what Krebber was doing.

The whole thing was an experiment, with a fixed time limit from the beginning. Since Krebber was an artist and didn't want to be referred to as an assistant, he called himself an "employee." Since he thought it was stupid that Martin no longer wanted to be called Kippi, he always referred to him as "Kippenberger." But he was ready and willing to do anything and everything. He practiced service as his form of art for a year, and his absolute devotion to a given idea or project is exactly what Martin liked, since that is what Martin always did: give himself 150 percent, whether fervently singing religious songs in the car as a boy, or taking drugs as a teenager, or being the wild impresario of S.O.36, or undertaking his Sahara Program.

Martin threw himself into the role of the lord and master, making the "employee" his errand-boy for everything. As a first step, Martin told him stories about our family all night—not always flattering stories, it seems—because he thought Krebber had to know these stories if he was going to work for him. Then Krebber had to put up Kippenberger posters in Café Broadway, before the eyes of other Cologne artists like Walter Dahn; had to take his dirty shirts to the laundry; had to paint pictures Martin had already sold before they even existed, and deliver them too; had to make sure there would be lentil soup in Teneriffe for the Christmas party. A passage from *Café Central* says what it meant to work for Martin, namely, to be on call around the clock; Krebber worked on the book, and it is impossible to know whether the passage was written by Martin, Krebber, or someone else:

> I am Kiprenbersher's emproyee and Im here at a inshtrallation in Teneriffe. The bossh says I can drink after work but I hafta trink til the lasht dishco closhes. Then geddup early in the moaning and go to the offish becaush itsh lunsh from 1 to 5. At 1 I hafta trink with the bossh on the beash. Then he takesh hish afternoon nap and Im back to the offish, and when he wakesh up he hash the crayshiest ideash.

They had ended up on the Canary Islands at the invitation of the Leyendecker Gallery, where Martin had an exhibition. They were working on the *Peter* sculptures. Krebber later said about his time working for and with Martin that it "gave rise to a common understanding in many areas." One important area of commonality that they discovered then, developed further, and exploited was their love of mistakes—the "unintentional poetry" (in Krebber's words) of mistakes.

Krebber tells the story in *Café Central* of how he went to a carpenter in Teneriffe with drawings, paper models, and a dictionary in hand, to explain to him how to build the sculptures. He went through everything, talked out and drew every detail, but the fact remained that "the carpenter misunderstood everything." Eventually they would take their leave of each other, politely, "with a gesture of Well, there's nothing to be done about it, what will be will be. The next day I would see whether the boxes looked the way I thought they would. Thus Art is born." Both MKs liked the misunderstandings so much that they built a few more into their sculptures on purpose.

Krebber's perceptions and his way of describing them, Martin later said, "can make people cry." Anyone who heard Krebber talk about gray suits, Martin said, would never see one on the street the same way again. Other people describe Martin's way of seeing in similar terms. "I can look," Martin said himself, "I don't only look at the canvas or look out the window, I can also look at people."

Krebber told Diedrich Diederichsen that what he (Krebber) offered as an artist was not "an object to look at and admire," a tangible thing, but rather ideas and conversations. His audience consisted of the people he was with, "who care about similar things, people where I like something about them and vice versa." There was mutual admiration between him and Martin, and mutual fear. But an imbalance remained: one MK was the boss, and the other MK was the employee, and when their year was up and they spent almost as much time together as before, there was still the subjective difference in their ages, which both of them felt. With Martin's high productivity and Krebber's long abstinence from artmaking, they were in fact many more years apart in their artistic careers than the one year between their actual ages.

Krebber described their relationship as a *liaison dangereuse.* When he describes Martin today, he casts him in terms that seem taken from Laclos's novel: as an older, jaded, melancholic figure feeding off of the other's youth and freshness.

"One mode of Kippenberger's thinking is to turn something upside down," Krebber said once, "and that's how I ended up while I was working for him." Martin took a lot of what Krebber told him—about things he had read, about his own life and thoughts—and appropriated it, turned it upside down, and spit it out in a new form. Martin took as uninhibitedly as he gave. He never added it all up later. Krebber, in contrast, kept a meticulous account. He had had a fixed concept in mind of how he would approach this year as an employee. He never protested against his meager salary, but in no way was he willing to let himself be "bought off," as he put it. When Martin wanted to give him art as a present, Krebber stubbornly refused. He did accept books, but it felt like he was being bribed. On the other hand, when Martin paid the bill in restaurants, that was different: "That was work, after all."

"Someone like Diederichsen," Krebber said later, "could say, 'Well, here comes Kippenberger, he'll humiliate me but I know that's what he'll do and that's OK, it's amusing.' Diederichsen could laugh about all that nonsense. He was on the outside. But I didn't have that distance. I was right on the inside, with my whole existence." Nevertheless, he didn't get up and walk away. "There was always something going on where Martin was."

Their *liaison dangereuse* stayed in effect after the year of "employment" was up. In the years that followed, they were often together day and night—excessive nights that were often spent in the company of Cosima von Bonin. She was Krebber's girlfriend (and later his wife); Martin was also friends with her and promoted her work.

Now Martin would use Krebber as his representative, his mouthpiece. In 1990, instead of giving his own lecture to inaugurate his guest professorship at the Städelschule, Martin put Krebber at the lectern: Krebber read the transcript of his extremely theoretical interview with Diedrich Diederichsen about his (Krebber's) artistic methodology and approach, standing so close to the microphone that almost no one in the audience could understand a word. The talk was torture for Krebber as much as for the audience; so too was the event the next day, where students were given the chance to ask him and Martin questions, except that Martin never showed up and Krebber was there by himself.

Martin arranged numerous shows for Krebber and for Cosima von Bonin, sometimes without asking them first. (He never managed to get Krebber a show with Hetzler, to Krebber's disappointment.) He ceaselessly praised Krebber so highly that it started to get on many people's nerves, including Krebber's own. Finally, Krebber and Bonin told Martin that they didn't want him to push and promote their work anymore. It made them feel humiliated and overwhelmed. In general, it annoyed Krebber that Martin stuck his nose into everything—for example, at a group show in Friesenwall that did not include Martin, he took one look and immediately started rehanging the pictures. Krebber's first reaction: "Always needing to get involved in everything!" But: "Then I unfortunately had to admit that the way he did it was better."

A Cologne colleague described the relationships between Martin and several of his assistants as "insanely Oedipal, with everything that goes with it: support, admiration, subordination, rebellion, rejection." Merlin Carpenter, who actually was much younger than Martin and had come to him as a brand-new college graduate from London (his final project was an homage to Martin), worked as Martin's assistant for a short while before working for Albert Oehlen and Werner Büttner; he distanced himself from Martin much more quickly than Krebber did. On the other hand, he published his patricide (as it were) only after Martin was no longer there to see it. In a book called *Guitars Not Named Gudrun* that Max Hetzler published in 2002 as an homage to Martin, Carpenter called Martin a "Back Seat Driver" (the title of his essay): someone who leaves all the work to others, who makes others drive and pay for the gas, who turns their stories into his own sculptures.

In any case, working with Krebber proved very instructive. Afterward, Martin worked a lot with others and, especially in the early nineties, often had students, assistants, and colleagues produce works—although he always wanted them to do more than just paint-by-numbers and do what he told them. He could do that himself. The others were supposed to give his work new facets, to enlarge it. He wanted to be surprised.

Unlike Jeff Koons, whose New York workshop and studio is run like the ones in seventeenth-century Holland, except with modern technology (he designs his pictures on a computer and a whole staff of assistants then transfers them onto canvas, accurate to the millimeter), Martin had a very open system of collaboration. Ideas were developed together in bars and restaurants, Martin made sketches at most, and within the framework of what they had discussed, the collaborators executed the ideas according to their own ideas. "He didn't want assistants to execute his plans," Uli Strothjohann says. "He wanted people to apply their own style."

THERE WAS REALLY A MUTUAL UNDERSTANDING THERE

When Michael Krebber—no more a craftsman than Martin— didn't know how to proceed with constructing the *Peter* sculptures, Uli Strothjohann came on board. Martin would have been only too happy to make him Krebber's successor, but Strothjohann didn't want to be an assistant. Being a paid collaborator was acceptable. And so a different mode of working together began for Martin, sometimes more intense, sometimes looser, according to the projects he was working on, but one that remained relaxed and friendly to the end.

They had met in Berlin, and in Cologne they went to the same bars, were part of the same scene, and liked each other. "Otherwise I wouldn't have worked for Martin. It's not like

I needed to." Strothjohann was, like Krebber, a year younger than Martin, and he protected his artistic freedom by earning money without having to sell his objects and sculptures. He used his ideas and craftsmanship in construction projects for fairs (he once built an entire miniature village out of styrofoam) and television (he also made a backdrop for the Rudi Carrell Show): "I had a knack for finding jobs that paid relatively well without taking much work." And he enjoyed his independence in a relaxed way, without bragging about it. In short, Strothjohann was so far on the margins of the official art market that he wasn't competition, and Martin ended up with one of the most likeable figures on the Cologne scene at his side, a man of integrity who was always himself, in his appearance, his clothes, his language, his work, and his dry humor. Even Martin couldn't ruffle his feathers.

Uli Strothjohann was making art at fifteen, and by sixteen he ran a gallery out of an old hat and glove shop in his hometown of Rheda Wiedenbrück. Since there were hardly any art journals in the provinces that he could learn from, he wrote to all the galleries that advertised in a national magazine and asked for information. "That's how I knew about Blinky Palermo when I was only fifteen." After fulfilling his mandatory national service outside the military, in a hospital, he moved to Berlin to study at the Academy of Art, leaving after only a couple of semesters when he found it too academic. He preferred to rent the floor of a factory with a few other artists, and he ran it as an open house— Krebber showed up sometimes, to lie in the bathtub. "The aversion against everything academic, musty, or slick, against strategically planning your art career, was something that Martin and I had in common," Strothjohann says.

Their close collaborations began in 1989-90, a time when Martin had no studio of his own and decided "to try out the Koons system": showing one exhibition three times, at Hetzler's in Cologne, Metro Pictures in New York, and Luhring Augustine Hetzler in L.A. "But of course that was too boring for him," Strothjohann said. Instead he did what he always did: smaller series, in this case with three variations on the same theme. For example, he had Strothjohann build a life-size gondola in three versions: realistic, as patchwork, and as a skeleton. Those were the only instructions Strothjohann got. So Strothjohann ordered a miniature souvenir gondola from Venice, sliced it apart to get a cross-section, drew the cross-section on graph paper (which Martin, who let nothing go to waste, would reuse later in drawings and paintings), and built the whole thing life-size from the blueprint.

During the intensive period of their collaborations, they would meet up every day, for meals, at bars, and "bounce ideas back and forth." Then it was up to Strothjohann to put them into practice. This was how various multiples were created, many of which Gisela Capitain published and showed: *Cineastes' Egress, Kippenberger You Can Touch, Mirror for Hang-Over Bud, Fake Yourself, If You Don't Know Me By Now—Artsy Model*, as well as larger works such as, right at the end, the *Spiderman Studio* and the crumpled subway stations. Strothjohann also worked on the sculpture series *Martin, into the Corner, You Should Be Ashamed of Yourself*, clothing the figures among other things. Since money was tight, as always, Martin had him get the shirt and pants and suspenders as cheaply as possible, so he bought them at Woolworth's, but they weren't quite right—Martin insisted that the sleeves be visibly taken in, like in the fifties and sixties, when "things you'd inherited were made to fit in this uncharming way."

Martin had found a congenial sculpture and multiple builder in Strothjohann. When Martin said "Can you make me a carousel with an ejection seat?" Strothjohann said sure, even if he had no idea how to do it. It was exciting for him, too, to work it out—that was why he was doing it. So he built a carousel with an ejection seat, which Martin saw for the first time only after it was finished. Later, Strothjohann put a fried egg in the middle.

"There was such basic trust, such mutual understanding there," Strothjohann says. "We didn't have to talk about the underlying basics." His refusal to fit into the streamlined art market—any more than Krebber, Jörg Schlick (Martin's close friend friom Graz), or Martin did—was part of their mutual understanding, in Strothjohann's view. And Strothjohann did not feel exploited or sucked dry in the process. Martin invited him to show, as an artist, in exhibitions he curated (in Graz, Kassel, Syros), and Strothjohann says, "I had the feeling of taking part in the process, of coming up with the ideas."

The collaborators didn't have to talk much, in any case, and certainly not all the time. Martin and Strothjohann could travel or just sit in a café and look out the window and not say a thing. "Half an hour in total silence." Martin's Graz friend Elisabeth Fiedler later said Uli Strothjohann "was one of the few people who was totally sensitive to Martin and understood him."

THE SPIDERMAN

I'm a gardener of people.
—MK

A fat spider was Cosima von Bonin and Michael Krebber's image for Martin in their obituary in *Spex*: "He was a fat spider who snatched up the things flying by on every side and then turned them upside down a few times, going from one room to the next, picking up things to use in his own work, and so on, back and forth, here and there. Always a new digestive path and so more stuff."

"He was like a vampire at everyone's neck," the artist Charline von Heyl said. "His listening was harvesting, picking, appropriating."

Martin said, "You have to be selfish. But that doesn't mean someone else has the right to call me selfish, not by a long shot, because that sounds like I never give anything back." His analogy was detox: he had to swallow something but then he spit it out along with something of his own—he always gave more than he got. He saw his works of art as gifts, gifts to the world.

He was no vampire lurking in the dark to pounce and suck blood; what he took, he took openly. "He was grounded in a strong network of relationships with friends," in the view of Bice Curiger, the curator, "and he proclaimed how much he valued them loud and clear, by collecting their work, hanging out with them, and candidly, flamingly plagiarizing them."

"He didn't use anybody," Uli Strothjohann says. "It was no secret that art was being produced in those bars, from those conversations."

And being produced nonstop. The Frankfurt artist Thomas Bayrle said that Martin was always on, always receiving signals, "like a computer that's always online. Every once in a while I'd do the healthy thing and take a break, to save electricity." Whatever Martin heard or saw, even out of the corner of his eye, was taken in, commented on, and reworked. Werner Büttner said Martin "heard everything and had eyes in the back of his head and was superhumanly alert."

It also was not true that Martin had no ideas of his own. On the contrary, it was more like he had too many pouring out. "He was always cooking up something," as the gallerist Daniel Buchholz said. But he threw everything he thought was interesting into his cooking pot, whether it came from himself or someone else, from an artist or a child. All he cared about was the quality of the idea. "Let it not be old, let it not be new, let it be good" was one of his favorite slogans.

At first, Albert Oehlen says, it wasn't easy for other people to accept that Martin just took what he wanted:

> Büttner said something and the next day there it was on one of Martin's posters or invitations. That happened a lot. It was kind of shocking how fast it happened. For a while we felt used, but we got over it. Then we thought, well, that's how he is. And eventually I also felt that actually he has every right to do it. If he makes something out of it, it's his. Bit of bad luck that you can't do anything with it yourself any more, but it would be petty to say no. That was his art, this constant putting to use all day of everything that came in. If you don't like it, you can just break off all contact.

One time, for example, they developed the idea together of putting stickers on oil paintings—but Martin was the one who did it first. "He always wanted to do everything faster, better, sooner."

Martin portrayed himself not as a spider but as Spiderman: someone who casts his web to make the world a better place, to help other people. He was a "networker" long before the word was in fashion; Rüdiger Carl called him "a connector" (and in fact, Rüdiger met his life companion, Bärbel Grässlin, at a concert Martin had arranged). He was someone who constantly brought people together, crossing boundaries between different camps in the art world that were often sharply defined. Even a passionate networker like the New

York gallerist Roland Augustine was "amazed, even jealous, how easy it was for him to start a conversation and create a relationship. He was always introducing someone to you or introducing you to someone else."

Werner Büttner described him as "fanatical at starting families": he would take people with various abilities and "bring them together into a clan," then "put himself right in the middle, decisively, elegantly, naturally playing the godfather." His catalogs overflow with "family portraits," so to speak, the most famous being the photograph taken for his fortieth birthday that he later used on the invitations to his 1993 Centre Pompidou exhibition. The picture was evidence, proof that he wasn't alone but rather embedded in a network of friends, women, relatives, and colleagues who gave him the support, recognition, and dialogue that the official art market with its critics and curators so often denied him. This clan—protectors, patrons, reservoirs of energy, cheerleaders, and audience in one—had to go with Martin from opening to opening, with Martin in turn making sure that everyone had a good time. There was no such thing as a VIP-only opening with Martin, where "important people" took precedence over his family.

But the members of this clan had to accept that Martin set the terms—that he was the godfather in charge of everyone else. When he organized group shows (which participants sometimes learned they were in only when they saw their names on his posters), it was typically Martin who designed the invitations, decided or at least had a say in which art works would be shown, and fiddled around with the works themselves. For example, Johannes Wohnseifer's piece for Martin's museum on the island of Syros was a museum guard's stool, and Martin vehemently insisted that Wohnseifer cover it in concrete, which Wohnseifer had had no plans at all to do.

Martin also had personal relationships with everyone who worked for him. He never had completely neutral relationships, except maybe with landlords or bank tellers, although even with them he felt an emotional connection, a feeling of hatred if nothing else. He was friends not only with gallerists, artists, curators, waiters, bartenders, and restaurant owners. His tax advisor and sometime travel companion was a childhood friend, Herbert Meese. His dentist, Heliod Spiekermann, was also a trusted friend, collector, and occasional collaborator, who wrote one of the books for his Kafka installation. As Martin explained in the publisher's note: "Mr. M. Kippenberger was responsible for the design of the book, not for the text."

Like every spiderweb, Martin's had inner and outer circles. There was the real Kippenberger Family, as it was called—friends, fans, collaborators, and relatives—as well as more distant relations, like Hans-Peter Feldmann. Martin and he rarely saw each other, and when they did it was usually in a personal context, but they felt very connected in their attitudes. Then there were the "substitute players," in gallerist Tanja Grunert's term: "When everyone else was gone, he called me up and I had to stand in. We went out to eat, it was very nice, very intense. We had good conversations, about ideas." But when the others were back and she ran into Martin in his bigger circle, she felt that he used her as a whipping boy, constantly insulting her. "At certain moments we were very close, and then the next day we barely said hello to each other."

Ultimately, slotting friends and acquaintances into his projects didn't happen only in one direction: his demands were often challenges that helped with the other person's own work. Andrea Stappert said that if Martin hadn't constantly forced her to take photographs—for instance, the time he'd fallen down a flight of stairs at a disco, showed up at her house, and had her take his picture like that, with a bandaged head, a cowboy hat, and a grin—she might not have become a photographer: she didn't know what to do after she'd finished art school, only that she didn't want to be a painter. He pushed people, encouraging the curator Barbara Straka to go back to school, Gisela Capitain to quit teaching and become a curator, the linguist Martin Prinzhorn to write about art, the gallerist Barbara Weiss to start her own gallery. His assistant Sven Ahrens said, "He had an unusually humane attitude for the art business."

I SEE MYSELF RIGHT THERE BETWEEN OTHER PEOPLE

For the people in his family—the "horde people," as Martin called them—there was no "I" and "you," and no artwork without its context. The individual piece was interesting to him only as part of a greater whole. "It's about your life's work, you have to achieve something lasting in life. That's the real stage direction you get from on high. Otherwise it's hell."

As a result, he always produced and presented his art in contexts, too. He worked almost exclusively in series. What linked his works was not a common style—he refused to give them that—but common motifs or themes that appeared and reappeared and connected his various phases and groups of work: the frog, the egg, Santa Claus, the lamppost, noodles, and especially, of course, himself. At some point he realized "that my style is there when the person is there and transmits this style through behavior, individual objects and actions, decisions, and a story grows up out of those things." His own life was the basis of his art, and other people were always a part of that life. "I see myself right there between other people," Martin said in describing his position as an artist. "Not alone in the desert sands." He always saw himself as part of a whole, part of something greater, in the history of art as well as in the present: "I work in a tradition, in any case. Everything I learned I learned from art. I love art."

Many people were amazed to learn that he was very well versed in art history, although it was not an academic knowledge—here, too, he had developed his own way of looking at things. "He had very refreshing views about what was important and what wasn't," his New York gallerist David Nolan said.

Martin often spun new strands of his web from existing art; many of his works were sequels. The point of art was to make new art from, as far as he was concerned. Andy Warhol had published a book called *a*, so Martin published *B*; Kafka had left his novel *Amerika* unfinished, so Martin helped it along to a happy ending.

Even as a boy, he had asked our parents' artist friends to send him things he could use as material; as a nine-year-old, he used Picasso in one of his own collages. Martin needed dialogue and engagement with other art as well as with other people. His works are closely linked with the world. In *Spiderman Studio*, for example, there are references to Jasper Johns, scientific discoveries (for instance, the fact that drugs affect how spiders spin their webs), personal experiences, Hollywood movies, and the bars and restaurants of Cologne— one window of the studio is from the Königswasser, where Cosima von Bonin had worked as a waitress, and it shows the shadow of a saxophone, a reference in turn to Matisse, who drew jazz with a pair of scissors and whose studio in Nice, a gallery by that point, was the first to show Martin's sculpture. In the middle of all these relationships crouches the artist himself as Spiderman, like a sprinter about to start a race.

Martin also had friends and colleagues design many of his exhibition posters as a way to define and expose the contexts he saw himself in: Michel Würthle, Jeff Koons, Uli Strothjohann, A. R. Penck, Christopher Wool, Albert Oehlen, Günther Förg, Rosemarie Trockel, Franz West, Clegg & Guttman, Heimo Zobernig, Markus Oehlen, Werner Büttner, Cosima von Bonin, Louise Lawler, William Copley, Sigmar Polke, Lawrence Weiner, Mike Kelley, Jörg Schlick, Matthias Schaufler, Ronald Jones, Günter Brus, Heiner Blum.

PICTURES OF AN EXHIBITION

"I realize," Martin said in his 1991 interview with Jutta Koether, "that it's more and more important to be permanently clear in your mind about what context you hang your work in and live in. To determine this for yourself, to build up your own network, is one of the artist's decisive tasks. That's what I'm working on now. And not only to create this context but to make it visible, make it indelibly manifest."

His own collection of art was one way to create this context and reveal it. For Martin, the collection—which contained a notable number of pieces by women—was part of his own artistic work. He already felt that any picture by another artist belonged to him "the moment I understand it"; if he had bought it or exchanged something for it, it belonged to him fully. Exchanging was better, of course, since that way the connection went in both directions. Martin never acquired pieces as investments, but only "when I could make something of it and knew how to relate it to something else." It might be the Gerhard Richter he later attached to one of his own sculptures as a tabletop, or a drawing by the musician Sven-Åke Johansson that Johansson himself described as a doodle.

Martin saw collecting as a labor-saving device: "If someone does something better than I do or someone has already done something but it's part of my labyrinth, I don't need to do it again. If it came off well, that's enough for me, I buy it if I have the money and exhibit it with my own pictures." For example, in St. Louis, where he showed his own works with works by artists like Richard Prince and Jeff Koons in a show he called *Pictures of an Exhibition.*

THE GAME WITH INFINITY

Martin always made new contexts for his own pieces, including them in ever-changing installations and new exhibitions and thereby creating closer and closer connections between each piece and the rest of his work. Kafka wrote his novel *Amerika* "heading off into endlessness," as he wrote in a letter to his fiancée, and Martin's Kafka project, into which he integrated earlier works of his own as well as works by other artists, struck the curator of the Copenhagen *Metropolis* exhibit as "like a game with infinity." "The dynamic of his constant reworkings ended only with his death," wrote the critic Manfred Hermes. "That is why his works often seem 'out of service' or inoperative in museums today."

In Martin's view, it was impossible to look at a single picture in isolation. The wall it hung on was already part of it, as were the floor it hung above and the room around it: "All of that is just as important as the art on the wall itself." That is why he paid so much attention to how his work was installed. Exhibitions, for him, were never just arrays of recent pieces—he always had a very precise idea in mind for their presentation, worked out in advance, to the gallerists' and curators' surprise. "He worked it all out in his head," his friend Franz Keller said.

Of course, the entirety he was working toward was not a closed-off whole—his work is one big collage. If something was whole, he would break it and put the pieces together anew. That is what he did with *The Raft of the Medusa*: he took apart Géricault's painting, had himself photographed in all the poses of the various figures in the painting, then drew, printed, or painted each pose as a self-portrait.

GRAZ

"You want to feel free and welcome in a city," Martin wrote in *Café Central*. That is how he felt in Graz. "In Graz," Martin Prinzhorn said, "Martin was the boss." People there did everything for him, and "asked him questions like, 'Might you have time to do a portfolio of work?'" according to Krebber. "In Graz he was in residence like the pope himself."

If Vienna was already a city on the periphery, Graz was even farther away: in southern Austria, half an hour from the Yugoslavian border, "the ass-end of nowhere's *socks*," as Martin complained every time he had to take the long and tiring trip there. All the more comfortable he was, then, when he arrived. He could walk to everything in the old city center. At the heart of the old town was Martin's regular café, the Glockenspiel, where he would find Herr Joszi from Hungary, his favorite waiter, of the old Austro-Hungarian type, whom Martin would immortalize on the cover of one of his catalogs. The café was his office: his gallerist Aki Bleich-Rossi was there too, always with the same small espresso, and the gallery itself was right around the corner, on Peinlichgasse. Everything was right around the corner from the Glockenspiel: the Frankowitsch (an old deli with unusual sandwiches), the Artelier gallery and publisher, the Fiedler piano shop, the Joanneum's Neue

Galerie, the Forum Stadtpark. The "plank shack" was not far, either—this was Martin's nickname for the strange, wood-paneled bar actually called the Braun de Praun, where artists, students, and locals would meet. Jesus hung on a cross in the corner, and the waiters didn't blink an eye no matter how crazy the nights got, whether Martin and his friends sung workers' songs in Nazi style or everyone just drank until they fell over or started fights. "We'd just scrub the blood away," the owner said calmly. "The eighties were a brutal time."

"Graz," an article in *Skyscraper* said in 1987, after Martin and Albert Oehlen appeared at a symposium there, "is an ideal world, where the avant-garde flourishes unbroken, where Arnold Schwarzenegger was born, where the bakers know all their customers' names, and *Gau* is considered a term from the Thousand-Year Reich."* It was an extreme city, but in an unusual way: bourgeois, reactionary, and progressive at once. During the Austro-Hungarian monarchy, retired officials of the multiethnic state, without a homeland of their own, liked to move to Graz, which was less expensive than Vienna and had a better climate. The city has an almost southern, Mediterranean flair, which became especially pronounced once students started to outnumber retirees. In the words of Michel Würthle, "Vienna is loneliness and suicide. When I picture to myself the Sundays, the old apartment, the Third District. . ." Martin told his Graz gallerist Gabriella Bleich-Rossi that he couldn't be in Vienna for more than three days without getting depressed.

In the thirties, Graz had been one of the major strongholds of the National Socialists and received the honorary title "City

---

* "Gau" is the medieval German term for a district or region, comparable to "shire" in English; the Nazis revived the term and used it for administrative regions in their regime, so that a Nazi governor was a "Gau-Leader," etc. Thinking of the Nazi re-gime as "the Thousand-Year Reich" (the Nazis' own preferred term) is a sign of rather unreconstructed political sensibilities.

of the People's Uprising" from Hitler himself. After the war, as a reaction against the lingering fascist culture of the city, a conservative politician had systematically promoted modern art and the city became "an absolute mecca for the avant-garde and their experiments" in the sixties, Martin Prinzhorn said. "You could be insane there in a way that was impossible in Vienna." The Forum Stadtpark was founded in 1960 as a meeting place for artists, including writers like Alfred Kolleritsch, Peter Handke, and Wolfgang Bauer. It defined itself as an "interdisciplinary labor of contemporary art," with concerts, readings, plays, films, and exhibitions of architecture, fine art, and photography.

Yet the city always reminded Martin Prinzhorn a little of a Chekhov play: "all these people with their international fantasies but who never made it out of Graz." Martin was just what the city needed: he brought the world with him— artists, students, assistants—and "attracted attention" to Graz, as Sabine Achleitner says. Everyone benefited. Elfie Semotan says, "Martin gave them the feeling that what they had done there was not provincial."

Martin transformed Graz just by looking at it in his own unique way. For example, Petra Schilcher says, there was "the horrible bar designed by Ernst Fuchs at the Erzherzog Johann Hotel—we from Graz were ashamed of it, it was so embarrassing. Then Martin walked in, and from then on the Ernst Fuchs Bar was *the* place to be." Martin liked the bartender there, Herr Manfred: "they were two of a kind, their styles went perfectly together. He was a gentleman from head to toe."

Martin had been brought to Graz by Jörg Schlick, who became one of his most important allies, closest friends, and eventually the best man at his wedding. Their first encounter, in Vienna, was not surprisingly an unfriendly run-in: they happened to be sitting at the same table at a bar one evening, Schlick accidentally picked up Martin's glass, and Martin got excessively angry, at which point Schlick ordered ten glasses of liquor "for the great German artist." By the end of the night they had planned an exhibition for Martin in Graz.

Auch Einer (Another One) is a whimsical nineteenth-century novel by F. T. Vischer, about the adventures of its hero, "A. E." (for "Auch Einer"). Martin and Schlick reprinted the whole text in the catalog they produced together, *Broken Neon*, which also gathered together such different artists as Beuys, Dokoupil, Fischli and Weiss, Franz West, and Zobernig. Schlick was "another one" himself, who immediately became part of the family—"our man in Graz," as Albert Oehlen called him (Oehlen, too, lived in Graz for a while and had many shows there).

Schlick, two years older than Martin, was another person who refused to let himself be pigeonholed. He was a conceptual artist, author, painter, curator, musician, and photographer, who made everything (movies, operas, plays, ballets), was interested in everything (contemporary art, music, literature), and had read everything (from philosophical theory to pulp fiction).

He, too, had gone to boarding school, was curious and enthusiastic, had genuine fun with art and artmaking, and (in curator Axel Huber's words) "led his rational mind around on a long rubber leash." A chain-smoker, a gentle person, a provocateur, a fun-loving and genuine person: Schlick was "right," as Mathias Grilj wrote in an homage after Schlick's death in 2005. Someone who patiently explained the art to exhibition visitors but "baroquely swept aside smart-asses with all their self-indulgent arrogance." The qualities Grilj attributed to him were the same as the ones Martin valued: "Art, attitude, directness, humor, friendship, bravery, carefreeness, discipline, nitpicking, naiveté, expertise, attention, loyalty, craftiness, feeling, pride, solidarity, lust for life, openness, responsibility, sarcasm, rage, calculation, consistency, generosity, strictness, insight, and forbearance." He and Martin spoke the same language and had the same sense of humor.

Schlick also liked to work with his students, supported and promoted them, and constantly engaged with the role of the artist in his work. Above all, he was also a brilliant networker, "pulling all the strings in the Graz art scene" as a musician said of him—he was someone who brought people together. Schlick did on a regional level what Martin did internationally. For example, in the *Eurostroll* exhibition of 1989 that Martin put together with Schlick's support, Martin's friends Luis Claramunt, Sven-Åke Johansson, and Michael Krebber were shown together; the 1994 Forum Stadtpark exhibit *Spoilsport* showed Cosima von Bonin, Mike Kelley, Jutta Koether, Jeff Koons, Hans Küng, Otto Muehl, Chéri Samba, Jörg Schlick, Uli Strothjohann, Peter Weibel, and Heimo Zobernig.

Elfie Semotan says that Martin "brought Schlick along" in more than just the literal sense when he took Schlick with him to America. Educated at an elite high school, Schlick knew Latin and ancient Greek but spoke only broken English—so badly that he avoided speaking it at all, since he felt that he could not carry on a serious conversation in it. Martin loved to play the big brother, showing someone around the great big world, while Jörg, who always seemed a little awkward with his big, heavy figure and gigantic glasses, found everything in St. Louis and San Francisco "Wonderful! Wonderful!" Martin was terribly disappointed when he wanted to take Jörg and his wife to Cipriani in New York and Jörg told him that he had already been to Cipriani, in Venice. Martin had never been to Venice.

Schlick admired Martin very much—"worshipped" him, Johannes Wohnseifer says—and photographed him constantly. As a consultant for Forum Stadtpark, he made it possible for Martin to put on shows and publish books that would have been impossible elsewhere; he gave him a platform "to try things out," as Peter Pakesch said, the same way Martin tried to get Schlick opportunities with his gallerists and curators. They greatly enjoyed collaborating, and Schlick was a proficient printer and bookmaker, so "it was fun for him to work on his subtle little delicacies and then paint the town red with Martin," in Sabine Achleitner's words. For example, there were Martin's *Canarybird* books of "scribble drawings" (Achleitner's term), which seemed to be printed on yellow paper but in fact the paper was white and the printing was yellow. Or the oversized book *This Life Cannot Be the Excuse for the Next One*: "it was totally insane, it wasn't parchment paper but just printed to look like it, then all the text was printed backward on the reverse side of the page so you could feel the letters when you held the pages, and then the stamped leather cover . . ."

They were allies, not least in the infamous Lord Jim Lodge. The critic and curator Marius Babias characterized the Lodge as a "mafia-like organization"—and that, Martin always felt, was the problem with Germany: its humorlessness. Jörg Schlick described the Lodge as an "anarchist utopia . . . the exact opposite of everything it was interpreted as." Its members weren't soldiers who followed the party line, but rather adventurous anarchists—that was the entrance requirement. Its motto was "Nobody Helps Nobody," which turned the idea of a lodge like the Masons or Rotary or Elks upside down. "Inside the Lord Jim Lodge awaited absolutely nothing," Daniela Jauk and Andreas Unterweger wrote, "no secret knowledge, no influential connections, not even, as Grilj's motto revealed, assistance from the other members of the lodge. The only thing that had changed was that you used to be 'outside' and now you were 'inside,' you belonged."

The Lodge was founded in 1984 or 1985—no one is sure of the exact date any more—in a Graz liquor parlor (as they are called). We do know that the writer Wolfi Bauer came up with the idea for the Lodge and gave it its name because he was reading Joseph Conrad's *Lord Jim* and felt that Conrad's protagonist fit the Lodge members' profile: Lord Jim was "a slightly suspect, but still idealistic character." Bauer himself was a hero in Graz and to Martin: he and Martin shared the same sense of humor, and when they were together, they feted each other as geniuses. Martin invited Bauer to his events many times, in Cologne, Frankfurt, and Umhausen.

The rules of the Lodge were simple. "Anyone who asks to be admitted will not be admitted. No one is asked whether or not they want to be admitted. No one, once admitted, is allowed to leave." (And the members had to be able to hold their liquor.) Since the Lodge kept no records ("there was no paper, no leader, no fixed meeting place"), it is difficult to say how many members it had, but there were apparently thirty to fifty: artists, scholars, and adventurous spirits, including Martin and Albert Oehlen along with Bauer and Schlick. One thing was certain: the Lodge was for men only. The exclusion of women, Schlick explained, was meant to making fun of "the boy's-club situation in the art business and in politics in general—we took it to an extreme." To mollify any women who might be upset, Bauer declared them all to be Goddesses. Schlick later said, "If I had been opportunistic and wanted to come across well, I would definitely have advocated for the inclusion of women, but I didn't want to take the easy route." As a result, the group was vilified as a sexist, reactionary mafia.

The Lodge became known outside Graz only because it adopted a logo that turned into an artistic concept and a magazine of the same name: *Sun Breasts Hammer*. The logo was born in a bar too, where Martin, Oehlen, Bauer, and

Schlick were sitting together. It was shortly before their group exhibition at the Bleich-Rossi Gallery, *Critical Oranges for the Digestive Village,* and the poster had turned out too small for Martin's liking—"we need a proper big one." It was Schlick's job to come up with a new poster, with the printer's deadline was the next morning. Since hardly anyone ever came to the openings in Graz, due to the difficult transportation connections, Martin had to make sure that all their activities there would be perceived in the wider world anyway, hence the catalogs, invitations, and posters that had to be big.

Schlick pulled a piece of paper out of his pocket and the group drew the logo then and there: legend has it that Bauer was responsible for the breasts, Oehlen the hammer, and Martin the sun. Schlick put the logo on the poster and so it went out in the world, from which it would not soon disappear. Schlick wanted to make the logo as famous in the art world as Coca-Cola was in the world as a whole, so he made coins, rugs, and games with it and made it the central theme of his art for years, to an even greater degree than Martin, who likewise used the logo and motto over and over again in his later works. When Martin's subway entrance was shown at documenta in 1997, with the logo at the center of the gate, Schlick felt that his goal had been reached; he put on one last exhibition with the logo and that was the icon's last hurrah. *Sun Breasts Hammer,* the magazine, was retired as the "Central Organ of the Lord Jim Lodge" as well.

Its short issues had appeared irregularly, with Schlick asking for images or texts from new artists every time. He published his own work and work by Cosima von Bonin, Michael Krebber, Albert Oehlen, Wolfgang Bauer, and Martin. The fifteenth and final issue was the "Ex-Bachelor Issue," consisting solely of photographs from Martin's wedding.

It was also Schlick who introduced Martin to his gallerist Aki Bleich-Rossi, another unconventional figure obsessed with art as collector and art-lover. He was a gentleman of the old school who kissed ladies' hands and never let on how sick he was; he needed dialysis several times a week. Which meant, of course, that he could not often travel as a gallerist.

Martin could go to "Bleichi" whenever he needed money—and he constantly needed money. Or the gallerist came to him. Martin would be at Innsbruck taking a cure and would issue a summons—"Bleichi, I need cashy"—and the gallerist and his wife would drive to see him and buy a few of his hotel-stationery drawings off him. Bleich-Rossi sometimes bought whole exhibitions as a package deal—"Martin liked that," Peter Pakesch said—and thereby got works at a good price that he could then sell to people in Graz, who may not have been the most knowledgeable about art but who had the money to buy it.

"First we admired Martin," Isabella Bleich-Rossi said, "and then we loved him. Wherever he was, he shined, and he included us." Their son Stefan (whom Martin called Benni, after the boy in the popular German soap opera *Lindenstrasse*) was included in Martin's work as well: Martin made a multiple for Stefan, *Cold on Canvas*, that his father then brought out. When he was older, though, Martin sometimes attacked Stefan so viciously in large groups that even the onlookers started crying on his behalf.

Martin's first solo show with Bleich-Rossi was called *Journey to Jerusalem*; his last, *Nada Arugula*, took place in an apartment. After the gallerist's death two years earlier, Isabella had had to shut the gallery, and she asked Martin to support her new beginning with a show. There was no question but that Martin would agree, and at the opening there were visitors lined up outside the door. It was a generous gesture with real consequences for the gallerist: "If Martin Kippenberger does it, others can follow suit."

Petra Schilcher of Artelier thought "Uh-oh!" the first time she met Martin: the tempo, the output, "he could get through five pieces in an hour." But the Schilchers were the right place for him. Ralph Schilcher, who already ran a silkscreen shop in Graz, founded Artelier gallery and publishers with his wife in 1985, to give artists a place to play around. Along with the printshop, there were workshops for woodworking, metalworking, and plastic. Martin went wild and silkscreened everything he could get his hands on: corrugated tin, Bariano paper, wood, Canson Mi-Teintes paper, patio furniture. He made books (including *Contents on Tour*) and had troughs, receptacles, and containers built and filled. His answer to the critics who criticized his overproduction was *Yet Another Kippenberger 5x*: a thick construction pipe filled with five silkscreen posters and sealed up with wooden covers.

The workshop was a dream, and Ralph Schilcher was someone who could make Martin's dreams come true, instantly grasping his intuitions and putting them into practice. "Martin produced artworks by the ton with Schilcher," Peter Pakesch says, "all he had to do was sit in the pub, say how it should look, and it was done." They often discussed only the necessary minimum over the phone, then Martin sent models or sketches from Cologne or wherever, and when he arrived he could get right to work, because everything was ready (and there was trouble if it wasn't). "He wasn't the type to futz around," Petra Schilcher says, and she called her collaborations with him "highly professional," with just one condition: "When he was there, there was no one else, we had to work only for him."

When they were done, he could do what he always liked to do: show his work on the spot, at once. "Production, publishing, and presentation" was his concept. He would show his editions at the Artelier Gallery in Graz, or at the Dependance in Frankfurt, which opened in 1990, or the Bleich-Rossi Gallery or steirischer herbst in Graz. Sometimes at more than one venue: following the example of Gilbert & George, who showed the same exhibition twice at the Sonnabend Gallery in New York, ten years apart, Martin did the same with a gap of one year, first at the steirischer herbst festival and then in the Artelier gallery.

Martin also produced and showed his *Elite 88* calendar at Artelier. He had been invited to open a disco in Vienna and had agreed, on the condition that he be put up in the best hotel. The organizers hadn't realized that the opening was during Festival Week in Vienna, so all the hotels were booked up—Martin was eventually housed in Pension Elite, a pension that was anything but. It was a typical, dusty, depressing Vienna bed and breakfast where the sound of a vacuum cleaner woke Martin up in the morning. He bought himself a new pair of large white underpants, stood in front of the mirror, bulged out his already fat belly in a caricature of Picasso's famous pose—a motif that Martin would later use in many self-portrait paintings and drawings—and took a series of pictures of himself. The resulting calendar's mix of first-class and second-rate was typical Kippenberger: "The photographs might be blurry and grainy," Petra Schilcher said, "but the paper had to be excellent and the date numbers perfectly printed in gold." A calendar offered numerous possibilities for such finesses, for example that the pages could be printed on both sides, or the year could begin not with January but somewhere in the middle. Then, when the pages were shown in the gallery in Graz, with Martin's fat belly and absolutely unsexy pulled-up underwear on display, he showed up at the opening "looking like a male model, long and lean," Petra Schilcher says.

His first edition with Schilcher was in 1987—*35 Mirror Babies,* containing photographs of pasta and people along with various sayings (including one of his favorites: "What is your favorite minority, who do you envy the most?") and the letter he'd sent to Manfred Schneckenburger, head of documenta, refusing to participate. His last Artelier edition was in 1996 and was another slap in the art world's face—this time the Biennale, which hadn't invited him at all and which he struck back at with humor. The photograph Martin's wife Elfie Semotan had taken on their honeymoon in front of the German Biennale pavilion in Venice was silkscreened as a poster, with the caption "Biennale di Venezia 1996"—a year in which there was no Biennale.

The Artelier was more than just a local home for Martin, it was a global one, and many of the artists he admired and valued did work there, including many of his friends: Thilo Heinzmann, Tobias Rehberger, Louise Lawler, Günther Förg, Heiner Blum, John Baldessari, Heimo Zobernig, Christian Attersee, Albert Oehlen, Franz West, and of course Jörg Schlick, who produced many of his Lord Jim works there.

"He liked being at home," Elisabeth Fiedler says. "He liked how Graz was like a village." Fiedler, an art historian who was the first non-artist to be Schlick's successor as the art consultant of Forum Stadtpark, was not only Martin's good friend but at the center of another of Martin's little families. Her house had an open door, and many artists visited; Fiedler's husband, Peter, ran a piano shop in Graz, and Martin got along with their son, Stefan, as well. Martin usually got along well with children—they liked him because he took them seriously and clowned around with them and was more fun and rude than almost any other grown-up. (Or else they were afraid of him, or hated that he competed with them for their place in the family.) It wasn't a matter of getting down on the floor to play with Legos or build sand castles, more like the other way around: he would have the children help him with his work. He talked to them the same way he talked to everybody, never in a special kid-voice; he liked talking to and working with children because they were what he always wanted artists to be: naive, playful, funny, rude, honest, open, genuine.

Once when Martin was visiting the Fiedlers shortly before Christmas, he slipped Stefan some money, at which point his mother protested: "Martin, you shouldn't do that." He quickly said, "No, no, no, I want something in return—there's a pile of all my catalogs, Stefan, go look at them and copy out the titles and write 'very good' after each one." Elisabeth Fiedler went on: "So Stefan disappeared and got all the catalogs and did it. But he didn't copy the titles, he described the pictures, with all his spelling mistakes. Stefan was dyslexic, too; he and Martin were a good pair."

A poor boy who is happy to finally be able to drink a
    Coca-Cola very good
A poor child looking at bread very good
A car starting to skid very good
An old wrecked attic very good
A punishing hand in the cow stall very good
Old and new shoes very good
The devil and the angel very good
Martin Kippenberger in front of a sunken city very good
An egg from old times very good
A negro and a boom box very good
A beautiful house on the ocean very good
A mother explaining something to a child very good
A room vull of pictures very good
A horse in a junk pile very good
Lots of carpetstands walking around very good

A duck in the water very good
A tomcat and a woman very good
A sailboat next to a cassle very good
A chinese showing another chinese his tongue very good
A hot stove very good
A trout with its head cut off by a bottle opener very good

Martin called it "art criticism" and later projected the nine-year-old's scribbles onto a canvas and painted them, white on white: *The White Paintings.* He wanted, among other things, to bring the American artist Robert Ryman, once famous for his white paintings, "out of storage" (but then decided that Ryman was "just a kitschpeter" anyway). In the end, Martin didn't hang the paintings on the wall, but embedded them in the wall, "so that you have the feeling there's nothing in the room," he said.

No other city seemed to miss Martin as much as Graz. "After Martin's death, it was a terrible time," Elisabeth Fiedler said recently, "there was a very deep hole, because we all knew: it's over. It was like that world had collapsed." It was a world that has since lost many of its other inhabitants: Aki Bleich-Rossi, Jörg Schlick, Sabine Achleitner, Wolfgang Bauer, and Peter Fiedler have since died as well.

Since an artist's action in 2006, Graz is probably the only city in the world with a Martin Kippenberger Square.

PURE EXUBERANCE

Meanwhile the art boom in Cologne was only growing: the glamour, the openings, closings, artist's dinners . . . "The revolution in Cologne has to be postponed," said a 1986 poster by Martin and Walter Dahn, with which they applied for an event at the Broadway: "The artists feel too weak."

Peter Nestler had already said, in 1985, that "the critical mass has been reached." The head of the cultural department of the city felt that Cologne had no need for more artists and gallerists. The international address book of the art world, *Art Diary*, listed fifty artists in Cologne in 1979 and two years later more than two hundred. By 1985, the community artist directory had six hundred names.

But there was still money to be made along the Rhine; the eighties were "pure exuberance," as Markus Oehlen said. A.R. Penck, an artist known for not liking to wash, supposedly passed out on a park bench in Cologne after a night of drinking, in a parka and sneakers, as usual, his face so overgrown that you could hardly see it, and with forty thousand marks in his pocket. The police arrested him as extremely suspicious, the story goes, and his gallerist had to get him out of jail.

Prices kept climbing and soon reached five figures—a big painting could cost between six thousand and twenty thousand marks. The prices were calculated based on how big the painting was, and how big the painter: length plus width (in centimeters), times the artist's multiplier (1 for beginners, 5 for stars). In Cologne, everyone knew each other's multiplier. Helge Achenbach, a so-called art consultant from Düsseldorf, declared that "Great art has no valleys, no zigzags, only peaks—the value always moves upward." In the eighties, art became in Germany what it had long been in the U.S.: an object of financial speculation. The Cologne journalist Willi Bongard called it "the most beautiful investment in the world that you can have on your wall." He invented the annual "art compass" in the journal *capital*, which listed the top hundred contemporary artists every November; Martin wanted to get to the top of the list.

The pioneers sometimes had the feeling that they had summoned up forces they could no longer control: "When it comes right down to it the eighties were shitty," Rudolf Zwirner says today. "That was when this damn business started of buying something just to turn around and sell it at auction." Art Cologne—today known as "the mother of all art fairs"—put the commercial side of art in the foreground, in Hans-Jürgen Müller's view: "Duchamp had said that when you take an ordinary object and put it in a museum, you change its aura, and it turns into art. We took art and changed its aura by hanging it in a fair, for sale. We turned artworks into merchandise."

Martin and his artist friends experienced both sides of the booming art market: growing success and recognition on the one hand, with lots more money (although Martin continued to be permanently short of funds) and increasing interest from the general public, but on the other hand increasing commercialization and pressure, with globalized competition and interest from people whom they were not interested in themselves.

In 1987, the year of the *Peter* exhibition, Martin finally achieved international, not just German, recognition. He had never had so many exhibitions so widely dispersed: his work was shown in Zurich, Copenhagen, Vienna, New York, Paris, Graz, and Antwerp, not to mention Cologne and Frankfurt. Meanwhile, the whole world was coming to Cologne, where an artist could feel at the center of everything. "There are only five significant galleries in Europe," Max Hetzler announced in 1988, "and five of them are in Cologne."

As a result, more and more foreigners came to the Rhine. Graz's Forum Stadtpark rented an apartment in Cologne for visiting artists, for example, and the city became a magnet, especially for Americans: Jeff Koons, Christopher Wool, Stephen Prina, Cindy Sherman, Julian Schnabel, and Larry Clark showed in Cologne, and there were partnerships between the Luhring/Augustine and Hetzler galleries, and between David Nolan (who had studied with Michael Werner) and Gisela Capitain. For gallerists, dealers, and curators, a trip to Cologne was a necessity, if one undertaken with great pleasure. Even New York was not as wild and fun as Cologne—political correctness had taken hold there much earlier, and the cosmopolitan residents acted much more blasé, not as passionate about art.

HOTEL CHELSEA

Martin had bet on Germany and won: "Patriotism pays after all." This made him the lone exception. It was a period when good German soccer fans enthused over Brazil, crossed their fingers for the English, wished the Dutch luck, and rooted for everyone except their own team. No one waved German flags at the 1986 World Cup. But Martin, having already won five hundred marks worth of free food at a restaurant and five hundred marks worth of free drinks at a bar betting on Germany, decided to try his luck with Werner Peters, who ran Cologne's Hotel Chelsea, and made a wager for a week in a double room, breakfast in bed, "and all the trimmings." Patriotism paid off once again. When Germany won on Sunday, so did Martin, and on Monday morning he was standing at the reception desk with his suitcase, demanding his prize.

He liked it there so much that he stayed.

He had a studio around the corner at the time, on Lindenstrasse, and came to the Chelsea's Café Central at least three times a day. He was living (that is, sleeping) in a kind of storage room under the studio, and he wanted to escape— also to get some distance from the studio, even if only a short walk. "I want to *go* to work." A hotel room was enough for him, and in any case he was hardly ever there: he went to bed at the Chelsea at three, or four, or even later when he was drinking with the hotel manager, and by eight or nine he was back downstairs, where he always had company waiting for him in the café. Only during the Fair did he have to make his room available—so he slept in the studio again for a few days.

Martin moved into the hotel in 1986 and stayed four months, and until his death he continued to use the Chelsea as his home base. He spent the night there when he didn't have an apartment—or an apartment in Cologne, at least—or when he had an apartment but just didn't want to sleep there. The Chelsea was his mobile home, his living room, his office.

When the owner, Werner Peters, met Martin in 1985, "Martin already had a name, and one to fear." Peters had just recovered from a serious case of hepatitis; the first time they met, Martin greeted him with a joke about livers.

They could not have been more different, Martin and the slight, frail man with a perpetual slight smile, who looked like a philosopher and was one. He had a Ph.D., though "no one knew exactly what he had studied," as Martin wrote in *Café Central.* "In any case it wasn't business and certainly not gastronomy. He is a slow person in a quick time and makes sure that his outfit never crosses the line."

Dr. Peters (as Martin loved to call him) did everything possible wrong and succeeded anyway. Martin loved to make fun of his ambitions: entering the hotel business out of left field, taking over a conventional city hotel named Maria Lentz, and rebaptizing it after probably the most legendary artist hotel in the world. Dr. Peters only gave a gentle smile, as usual, in response to Martin's teasing. He admired Martin's honesty, his authenticity: as he said, "the fact that he lived how, who, and what he was. That he didn't care about conventions." Martin, of course, wanted to show him how it was done, over and over again; he took over the hotel's fifth anniversary party in 1989, for example, and Rüdiger Carl played, Wolfi Bauer read, and Udo Kier was there. The party lasted from noon until noon, twenty-four hours.

Martin paid for his room with pictures: his own and others' from his collection. The walls were too bare anyway. Only large paintings, since Peters didn't have the money to insure the art and big works couldn't be stuffed in a suitcase and stolen. Martin paid cash in the café and was there every day and every night. He sat at the table and drew, held court, did business, met with his collaborators, and ordered people to run errands for him. Since the Chelsea eventually did develop into *the* hotel for the art scene—thanks in large part to Martin's constant presence—he met countless foreign visitors there, too, without it being necessary to make plans with them first. There was no getting around Martin in the small café.

Martin was the frontman at Café Central, as another Cologne resident said. The staff obeyed him. He got whatever he wanted—bloody marys for breakfast, a breakfast egg for dinner—and could do whatever he wanted, too. "He demanded that others pay court to him," Peters said, "and that he call the shots. He could be loud. But he was never offensive." After a lot of whining, he even finally got his beloved noodle casserole there. Just not the way he wanted it.

ONLY MADE BY MOTHER

The gallerist Christian Nagel said, "He always needed something in his mouth—something to eat, or drink, or smoke." He ate for consolation when things were going badly in Berlin—his favorite dishes were always comfort food (plain cooking and dishes for children)—and he had Uschi Welter cook him spaghetti whenever he needed it, even in the middle of the night. Rudolf Augstein once said "Kippi can't even make himself a sandwich," but it wasn't a question of ability: he thought it was much nicer to have someone else make the sandwich, and buy the bread and sausage in the first place, and wash the dishes afterward. Much nicer to feel taken care of.

Martin reprinted Augstein's comment in *Through Puberty to Success* and he knew that his eagerness to be coddled was part of both his adolescent behavior and his success. That was also why he liked to stay with friends and in hotels: someone made his bed and cleaned his bathroom, which left him completely free, with nothing to worry about. Except art.

On a fundamental level, Martin was not especially interested in eating as such; he was no gourmet. Food was like money: something you need to stay alive. "The only thing that bothers me is that I have to eat," he said in 1991, a period of his life when he seemed tired of many things. Eating bored him, he said: "there's nothing new for me in it." He wasn't a big eater, and the more he drank, the less he ate; by the end, he only "nibbled," as a girlfriend said, but even then he never ordered something light—God forbid a salad! He ordered roasts or innards, then shared his portion. This was one reason Martin liked to eat in his Chinese friend Davé's Paris restaurant: the food was "really very, very fine," but Davé was not insulted when Martin left some on the plate. He often ate it all just to please Davé and proudly showed him the empty plate.

He was not a big eater, but he was a grateful one, who could enthuse about Sabine Grässlin's or our sister Bine's culinary skills as much as he did about artists. He had done that as a child, too. In a letter from boarding school in Honneroth, insulting the circus and the teachers, he praised only the new cook. "She cooks unexpectedly well. She uses amazing spices and makes only the best food: muesli, spagetti, egg ravioli, all sorts of stuf like that."

Eating was first and foremost an occasion for talking, for getting together. It was something you made plans to do. Nothing could be more wretched than the scene his ghostwriter described in his little book *1984: How It Really Was, Using the Example of Knokke*: Martin sitting all alone, in a hotel room that was already depressing enough, ingesting a breakfast of three rolls ("rather big but almost brittle") that tasted like nothing, with equally tasteless mystery-marmalade (the fruit indiscernible under the pinkish-red and orange color), served on a plastic tray.

In fact, Martin absolutely never ate alone, just as he never drank alone. When he wasn't living with someone or spending the night somewhere where he was cooked for, and when he didn't have an invitation to a meal, he went to a restaurant, two or three times a day.

He liked it best when he could eat with one hand, keeping the other hand free to talk with, sketch, and make notes. He thought that food should be "monosyllabic"—after all, he talked enough himself. Bread dumplings *and* noodles in a soup was already too much for him. Disks of pickled rhubarb sliced with an asparagus peeler on a delicate ribbon of mint purée, with a semolina cake on top, a paper-thin leaf of cinnamon pastry, and rhubarb ice cream, garnished with a little stem of dark chocolate—such a dish would have left him completely helpless. So many sensations and combinations, each one demanding his full attention, were much too stressful for him. He wouldn't have wanted to have to stop and think about whether that green purée was mint or spinach or gooseberry, or wanted or pay attention the cinnamon dough—only to the person across the table from him and the conversation. Everything pretentious was foreign to him; when a maître d' held out the cork of an expensive bottle of red wine for him to sniff, he would stick it in his eye. He made fun of modern dishes with a floating sculpture: *Santa Claus Disguised as Frog on a Fried Egg with a Streetlamp Disguised as Palm Tree.*

Life was eventful and exciting enough—food should be simple and honest, like the blood sausage and oysters he so loved to eat at the Paris Bar. That was why he loved Italian cooking so much: it was like him, open and direct, complex in its apparent simplicity, straightforward, never sophisticated. In Italy, the food in the best restaurants was like home cooking. It was a Mama's cuisine.

He liked that Italian cooking was based on traditions and recipes handed down from generation to generation, not on trends. So it was all the more disheartening when some fashionable trend fundamentally misunderstood and diminished it, as in the art world of the time with its beloved mozzarella and tomato bruschetta and spaghettini. Nowhere were the fussy affectations and craven conventionality of the art business so obvious as on the plate. Martin wrote on one of his paintings: "We don't have problems with mozzarella and tomatoes with basil, because we pay back with Tiramisu."

Martin ate pasta no matter where he was—Belgium, Greece, even Dublin, "and their misunderstandings of Italian cooking are by no means the worst." He rejected good taste—"bad food is good, good food is bad," just as bad painting was good in his view, and paintings with impeccable craftsmanship were bad. This doesn't mean that he always ate badly and painted badly, only that he was especially fond of mistakes. In his book about the Easter vacation he took in Tunisia with his girlfriend Gabi Marzona, *Kippermann as Neckermann* (Neckermann is a famous packaged-tour company), he noted: "Finally, mealworm bolognese—specialty of the house. Gabi says: 'Tastes terrible.' — Kippi answers: 'I won't let the noodles down.' (Doesn't matter who, where, when — Everyone does the best he can.)"

Pasta is "the friendliest foodstuff you can find on a plate," he wrote in *Café Central,* "smooth, soft, and unbelievably aesthetic." As an artist, too, he liked it. It was inexhaustible material, in its variety of form if nothing else: thick and thin, very thick and extremely thin, long and smooth, shell- or spiral-shaped. It had great comedic potential.

Pasta appears over and over again in his work. He called one of his early shows, in the Petersen Gallery in Berlin, *Kippenberger in the Noodle Casserole Yes Please!* (a macaroni curtain covered in red pearls). He titled one of his paintings *Spaghetti Full Moon,* another *Painted Under the Influence of Spaghetti No. 7,* and garnished his bronzes called *Badly Filled Noodle Casserole* with a few stray strands of spaghetti. The photographs he reprinted in his catalog *Homesick Highway 90* include himself eating spaghetti, the *Transporter for Social Boxes* with the pasta crate, and his *Homesick Highway* installation in Barcelona: a macaroni curtain, which he also produced as a do-it-yourself multiple (macaroni, string of pearls, and wooden balls), called *Per Pasta ad Astra.*

What Martin found especially gripping about pasta— as with the egg—was the insignificance of the material. In his view, to make something out of nothing was always the highest form of art, in cooking no less than in painting:

> The egg is white and insipid, how can a colorful picture result from that? You can turn it this way and that and you always discover something new. Sometimes sociopolitical things, or humor, besides, it does have a beautiful shape after all, just like breasts have beautiful shapes. It's like with spaghetti, you never get bored eating the same thing over and over

again. There is always the same thing on the menu, and then suddenly you have something else, the surprise special, and it's not the same.

The art lay in the constant variations on an identical theme.

He made art out of noodles because they were what lay closest to hand—the most commonplace thing, the most emotional thing, and therefore exemplary. Pasta became his artistic leitmotif and his trademark precisely because it was right there on the plate, beneath most people's notice—and because it was a central part of his life. Diedrich Diederichsen called Martin a happy revolutionary, in the *Rent Electricity Gas* catalog, because the pasta that was "the inexhaustible reservoir of metaphorical beauty" in his work was food he really and truly loved to eat. For Diederichsen, this was proof that Martin was a critical artist but not one locked in bitter mortal combat against the world.

If there was anything even more noodly than noodles, it was noodle casserole. As he wrote in a poem, "Puerto Escondido (Mexico)," about an unhappy moment of his travels in Mexico in the seventies: "Beans / Pesos / Diarrhea / Around the shack / And 3 wishes inside: // Loden coat / Noodle casserole / Tiled bathroom." Noodle casserole as longed-for paradise.

Noodle casserole was the absolute epitome of home and homesickness. In *Café Central,* Martin describes how he

fought for three years for lentil soup with nice spicy sausage. Now that I have this dish on my plate, and I've tried it in various moods and conditions, I don't eat it anymore. The application process for noodle casserole has stretched out even longer. I preached noodle casserole, I praised noodle casserole, gave hints, gave damn good advice. When it comes right down to it it's the one food I know by heart and really understand. Granted, whole memories of deep wounds in my life's happiness are bound up with macaroni. OK. The day arrived. The preparations were underway. "This weekend," they said: the key to unlock the door of my contentment. Sunday evening I came in as usual, sat down, and ordered noodle casserole. To make a long story short: Not for me. Other people might have eaten it after three years of waiting and more.... Another two weeks went by, begging and pleading, with various conversations with Dr. Peters: whether it might be possible to obtain a new casserole for preparing the dish.

Again it seems ready, and Martin has it brought to his room. Alas, it "was prepared French-style. Nouvellcuisinic thin slices draped across the plate. It was too bad they hadn't fried it up in the pan, they warmed it up in the microwave oven upstairs."

The book also lists his various favorite foods:

Cabbage roll, meat roll, good old bratwurst, fried slices of blood sausage with burnt onion rings, burnt butter sauce, and potato purée, there could also be some kidneys, a nice piece of liver from Tönshoff [a local supermarket from his childhood]. But when the waiter or owner where Kippenberger is a regular bent over the plate and criticizing it asks him "How are we supposed to make it then? How should it be?" the incontrovertible answer comes: "Like my mother does it!" His mother was hardly a master chef but she couldn't go driving to restaurants in the city every afternoon and evening with the five kids and the au pair (she couldn't cook but she did it right).

The search for noodle casserole was a guiding thread of the whole homesick highway of his life. In New York and L.A., Sevilla and Syros—everywhere he went he asked for it, nowhere did he find it. As it says in *Café Central*: "Let the noodle casserole be only made by Mother and reheated by her the next day."

SPAIN

Albert Oehlen no longer quite recalls how he and Martin came up with the idea to go to southern Spain, in early 1988. He can only guess: "We were talking and realized we didn't have girlfriends, no pressing exhibitions, we could actually do something. And then Juana was there and she said, 'Come to Spain!'" Juana de Aizpuru was their gallerist in Sevilla and Madrid, a Spanish grande dame with a towering hairdo and a voice "that you never forget," as Georg Herold said. He described her as "sophisticated and unbelievably nice and charming." So they knew Juana would take care of them, and Albert spoke Spanish.

The house in Carmona could not have been uglier, the neighborhood could not have been more horrible. Martin wrote in a letter to Michel Würthle, later reprinted in the *Joints I* catalog:

A nouveauriche bungalow on the townedge with a garbage dump around the corner. Inside needing well-trained west-central european corrections eyes + hands needless to say. The tendency to throw mothball parties must have been a predilection of the landlord (instead of giving hot zipper/sausage parties a chance). After 3 evacuations + attempts to transform the furniture with the most suitable sewed-on beautiful fabrics (which didn't work; since here & there the past still showed through). The 4th deportation now planned for the weekend.... If you dont feel so good, bars on the windows and doors keep you from jumping out of the ground-floor into the cold swimming pool.

Again the two men spurred each other on, for the last time with this level of intensity and only after a certain warm-up period: "for a few weeks, maybe even months, we didn't do anything, or only crap," Albert Oehlen says. "But at some point it clicked, for both of us at the same time. Spain was extremely productive for us, totally extreme, for me it was the start of my abstract paintings, a radical revolution in my painting, the decisive step in my development." As for Martin, his first cycle of self-portraits in underwear dates from Carmona. He showed them in Juana de Aizpuru's Sevilla gallery. He also started to draw and designed new sculptures: *Streetlamps for Drunks* and *Chicken Disco* would later be shown at the Aperto at the Venice Biennale. "It is not so simple to free yourself from 'wanting to make art at all costs,'" Martin wrote to Michel. "Again and again free thoughts are undermined by especially crazydumb bright ideas.... I sometimes get the feeling that someone has slipped the right thing into my drink + that here between the olive pickers I've really found a good place."

There was little to distract them: only occasionally a visitor from Germany. The high point of the day was the hike through the thickets of undergrowth to the village restaurant. "The garbage points the way and lots of tree stumps are charred," Martin wrote to Detlev Gretenkort. "In general you're glad to find a camping vibe in all the filth. People just throw things on the ground, that's why I still dont know the Span. word for ashtray. But back to our route. Lemons fall from overhead on either side, a used stroller lies crumpled up half off the path." The restaurant didn't look much better: it was like a big hall with everything thrown on the floor, fluorescent tubes on the ceiling, and a propeller on the wall. But with Manölchen (Martin's nickname for Manolo), Martin found another of his innkeeper families who loved him—father, brothers, and sisters, including Carmen, a teacher he dated. The restaurant was also Martin and Albert's telephone switchboard: they took calls there between eleven and noon, then returned to work through the wasteland until it was time to come back for dinner.

They sometimes drove to nearby Seville, and in a bar there Martin discovered Luis Claramunt, an outsider painter he befriended and included in numerous exhibitions in Kassel and Graz. Or they took trips to Madrid, where the nightlife was definitely wilder than in Carmona. Martin liked the Spanish rhythm, where life only really gets going late at night. At the end of the year, Albert and Martin moved to Madrid, but Martin didn't stay long. He celebrated New Year's Eve in Spain with his girlfriend, Gabi Hirsch, and then moved back to Germany. She was pregnant with his child.

CHAPTER SIX

COLOGNE YEARS:
THE TURNING POINT

"On November 9, 1989," the Berlin gallerist Bruno Brunnet said, "Cologne was finished." That was the date of the fall of the Wall, which led to the end of the Republic of West Germany and Bonn as its capital. Berlin became the German capital again, first politically, and then a few years later the art capital as well. Cologne turned into a media city, with private television networks establishing themselves there—and then typically moving to Berlin.

The art dealer Rudolf Zwirner told me that until 1989 he saw Paris, a couple of hours by train from Cologne, as his "natural capital city," but that changed, too, and he moved to Berlin in 1992, while his son opened a successful gallery of his own in New York. Paul Maenz, who had represented the Mülheimer Freiheit artists, closed his gallery in 1990 to move to Berlin; Max Hetzler moved in 1993. "It was a big step," Hetzler said, "and a big cut": he stopped representing all of his former artists except Albert Oehlen.

In any case, the Hetzler Boys' time together had long since ended; they even began to lose personal contact with each other. Their attitudes were no longer compatible. In Hetzler's view, "Martin's overflowing creativity, these hundreds of thousands of exhibitions, were more than a gallery could handle." Every month another opening—and Martin would rather have had it be every week—and in such insignificant cities, too: Innsbruck, Stuttgart, Graz. Betsy Wright Millard, a young curator at the St. Louis Forum for Contemporary Art, was amazed when Martin once asked her, over a meal in Frankfurt, if he could have an exhibition with her. She bravely said, "'Hey, you want to come to nowhere in the middle of nowhere?' and his eyes lit up: 'Yes!' He didn't even know where St. Louis was. But I got the impression that he wanted to experience everything, try everything out."

This pioneer spirit, the pleasure he took in making and promoting art, impressed the young American. Hetzler, on the other hand, felt that all these excursions into the hinterlands were extremely bad strategy, even counterproductive. He would have liked to steer Martin, and especially put the brakes on him, but Martin never allowed that—he was always his own master. If anything, it was he who told his gallerists and curators what they should do and whom they should show, and he dragged his friends and students along to do it; especially the younger gallerists and curators had no hope of withstanding him. "You didn't contradict him," said Daniel Buchholz. "The orders came down from on high."

Martin was not interested in following the shortest path up the career ladder—his path was horizontal, not vertical. He spread himself around with all his various projects, and in fact this multilayered complexity, Michael Krebber thought, was Martin's guiding principle. Jutta Koether said:

> Martin wasn't arrogant, he never thought here or there wasn't good enough for him, this or that gallery is only B-list or C-list. He wasn't disturbed by those hierarchical relationships, which already back then were beginning to establish themselves. Instead, he disturbed them. Especially in America, everything is extremely hierarchical today and the least little movement is registered: if you show here or there,

your market value goes up or down. And that's what people pay attention to—that is the standard of worth. The idea of art and the production of art are warped accordingly. It was different back then.

This is not to say that Martin was always delighted out in the sticks. Of course he would have preferred a show at the Museum of Modern Art in New York to one at the Institute of Contemporary Art in Philadelphia, where he had to share a room with Christian Nagel, the young gallerist he had brought along for company and as his "porter" (in Nagel's words). That in itself was fine—it meant Martin never had to be alone—but the whole thing started to seem a bit piddling. He caused trouble at the show, which was called *Not to be the Second Winner*: Nagel recalls that when the crates arrived with the work, "Martin said he wouldn't unpack anything, everything there was too stupid. The curator almost flipped out, but she bravely went to the museum director and told him what was going on—but we all went out for margaritas that night, and then Martin said he'd unpack some stuff after all." Not everything, but most of it—he kept a couple of pieces in their crates, and wrapped some others with bubble wrap and masking tape, adding a label (in English): "I hold myself closed."

Martin bypassed his gallerists not only to arrange exhibitions but also to make sales, which they liked even less. And the more products Martin had circulating out in the world, the harder it was for them to keep track of them all. That was one of the reasons that tensions developed between Martin and Peter Pakesch, even before Pakesch closed his gallery in Vienna in 1993. Business in Vienna was following the same path as in Germany, with the booming eighties followed by a slump in the early nineties. Pakesch no longer wanted to be a gallerist and became a freelance curator; he traveled to America often before becoming head of the Basel Kunsthalle, which would eventually show an exhibition of Martin's self-portraits.

The beginning of the end of Martin's Cologne collaborations had already come in 1988, when Hetzler moved gallery spaces within the city. He had the architect Oswald Mathias Ungers make an expensive new building for him on Venloer Strasse, all stern right angles of course; Albert Oehlen, Werner Büttner, and Günther Förg, the most successful of Hetzler's artists at the time, also bought space in the building and thus helped to finance it. Martin hated the building, which a visitor described as "a housing project in aristocratic style." "As an artist I can no longer work in a gallery like Max's the way Ungers built it," Martin told Jutta Koether in 1991: even the dark floorboards "bring you down so much." He thought Eskimos knew more about architecture than this star of Cologne architecture, and he made fun of the building with a sculpture he designed in Spain, *Chicken Disco* (a disco floor of colored squares not unlike the building's squares of color). He nonetheless continued to show work there—he didn't want to give that up. But he no longer truly felt comfortable and at home in the new space.

The Hetzler Boys had grown up by that point. They appeared in public as a gang less and less often, preferring solo shows. Now that they were established as artists, they drifted apart as a group, with each one following his own path, with greater or lesser success. Martin's attempt to ride the coattails of the *Truth Is Work* show with an exhibition in Munich called *Painting Is Elections* (*Malen ist Wahlen*, riffing on *Wahrheit ist Arbeit*) turned out to be a misstep: Oehlen and Büttner felt exploited and resented not being consulted when Martin showed their works from his own collection without asking them first, and they hated the show's title. They accused him of stabbing them in the back. "There was no back-and-forth," Oehlen said. "In his eagerness he just took the whole thing in hand himself. He was under such pressure with all his projects, he took on more and more assignments until the whole thing took on a life of its own. He didn't have time to listen to you." Oehlen at that period had "taken a step back" in any case. "It bothered me that Martin's show gave second-rate artists, random idiots, the same status as others." He preferred to spend time with Martin in smaller circles.

Oehlen had been leading a healthier life for some time, cutting short the long nights out, going for hikes and bicycle rides, and retreating to Spain. Günther Förg likewise withdrew to Switzerland, Werner Büttner to a professorship in Hamburg, and Georg Herold to spend time in New York. Martin himself didn't entirely break camp in Cologne, but he spent more and more time elsewhere—L.A., Syros, Frankfurt, Tokyo, Sankt Georgen—whether to get a little distance or in search of a new home.

FAREWELL TO EXUBERANCE

The art market was in crisis, with the boom of the late eighties leading to the recession of the early nineties. The bubble had popped, and pictures that had just recently cost a hundred thousand marks were suddenly selling for twenty thousand. With the start of the first Gulf War in 1990, American collectors said that it was difficult to buy art anymore; war broke out in Yugoslavia and would continue for years; in Germany, the euphoria that had accompanied the fall of the Wall gave way to new low spirits. Work by American artists like Mike Kelley and Jeff Koons was still selling for high prices, which hurt Martin's feelings, since he knew the prices his own works were selling (or not selling) for. Money was so tight at one point that Martin's assistant, Johannes Wohnseifer, was paid his salary three months late.

Painting had become yesterday's medium—totally eighties. Photographers of the Becher school from Düsseldorf were all the rage, and their pictures were everything Martin's art wasn't: regal, monumental, uninhabited, and technically unimpeachable. Before long, the practitioners of Brit Art would be causing a sensation—and showing what they had learned from the Germans.

Cologne quieted down. Franz Keller had had to give up his restaurant at the end of the eighties and had left the city; the Hammerstein was no longer what it used to be. To fight the financial and art-business crisis of the nineties (which would last until 1997, the year of Martin's death), the remaining galleries in Cologne banded together, with younger gallerists like Esther Schipper, Sophia Ungers, and Daniel Buchholz playing important roles. They were trying to make the art scene more youthful and fresh again. Martin liked working with younger colleagues; he showed with Sophia Ungers and developed projects with Schipper and Buchholz.

One of these projects, probably from 1995, never came to pass, but developing the idea was enjoyable enough. Martin wanted to sit in Daniel Buchholz's gallery, located behind his father's used bookstore, so people could buy something in front ("You know the kind of thing I like, fried eggs, Frank Sinatra") and bring it to Martin's table in the back, where he would draw on it. Buchholz would pay for the pens and the wine, and they would split the profits. "You'd be able to buy something for twenty marks, but also for a thousand. The funny thing would be that a felt pen can make an engraving worthless, or can make it more expensive."

Everyone in the Cologne scene was having more or less as hard a time as everyone else—harder than in previous years, certainly. But that had its positive side, too. The photographer Andrea Stappert, for example, felt that "there were moments when you thought, *Ah, humanity returns.* There was a new openness, fewer rigid boundaries. Everyone had to work on a smaller scale, there was less arrogance. No more swank."

ONE FAMILY ONE LINE

Do you feel lonely?
There is no such thing as loneliness for a family man.
—MK

The German word for the fall of the Wall is *Wende,* a "turn" or "turning point." 1989 was a turning point in Martin's personal life as well. That was the year our father died and Martin's daughter, Helena, was born.

Martin was amazed to watch how our father fought against his cancer, year after year. Even long after our father's death, Martin was obsessed with the question of, as he put it to Jutta Koether, "wanting to survive, wanting to keep living, where do you get the strength? When you are doing badly, where do you get the strength to believe, to keep living? Why? How?"

Our father knew why. In 1988, he wrote to Martin in Spain from the hospital where he was a regular patient with one new metastasis after another. After advising Martin that "in Jerez the sherry tastes best outside, in the sun, at a little marble café table," our father wrote that he wanted to live long enough to see Moritz, his youngest son, then fifteen years old, "find his footing. The way I feel these days, it must surely be possible." But it wasn't—he was dead a year later.

Painting was our father's consolation and delight in those days, and he enjoyed doing it in the hospital, "sitting as well as standing. It's a real hobby." He regretted only that he had not succeeded in making a career out of art, any more than his grandmother had. "So it's good," he wrote to Martin in that same letter, "that at last you've been able to give art its due." Martin saw his role in the family in similar terms: "I rose in the world, for example—my great-grandmother was an art student in Düsseldorf, my grandmother painted, my father painted, but none of them did it professionally. I am the first one to do it professionally and really pull off the concept of Kippenberger Art."

Martin wrote on our father's gravestone "One Family One Line." He designed the stone with Hubert Kiecol, and it was responsible for the fact that our father had to be dug up from his grave: the simple stone was laid lengthwise along the grave, rather than across the head, as per German cemetery regulations; the sculpture director of the Marl museum tried in vain to declare the stone and thus the grave a protected work of art, but the city council was merciless. So our father had to be reburied, in a corner, where, it was hoped, he would cause less offense.

Martin's friends were shocked when they first met our father. Carmen and Imi Knoebel said, "We always thought Martin was the original," until they met him, who had the same total lack of inhibition in public, whether dancing, giving a speech, or singing—the same sentimentality, excessive artistic production, need to arrange everything and enforce good cheer, and striving toward an all-encompassing total work of art. Some of Martin's friends thought our father was even worse than Martin; Albert Oehlen called him "the extreme version of Martin."

In his wedding newspaper, our father had requested "pictures in all sizes and price points" and hoped for "a son with red hair and jutting ears"—he even drew the son he wanted, exactly the way that Martin would later portray himself as a child, with jutting ears and a crew cut.

As for Martin, he said, two years after the birth of his daughter, that he under no circumstances wanted a son himself. "They look like you and say the same things, too." He knew that there was no escape: as he wrote in a poem in 1981, "Whether in Stuttgart, Rome, or Frankfurt / I am always the son of Gerd."

They were both Pisces, with Martin born on February 25 and our father on March 1. "My father always signed his paintings, drawings, and photographs with 'Kip,'" Martin said. "That's why, when I was seven, I came up with 'Kippy.'" Gerd signed his letters to us "Your father," while Martin signed his "Your brother," as though to make sure of their roles. "I will have no other God but me," our father told our mother once, and he called himself "a textbook egoist": "The only thing I do energetically is what I want to do. That's why I sometimes manage more than other people in such cases." Martin could have said the same.

Martin learned from him that you can't wait to be discovered. You have to take matters into your own hands: organize your own shows, publish your own books, build stages for your own performances. And no false modesty, either: our father always said that his pious grandmother had told him to put his light *on* the bushel, not under it. That's what it actually says in the Sermon on the Mount, after all.

Our father's taste in art shaped Martin's while at the same time provoking a reaction in the opposite direction. Martin felt Gerd's skepticism as an incentive: he wanted to prove to his father that it actually is possible to make a living as an artist. Martin often told the story about how our father had said that an artist needs a style, so he, Martin, had tried with all his might to find his style, until he realized that his style was to not have a style. He also told a story about how our father promised a one-mark reward to whichever one of us found the best painting in the Folkwang Museum in Essen, so of course we looked for the one we thought he liked best. In the end, every one of us got a mark, which Martin thought was especially awful.

Martin's view of art was different from our father's, but Martin was always proud of him and his work, no matter how unlike his own work our father's was. He gave Gerd's books to his friends, for example. He was proud of the family he came from, too, even if he had very little in common with most of its members. He was proud that our father, too sick to walk after a new bout of cancer, had had himself carried to Martin's opening at Gisela Capitain's gallery. It mattered to Martin that Gerd meet his gallerists. Martin brought Max Hetzler to a show of our father's at a barn in Marl. "He didn't make fun of it," Hetzler said. "He respected it." Our father was proud of his son, too, who was living the life he had only dreamed of for himself. Once, when Martin did not have a single work on show at the Cologne Art Fair, he rented rooms in the city to show his work after all, and our father stood on the street in front, in a white scarf, pointing the way to interested parties.

There was one thing our father may have been too proud to do: buy his son's pictures. It may have been painful for him, too, seeing the wild, free life he himself had missed out on—where you can do whatever you want and nothing but. Martin had celebrated *1/4 Century Kippenberger* as an extravagant "happening" in S.O.36, filled with excessive behavior. When our father turned 25, by contrast, he had just escaped the war after six years. As he later wrote in one of

355

his many autobiographical texts, "We were a Nazi, militaristic generation of young people. We let ideas that weren't our own seduce us and wrap us around their little fingers. We didn't resist as much as we needed to. I can only hope that our children realize better than we did which way that path leads."

Along with their mutual pride, however, there was another feeling, on both sides: jealousy, unfulfilled longing, competitiveness. Hubert Kiecol sensed it the first time he met our father, when Gerd sang the miner's song *"Glück auf"* after an exhibition opening, as Martin himself liked to do with his drinking buddies at midnight. But while Martin contented himself with a single verse ("For they wear leather on their asses at night..."), our father sang ten or more and still didn't stop. "It was one too many," Kiecol said.

One time, Martin had a show together with our father, in the CCD Gallery in Düsseldorf: *Sand in the Vaseline.* The show included photographs by both of them—Martin's from Brazil, from 1986, and our father's from Zandvoort an Zee, from 1968. But Gerd wanted to be more than an adjunct or a point of contrast; he wanted to have pictures he had chosen himself shown in a real gallery, a wish that Martin never fulfilled for him. When our father showed up at Gisela Capitain's gallery with a pile of drawings he had made blind, in a dark theater, Martin quickly disappeared. "It was embarrassing for him," Capitain said. Martin later asked Peter Pakesch in Vienna— far enough from Cologne, no doubt—if he would show some of our father's pictures, together with work by Oehlen's father. Pakesch says,

> It was important to Martin that he organize an exhibition for his father before his father's death. That was another reason he and I were not on good terms for a while, because it didn't happen. But I had told

him, OK, you can do it, I just don't want to do any of the work, you have to do it yourself. Then the whole thing melted away.

After our father's death, Martin considered publishing Gerd's books with Martin Prinzhorn in an edition annotated by Prinzhorn. Prinzhorn was always seated at our father's table at exhibition openings and parties, "because Martin thought I would understand him and the others wouldn't." Martin always made an effort to get our father's praise and approval, which made him seem like a little boy: "he couldn't use his usual weapons and defuse tense situations with irony."

When Martin came home for family holidays (Christmas, weddings, baptisms), he was calm, fun, uncomplicated, "normal"—never the wild man. Of course, he couldn't keep it up for long, and by the time night rolled around at the latest he would be off, to a bar with our brother-in-law Andreas, or to the Marl disco with our little stepbrothers Jochen and Claus, furthering their education (for instance, teaching them how to get past the bouncer).

Martin surprised us by coming home for Christmas as usual in 1988, when our father was so sick. He called at noon on the 24th from the Recklinghausen train station, and the surprise was a happy one. Both father and son were moved. It must have taken a certain amount of willpower for him to come—he may have been fearless about everything else, but coming into contact with death scared him. When he visited our father in the hospital, he had to drink for courage and bring friends for protection; he had to gather all his strength to be at home with our father when he died. He popped copious pills to survive the funeral.

That summer and fall our father had been in bad shape: confused and apathetic like never before. But for Christmas, the family holiday, he too pulled himself together. Martin called it "furnishing proof." "It's about proving yourself. The same with me. I'm not so different from my father that way." Our father wanted to make it to January, to his first gallery opening—our sister Babs, a lawyer, had recently opened a gallery in Cologne, the K. Gallery. (Martin hadn't wanted her to use the name Kippenberger—Cologne was his domain when it came to art.) Our father, dressed up and lying on the sofa, held court at the opening, and on February 22, three days before Martin's birthday, he was dead.

Six months later, Martin's daughter was born. Two years later, Martin would say, "Just as she was born, he died. I saw him lying in bed like a baby. The rhythm, it makes you think.... The real reason I had a child was because my father was dying. I wanted life to go on." He gave his daughter our mother's name: Helena Augusta Eleonore. If it had been a boy, he would have been named Hans Otto Oskar (Hans and Otto were our grandfathers' names).

Martin had always been thrilled to be a godfather: first for our half-brother Moritz and later for Reiner Opoku's daughter. Now he had decided to start a family of his own. A big family, too. When Joachim Lottman asked him in 1989 how he imagined his future, Martin said: "I will live to 72, have four children, all girls. If it's a boy I'll put him out on the street, with a sign around his neck: Please don't send me home. Bundled up nice and warm of course." It was easier to cope with girls, he thought. "If only the mothers weren't around."

He was obsessed with the idea of becoming a father and ran around the bars and restaurants of Cologne announcing it. And then he found the woman who would be the mother of his child: Gabi Hirsch, a young, beautiful, lively, and good-natured woman who was a family person, like him. They had just started dating when she got pregnant. Martin soon realized that the reality was different than his fantasy: more stressful, complicated, and banal. Gabi's pregnancy had complications, and she was put on bed rest at the hospital. Martin couldn't handle how she changed under the influence of her hormones, and his friends had to give him some private tutoring about the female condition. They were shocked at how little he seemed to understand about women.

Helena's birth on August 24, 1989, was the most emotional experience of Martin's life. He called up friends and family afterward, ecstatic and excited, and described the birth "almost like a science fiction movie," Martin Prinzhorn said, "as though some alien life form had appeared." He was normally scared of blood, "and I absolutely can't stand screaming," he said, but none of it bothered him during the birth, not even the afterbirth: "I was so overjoyed." One female friend said, "He was so happy that you simply had to be happy with him." In the years to come he would say again and again, and always with the same astonishment, "that new worlds open up when a child is born, just like a little green man on the runway, out of nowhere, and everything is perfect and everything is there, I didn't make it, you wonder where it came from." From biology, the person he was talking to might say. "Well maybe I wasn't paying attention in class," Martin would answer, "but I'm no Maya the Bee" [a popular cartoon character; "the birds and the bees" are used for sex education in Germany as well]. Biology was not the answer to the questions he was suddenly starting to ask himself, which wouldn't let him go and which he couldn't explain. "It's such a decisive break in your life."

When an interviewer remarked how surprised he was that Martin was talking so much about his daughter, Martin said that after all she was a part of him: "Intelligence and beauty from her mother and the rest from me. Half is definitely from me. What we can't decide is where she gets the hysteria from, her or me."

The birth announcement, which Martin later used as a poster, is the photograph of a family that could not be more beautiful, happy, and perfect.

They tried to lead a family life for a while, but maybe their twelve-year age difference was too large, their interests and views of life too different. They led that life in the apartment on the Hansaring in Cologne, then in L.A., and then he bought an apartment on Eifelstrasse back in Cologne; Gabi renovated and furnished it, "everything really great, almost finished a year later, almost finished, almost finished, then you realize: That's not the apartment you want at all."

"I have a commandment for myself," Martin told the *Artfan* interviewer two years after Helena was born. "I will never ever go back to a double cell, or six-person cell, or four-person cell, whether it's boarding school or a kid's room or whatever, I will never set foot in them again. I think I'm damaged, I wouldn't want to live in the same room with a woman either. I managed it once in my life [with Inka Hocke in Hamburg] but there I had my own apartment too, and slept with the woman every night. That was different. Together in a single apartment, that would be hell. Sometimes I am not strong enough to rely on myself, so you cling to the next person you want to rely on. Doesn't work though. Won't ever work. I have a much much greater number of weaknesses than other people maybe, other people can accept the situation, I never accept it. I just get annoyed. I'm too sensitivey for it."

Martin repeated the rituals of his childhood with his new family: vacations in Holland with Gabi and Helena; French fries and croquettes there; visiting our uncle in Siegen; traveling with them and Bine and her family to

Cappenberg to spend St. Martin's Day with the Jansens; and spending almost every Christmas together with us, whether in Cologne, Holland, Berlin, or Jennersdorf, complete with turkey, presents, and a Christmas tree. That's what he wanted, and even when they were separated, Gabi always came with Helena. But all Martin's ritual activities didn't help. You can't go home again.

Homesickness could not be reconciled with the highway. As soon as he could, Martin took flight—into his work, to another place, to friends. "Father insisted on freedom!" he said by way of explaining his first separation from his family, in L.A. "The new situation made me too tense." He had pictured an idyllic existence with a family that was simply there and that supported him, the artist. He hadn't counted on the banality of everyday life. "Everyday life," his friend Uli Strothjohann said, "was poison for him."

Martin carried Helena in a sling when she was a baby and later pushed her around in a stroller. When Meuser was there with his daughter, the same age as Helena, Martin used to brag about his own daughter: "Yours is cross-eyed and mine has beautiful eyes and long lashes too." He took mountains of photographs of her and bought presents by the bagful—stuffed animals, T-shirts, but also Munch's *Scream* figure as a life-size inflatable doll. He loved her very much, but he couldn't live that love. Later, too, when she came to stay with him, he didn't try to make up for lost time—he continued to paint and see friends. And then he was proud and moved when she fell asleep next to him in bed. His relationships with other children were usually fun and uncomplicated, but he seemed almost bashful with his own daughter, as though she remained an alien being for him. Still, there was an intensity between father and daughter that you can see in the photographs Elfie Semotan took of them together.

"As soon as you have some warmth," Martin once said, "you don't know how to handle it. I'm the world champion not-know-how-to-handler."

Gabi and Helena remained permanent parts of our family, and that was important to Martin—he knew that he could never have found a better, more loving mother for his child. But the project of a happy little family of his own had failed. It was the greatest defeat of his life, and he fell into despair.

MARTIN, INTO THE CORNER, YOU SHOULD BE ASHAMED OF YOURSELF

Finally, 1989 was also the year the public backlash against Martin began, over the course of which, as one Australian critic was amazed to discover, Martin was increasingly presented in the German media (when not ignored altogether) as a "neo-Nazi playboy." Two legendary articles were published in 1989 in which the authors absolutely pounced on him. One was simply a tirade of hate, and the other was a strange combination of repulsion, envy, and admiration.

"HE is disgusting. HE boozes, farts, and says 'cunt' to every woman. But HE is probably the greatest German artist since Beuys. Joachim Lottmann brings you Martin Kippenberger the way you never wanted to see him": this was how the April 1989 issue of *Wiener* put its readers in the mood for Lottmann's article. The New Journalist seemed to get almost carried away, bringing up everyone from Muhammed Ali to Adolf Hitler as Martin's forebears ("A man like him could scare Khomeni stiff"; or, he wrote, after one of Martin's endless shows, he collapsed "like old Adolf used to do after his five-hour speeches in the beer cellars of Munich, sinking into desperate dreamless unconsciousness"). Then, having launched Martin into the pantheon of evil, Lottmann (who had himself done assignments for Martin, such as writing the essay "Mr. Kippenberger" and conducting the interview with Michael Krebber for *Café Central*) tried to bury him in the depths of harmlessness: "The man is a child. His art is good, but the child himself is a disaster. He is unbearable. He is a world-champion blowhard who ruts around like a filthy pig."

Throughout the article, Lottmann consistently referred to Martin as "Kippi." Martin hated when people continued to use his nickname years after he had put it aside. He liked "Kippilein" even less, as Kaspar König's then-wife used to call him—"I can't be the baby in public my whole life, can I?"

Even Lottmann's article was much too positive for Wolfgang Max Faust's tastes. Faust portrayed Martin as not only a sexist pig but also homophobic, racist, petit bourgeois, cynical, and a coward. His article in *Skyscraper* was called "The Artist As Exemplary Alcoholic." Martin's answer was the sculpture series *Martin, into the Corner, You Should Be Ashamed of Yourself,* which went over so well that instead of the planned three figures he had Uli Strothjohann build him six.

It was a time when many people talked like that about Martin, even if few of them dared to do it so publicly. This caused Jutta Koether, in turn, to publish an article in *Artscribe* that same year, 1989, which took the opposite position. In "Who Is Martin Kippenberger and Why Are They Saying Such Terrible Things about Him?" she tried to explain the phenomenon of Kippenberger and his artistic attitude.

CHAPTER SEVEN
AMERICA

"It was a land of possibility," Max Hetzler said, "and impossibility."

They wanted to conquer the West. Hetzler's gallery was a success in Cologne, as was Lawrence Luhring and Roland Augustine's in New York, and now these three gallerists wanted to try something new together, something different. The omens were good: German artists were showing in the United States, Beuys had had his major show at the Guggenheim Museum, Günther Förg was enormously successful, and the other Hetzler Boys had regular exhibitions. The West Coast was virgin territory in the art world, certainly compared to New York. The Luhring/Augustine/Hetzler Gallery opened in Santa Monica in 1989—and closed in 1992. There was not much competition, but also not much of an audience. Los Angeles at the time was, in Ed Ruscha's words, "the Australia of the art world": very far out of touch. The art boom would hit L.A. only later.

For Martin, it was a dream to go to Hollywood, have his international breakthrough, and maybe even make it work with his family. It was another instance of his pressing ahead: leaving Cologne, where he had reached a dead end, for a place where, if nothing else, the gallery would provide an anchor. His dream, like the dream of so many others who come to L.A., was to be a star. Instead, he remained what he always was: "a one-off." No matter how hard he tried, he "had to Keep Out." After going to California in 1989, he went back to Germany in 1990 and in 1991 summed up "the knowledge gained during my stay in America" as follows: "L.A. is a sprawling pit."

America was the land of our childhood dreams. Everything we saw on TV came from the U.S.: *The Little Rascals, I Dream of Jeannie, Bonanza.* "In Color!" the opening credits bragged, even if our own TV set, like most at that time, was black and white. *Fury, Lassie, Flipper*: we knew all the theme songs by heart and played America on our school vacations in Trier. Martin threw himself into the histrionic hero's death from Western movies or waddled down the street with a hat and cane like Charlie Chaplin. One of his sayings was: "Whoever films *Bonanza* himself / understands the world that much better." *

Our big sisters were into blue jeans and black men; we younger siblings longed for Milky Ways and Mickey Mouse. Everything was different in America, everything was modern—the clothes were made of paper, the milk came in cardboard, the cars were enormous, and the buildings scraped the sky. The Americans had John F. Kennedy, while we Germans had Ludwig Erhard; they flew to the moon, while we sailed on the Moselle. Anyone who went to America, we thought, would come back a different person, and that turned out to be true, to a certain extent: our grandmother came back with purple hair and a manicure; our sister came back with five or ten extra pounds.

America was the land of freedom and adventure, Hollywood and rock and roll, LSD and Dennis Hopper, Andy Warhol and *Hair.* It was a faraway, foreign land: flights were very expensive then, as were phone calls, and there was a lot less American culture in Germany—no muffins or

---

* A rhyme in German: "*Wer Bonanza selber dreht, der die Welt umso besser versteht.*"

bagels, no Gap or Nike. In Frillendorf, the opening of the first French fry stand was sensational news—we wouldn't hear of McDonald's or Burger King for years. America was also the land of forbidden pleasures: chewing gum (vulgar), comic books (trash), and fast food (unhealthy).

Later, the underground would come from New York to Berlin. Iggy Pop and David Bowie played at S.O.36, as did John Lurie and Christine Hahn. In 1979, when Hahn, the drummer of the artist-band Static, went back to New York after playing in Berlin, Martin heaped cards and kisses and phone calls on her and soon followed.

Martin had always liked the Leonard Cohen song "First we take Manhattan, then we take Berlin." Now he was trying it the other way round.

He won over Christine Hahn: "he was very romantic with me," she said. They saw New York together and "he was so hungry to take everything in," from the clubs to the museums to Coney Island on a dull winter day when everything looked abandoned, almost spooky. They went to the movies, too, and saw *Apocalypse Now* on a giant screen with a top-of-the-line sound system. Martin was impressed by the technology (how real the helicopter and gunfire sounded) but less taken by the content: "He was mad about it, really upset. He probably thought the movie was too pro-war." But Hahn was often not sure if she really understood him (Martin's English was quite bad at the time), and whether the confusion was because of the language or her or him. "He was very theatrical," so was he being serious when he asked her if she would marry him at the Wedding Chapel in Las Vegas? She thought it over, "but I didn't want to be a joke." For breakfast he ordered "two eggs looking at you," with a scotch (the German for "fried egg" is *Spiegelei*, literally "mirror-egg"). He told her stories about our mother and said that he'd never gotten a driver's license because our mother had died in an automobile accident—not exactly a lie but not exactly the truth, since our mother wasn't driving, and besides, Martin was twenty-three when the accident happened, long past the age when he could have gotten a license. In any case, it made Christine all the more willing to drive him around.

And so he criss-crossed New York in search of adventures, encounters, and noodle casserole: he asked for his favorite food everywhere, but they didn't know what he was talking about. It was his first disappointment in a country whose possibilities, he soon realized, were limited after all. "He ended up with spaghetti."

Martin was a European and wanted to stay that way, not disappear into the melting pot like other German artists. He wanted success in New York as Kippi Kippenberger from Berlin, not to be a New Yorker. "He wanted to set up a home base in New York," Hahn said. So he presented her with a very detailed list of the people he wanted to meet—"he had antennae for who was really interesting." He was hungry for exchange and interaction and made plans to meet people even over breakfast. After all, he wasn't in New York on vacation: everything he did, saw, and took pictures of (he was always in front of or behind the camera) would later be material for his postcards, posters, and catalogs.

Many of the people Martin did meet later appeared in the zine he put out in Berlin: *sehr gut, very good.* If no one else would praise him, he would just have to do it himself. The zine cost three marks and in the end he had so many unsold copies left over that he stacked them under his bed to support the mattress. The issue (there was only one) opened with a kind of family photo album as table of contents: Jochen Krüger, Middendorf and Fetting, James White, Scott B., Meuser, Kippenberger ("boss"), Eric Mitchell, Christine

Hahn, Klaus Krüger. Along with the photos of these artists, musicians, and filmmakers from Berlin and New York, there were also photos from S.O.36 and Kippenberger's Office, of course, and photos that didn't show the people they were said to depict (the one captioned H.P. Feldmann, for example, was not of H.P. Feldmann).

Martin was so excited by his meeting with the filmmaker Eric Mitchell that he invited him on the spot to join the band he had started with Christine Hahn: Luxus (Luxury). The name was a provocation—he wanted to be the exact opposite of the artists of the time who showed off their poverty by going around in torn rags—and the band itself was a fiction that existed only on its one single ("New York—Auschwitz") and the posters he and Hahn put up all over the city, the way musicians do.

But who were these musicians? No one knew—everyone was waiting for their first concert, but in vain. That was the concept. Hahn said later that Martin swept through New York like a whirlwind; to her he felt like "a breath of fresh air." Artists in New York didn't act like that: so theatrically, so playfully, so curious. No one tried to win over the whole city at once. "New York artists were so serious back then, dead serious. Everyone wore black." That was the big reason she and other artists had gone into music: "We wanted to have some fun."

Martin made these New Yorkers a bit unsure of themselves, with his boozing and bragging, his tight leather pants and his dress shirts and ties. "They didn't know what to make of him." They didn't understand this unknown but extremely intense German artist (at least he said he was an artist—no one had seen any of his work), but they were certainly curious. What more could he want?

Martin would often return to New York—you couldn't get around it. His home base gradually came together, but never quite all the way: he never managed to found a Kippenberger Family in America, "a group of people you could count on and trust," as Wilhelm Schürmann said. He found a steady gallery to represent him in 1985, Metro Pictures, where the gallerists Helene Winer and Janelle Reiring were, like him, more interested in ideas than in painting. His first show there was called *Selling America & Buying El Salvador*. Martin hounded the gallerist David Nolan (a specialist in works on paper, like Gisela Capitain at the time) so persistently that Nolan finally gave in and started working with Martin, which in this case meant keeping Martin company on nights out. Helene and Janelle were spared that. Martin was also friends with Hetzler's partners, Lawrence Luhring and Roland Augustine, and with Thea Westreich, an art dealer. Julie Sylvester became his closest friend in America and his companion, publishing many of his editions, including his shrink-wrapped used socks and *Disco Bombs* (disco balls with ladies' wigs). Friedrich Petzel, the young German gallerist, accompanied Martin through the city and brought along Martin's alcohol-free beer (it was a phase when Martin wasn't drinking, and alcohol-free beer wasn't readily available at the time). Tracy Williams and Martin were a couple for a while. He had his regular hangouts too, of course—a bar in Soho, on Prince Street, where he could get his morning screwdriver, and an Italian restaurant in Tribeca, Barocco. They kept a table in the corner reserved for Martin whenever he was in town, and he designed the restaurant's matchbox; obviously everyone there knew him immediately, from the dishwashers to the maître d'. "We'll expect you in October," Julie Sylvester wrote to him on a postcard once, "Barocco Pasta Factory will make bratwursties and cabbage rollies."

But Martin would never be as fun, lively, and playful on his later trips to New York as he was the first time. The pattern was always the same: do everything, take in everything, try everything, take limos, look at exhibitions, meet people, go dancing. New York was the clubbing capital of the world in the eighties, with Studio 54, the Limelight, and the aptly named MK—which, in Martin's opinion, looked exactly like the Pop-In had looked in Essen, twenty years earlier.

"New York is misery," he said once. He never worshipped the metropolis—he called it "Greater Ibiza." Nor did New York worship him. The indifference that bothered Martin was something David Bowie liked about New York: "People don't care what you do, they pay attention to their own thing." And if David Bowie didn't turn their heads, Martin Kippenberger sure wouldn't.

In 1979, Martin raced through America for a few weeks with Achim Schächtele, his partner from S.O.36 (and possessor of a driver's license). S.O.36 had closed, and, Schächtele said, "We were on the lookout for new horizons. What can we do there? What do people do there?" So, camera and Super-8 in tow as always, they were off through the land of pioneers, "outfitted in style: beautiful suitcases, flannel suits." They tried everything, gambled in Las Vegas (Martin lost two thousand dollars in a single night), rode horses through the Grand Canyon like cowboys, stayed at "adults-only" hotels, and tried to follow the trails of rock stars like Patti Smith, ending up, for example, in the Tropicana Motel with its black swimming pool, surrounded by musicians. At a peep-show, Martin realized that there was no glass between him and the stage and clambered through the window; in New York, they saw the pope, Andy Warhol, and Joseph Beuys all in the same week, and they went to museums, concerts, and other performances. Everywhere they went, they posed and took photographs, especially on movie sets.

And of course they made art out of it all when they got

back: the *Slaves of Tourism* show at Café Einstein (discussed above). Many of the photographs showed up in various forms in Martin's work later, too: as models for the *Dear Painter, Paint For Me* series, book covers, or catalog entries. The last of a series of pictures he later showed in a performance at Café Einstein was taken by Gisela Capitain at Alexanderplatz: Martin and Achim as cowboys in East Berlin.

Still, Schachtele says, they never really connected with the U.S. "There was no common ground, no people with the same sorts of ideas. We put on a pretty big show, we wanted cheers and applause, but there was no real relationship between what we put out and what we got back." They didn't even have the success they were used to with women: the Americans didn't like being hit on so aggressively. "What takes a couple days in Berlin takes a couple weeks in America."

They had planned to stay in America for three months but went back to Berlin after six weeks.

Nevertheless, America was a treasure trove for Martin: this "smoke-free, cholesterol-free, fat-free, zero-calorie, no problema America," as Jan Avgikos described it in Martin's St. Louis exhibition catalog, was the source of the stickers Martin plastered all over his paintings ("I love . . ."), the "Don't Wake Daddy" board game, the "Fred the Frog" character in old Bermuda shorts. New York was big, fast, exciting, made for Martin—but maybe it was *too* big, *too* fast. Maybe also too small and narrow; he sometimes felt like he was in a small town: "after a while you never get out of Soho."

And he missed having people who spoke his language, understood his jokes, and would spend nights out with him. He often took his own gang with him as a precaution— Gisela Capitain, Uschi Welter, Max Hetzler, Jörg Schlick, Uli Strothjohann, friends, assistants, students. Once, when he said to Georg Herold, "Sheorsh, come with me," and Georg said he didn't have any money, Martin bought one of his works on the spot so he had no excuse. Herold, born in Jena in East Germany, said that New York reminded him of the East at first: "Everything was so run down."

Martin shocked and fascinated the Americans with his uninhibited openness and spontaneous way of saying whatever he saw and felt, whether making a comment to the curator of the Museum of Modern Art about the curator's bizarre haircut or telling Mrs. Pulitzer at a dinner in St. Louis—*the* Mrs. Pulitzer, a white-haired lady in a white suit—"You are the whitest white woman I have ever met." The first time he went to the curator Betsy Wright Millard's house, where he was to spend a week with Jörg Schlick, he didn't politely compliment his hostess but instead burst out with "Oh my God, my worst nightmare has come true!" The ground floor was full of paintings by the New Wild Ones, the Mülheimer Freiheit painters, and the Moritzplatz group. "But," Betsy said, "he didn't just turn around and leave," and so he saw the Oehlens and Kippenbergers hanging on the second floor.

What Americans may have found new and refreshing at first—all the loud ringleading—soon turned them off. Americans were suspicious of heavy drinking like his; that sort of thing was no longer done. If you needed to calm down or pep up, you did it in private, with pills, not all pushy and out in the open. In America, an artist who drank was seen as a junkie or a loser. Why drink when there was AA? As Peter Schjeldahl, a critic with an ambivalent relationship to Martin ("I sort of despised him, and he sort of fascinated me"), wrote in the *Village Voice*, Martin's sculptures of drunken, swaying streetlamps really took him aback: they struck him as "civic monuments of the phantasmagoria and sorrows of alcoholism. As a citizen of self-help America, I find it hard to get with a culture that still issues points for fuckedupness. But there it is."

Martin's student Ina Weber said, "I think America stressed Martin out: this perpetual insistence on being polite, always speaking in code." *How are you, I'm fine, have a nice day, that's nice.* Martin's style of saying hello was more like, *Hey asshole, Hey nigger.* He could only mock the American jargon of meaningless niceties and American bigotry, which provoked him to further provocations and only cemented his reputation as a bad boy. The more politically correct New York became (long before there was any such thing in Germany), the more people reacted against him. Americans went out of their way to avoid someone with the reputation of being anti-Semitic, racist, sexist, and homophobic.

Martin himself was annoyed by different things. All the money, for example, and that it played such a big role even in the art world. His shorthand description of New York was "A dollar a step," not only because everything was so expensive, but because of the homeless people in front of every doorway and shop window in those pre-sanitized days, none of whom St. Martin could walk past without giving money.

Martin was also disappointed at the superficiality he found even among the collectors. "It's unbelievable that they're still so sure of themselves even now. They don't have the slightest idea of history. They think that what happens tomorrow is what counts." And he was irritated by the self-contradictory conformity—that Americans would "slurp down one hamburger after another but not have any spaghetti bolognese, because they're healthy."

Still, he kept coming back. He wanted to be a successful artist, which was impossible without America. Martin belonged to the generation of German artists who found international recognition even in their early years. He had many exhibitions in the U.S., not only in New York and L.A. galleries but also in the San Francisco Museum of Modern

Art, the Hirshhorn in Washington, the ICA in Philadelphia, and the St. Louis Forum for Contemporary Art. "He caused trouble in Germany and caused a sensation in America," the *Berliner Zeitung* wrote after Martin's death—even if that wasn't exactly true, he still found in the U.S. some of the official recognition that was denied to him in Germany. The Museum of Modern Art showed him in their 1987 group exhibition *BerlinArt* and today owns more of his works than all the German museums put together. In 2008–2009, MoCA in Los Angeles and MoMA in New York put on a huge and widely reviewed exhibition of his work.

"Martin Kippenberger, widely regarded as one of the most talented German artists of his generation, died on Friday at the University of Vienna Hospital": this was the opening sentence of Roberta Smith's obituary for Martin in the *New York Times*, a sentence no German newspaper would have printed. "His penchant for mixing media, styles and processes influenced younger artists on both side of the Atlantic. Yet the German art establishment seemed to have difficulty with his antics, which included buying a gas station during a trip to Brazil in 1986 and renaming it the 'Martin Bormann Gas Station.'" Even ten years before the obituary, Smith had discovered in the rawness of his work something delicate and tender, in contrast to the perfect, smooth, extremely expensive sheen of the sculptures of the time.

How did the Americans understand him and his art? They didn't, according to his New York gallerists today: "He was an artists' artist." Jeff Koons, Julian Schnabel, Stephen Prina, Christopher Wool, Christopher Williams, John Baldessari, Ronald Jones, Mike Kelley, Sam Samore, and Willem Dafoe were among his early fans, but he was not an artist for American collectors. Unlike in Europe, Martin could never build up a real base of regular collectors in America—

he was too unpredictable for their taste. What his friends so liked about him, in New York as well—that he was always trying something new—scared off many potential buyers. "Collectors like consistency," a recognizable style, pristine pictures, no crumpled subway entrances, no sculpture shows making the gallery look like a junk room.

Many of Martin's works had to be sent back to Europe unsold after his shows in America. Maybe, in the land where success is everything, it was particularly hard to understand someone who pulled his pants down, celebrated failure and defeat, and practiced "bad painting." Exhibiting your weaknesses rather than hiding them away is exactly what fascinates artists like Jeff Koons to this day.

Martin respected Koons, admired his success, and coproduced an issue of the art journal *Parkett* with him. What especially impressed Koons was that "he was always looking, always in the moment of art." He liked Martin's playfulness, his cheerful aesthetic, the freedom of his work. "Some people have a lot of anxiety, and that anxiety confines them. Martin didn't have this anxiety. When I think of Martin's art, I think about life. Art in New York at the time was an inanimate object."

Martin didn't fulfill the Americans' expectations of a German artist the way Kiefer, Lüpertz, Immendorff, or Baselitz did—in fact, he talked trash about them to American collectors whenever he could. He was an artist who was German, that's it: nothing to be ashamed of, but nothing especially worth promoting either. His Germanness didn't involve any flag-waving. The canary flitted through his work, not the German eagle; irony, not lugubrious pathos. Martin drew his material from German everyday life—soccer, politics, tabloids—but who in New York had ever heard of Loki Schmidt or Hansjörg Felmy?

Above all, his language was German and the games he played with it were hard to carry over. Taschen Verlag, the publisher of the 1991 volume *Kippenberger*, wore out several translators trying. How could you convey the title *Lebendige Freizeitgestaltung am Stiel* (Lively Leisure Activity on a Stick), for a picture of Helmut Schmidt punting on the river? What about Martin's trademark greeting, "Hallöchen," never mind "Hallööööööööchen"? It is translated in this book as "Howdy-do," while past translations have included "a little Hi-there" and "hi-i"—none as whimsical and winning as the original. The curator of his show in St. Louis was glad to come across anything she could label *Untitled*.

LOS ANGELES

New York always seemed cold to Martin, as it did to a character in Kafka's *Amerika* who battles "the snowstorms in the long straight streets of New York! . . . If you walk into a swirling headwind, you can't open your eyes even for a second, the wind is incessantly rubbing snow in your face, you walk and walk and get nowhere, it's quite desperate."

All the more appealing, then, was sunny, relaxed California. Andy Warhol once answered the question of where he would be in ten years by saying that he didn't know yet. "The only goal I have is to have a swimming pool in Hollywood. I think it's great, I like its artificial quality. New York is like Paris and Los Angeles is so American, so new and different and everything is bigger and prettier and simpler and flat."

In L.A., Martin managed to do what he couldn't in New York: leave a real trace behind him. Young artists in L.A. still talk about Martin, his appearances, his parties. He made "a powerful impression there," in the view of the Austrian artist

Hans Weigand, who lived in L.A. for a few years himself. But there, too, Martin failed to find a real home. What was someone without a driver's license supposed to do in a city where everyone drives? How could someone who constantly needed other artists around, who needed interaction the way others need solitude, possibly make it in a city where everyone lives and works on their own, miles away from each other? Where everything is planned out days in advance, where you spend hours talking on the phone? In L.A., Max Hetzler said, it took an hour to drive to Mike Kelley's, "and by the time you got there, you were no longer in the mood to see him." Hans Weigand said,

> once in a blue moon there's a party or an opening, but there's no artists' bar. A city of eighteen million people with no artists' bar! That says it all. There is no social life there—nada, nothing—people just sit around the house. In Vienna you knew that if you went down to the Engländer you'd meet a few people. There's nothing like that in L.A. There are no accidents. Everything has to be planned down to the minutiae. Organizing a meal for a couple of artists is like planning a state dinner.

Still, Martin did what he always did: spread out and took over. Within days, Luhring and Augustine said, he had marked his territory—a place to live, place to eat, place to dance, place to work. "It would be an understatement to say that Martin got settled in L.A. quickly. His arrival was more like a Santa Ana, literally taking possession of Venice and Santa Monica."

In both of those parts of western L.A., there were at least a few bars and restaurants Martin could get to on foot. He was always at his best on foot; he took long walks, his way of seeing the world, and everywhere he went he found new material for his art. It was in front of a bank in Venice (California), for instance, that he noticed the gondola up on shore that inspired his gondola sculptures. With Reiner Opoku at his side, Martin even did what no white American would do: he walked across the whole city. They ran into the most trouble in Beverly Hills, where the police stopped them. They set out at six in the morning from Venice and arrived at nine at night on Sunset Boulevard. Martin's summary: "One person has a garage, someone else has two. That's the only difference. Nothing else is going on."

Martin had no garage at all, but he did have two cars: a huge pink boat of a classic Chevy Cabrio he bought for Gabi (who learned to drive in L.A.) and a big black BMW. Later, the BMW ended up in a show with a gondola on its roof, but until then Martin's assistant Jory Felice had to drive him around in it. Even in uniform once.

Jory Felice, a younger artist, lived just ten feet away from Martin's pretty little bright, modern house in Venice. The studio was downstairs and the apartment was upstairs; Albert Oehlen moved in later, too. The night after he first met Martin, Jory knocked on the door and offered his services as an assistant—he had never seen a show of Martin's, he only knew his work from magazines and catalogs, but he liked it and the freedom it radiated. He had gone to art school, where it was "very serious, stifling creativity more than anything else." He liked Martin's looser ways of handling material: "Martin didn't have too much respect for history." And he had never met an artist who talked all the time about art: at the openings Jory was familiar with in California, people talked about the business, the market, who was doing what where and when; a lot of people didn't dare say what they thought of a piece, for fear of stepping on someone's toes. Martin said what he thought. "Other people thought it was impolite"; Jory thought it was generous.

Jory also said, later, that he had no idea what he was getting himself into. In his mind, an assistant was someone who stretched canvases, washed paintbrushes, maybe ran a few errands. Martin, on the other hand, expected his assistants to be always on duty, just like him. The next morning, at nine, it was Martin knocking on Jory's door, and the knocking never stopped, day and night and every hour in between. Martin expected Jory to drop whatever he was doing and be at his service: drive him through the giant city, accompany him to lunch at a restaurant and drinks at a bar, give him music tips. He expected perfect service. Once, at the beginning, they got lost and arrived late for an appointment—Jory Felice had a driver's license but no sense of direction and had never in his life used a city map—and "Martin was furious. He hated to keep people waiting." Sometimes, Felice said, he had the feeling that he wasn't German (efficient, meticulous) enough for Martin.

Felice called their work together "confusing." Half the time, he had the feeling that he wasn't even understanding what Martin said: "His English was okay, but it took months to realize that he spoke his own language." Jory never knew if something Martin said was a game with language, or a mistake, or a misunderstanding. Once, when Martin asked for some "tooth pasta" (because "pasta" and "paste" are the same word in German), Jory thought that it must have something to do with pasta, since Martin loved pasta so much and was always making fun of the phrase "al dente." "Sometimes I pretended to know what he was talking about when I didn't have a clue. It was frustrating. But funny."

The empty house quickly filled up with furniture. One of the first things Martin bought, right at the start, was a gigantic TV, on which he would later watch World Cup soccer games with a huge crowd—the parties were legendary. Jory drove through L.A. early one morning with Tanja Grunert (who had to furnish her booth for an art fair to which she and various other Cologne gallerists had been invited) and bought tables and chairs at junk shops for a few dollars. The designer pieces came later: classics of American modernism. Charles and Ray Eames's workshop was located right around the corner.

Martin set up his own little world there, as Jory Felice said, "a pretty great little world." A world of art. Thea Westreich once said that wherever she visited Martin, she never had the feeling that he was really there in whatever apartment he had. The house in Los Angeles, too, she felt, was more like an exhibition, a workshop. "I don't think he was a nesting animal. So with Martin—what else would you make of a house but art? Not a home."

Even his bed was an art object—an allusion to the works of his German sculptor colleagues. Jory built it out of plywood, following Martin's instructions. To separate it from the open living room, Martin designed a divider that recalled the Berlin Wall; it had a bookshelf on one side and a New York artist's tapestry on the other. Pictures by Jeff Koons, Zoe Leonard, and Michael Krebber hung on the walls, and there was a giant photo of Audrey Hepburn in the studio.

Jory recalls a few moments of domestic bliss: Martin and Jory drawing at the enormous conference table Jory had found and covered in linoleum, Gabi at the stove, Helena in her baby bouncer. Martin called his daughter "Schmusi," and already she was just like him, even if she looked different. Jory thought that even when she was just a few months old, she had her own personality and a great sense of humor: "As if she was making her own jokes."

But before long the fights would start again. The relationship was in crisis. As Martin said later, there wasn't much joy there so he had to supply it himself, which he did by throwing himself into his work. He took a "Runaway Forward Tour" to Stockholm, Milan, Paris, Nice, Graz, "the first time that a tour fit with my life. An exhibition every three days, always in a new city. Still, pretty stressful."

HOLLYWOOD

Martin later brought the American furniture back to Germany and used it as the basis of his biggest work, *The Happy End of Franz Kafka's "Amerika."* Martin had Kafka's unfinished novel with him in L.A., and Jory thinks he remembers that Martin actually wanted to make a movie of it. Like Kafka, who never set foot in the U.S., Martin was less interested in the real country than in his childhood dream of it: one of his drawings that he stamped with "The Happy End of Franz Kafka's 'Amerika'" contained the words "Fury? Lässy? Flipper?" Kafka's novel reminded Max Brod of Charlie Chaplin, who had also fascinated Martin as a child—he dressed as the Tramp character for Carnival one year.

Martin never cared about theater or opera, only the movies. He learned important lessons from the silver screen and its heroes: romance, comedy, adventure, melodrama. That was his metier. Movies survive on exaggeration, on being "larger than life," and yet, unlike opera, "true to life" at the same time. That was another reason he had hired a movie-poster painter in Berlin for his large-format *Dear Painter, Paint For Me* series. If he couldn't make it as a movie star, he wanted to be at least as big an artist as Fassbinder's star Hanna Schygulla, or Bud Spencer. He had had three small parts in

movies during his years in Berlin—in *Gibby West Germany,
Love and Adventure,* and *Portrait of an Alcoholic Woman* (a.k.a.
Ticket of No Return)—and was eager to play a policeman with
a German shepherd. But the roles didn't lead to anything.

He loved the pace, intensity, and complexity of the medium
and felt that the interplay between the actors' performances,
cinematography, sound, story, pacing, and editing added up to
a true *Gesamtkunstwerk.* He loved the terse storytelling of the
movies, where everything had to be said in ninety minutes.
He said once that you would have to go see thirty thousand
exhibitions to get the intensity of one *Kramer vs. Kramer.* He
believed in the power of cinema—its heroism, its stars. When
Christine Hahn told him that she had been with a man who
looked like Jack Nicholson, Martin (who looked rather like
Nicholson himself, friends said) was appalled: how could she
break up with someone who looked like Jack Nicholson?!

He loved the New Hollywood films of the seventies:
Scorsese, Spielberg, Nicholson, De Niro, Ben Gazarra in
Cassavetes's *Killing of a Chinese Bookie.* He did *Taxi Driver*
imitations in bars and was "totally fascinated" with Spielberg's
Close Encounters of the Third Kind, according to Angelika
Margull, especially with how Richard Dreyfus heaps his
mashed potatoes into a mountain and discovers his vision.
"He sang the score over and over and over again."

Martin wanted to be a star like them and was over the
moon when *Vogue* put him on the same page as Richard Gere,
Kevin Costner, Matt Dillon, and Spike Lee in response to
the question of who the New Man was. Martin also felt a
connection with Fassbinder and his clan (Martin's mirrored
screen in the *Peter* show was titled "Rainer Werner Fassbinder").
Now that was great cinema—that was pure melodrama. He
felt a similar connection to the John Huston movie *Under the
Volcano,* in which he recognized himself; he had never seen the

life of an alcoholic presented as realistically and intensely as it was by Albert Finney standing in the shower. Martin then called one of his shows *Give Me the Summer Downtime (Under the Volcano, Part II)*.

He turned scenes from movies into his own works again and again. His whole subway system was inspired by the movies (Truffaut, Buster Keaton, Marilyn Monroe); he naturally went to see the hotel from Billy Wilder's *Some Like It Hot* while in California. He reworked one of the last scenes in Hitchcock's *Rear Window* into his *Hunger* sculptures. He even wrote a piece of film criticism, for *Spex*: a review of *The Color Purple*.

Martin loved the movies, and as always he caricatured and mocked what he liked—for example, by going around in movie costumes, striking Hollywood poses, and having Achim Schächtele take his picture like that for *Slaves of Tourism*. One reason Martin wanted to go to L.A., he said later, was to "get free of his childhood dream." He wanted to appear in one major American movie, even if only as an extra, to show that he had made it. He wanted to be the hero of L.A., Jory Felice said. He imagined it like a scene out of a movie: being welcomed by Hollywood with open arms, the way he himself had welcomed American artists. (Jeff Koons said how welcome he felt when he came to Cologne in 1986, for his first show with Hetzler: "I felt totally at home, Martin took us artists under his wing.")

Instead, Hollywood gave Martin the cold shoulder.

He had pictured Hollywood as wilder and crazier, swankier, not so tame and health-conscious. And he resented that the big stars didn't spend their piles of money on art. (Lawrence Luhring: "Hollywood in general is not interested in art. Their egos are too big.") Martin did not succeed in penetrating the world of the stars. In Hollywood, it wasn't enough to say "Howdy-do, here I am!" "You need someone to introduce you, someone to bring you inside the circle," Jory Felice said, and Martin didn't understand that. You need an agent if you want to be in a movie, even if you don't want to get paid for it. He went to a lot of restaurants frequented by stars like Jodie Foster; once he even managed to talk to Peter Fonda and was thrilled. He liked it less when he saw Sylvester Stallone sitting with his lawyer at the next table—the actor really did behave like Rambo. And it hurt Martin's feelings when Dennis Hopper, who lived near Martin in Venice, didn't even bother to decline when Martin invited him over: "He took it a bit personally," Jory Felice said.

"He seemed to be obsessed with the Hollywood thing," Lawrence Luhring said. "But we didn't go to see any movies, or talk about movies—we only talked about Hollywood power and Hollywood politics."

In Cologne, Stephen Prina said, Martin had his audience in the palm of his hand; in L.A., people simply ignored him. He was used to rejection or hate—that was just a challenge. But he couldn't handle indifference and disinterest. At a party John Baldessari gave in his honor, Martin started telling his jokes as usual and people listened at first but then gradually drifted back to their previous conversations. He was left standing there all alone. Only Raisin, Baldessari's elderly dog, still stood there looking at him—and Martin looked back down at him.

He bought a share in a restaurant called Capri, fittingly enough. "I walked in and saw a woman and knew right away: My people! And of course she wasn't an American. Her roots were somewhere else. She was Swedish." Alona Hamilton Cooke became a friend, and he felt that she understood him. She hung a "glow worm" in the backyard (a chain of tiny little light bulbs) and served noodle casserole at Capri the way he liked it—simple, no poppycock, sometimes just butter or lemon. As an owner, he had bought himself the right to "enforce happiness" on the other patrons with his speeches and endless jokes; no one could defend themselves, and if someone did ever venture to stand up and leave, they wouldn't make it out the door unscathed. There was only one door, and Martin was standing next to it.

John Baldessari was a big fan of Martin's, and Martin saw in him another impassioned networker, teacher, and art enthusiast—a kindred spirit. Baldessari thought photography, painting, and sculpture shouldn't be cordoned off in separate ghettos; he also disliked New York and, like Martin, had only to look at a newspaper to start laughing, because the world was so absurd. And he wished more artists had the courage to fail sometimes: "They think things have to be right from the start. Sometimes I have the feeling that artists are not doing what they really want to do." Baldessari made a poster for Martin, too, as did Jeff Koons.

Despite his feeling so isolated in L.A.—or because of it—Martin's time there was productive. He created lots of sculptures there, his latex pictures, and his "Fred the Frog" series of paintings. Finally, Martin achieved one great success in California: he met John Caldwell, curator of the San Francisco Museum of Modern Art, at the Luhring Augustine Hetzler Gallery, and asked him when he would finally get an exhibition—even Förg had already had one. Caldwell thought it over for a moment and said, "In September?" Martin was speechless. No curator had ever said yes to him so spontaneously.

The show at SFMoMA in 1991 was pure pleasure for Martin. He had finally found a museum person he admired and respected as much as they did him. John Caldwell was a Harvard graduate from a liberal Southern family and was known as a pioneer, even a visionary, of contemporary art on the West Coast. He had already exhibited Richter and Polke. "Howdy-do," Martin faxed from San Francisco to Gisela Capitain, excited and proud and ecstatic: "Everything not cobbled together here, over the moon."

He played accordion with Rüdiger Carl at the opening, dancing around the sculptures. Carl later said that in the photographs, "I always look like the amateur and he looks like the professional. We rented the most beautiful old accordions from dusty music junk shops, usually from old Jewish people. They didn't sound so great any more, but they looked magnificent—like classic old Buicks or Oldsmobiles."

"Well, to have an exhibition in America," Martin said to Jutta Koether in 1991, "I guess you have reached some sort of goal in that! And you'll never achieve that again, the feeling, the first real solo exhibition in a major gallery, or in a foreign city.... San Francisco is something great, I mean, Polke has had exhibitions and installations there."

The exhibition didn't lead to anything, though. Especially not in Germany.

Martin and Max Hetzler in
Hetzler's gallery, in front of
the series "8 Pictures to Think
About Whether We Can
Keep This Up" (1983)

Opening of Martin and Albert Oehlen's show "Women in My Father's
Life," in the Erhard Klein Gallery in Bonn, 1983. Max Hetzler, Werner
Büttner, Albert Oehlen, and Martin singing the miner's song "Glück auf,
Glück auf"

387

The First Viennese Carriage Race, 1985. Competing: Martin and Albert Oehlen. Audience: Three spectators

Martin and Albert Oehlen at the "Officer's Casino"
artist's vodka-drinking contest, Vienna

Martin with the Viennese art dealer and restaurant
owner Kurt Kalb in Club 45

Martin in Peter Pakesch's Vienna gallery (Pakesch on
right; Max Hetzler sitting)

Martin and Gisela Capitain in the *Petra* exhibition, Galerie Gisela Capitain, 1987

Martin signing books with the Cologne book dealer Walther König

Martin after the opening of his *Heavy Fella* show in Cologne, 1991. This speech lasted ca. 150 minutes.

Hans-Jörg Mayer, untitled, 1991 (l. to r.: Charline von Heyl, Michaela Eichwald, Jutta Koether, Cosima von Bonin, Isabelle Graw)

MK1 and MK2: Martin with his collaborator and friend Michael Krebber

Museum Kippenberger: MOMAS on Syros

Martin with Michel Würthle in Rotterdam, 1994

Martin with Kazu Huggler in Tokyo, 1995

Martin with Thomas Bayrle at a noodle restaurant in Tokyo

Martin and Gabi Hirsch with Helena, August 24, 1989. Martin later used this birth-announcement photo for an exhibition invitation.

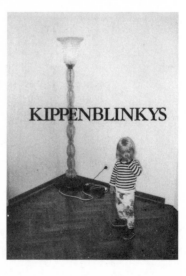

Picture of Helena as the invitation to the *Kippenblinkys* show at David Nolan's gallery in New York, 1991

The Grässlin family, 1993 (l. to r.: Martin, Sabine Grässlin, Anna Grässlin, Franco Ubbriaco, Thomas Grässlin, Grandma Haas, Bärbel Grässlin, Bernadette Grässlin, and Rüdiger Carl)

When Thomas Grässlin got a slot-car racetrack for Christmas in 1981, it was Martin who played with it the most. The Grässlin Family gave him one of his own for his 40th birthday.

Martin and the frog he had carved and crucified

Playing mau-mau in the Paris Bar, Christmas 1995: Martin with his niece Elena

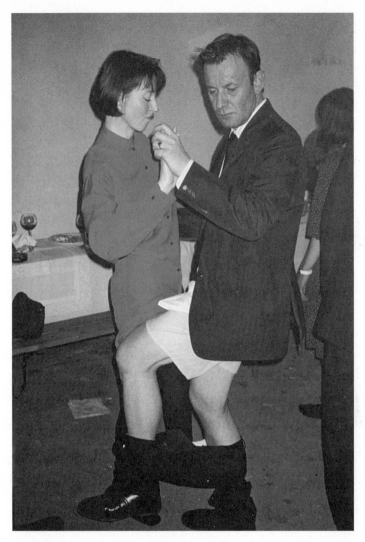

Martin and Gisela Capitain in the Jennersdorf studio

Wedding, 1996, Vienna and
Jennersdorf

Martin and Elena doing the chair dance

Catherine Würthle, Martin, and Michel Würthle

St. Mark's Square, Venice

Martin and Elfie Semotan

399

The egg wagon in Jennersdorf, 1997

The window of Walther König's bookstore with all of Martin's artist books,
arranged the night after his death

CHAPTER EIGHT

FRANKFURT AND KASSEL

For Bärbel Grässlin, who moved to Frankfurt in 1984 to open her own gallery after her years with Max Hetzler, Frankfurt was a no-man's-land. There was no infrastructure for contemporary art in the banking capital, as there had been in Cologne, although Hilmar Hoffmann, the city councilor for cultural affairs, was interested in creating one. The Schirn Kunsthalle opened in 1986, and three years later Kaspar König became head of the Städelschule and served as Founding Director of the Portikus exhibition hall. The Frankfurt Museum of Modern Art opened its doors in 1991, under the direction of Jean-Christophe Ammann.

Frankfurt was also new territory for Martin when he arrived in the fall of 1990 to teach at the Städelschule, though it was a hub between the Black Forest and Cologne, with good international connections. Family connections, too: before he got an apartment of his own, he spent nights at Bärbel Grässlin and Rüdiger Carl's. He would "yank on our sheets bright and early, before we were even awake," Carl said, and would ask for a Bloody Mary, his first cigarette in his hand. Even after he'd found a place, he would often call the gallery at lunch time, twelve noon on the dot—"You could set your watch by it"—or show up at the door in person with a "Howdy-do." After his midday nap the show went on in the evening: eating, drinking, talking, and singing until late at night. Sometimes Grässlin and Carl just didn't answer the phone or turned off the lights in their apartment and sat on the couch in the dark, pretending not to be at home. "We thought: What if he comes by again! What if he comes by again! We just wanted a break, a little peace. We didn't have the energy." They knew for a fact that Martin would never take no for an answer—"You couldn't not be there too often, or it meant you didn't love him." It was a demanding time, Grässlin said. Only after he started his job at the Städelschule and turned his students into constant companions did it get easier—or at least a little easier.

Even before Martin moved to Frankfurt, he had often shown work there: the *Hunger Family* with Bärbel Grässlin and her then-partner Heinrich Ehrhardt, the *Rest Center for Mothers* and *Profit Peaks* pieces, bronze skeletons and bath mats in the *Handful of Forgotten Pigeons* show. According to Grässlin, though, it was "difficult, very very difficult," to sell his pieces in Frankfurt, whether to collectors or institutions. They usually went, in the end, to the people who were Martin's collectors anyway: Uli Knecht in Stuttgart, the Grässlins in Sankt Georgen, or Thomas Borgmann in Cologne. The trade fair organization in Frankfurt did buy one piece, *Two Proletarian Inventresses on the Way to the Inventors' Congress* (recently donated to the Städel), as did Bernd Lunkewitz.

Lunkewitz was a real estate investor with a leftist past; he had bought the Aufbau Verlag (the leading literary and cultural publisher of East Germany) after the fall of the Wall, and the newspaper *Die Welt* had once called him "the Che Guevara of Kassel." Grässlin had arranged with him to rent Martin a place: a big, beautiful prewar apartment on Hedderichstrasse in Sachsenhausen, newly renovated according to his wishes. It was an apartment where Martin really lived, with a long Shaker table as the centerpiece. He received many visitors and students there, there were parties and meals and work, and Martin hung or displayed works from his collection, such as Franz West's day bed.

The rent was much too expensive for him (2,700 marks a month, when he also had the large apartment with Gabi and Helena on Eifelstrasse in Cologne), but the housing that the Städelschule had arranged for him was too depressing. So Martin invited Lunkewitz and his young actress-girlfriend over with Grässlin and Carl, the Filipina cleaning ladies took care of the cooking, there was charm and haggling and negotiating on both sides, with Martin trotting out all the gangster tricks he knew from all the film noir he had seen, and finally he got what he wanted: "A good picture for a good apartment." Martin lived on Hedderichstrasse for two years, rent-free. And Lunkewitz missed his chance to pick a picture—after Martin's death, he thought, it was too late.

Frankfurt was not one of the cities that Martin conquered. He probably never really tried, focusing instead on a few places, some of them private, and a small fixed circle. He only rarely made his presence known beyond that circle—for example, in a reading he organized, which Martin Prinzhorn remembers with a shudder: "He really threw me to the wolves there." Martin insisted that Prinzhorn give a theoretical lecture, which was obviously too dry and academic for the literary audience there (the previous day's speaker was Günter Grass). "It was torture, one of the most painful experiences of my life. Albert Oehlen was there, too, sitting in the second row, actually cringing in pain." Then, after Prinzhorn's theoretical lecture, Martin told Opel Manta-driver jokes* for a whole hour, which didn't go over any better. "Everyone hated us so much, I had never felt anything like it. And that was what he had planned. He had arranged for crazy honorariums, too, and rooms at the best hotel—he always did make incredibly sure that his collaborators were paid well."

---

* The approximate equivalent in German of male "blonde jokes" or "New Jersey jokes."

Martin had a local restaurant in Frankfurt, of course: the Gemalte Haus (Painted House), right around the corner from his apartment. It was an Apfelwein cider bar where he went for breakfast, cheese plates, and lively conversation at the long communal tables. He was on a first-name basis with the retirees who spent their days there, and he even charmed a few single older ladies, according to Carl, until they got to be too clingy and he temporarily took flight. He had other options: he could eat for drawings at the upscale Gargantua, with its brilliant owner Klaus Trebes; he painted a picture of a drunken streetlamp and attached little light bulbs to it for the Colosseo, his regular Italian restaurant. When, after Martin's death, a later owner of the restaurant learned how important Martin was, he took down the picture with its light bulbs and sold it through Sotheby's to Charles Saatchi.

"I wasn't born for school," Martin liked to say, and he didn't like the institution at all. On one of his *Mirror Babies* from 1987, he wrote: "What my father learned in school: French women don't wash, they wear dirty underwear. (I learned a lot, too, but I didn't pay attention.)" Art schools were even worse: he called them "dusty" and "totally unnecessary," "the dumbest educational institutions in the world." The only reason anyone went there "was so you could tell Mommy you'd gotten a degree." He couldn't stand academic types, saying once that "Kippenberger's better academic training" was "feeling, understanding, experience." In his opinion, too much education was damaging for an artist: "The more intelligent types just get in their own way. Naivete is what lets anything elemental show through." Anyone who had been rejected from school, like his assistant Johannes Wohnseifer, or who had left after one or two semesters, like Uli Strothjohann, was automatically on Martin's good side. He recommended that Anna Giehse, a young woman who worked for him in Spain, submit boxes of pralines to the Düsseldorf professors as her application. (She did, and was rejected.)

Martin was firmly convinced that you were born an artist or you weren't—you could learn techniques, but that wasn't art. "Everything else has to emerge from life." And so that was what he told art students: "Get a life!" Another recommendation: they should make catalogs, whether they had an exhibition or not. "A catalog expands your audience and gives an artist a voice outside of critics and criticism. Trade your pictures for food, for a catalog."

It was a real challenge for him to be a teacher, with all the memories of his youth that teaching brought with it. "You have students who are insecure and looking to you for direction, and then you do something or another wrong, I'm responsible for them to some extent," he told Jutta Koether. "And I realize how often I'm talking shit. It's stressful, you can hardly do anything else if you're serious about it. And you get the feeling that you have to start over again from the beginning yourself. It kind of rubs off on you!"

But art was "about developing," for Martin, and he liked helping others develop. "Pedagogy," in Peter Pakesch's view, "was an important driving force for him. He was always a great explainer, he believed in Enlightenment. He wanted to improve people's lives." Martin gave guest lectures in Nice and Amsterdam and at Yale in his later years, and when Isabelle Graw, a guest lecturer at the time at the Vienna academy, met Martin with her students—first at his show, later in a coffeehouse—she was deeply moved to see how patiently he made himself available to answer their questions "for hours and hours."

So now, without a high school diploma, Martin was a guest professor for a year at the Städelschule.

It had been the students' idea to invite him. One lecturer

was skeptical and thought they had chosen him only because he was "hip," but in the end he was offered the position. As a result, he had a fixed salary for the first time in his life—not that he kept much of it himself, spending most of it right away, mostly on his students.

As a teacher, he was free to do what he so liked to do: talk, lecture, make demands, order people around, say what he thought, and show off. "One of my most noticeable characteristics is simply that I show off!" Martin once said. "And then, if you put 'Professor' in front of your name, that is Level 3 Showoffery (works well on taxi drivers)." It was also an opportunity for Martin to meet pretty, young female students and collect a new clan for himself. But it was impossible in the long run to turn into a teacher for life, a public official— that was not his goal. "A little of everything, but all of it intensely" was his motto. So he threw himself into his duties. Teaching became another mode of being an artist, which he wanted to plumb the depths of in all of its forms. The school turned into the stage for his performances, with the students as his costars and audience. They were a loyal public, many of them hanging on his every word. Even before Frankfurt, Martin had undergone a generational shift in his life: he was no longer the ringleader of a group of peers but instead had started collecting younger groupies. His girlfriends were getting younger and younger as well.

The first thing he told his students was that he could not tell them how to make art. You were born an artist or you weren't. At the same time, Martin didn't turn art into a mystery; there was no secret, he said, he never had secrets. He invited anyone who was interested to come visit his studio; he explained his work to them; he worked in public, in bars and restaurants, developing ideas before everyone's eyes. He would show his students whatever he could show them: all the trappings of the business, the mechanics, the players involved (collectors, gallerists, artists, curators); how to put on an exhibition and make a catalog; how to introduce yourself to gallerists or talk to collectors. What he could teach them was an attitude; what he wanted to take from them was their illusions.

And he jumped right in. His strategy for picking students was to weed out the weak ones by scaring them away, beginning with the inaugural lecture he gave in October 1990—or rather, had Michael Krebber give. Almost no one could understand a word of it, and then there was a question-and-answer session the next day that Martin again left to Krebber, not even showing up himself. Out of the twenty-five or so students who enrolled in his class, about half couldn't take Martin's behavior and withdrew. Then there were a few guests who weren't Städelschule students, like Andreas Höhne and Matthias Schaufler, and auditors like Nicole Hackert, a future gallerist who was studying art history.

The students saw right away that Martin was the boss, someone worthy of respect, who seemed significantly older than he was. In fact, he was only thirty-seven, a young man, but to one of his students, Valeria Heisenberg, he came across "like he was fifty." He preached independence and demanded obedience; for the one-time bad student, it was a treat to be the strict teacher, and he went after his students' work rigorously, with a lot fewer carrots than sticks. Nicole Hackert says it was "sometimes totally cruel." When he praised someone—and clearly it was hard for him to give praise—it was often only to keep the student afloat so that he could torpedo him again. "That's how the boys were toughened up for the business."

Tobias Rehberger, a student who had been instrumental in inviting Martin to the Städelschule, said that during

Martin's first studio visit, "the first thing he did was trash everything. There was nothing there that he thought was the least bit good, it was all shit." Bärbel Grässlin said that Martin came back from this first visit truly depressed, thinking it was all worthless, "except for one student with his jigsaw work, that was Rehberger." Classmates say that Rehberger, twenty-five years old at the time, was the only one Martin saw as an artist, not a student. That didn't mean he received much praise—on the contrary, Rehberger felt like the black sheep whenever he disagreed with Martin, or didn't join him at the bar when he'd already made plans to see a movie with his girlfriend. It may have been because Martin saw him as an artist more than he did the other students, Rehberger said, that he "took more blows."

If the students had decided to go to school, Martin was going to make sure it felt like it. Laziness was not tolerated; there were massive homework assignments. The students had to prove themselves with classic exercises, like a drawing of their own hand, an abstract oil painting, and a painted still life (of spaghetti bolognese); they had to take photographs (the Jewish Museum in color; a nude in black and white), write poems, make a record, produce a multiple, keep a journal, make a poster (and attend a silkscreen and work-on-paper class for it), and, finally, produce "1 Kippenberger." The best pieces would be exhibited in the Grässlin-Ehrhardt gallery under the title *Virtuosos of Their Time.* Hundreds of young people came to the opening.

The lesson plan also included playing mau-mau, with the rules printed in the student handouts. Once, when Martin took his class to the Black Forest to visit the Grässlins and tour the Grässlin factory (a field trip called "Where does the dough come from & who hands it over where?" in the syllabus), they played mau-mau, of course, and the pot kept being doubled until one student ended up having to paint the Grässlins' warehouse for a week to pay off his debt. When Thomas Grässlin lost sixteen thousand marks, Martin told him on the spot that he had to pay it by financing the catalog for the student show.

It was called *Virtuosos Before the Mountain* and listed Matti Braun, Andreas Höhne, Adam Kuczynski, Martin Liebscher, Tobias Rehberger, Matthias Schaufler, Markus Schneider, Tatjana Steiner, Ronald Wullems, and Christian Zickler as authors. It was a guidebook through the art world as the students had come to know it through their numerous class trips to Stuttgart, Cologne, Berlin, Zurich, Vienna, New York, and Dublin, and proof that they had learned their lesson. They put together an associative collage in the Kippenberger spirit of names, places, pictures, and events, their own and others' photographs, real and fake quotations. "We thought we owed it to Martin," Rehberger said, "not to make a normal catalog with our works, but something special. We also didn't think it was really appropriate to make a book of our works when Martin didn't think they were so great."

Obviously, Martin didn't guide his students through the major museums on their class trips like a normal professor. They went to the Wilhelma Zoo in Stuttgart because he thought it was pretty, or to the fair in Sankt Georgen. Instead of showing them noteworthy local sites like castles and churches, he introduced them to noteworthy local sandwiches; he took them to see bars more than to see art. In Graz, for instance, students were sent straight to the Frankowitsch, famous for its unique canapés; in Vienna, they went to a cellar bar where you could get "Storm," a kind of Federweisser (a cloudy, fermented grape juice), and then to the King of Hungary for a drink of the house vodka Martin spoke so highly of, before going to a gallery opening.

Martin taught according to Beuys's motto: "Wherever I am is the classroom." That might be his apartment in Sachsenhausen, David Nolan's gallery in New York, on a walk, in a bar, or on the train. Martin rarely set foot in the school itself, so great was his dislike of institutions. He never painted in the studio the school had made available to him as a teacher—he rented one himself, on Bockenheimer Landstrasse, where he worked on his self-portraits and *War Bad* pictures—so they tried to figure out what to do with the space and ended up turning it into a club room, à la Oxford or Cambridge. Of course, every true club needs a club jacket, so the students headed out to the flea markets, found dark blazers, and sewed on the "Friendly Kippenberger Class" emblem. It was a game that had to do with drawing boundaries, demonstrating difference, and showing a bit of arrogance, too, according to Rehberger: "we wanted to piss other people off a bit, pull them out of their comfort zone." And they did.

There was no escape for the students—attendance was mandatory, and not just for a couple of class hours but round the clock. At night they went from bar to bar, drinking a lot, some of the students probably more than was good for them. Not that Martin was ordering them to, "but that's how it is with students sometimes," Rehberger said. "They take it too far or try to be crazier and more out of control than the teacher. We wanted to please Martin, too, and show him how edgy we were. It was all about taking on certain things from Martin and being wild." The next morning, though, Martin would be the first one up, dragging the students out of bed. They weren't there to sleep, after all.

Martin looked at their work and judged it and told stories from his own life, often the same ones over and over. "We spent an enormous amount of time together," Rehberger said:

and no one has *that* many stories that they can tell without repeating themselves. It was strange, though, it usually wasn't annoying, we were glad to hear the stories again. Of course it did happen sometimes, we were like, "Hey! not again, Martin, we've heard that one five times already!" Then he'd say, "What?! Shut up! I'm telling you something! If you don't like it, I'll tell it five more times." He wanted to tell a story and so he had to tell it—not primarily to communicate it to anyone, but so that the story would be told. It was like he wanted to tell it again to himself. He felt at home in these stories.

He also liked to have other people tell him stories—sometimes so he could add them to his own repertoire. As he warned the young gallerist Friedrich Petzel once: "Don't show up in a bad mood, show up with a good story!"

He brought his friends into his classes—Krebber, Carpenter, Schlick (who gave a talk on the Yugoslavian War), Isabelle Graw. Even as a teacher, he didn't see himself as acting alone. He once proposed to Jan Hoet, head of documenta, that he be given a full professorship but that his salary be used to pay for guest speakers to come and give lectures, two or three days per person. Hoet was enthusiastic—"New people all the time, from all over, that would be fantastic!" Then Martin laughed, "Yeah, then I wouldn't even need to show up."

Martin was the magnet and motor for the group—after he left, the cohesion fell apart and everyone went their own way—and the group developed a dynamic of its own, which sometimes included conflict with the other classmates. Sometimes Rehberger caught himself thinking exactly the way Martin thought, "and then I had to wonder, do I really believe that? He was an incredible whirlpool. It was torture

411

sometimes, trying to strike the right balance between the group and myself." He didn't want to do what some of the others did: give up their selves and only do what Martin thought was funny and good. But he didn't want to throw in the towel and run away either: "I was too curious. It really did offer incredibly much . . . I liked Martin, I liked being around him." Especially when they were traveling somewhere together, "he could be supernice, totally like a father."

Martin enjoyed being a father figure and taking students under his wing, and he didn't always understand it when they wanted to have their own experiences without him. Even as a child, he used to call himself "Dad" and always liked taking care of others—on his own terms. He outfitted his godson, our half-brother Moritz, at Brooks Brothers in New York, and gave our nephew Philipp a taste of the world in Cologne by buying him expensive sunglasses, ordering him oysters, and sending him to a whorehouse.

"It made him proud to show us around New York as his class," Rehberger said. "He liked that he was our Daddy." He invited them to take part in his life—at least in his artist-life— and interfered in their private lives in return, "thinking about everyone's life and making suggestions, both good and bad." He told Rehberger, for example, that he had to break up with his girlfriend or else he would never be a good artist. When he didn't, Martin "kept the pressure on for weeks." Martin crossed the same line around others that he had drawn around himself to protect his own private life.

The students liked that he was interested in them, truly interested. Such a close relationship was rare. As Valeria Heisenberg called it, "mutual exploitation." Maybe it was too close. "There was no distance."

THE HOT TOUR

Martin's most devoted student, Matthias Schaufler, who made a policy of submission and devotion (as a classmate put it), asked Martin to give him a particularly hard assignment, and so he did: walk across Africa. The "Hot Tour" was a continuation of the "Magical Mystery Tour," except this time, Martin didn't suffer through it himself—he had a representative do it. "But I wouldn't do it to Schaufler if I wasn't willing to do it myself." He sent the slight, shy student, raised in a Pietist family in the Swabian Alps, off on a thousand-mile trek through Tanzania and Zaire; the journey ended up being almost twice as long. Schaufler had postcards from the "William Holden Company" in his backpack that he had to send to Germany, pre-addressed and preprinted with sayings like "In Search of the Happy End of Franz Kafka," "How many times has Germany won the World Cup and who invented Mickey Mouse," or (in English) "Watch it! All animals are dangerous!"

Martin explained the William Holden Company by saying, "An artist should be curious about the world, a kind of research traveler." The name referred to the Hollywood star who had appeared in several Billy Wilder films and himself owned a safari club in Africa. Holden was a romantic and tragic figure, a hard drinker and heartthrob, who had died, ten years before Martin went to L.A., of the consequences of a drunken fall; his body was found days later. "I don't really know why," Holden had said once, "but danger has always been an important thing in my life—to see how far I could lean without falling, how fast I could go without cracking up."

Matthias Schaufler was on the road for three months—June to September 1991—and his travel report, reworked by Martin, was exhibited that same year in the Wewerka & Weiss gallery along with pictures by the African artist Chéri

Samba, from Zaire, whom Martin first heard about from Michel Würthle.

Martin wasn't a teacher who gave lectures and afterward felt drained and exhausted. "It wasn't a professorial passing-on of knowledge," Thomas Bayrle said, "but an exchange, a give and take." Martin was an artist, not a pedagogue: he wanted something from his students, too, and he got it. He made their works his own—his students drew and painted and made sculptures for him. Adam Kuczynski, for example, made a series of watercolors, each showing a book with a magnifying glass resting on top, as Merlin Carpenter had also done for his first show in Hamburg. (Kuczynski now works as a doctor in London.) Rehberger built sculptures for Martin's exhibition at the Pompidou Centre (brooms on carpets); Andreas Höhne and Tatjana Steiner added things to Martin's paintings. He was not a master who expected his pupils to imitate his style; he wanted them to work for him, in his spirit, but in their own way. "That was something you could handle only if you had the right stuff yourself, intellectually," in Bayrle's view. "For others, for the people who internalized it too much, it was a dangerous game."

He didn't say that the best artist in his class would get a show at Forum Stadtpark in Graz—he took the students to Styria, everyone went to the casino together, and "poor Bleich-Rossi had to hand each of us a thousand marks in cash," Rehberger said. "Whoever lost the money fastest—it ended up being Tatjana Steiner—got the exhibition. It was a kind of performance piece of Martin's." The curator Elisabeth Fiedler interpreted the action like this: "He didn't want to give preference to anyone, so he made a game out of it."

Rehberger said that he didn't feel exploited—he thought it was fun. "It was clear from the beginning that we would be making work for him. That was part of the education, and it was also important to get a handle on this whole question of authenticity, of authorship." What does the artist do himself, what do others do for him, and how does he integrate the two? Martin shook their image of the artist to the core. In addition, Rehberger said, Martin was very generous, going out on the town with them, buying them meals and drinks, and sharing his knowledge and his contacts with them. "So it was fine to give a little back."

Aki Bleich-Rossi in Graz was only one of the many gallerists Martin introduced them to. In New York, for example, they met Leo Castelli, Andrea Rosen, and David Nolan. His goal was not to give his students sales opportunities or launch their careers as much as to show them, as promised, the art world as a real place. He was doing the opposite of what most art schools do when they create a protected space in which their students can explore without any thought to exhibitions. Valeria Heisenberg said, "He challenged us to work more consciously, reflect more, be more self-aware. He was very critical of everything romantic and ineffable and always resisted the idea that there was anything you couldn't talk about."

Martin told his students, "I can't make a masterpiece every day." That was one of his most important lessons, says Rehberger, who is himself now a professor and prorector at the Städelschule, "the fact that quality emerges from an oeuvre, from an interaction, not just from an individual work." Martin also taught him a certain amount of defiance, "that you have to never throw in the towel, but always keep going, keep scrambling and pushing on." And always keep a certain mistrust of yourself; bet on discomfort; don't relax when you think you've found something good; don't always continue along the safe track, but look for new paths. "That you don't say *I always put green on top and blue on the bottom, because it works so well,* but instead you're suspicious of green on top and blue on the bottom and try to get a handle on what it's really about by putting orange on top and pink on the bottom. That you always approach your own work differently every time."

Martin didn't influence only the students. He left his traces at the Städelschule, too, Thomas Bayrle thinks: "He brought dynamic thinking, the courage to try collage as a form of art and of life." After two semesters, though, Martin's time as a guest professor was up. He would have liked to keep teaching in Frankfurt—he liked being with young people and influenced many young artists. "He opened their minds," his New York gallerist Janelle Reiring said, "precisely by being so open himself and because there were no sacred cows for him: he called every rule and every fact into question." But Kaspar König, the head of the Städelschule, had no interest in keeping him on. Bärbel Grässlin had noticed Martin and König "suspiciously eyeing each other" in Frankfurt; with their huge egos and need to take charge of everything, they were too similar to like each other.

König was a real down-to-earth character, ten years older than Martin, who had left school to apprentice with Rudolf Zwirner and was known as the curator of several important shows: *West-Art* in Cologne (1979), *from here* in Düsseldorf (1984), and *Sculpture Projects* in Münster (1987). He had once called Martin's art "party-basement painting" and never included him in his exhibitions. But they were two of a kind, and König was as serious about art as Martin. Before he came to Frankfurt, he had taught "Art and the Public" in Düsseldorf—exactly Martin's specialty. Martin said to Jutta Koether in 1991 that "Kasper is the best" museum person "in Germany. Because he really travels around and looks at lots and lots of things. At least he has the information he needs to turn it into something." Similarly, Max Hetzler said that "Martin didn't despise König," unlike so many other curators, "because he knew that he wasn't corrupt." Today, König is director of the Ludwig Museum in Cologne, and in the end he did invite Martin to show work at a sculpture exhibition in Münster—in 1997; Martin did not live to see the opening. Bärbel Grässlin saw the invitation as a "late atonement."

KIPPENBERGER'S DELIGHTFUL CLASS

Martin's Frankfurt students hardly noticed when the official semester was over—the instruction had never been limited to school, and the students continued to travel with their teacher to his openings. Martin kept his Hedderichstrasse apartment, too. "When Martin was in town," Rehberger said, "you got a call at 10 a.m. saying where you needed to be at 11, usually the cider bar, then you talked until 2:30, Martin had his midday nap at 3, but by then you had already made plans where to meet that evening, so at 6 or 7 you met up again out somewhere, or went to his place and cooked together."

In fact, the crowd of students only grew, since students from Kassel joined and mingled with the students from Frankfurt. Martin taught one more semester, Winter 1991–92, at the polytechnic (*Gesamthochschule*) in Kassel, and this time it was a professor who invited him, since so many other teachers were about to retire or had just retired. Why not? Kassel was hardly an elite academic institution—it was a polytechnic—and Kassel itself was strange enough to be interesting: a capital of contemporary art every five years, for documenta, and a provincial wasteland in between. It was a hybrid location, but with good train connections, and not far from Frankfurt, where Martin continued to live when he wasn't in Cologne or somewhere else.

While teaching in Frankfurt, he continued to travel

constantly; Bayrle said he would hop into a train to Cologne at five in the afternoon and sometimes came back to Frankfurt that same night—"and if he missed the last train, he would get someone to drive him." All while squeezing in a few days in Graz or Vienna, a side trip to Kassel, an exhibition in New York, a stay in Syros... "He always had to be jumping back and forth between four or five places. It was like a transportation hub with shipping containers being transferred from one train to the next." Bayrle used the well-known image from Einstein's theory of relativity to explain Martin's overcoming of space and time: "Several trains are passing each other at the same time but at different speeds. That's how he overtook time itself. Actually, he was as fast as the stock market: when it closes in Hong Kong, it opens in Frankfurt." As a result, Bayrle wasn't surprised in the least when Martin showed up one day in precisely the noodle bar in Tokyo where Bayrle was sitting with his wife, "and Tokyo has thousands of noodle shops." The first thing Martin said was exactly what the Bayrles had just been thinking: "The owner looks like Bill Clinton."

Martin continued his work in Kassel with different students but the same methods. Again he chose his students by scaring everyone else away: he had just returned from L.A., with jet lag, and thought he was there only to sign the contract, when in fact he was supposed to give his inaugural lecture. So he told jokes for ninety minutes. By the end, the hundred or so listeners were down to six, so he stopped and told them, "OK, you're my students. Now that you survived that, let's go get some Italian food."

"Wow, super!" thought Sven Ahrens, today a gallerist in Cologne. For three semesters he had felt "stalled at the polytechnic, with the motor running but going nowhere. Now we were off." Ahrens was quickly made the class representative, and the Kassel class had its emblem, too: a waiter's arm with a napkin draped over it. Again there were homework assignments like "draw what you feel like on the inside." At one point Martin prescribed a journey into the self, without food or drink—he himself was on a fasting cure when he started teaching in Kassel.

The Kassel students had not only a class trip to New York but also an exhibition of their own that he had arranged with his gallerist David Nolan. They showed their little bronze worms. "Sucking on candies," Martin called it, "to test out the system by throwing them into the middle of it. They flew to New York as artists and were faced with real little illusion-killers." "He let us do it," his student Ina Weber said, "but at the same time he told us, 'You're my students, don't embarrass me!'" He co-financed the catalog, and before they left (he didn't go that time), he assigned them drawing homework, corrected and signed the results, and handed them back for the students to sell to Nolan for a good price, so that the poor students would have some spending money in New York.

In return for his giving them "comfort and drinks" (as he put it to a journalist), the aspiring artists had to find him information on train connections or go save a scarf he had left behind in a hotel room. After all, the Kassel class's motto was "Independence." In place of the usual academic fare, he offered them "confrontation with all sorts of information," which included going to the movies or soccer matches with them and holding class in an Italian restaurant, a hotel room, a dining car, at the opening of the Bruno Brunnet gallery in the only pedestrian zone in Berlin—anywhere but in school. "He thought the atmosphere there was horrible." And the point wasn't to paint as a group, but to talk with each other. "It was always exciting when he was there," Ahrens said. One time, "Kippenberger's Delightful Class" (as he called them) showed up for a Great Battleship Tournament against

Werner Büttner's class from Hamburg: high noon in front of the Hochzeitshaus in Hamelin, as announced in the city newspaper, and "Captain Büttner and Captain Kippenberger are expected to attend in person." Martin was seriously upset that Büttner's students won.

Ina Weber joined his class as "a great fan, he was a hero of mine." She later said that the whole course of instruction was "a tug-of-war, a test of strength. Martin was very generous and supportive, but he could also be very cruel. You had to be able to stick it out."

He bought sausages and mulled wine for the students at the Kassel Christmas market, gave them assignments (they had to sing "The Glow-Worm"), and suddenly announced: "OK, now we're going to see the head of documenta, to talk about whether I'm taking part." Jan Hoet's office was right around the corner, so in they walked, a crowd of eight people, with a "Howdy-do!" As Sven Ahrens described it, "Jan Hoet was extremely scared at first, and then masterful." The conversation lasted two hours and later filled an entire issue of *Sun Breasts Hammer*, the journal of the Lord Jim Lodge. "Martin was trying to take the ball right into Hoet's court, and Hoet kept trying to give it back." The result: Martin was still not included in documenta IX (1992), but he would make a poster for it. And it ended up being something pretty substantial: a moving, funny self-portrait as an artist.

Martin set up one of his drunken lampposts in front of the neoclassical building on Friedrichsplatz in Kassel, replacing the inscription "Museum Fridericianum" with the word "MELANCHOLY". The lamppost was bent, with a large teardrop on its crown, and looked like it was bowing its head to the museum or to Walter de Maria's *Vertical Earth Kilometer*, which Martin had set his gaudy lamppost right on top of.

For the sixth documenta, in 1977, de Maria, the American

minimalist, had drilled a hole a kilometer deep in Friedrichplatz and filled it with two-inch-wide brass rods attached together. Martin liked to make fun of de Maria's divalike appearance— for instance, the way he wore a hat and sunglasses so that no one would recognize him but thereby attracted even more attention. He was very proud to have the only photograph of de Maria, who never let himself be photographed—and he made a poster out of it. But he respected the artist's work. Whenever he was in New York, he told Jutta Koether, he went to see de Maria's 1979 *Broken Kilometer*, a sequel to the Kassel piece that was permanently installed there: "I need that, just to take a peek into the room and feel good, then leave. I have no idea what de Maria was really trying to do when he made it."

He continued de Maria's work in Kassel with his own methods—documenta visitors couldn't see Martin's lamppost any more than they could see de Maria's underground kilometer, because it wasn't there. He had placed it there only to take the photograph for the poster.

The documenta IX poster contains everything about Martin as an artist: his irony and melancholy, respect and irreverence, calculation and improvisation, the possibilities and impossibilities, and the juxtaposition of modern popular culture at its most trivial (Martin had found the motif of the drunken lamppost on a joke postcard) with European cultural history (Museum Fridericianum, opened in 1779, is considered the first public museum on the European continent)—a light bulb in front of the Enlightenment. It thematizes both the artist's solitary existence and the artist's context in history and contemporary life: the contexts in which he finds himself and into which he inserts himself. It's all there, everything we know about Martin, including the chutzpah with which he occupied another's artwork and put the profane right in front of the sublime, confusing the public and annoying the organizers. This poster of a weeping lamppost shows how Martin managed to be "in" and "out" at the same time, participating in the art world and evading it—and also how other people managed to include him and nonetheless exclude him. Finally, the poster is proof of the power of the spoken word: it was only through talking that Martin managed to be allowed onto documenta's wall of posters at all (even if not into the show itself). "Never give up before it's too late," as one of his slogans runs. Without fear of embarrassment or humiliation, he simply charged right up to Jan Hoet's office and quoted the German equivalent of the saying about the light at the end of the tunnel: "When you think you can't go on, a little light appears from somewhere." Martin liked Hoet's idea of putting a lamppost on the de Maria: "Someone has to protect art," he laughed. "And art always starts with a light going on somewhere." (The German term is *Erleuchtung,* an inspiration or epiphany.)

Being included in documenta was actually Martin's greatest wish. As mentioned above, he loved to tell the story of how our grandfather had taken him to the first documenta in a stroller, when he was two, in 1955. He was invited in 1986, by Manfred Schneckenburger, but in the end he turned it down because no one got in touch with him after the initial invitation to discuss what he wanted to do. He thought that an invitation would mean involvement with him as an artist. Finally, eleven years later, he was in documenta with his subway entrance—but he died before the opening.

KIPPENBERGER ART ASSOCIATION

"Revises his address book, parting from several friends": when Martin wrote his artist bio, this was his entry for 1993.

Becomes increasingly convinced that the music world is defunct and the theater is insular. From now on, concentrates on recommendations from people previously unknown to him. Is constantly at odds with the art market (which thinks him crazy). Runs the 'Kippenberger Art Association' in the Fridericianum in Kassel until 1995.

Veit Loers was the head of the Fridericianum Museum Kunsthalle, an effort, dating from 1988, to give contemporary art a forum in Kassel during documenta's off years. He invited Martin to exhibit there, and Martin wanted to set up a kind of anti-documenta, but that would have been too expensive. Instead he created an anti-art association, because against Loers's will, the Kassel Art Association had been moved inside the museum. For two years, Martin used the Kippenberger Art Association to show works by his friends: Uli Strothjohann, Cosima von Bonin, Albert Oehlen, Michael Krebber, Johannes Wohnseifer. He also showed erotica from his collection. He had given up teaching by then.

COME ON, JUPP, LET'S SPLIT THE PIE

In the same artist bio, Martin described his student days as follows: "1972: Starts educating himself at the Academy of Fine Arts in Hamburg. Breaks off his studies after sixteen semesters." Of all Martin's father figures, models, and teachers, Rudolf Hausner, his professor in Hamburg, was doubtless the least important. Sigmar Polke played a much bigger role; Martin had known him for a long time when he came to teach at the academy toward the end of Martin's time there, and Albert Oehlen and Georg Herold had already studied with him. "Even though I was not one of his students, I followed him around everywhere." He saw Polke in bars and restaurants, not in the school. They were both regulars at the Ganz.

Polke, as cofounder of "capitalist realism," had taken on the real world (with themes like "Office Party" or "Weekend House") in a period when abstraction still ruled in art, and he did so in a style that took up *"Bäckerblume* aesthetics,"* as Werner Büttner put it. Postwar German art had seldom seen so much trash, so much irony, and such variety. Polke was the great liberator of postwar German art and, at twelve years older than Martin, a leading figure for him. When Martin was given a show at the San Francisco Museum of Modern Art, the fact that Polke had also exhibited there that was one reason Martin thought it was "great," and it was also a special challenge: "It doubles the risk, of course, you better not show shit." No distance was too far to travel to see a Polke show. And in 1990, when Martin already had quite a name for himself, he told Heliod Spiekermann, full of pride, "Polke said hi to me!"

An American critic once called Martin "a child of Duchamp and a student of Polke." But despite Polke's importance to Martin as an artist, he played a much more ambiguous role for him as a person. Known in the seventies as a "party terror" (in curator Bice Curiger's words) and "an epicurean radicalinski" (Sven Ahrens), Polke grew more and more hostile in his later years and could sometimes be downright poisonous. "He's vicious now and then," Martin could report from personal experience. When they met in Cologne after both of them had moved there, Martin expressed his admiration for Polke, who brushed him off and showed his contempt for the younger man. Polke in person was as humorless as his pictures were witty (although by the eighties, in Curiger's view, Polke "was

---

* *Bäckerblume* is the journalistically lightweight newspaper given away for free in bakeries across Germany, comparable to *Metro* in the U.S.

finished with irony," too). There was a love-hate relationship between Martin and Polke.

With Beuys it was different. What Martin liked about Beuys, the über-father, were precisely his personal qualities: his warmth, humor, generosity, melancholy, pedagogical engagement, and, not least, the fact that he was a family man. An English critic wrote, with reference to Martin's Tate Modern show in 2006, that Martin hated Beuys; nothing could be further from the truth. Along with Fassbinder, whose intensity in even the longest movies Martin so admired, Beuys was for Martin the great exception in German art. And, he said, "I'll be an exception someday, too. The others can't keep up with that speed of life."

"Warhol and Beuys were Martin's two important models," in Gisela Capitain's view: they had pushed back the boundaries of art, or moved past them altogether, and shown that being an artist meant much more than standing in your studio hard at work in front of an easel. In addition, neither was competition for Martin, a fact he especially appreciated. Warhol and Beuys embodied the seventies, he thought, while he embodied the eighties. As Veit Loers, the curator, said, Martin's "ambition was to be Beuys's successor."

"Come on, Jupp," Martin said to Beuys once (according to Meuser), "let's split the pie." Meuser said, "He loved him. Except for the shamanism, that didn't mean a thing to Martin."

Joseph Beuys, like Martin, stood behind his art with his whole being—he just put it out there and brashly said, *That's how it is.* He made people pay attention to contemporary art and the figure of the artist like no one else in postwar Germany; he was the first artist to become famous outside of artist circles. And Beuys bought his famous hats in London, along with all his clothes, from shirts to shoes, only the finest quality. He liked to drive Cadillacs and Bentleys occasionally.

—These were also things that Martin liked about him, of course.

By the late seventies, Beuys was the best-known German artist and also the one whose work fetched the highest prices. He was the first German given a solo show by New York's Guggenheim Museum (although Beuys had an ambivalent relationship to America, much like Martin's). There was no getting around Beuys for a young German artist, especially one who loved publicity and self-presentation as much as Martin did.

Beuys, Warhol, and Bruce Nauman were "the bellwethers, the superstars" that Martin criticized Jan Hoet's documenta for not including—even though Martin had no patience for Nauman's privacy and avoidance of public appearances ("he never sets foot outside his little house"). Warhol and Beuys put themselves out in the world, "with love," too, as Martin emphasized. "You have to have an artist who conveys that, but he also has to be ready to show himself in public. Like Mr. Picasso, he stepped into the bullring and let everybody gape at him and did it with love."

Martin referred to Beuys over and over again. His poster for the Forum Kunst Rottweil exhibit in 1982 had depicted him in a Beuys-style felt suit. The Darmstadt Landesmuseum had the most important collection of Beuys's work at the time, and Beuys had famously had himself photographed there in front of a dinosaur skeleton, so Martin's invitation for his show there depicted Martin in front of a (smaller) pair of antlers. The Darmstadt curator, Johann-Karl Schmidt, interpreted Martin's message like this: "I am the little Beuys. I am the next Beuys. I am the parodic Beuys."

In 1972, at a panel discussion at Kunstring Folkwang, someone accused Beuys of talking about everything under the sun except art, and Beuys replied, "But everything under the sun is art!"* At a time when everyone at the Düsseldorf Academy "was kept miles away from anything concrete," as Meuser knew from personal experience, "where Informel was king, and then Minimalism," Beuys the Fluxus artist was the man who opened the doors and the windows.

Beuys had also made his own life the foundation of his art; his works were, in fact, much more autobiographical, more private, than Martin's. Martin didn't have any patience for the messianic element in Beuys or for his political involvement with the Green Party (he was one of its cofounders in 1979). Martin had his feet too firmly planted on the ground for anything mythical or magical; but he liked how the Master used earthly materials, like margarine, or stuck a light bulb into a lemon and called it a "Capri Battery." Or that Beuys supposedly once told his student Blinky Palermo (an artist Martin also admired), "Throw away your pipe, it'll make your paintings better," since in the teacher's opinion the student had something about him that was too stocky and complacent, "like a real pipe-smoker." It was a piece of instruction that could have come from Martin. He didn't agree with Beuys's view that every person is an artist, but he no doubt appreciated that Beuys took the side of the applicants rejected from the academy, occupied the academy offices with them, and had to leave the academy as a result.

Artfan asked Martin what his relationship was to Beuys, and he gave a very detailed answer:

> He was a man with an aura, and I was in the very last generation. I met him here and there over the years. We had our little jokes. Little private jokes. One time he came to the academy in Hamburg and

* The German phrase for "everything under the sun" is "God and the world"—Beuys literally said, "But God and the world are art!"

went through my absolutely dumbest pieces and then discussed them with me in private. And then scolded me. That must have been one of the worst hours of his life. But on the other hand there were sympathies that lasted many many years. I was always the good-for-nothing, that's how I felt. I mean, he was *the* super-being. If you haven't spent time with someone like that, it's impossible to understand. To see something of his appearance, his sweetness, his humor, it was really something. He was born the same year as my father, from the same part of the world, there were a lot of parallels. Today I'm a bit more critical of him but he put out so much power, so much material, the thousands and millions of mistakes too that he made out in the open just as publicly available as the rest, it was all very public.... I saw his kids growing up, from documenta to documenta, when they'd turn up. They kept getting bigger. They used to be so tiny.

There were other contemporaries who influenced and inspired Martin, of course. Dieter Roth, for example, a friend of Michel Würthle's who was also a restless spirit, constantly changing addresses and bringing together his life and his art. "This endless creativity in Roth, it influenced Martin," Max Hetzler said. "He measured himself against Roth's hyper-productivity." Gerhard Richter's elegant personal appearance impressed Martin in his early years; he didn't understand Richter's paintings, as he later said himself, "but I liked them, and they took me a few steps farther along my own path." Later, Martin felt that Richter was making things too easy on himself.

Picasso, the epitome of the modern artist in our childhood, interested Martin as a person—as *the* art star of the 20th century. He measured himself against Picasso's fame and productivity, while also making fun of Picasso's vanity by copying his famous pose in underwear. But as an artist, Picabia was more important for him. A French Dadaist and colleague of Duchamp's (whose ready-mades were, of course, an enormous influence on Martin), Picabia was a master of bad taste far ahead of his time. As an "artist's artist," he is considered an important forerunner of Pop Art: he worked from photographs and other models and constantly changed his style (Impressionist, Cubist, Dadaist, orphic, ironic, Surrealist, erotic, realistic, Informel), but not out of insecurity. "I am always completely convinced by everything I'm doing," he said. The critic David Hickey wrote of Picabia that he left no stone unturned, no rule unbroken, no boundary uncrossed, and that he did not take any style for granted. Picabia himself once said, "The head is round so that thinking can change direction." And "I hope I can someday write on the wall of my house: 'Artist in every area.'"

CHAPTER NINE
COLOGNE YEARS: THE END

At the beginning of the economic and political crisis, Max Hetzler returned most of his artists' archives to them before he moved to Berlin, in effect giving them notice. "Hetzler's handing out pink slips," Martin announced at his last show with him, in November 1992. From then on his main gallerist would be Gisela Capitain. Hetzler's actions deeply wounded Martin, for whom loyalty was always so important. That said, the break was not final, probably because Martin was too loyal to allow it; a few months before his death, he showed his Jacqueline pictures in the Paris gallery run by Hetzler's wife, Samia Saouma.

At least since Hetzler's move to the Ungers building, Martin had felt more at home with Capitain anyway. She originally focused on smaller pieces (drawings, editions, illustrations, multiples), and her gallery was smaller, with a more intimate atmosphere (not least because there was less money involved). Hetzler's motto was "If it's small you get nothing at all, Make it large so you can charge." But big paintings required a bigger infrastructure, more risk, more stress.

Martin didn't give up painting—he continued to paint until his death—but in the late eighties he had discovered a new medium, one that fit perfectly with his constant roaming around and, in fact, grew out of it: he started drawing on hotel stationery. Here, too, necessity was the mother of invention: since he was so often traveling to places in the world where he couldn't get the paper he was used to drawing on, he simply took what he found in his hotel rooms. This gave him a working foundation that had what he always wanted: variety, surprise, a challenge. "Every kind of paper behaves differently with the pen. The result is a kind of dialogue." Another kind of dialogue resulted from the hotel's logo and font and his drawing: every one of the pictures turned into a collage. Martin was so excited by his discovery that he had people bring back or send him hotel stationery from all over the world.

He could draw anywhere—on a Greek sidewalk café, in Capitain's gallery, at his curator's kitchen table in St. Louis. Betsy Wright Millard said, "It was like he wouldn't have known what to do with his hands otherwise." Now he had drawing as a way to work alone without being alone.

Martin went to the Gisela Capitain Gallery on Apostelstrasse every day, drank his wine there, drew, told stories, gave advice. Martin had an "exclusivity system," Capitain said. "If you were there, you were there for him. Completely." She was Martin's oldest and closest friend, his favorite dancing partner as well as his gallerist, and he could talk about anything with her, including things he didn't bring up in public—and there were such things, even though everyone thought he spread his whole life out for everyone to see, at the restaurant table, in his books, and on his canvases.

Capitain had already handled personal tasks for Martin—leases, bank transactions, correspondence with health insurance companies, communications with his tax adviser. He knew how organized and meticulous she was, and she managed not only his various moves but really his whole life. Even when Hetzler was still officially representing him, Martin had hired Nicole Neufert to run a new incarnation of Kippenberger's Office (this time really just an office) in Capitain's gallery's back room, with its own visiting cards and stationery. Capitain had trained Neufert, preparing the important shows in San

Francisco and for the Vienna Festival Week (*Deep Throat*) with her and Uli Strothjohann. When Neufert got sick in the summer of 1992, while Martin was still in Syros, Capitain hired Johannes Wohnseifer as her successor.

Wohnseifer professionalized the Office. He spent his first few weeks organizing the photographs, slides, and correspondence from recent years; later, they took back all the work Martin had stored in an expensive art shipping company's warehouse to store it themselves. This material included not only Martin's unsold works and his own collection (in fact, it was in the early nineties that he seriously started buying and trading other artists' work) but also his mountains of boxes containing source material.

For Wohnseifer, it was a "dream job." A native of Cologne, he was a long-time fan who had been interested in Martin and his work since he was a teenager and had read about him in *Twen* in 1982 when he was 14. He had all of Martin's catalogs. He had observed him in the Alter Wartesaal restaurant and disco in Cologne and listened to him at the Broadway—"I had never seen anything like that, an artist working in interaction with others"—and he studied the sketches that Martin left behind on napkins and scraps of paper there. But he had never dared to talk to him.

When Martin came back from his stay in Syros and first set eyes on Wohnseifer, he was furious: until then he had always found his own assistants, all real firecrackers, and now here was someone just stuck in front of him? When they sat down and started to work—Wohnseifer tense and insecure, Martin surly and in a bad mood—Wohnseifer brought out a photograph he had taken for Martin of an engraving of an Indian chief in the window of the Buchholz antiquarian shop. Wohnseifer had realized that the Indian looked remarkably like Martin. "Then he was suddenly fired up—'Where'd you

get that? Unbelievable! Come on, let's go, we need to talk.'"
First they went to the store, and the engraving was gone,
but Buchholz gave him a copy, which Martin would use in
1994 for the invitations to his birthday party in Rotterdam
the night before his major opening *The Happy End of Franz
Kafka's "Amerika."* Then they went to a beer garden, where
Wohnseifer ordered his usual cola. Martin was highly amused
to suddenly have an assistant who never drank alcohol except
at openings.

Despite his worship of Martin (or perhaps because of it),
Wohnseifer always kept a certain healthy distance from him
and never became one of the groupies who thought they had to
do everything Martin did, but even worse. He not only didn't
go drinking with Martin, he also used the formal "*Sie*" with him
for a long time, and called him "Mr. Kippenberger" ("for me
he was someone worthy of respect"), which Martin liked very
much at first, until finally it got to be too ridiculous. Wohnseifer
was fourteen years younger than his boss and a gentle, slight,
cheerful person; the difference between their temperaments
and the distance Wohnseifer maintained resulted, after the
difficult beginning, in the most relaxed assistant-relationship of
Martin's life, which lasted until Martin's death. "We had a lot of
fun together," Wohnseifer said.

A certain geographical distance was probably good for the
relationship, too. They discussed a lot on the phone or by fax
while Martin was living in Frankfurt, Sankt Georgen, Tokyo,
Syros, and Jennersdorf, and working in Paris or Rotterdam or
traveling somewhere else.

In between, when Martin did come back to Cologne,
Wohnseifer was always happy: "We had four or five days
of causing a ruckus." They discussed everything intensely
over lunch at Ezio, an Italian restaurant, and Wohnseifer
enjoyed the long nights, since there were only a few of them.

Sometimes they would sit back down together at four in the morning to take notes and make plans, and Martin would give precise instructions about things Wohnseifer would have to do the next day. "It was extremely concentrated."

During these same short visits to Cologne, Martin also discussed sculpture projects with Uli Strothjohann, looked at books at König's, maybe planned one or two new books there, too, met with friends and with his "favorite collector" (as he called Thomas Borgmann—unlike some collectors, Martin thought, he was a dealer with a real sense of art), visited Gabi and Helena, and ate pasta and talked with Capitain at the Trattoria Toscana. And he always invited himself over for some home cooking at the house of Gundel Gelbert, the used book dealer, and her husband, Hans Böhning; they had started collecting Martin's works back in the early eighties. He felt at home there—they were a pleasant change from the many pretentious denizens of the art scene. He also got someone to drive him out to the Bergisches Land (often overnight) to visit his dentist Heliod Spiekermann, her husband Hubertus, and their daughters in their idyllic, isolated house. He was spoiled in the maternal atmosphere there and by the housekeeper as well, whom he asked for a peeled soft-boiled egg in the mornings, in a glass, with chives, and fresh squeezed orange juice. Her reaction: "Mister Kippenberger is a real gentleman." All the solicitous care he received didn't stop him from wanting to seduce the young daughter, however.

Unlike most of his assistants, Wohnseifer rarely painted, drew, or built sculptures for Martin; most of his duties concerned organizing the various exhibitions. After Krebber had lifted Martin out of a depressive moment once with the comment "Art is an allotment garden," *Schrebergarten* in German, Martin was interested in the history of the Schrebers: the strict father, who had invented that type of gardening and after whom it was named, and his gifted, sensitive son, Daniel Paul Schreber, who took refuge in insanity. Wohnseifer had to get Martin a copy of Daniel Paul Schreber's book, *Memoirs of My Nervous Illness,* in which Martin found lots of wonderful sentences and phrases that he had printed and cast in plexiglass. Then they assembled pictures together: Martin squirted paint onto the canvas with a caulking syringe, Wohnseifer blindly pulled the plexiglass sayings out of a cardboard box ("each one was as good as the next anyway"), and they affixed them to the picture. Only when it was time to put one on the forehead of a portrait of Schreber did Martin say, "now we need an especially good one," but Wohnseifer reached into the box blind again—and ended up with an especially good one: "This is to a certain extent unbearable."

"That was a great aspect of working with Martin," Wohnseifer later said. "This balance: allowing in chance, but still knowing exactly what he wanted."

SYROS

He had to get away—from Cologne, from Frankfurt, from Sankt Georgen; from the art business, the ever-increasing pressure, the alcohol. The farther away, the better. And so Martin headed off to the edge of Europe, a small, hard-to-reach Greek island in the Cyclades that had nothing to offer but work and weeds, ruins and comfort. In the globalized art market, with every place like everywhere else, Syros managed to be somewhere different: in the middle of nowhere. Starting in the early nineties, Martin spent a couple of months a year there with Michel and Catherine Würthle.

"Between stubby laurel bushes" and "chunks de stone," he wrote in a letter, he had the emptiness he needed, the emptiness "that is open to so many things." He could experience on Syros "the changing acupuncture from coming there + flying warmth—little lightning bolts of good mood beams, an adorable jellyfish hugging you unmoist roughguy frontfan + last of all 1x/wk kidfishsticks fried with lemon + a little Heinz ketchup."

When Michel told his wife for the first time, in 1991, that Martin was coming, she was "terrified. I thought now we'd have to go out every night and booze and cause a scandal." But when he stepped off the little plane beaming, she was disarmed. They would end up having a lot of fun together. Martin was happy to drink milk while on Syros.

Catherine knew the wild life only too well, having spent most of the seventies and eighties with Michel in Berlin. After the birth of their daughter, Carolina, she returned to her native Greece to spend most of the year in the house on Syros with her mother next door, and Michel came whenever he could get away from the Paris Bar. Martin stayed in their little guest house in the large field, drove with Catherine when she took her daughter to school in the village in the morning and opened her small store, sat in the café, Greco, with its view of the port, and drew on hotel stationery. In the studio back at their guest house, he painted, including the large series of self-portraits *Handpainted Pictures*. There was lunch at two, the big event of the day: "What's for lunch?" Martin always asked Catherine. "There'll be something." "Yeah, but what, what?" he pestered her before going back to his room so as not to spoil the surprise after all. When they had chickpea stew, she let him "put his little hot dogs on the plate too."

In the afternoon, a siesta and then more painting; in the evening, they watched videos, often one after another, or went to the taverna, where Martin had the overcooked camping spaghetti he so dearly loved. At night, mau-mau with Michel, sessions sometimes lasting until the next day and into the following night: "it was a lot of fun, but also a matter of honor, a real wrestling match." The stakes were usually drawings, "and Martin insisted that the debts be paid." He encouraged both Michel and Catherine to draw and paint.

Whenever someone visited them, "Martin was charming," Michel said. "The more ordinary the person, the better he got along with them"—for example, the farmers from next door, who didn't know any more English or German than Martin knew Greek. Helmut Middendorf, who often visited Martin in Athens, said that in situations like that, Martin "didn't need all that self-display performance nonsense. In Berlin and Cologne it was like they flipped a switch to turn him on and he had to give them the Martin." In Syros, on the other hand, even phone calls bothered him. He considered building a monk's tower in white on the Würthles' land: a simple building with a room to sleep in and a room to work in, modeled on the pigeon towers on the island of Tinos. "Fantasies of solitude," Michel said.

Catherine was lively and loved to laugh as much as Martin; their daughter Carolina "adored him, he always treated her like a little lady, brought her presents." Michel puttered around in the fields, where new houses and patios were constantly springing up; Martin gave him a Ferrari tractor for his fiftieth birthday. Martin even joined Michel on his boat, though he didn't like it: he needed people, not an ocean, and longed for civilization in nature. "When we landed in a solitary bay with no taverna, it was terrible!" Michel said. All three of them drank little in that period, though they smoked all the more to make up for it (Catherine died of lung cancer in 2005). "He looked as healthy as a baby," Michel said. "The days could be really peaceful—and then there'd be another madhouse." Martin started drinking heavily a couple of times: once when he was preparing his exhibition for the Hirshhorn Museum in Washington, another time when Catherine told him that the red splotches on his neck came from drinking. "He didn't want to hear a thing about alcohol," and for ten days he didn't speak a word to Catherine, only drank.

Things were wilder during their trips to Athens. "There he caused more of his little scandals," as Michel put it, careening through the city insulting artists and collectors. He told one collector, the first time they met, that if it were up to him he would throw his whole collection into the garbage. Eleni Koroneou, the gallerist, was afraid that Martin was scaring off a potential client. "But the collector liked it, better than all the brown-nosers." A few months later, he bought several of Martin's pictures.

Martin had another of his substitute families with Eleni Koroneou; her daughter, Alexandra (Martin promised the twelve-year-old that he would marry her when she turned eighteen, and she liked that, "it wouldn't be boring!"); Eleni's husband, Helmut Middendorf, Martin's colleague from the Berlin days; and Eleni's parents. They were part of the group Martin liked to eat noodles with on the patio. He especially liked that Eleni's father looked like Picasso. He put on two shows with the Athens gallerist—*Handpainted Pictures* and *Made in Syros*—and at one of the openings he introduced her by saying, "This is Eleni, the wife of the only German artist who has discovered the color blue." An hour earlier, he had been wandering around the old town buying kitschy souvenirs and gluing them to a table in the gallery. Middendorf crawled the bars with Martin and after three days needed a week to recover, "but I've never met anyone I had so much fun with. No one came close. As an artist, either." Even at the bars, Martin drew: another self-portrait, naked, from behind, on a barstool, with "Only waiting for a girl" written on it. The next morning at eight he was standing on Eleni's doorstep again and asking for beer for breakfast. Once they were at a party where drunk people were jumping into the pool, and Martin told her, "If you do it, too, you're not my gallerist any more." "He could be very conservative," Koroneou said. "Etiquette mattered to him."

On Syros he launched two of his biggest projects: his Museum of Modern Art and his subway stations. As early as 1988 he had planned to take a year at some point and "have no exhibitions and take a break." Now, on a distant Greek island, he had a better idea: to put on exhibitions almost without art, with practically no public audience (certainly without the art-world crowd), with only a few friends, by running a museum that was merely the idea of a museum. It had nothing to do with the art market—in fact, his MOMAS (Museum of Modern Art Syros) was his statement against the globalized art business.

"All there is is garbage," Martin said once, "and the beauty *in* the garbage." He had found Greece overflowing with both—for example, an unfinished slaughterhouse stuck on a hill, a concrete skeleton, suggesting, if you saw it from a distance, a columned hall as antique as it was modern. It was almost sublime, "but then," as the American artist Stephen Prina said, "it doesn't look right. For most people it would have been a failed building, but for Martin it was a monument to Western civilization. He saw the Acropolis in what it was." And he turned this useless ruin, this failed meat factory, into a museum without walls and almost without art, a museum of possibilities that remained open to everything.

It opened in 1993 with a "show" by Hubert Kiecol—who else? Kiecol didn't even need to make any of his little concrete sculptures; there were Kiecols standing around already. For the opening and the openings that followed, Christopher Wool scattered signposts around the unkempt island, Jörg Schlick put up stickers, Lukas Baumewerd produced a computer simulation of the finished museum (complete with cafeteria), Uli Strothjohann filled in a hole in the ground, Christopher Williams showed avant-garde movies about slaughterhouses at an open-air cinema in Ermoupolis, and Cosima von Bonin served a meal of spaghetti in macaroni on a long table—every show needs an opening-night dinner, after all, and Martin invited Christopher Williams, Heimo Zobernig, Stephen Prina, and Michael Majerus. Martin had asked the young gallerist Burkhard Riemschneider who he thought was his most talented artist, and when Riemschneider said Majerus, Martin added him to the exhibition list on the spot. He got to spend a week on Syros with his girlfriend.

MOMAS was an excuse, of course, to have parties with friends—every opening another Anti-Sahara Program after weeks of moderation, a transition back to Germany. They were relatively intimate gatherings: other than Martin, the Würthles, and the artists themselves, only a few visitors came from Athens for the openings.

There was a big party on the island in September 1993, though: Michel's fiftieth birthday. It was the perfect opportunity for Martin to christen his subway station before a large audience. Again, a local piece of construction was the start of the piece, in this case an ornate railing in a field. If the Museum was a constructive misunderstanding, the subway entrance was one of his much-loved incomprehensible constructions: an entrance that led nowhere, consisting of nothing but a short flight of stairs down to a gate with the Lord Jim logo on it (breasts, hammer, sun), built by a local contractor, with the railing up above. A subway entrance without a subway, but nevertheless, two years later, it would link up with an exit on the other side of the world, in the mud and scree of Dawson City in the Yukon in Canada, even more isolated than Syros, where Reinald Nohal, Michel Würthle's partner from the Paris Bar, ran a hotel, the Bunkhouse Hostel, and where Oswald Wiener and his wife also lived several months a year. This time, due to the icy temperatures, the entrance would be made of wood, not concrete. Gisela Capitain helped paint the gate, which wasn't quite finished—they had traveled together, first visiting a collector couple in California. She later said the opening was hilarious: a stage was built that the whole village could dance on, the cowboys rode out of the forests to celebrate, and a ribbon was cut. Martin explained his work at great length to the young reporter from the *Klondike Sun* who had come to cover the event, and who had never written about art in his life. They all sat at the bar that night, where Martin made more drawings.

"It was very nice, in a personal sense," the Cologne photographer Albrecht Fuchs said later; Martin had summoned him to Dawson City for the occasion. Together they visited Indians and took pictures of Martin in front of "Guggieville," which Martin already planned to use as a poster for the Guggenheim Museum—unfortunately, he never had an exhibit there.

Fuchs photographed Martin like Buster Keaton in a Caspar David Friedrich pose, wearing a flat boater hat and a long coat. Martin's most important model for his "METRO-Net" subway system was in fact Keaton's movie *The Frozen North*, in which Keaton guards a fake subway exit in the snowy arctic wasteland. Martin had not a little in common with the melancholy comedian and drinker. The Swiss curator Daniel Baumann remembers Martin as sad—"his sadness was very moving"—and the saddest thing, Baumann said, was how he put on a jacket, "like Buster Keaton."

The Dawson City station would be followed by others

in L.A., Kassel, and Münster; stations were also planned for Normandy and Tokyo, and one would appear in Venice after Martin's death. Martin opened the first station, on Syros, in 1993, the same year that the internet took off: for the first time, anyone could download a web browser with graphic capabilities for free. The internet was open to all; Martin's network was the opposite: real and ideal, an ironic utopia, "condensing and fusing the continents together through the imagination" as one critic put it. "The whole thing is useless, but not meaningless."

ART NEEDS TO HANG

Meanwhile, in Cologne, a new generation of gallerists had sprung up: Schipper, Buchholz, Ungers, and especially Christian Nagel. Just as Hetzler had set the tone in Cologne in the early eighties, Nagel did in the early nineties.

Nagel had run the Christoph Dürr Gallery in Munich with Matthias Buck in the late eighties, where Martin had shown several times. Both gallerists were very young—Nagel was still studying art history—but they thought Martin's work was interesting, and when they asked him if he wanted to do something with them, "he was on board right away. He didn't even know us." He got to know them fast. When they met in Cologne he spent three straight nights talking with Nagel: "we talked, talked, talked, who liked what, how to run a gallery—he said we should start a newspaper, define our own era, the best thing would be no more openings, no invitations, just a handful of interested people, we definitely had to show Krebber...."

Munich is the only major German city where Martin never lived. Though Martin's good friend Uschi Welter had moved there, the slick chi-chi scene was too much for him. Once, when he was sitting with Nagel at a café on Maximilianstrasse and saw a car drive into another car, he clapped—and when the people around him threatened to beat him up, he applauded even louder. "That was the spirit of Munich, he felt: everyone drives a BMW, everything is expensive, but none of it is really good." Martin went further in his *No Problem* exhibition at the Dürr gallery when he showed, on a loden-covered pedestal, a T-shirt with "Pas de problemes from the Côte d'Azur" printed on it. Price: six thousand marks. "It was sensational, no one understood how a T-shirt could cost so much money." It was in Munich, where everyone always dressed to the nines, that Martin bought himself a complete Burberry outfit in a Burberry store and wore it for a few successful performances.

Nagel left Munich for Cologne in 1990, starting a second camp. Alongside the commercial hedonists of the eighties— the Hetzler artists—there were now the unwieldy, political, institution-critical artists of the nineties: the Nagel artists. Martin, of course, simply crossed the line between the two sides. He was already friends with Nagel, who was Karola Grässlin's boyfriend; he had shown up at Nagel's door more than once. "Martin took Nagel under his wing," Peter Pakesch said. "Nagel had a kind of intelligence that Martin was very sympathetic toward." Martin had fights with Nagel—for example, over the fact that Nagel only wanted to show art about art—but at the same time bought from him: both works by artists from Martin's circle that Nagel represented (Michael Krebber, Cosima von Bonin, Merlin Carpenter) and works by other artists, such as the Americans Louise Lawler and Andrea Fraser. Martin was always interested in new approaches: "He wasn't phobic about Contextual Art," the critic Isabelle Graw said. "In fact he explicitly supported some of its formulations." When the aluminum smiley faces that

Martin had bought from Fraser kept falling off the wall, he told her, "Art has to hang." She used the phrase later as the title of a performance in the Nagel Gallery after Martin's death, in which she imitated one of his infamous appearances and told jokes and provocations for half an hour. Her appearance went over in two very different ways: some in the audience took it as an homage, others as a settling of accounts.

The mood had changed in Cologne by the time Nagel moved there. In 1990, Graw and Stefan Germer founded *Texte zur Kunst* (Texts on Art), a journal that reflected as much as it shaped the new climate in Cologne. Everything became much more heady, heavy, academic, theoretical, political, and politically correct, a turn strongly supported by the corresponding shift in the United States. Diedrich Diederichsen and Jutta Koether are still among its regular contributors and Martin Prinzhorn is its Vienna correspondent. For the first issue of the magazine, it was clear to Graw (as she herself says) that she should ask Martin to make the first of the artist-editions she would use to finance the journal. He did it immediately and with pleasure: *Ricky Model: From Head to Gullet.** Cologne was becoming more and more like a village: more rigid, more claustrophobic. Everything was too close—there was no escape, no private life, no secrets.

I JUST HAVE TO GET THROUGH THIS YEAR

In 1991, Martin reached a new turning point. As he told the *Artfan* interviewer, "I have to change certain defined structures

---

* Kippenberger commissioned a large wooden bust of Richard von Weizsäcker, Germany's president, then photographed it and sawed it into slats of different lengths, a reference to the slats produced by Georg Herold in the early 1980s. Little photographs of the destroyed bust, in plastic cases, dangled from each slat like keyrings.

in my life, totally change them, so that I can take things in, new things, too, see them differently. And I need to get rid of almost everything I have so I can get at other things.... I just have to get through this year, I mean with my health. But if I survive this year, boomtown."

His doctors had told him very clearly how serious his liver problems were and how dangerous it was to keep drinking. He had not yet officially separated from Gabi Hirsch, but it must have been clear to him by then that Project Family was not going to work out, or maybe had already failed. The prices his art was fetching were in the basement, if it was selling at all; the Hetzler group had drifted apart; the art scene was a vacuum, with Berlin not yet what Cologne no longer was. He didn't know where his home was. To console himself, he described himself as the hero of a bygone era: "They'll say about me that I was the eighties, and that's important to me."

He made this comment in 1991, in his interview with Jutta Koether that appeared in the catalog for the SFMOMA exhibition. The whole interview reads like an accounting of his life as an artist: a manifesto and confession. He gave other interviews as well around that time, as though reflection and contemplation were more appropriate forms of expression for this period than producing art itself. Never before had he spoken publicly about such private matters. It was more than just capturing a moment in Martin's melancholy mood—it was a long-term project, initiated and financed by Martin himself, with various interviews taking place over a six-month period: a few in Cologne's Café Central, one in his Frankfurt cider bar, one with Diedrich Diederichsen on a train between the two cities. Martin had sought out Jutta Koether because he admired her work: she had conducted a lot of interviews with film people and musicians. Martin had known her for ten years, he trusted her but had the necessary distance—and she was a woman. "I had the feeling," she later said, "that he was a bit desperate at the time and just wanted to talk to someone."

It was never intended to be a typical interview—journalist asks, artist answers—rather, as Koether said, "a self-display, meandering from one topic to the next as a way of showing his method, his way of working and thinking." It was an open-ended conversation, and neither of them would know in advance which way it would go. The transcript was shortened, reordered, and otherwise edited, but not smoothed out; Martin's voice is on the page, his cryptic way of jumping around while he talked. "This distinctive way of talking is like the line of my paintbrush," he said. Martin himself changed almost nothing from the transcript, leaving in even very personal passages.

Koether felt that she was the "sounding board" in this experiment:

> What I thought was interesting was this extremely voluble talking, this desire to communicate so much, expressed in such an unusual, nonstandard, scrambled, crazy way. For me, you couldn't understand Kippenberger's way of talking in terms of words or statements, but as part of a performance, almost like a concert. I was the audience at this performance, and to begin with I had to stick it out myself.

Martin asked her over and over again in the interview what would happen with it, whether anything would come of it, "because I know that it won't work with me next year, so I have to know that something will happen with it." Something did happen with it: it was published in book form for the SFMOMA exhibition, and an excerpt was published in *Texts on Art*. Koether recalls that the excerpt "caused an unbelievable shitstorm. You just cannot imagine how much I was criticized over it." One critic (who later, after Martin's death, wrote a very long, positive essay about Martin) was so angry that he lectured her about it for a whole night. The Berlin scene, in particular, attacked her for letting someone like Martin just talk, giving him so much space without pushing back. "That went on for a few years. Only after his death did people start saying, 'Oh, what a fantastic interview!'"

EVERYTHING'S IN THERE

Taschen's monograph about Martin was published in 1991, and Martin used it to spread his fame far beyond the art collectors and cognoscenti. It contributed greatly to his popularity, especially among younger artists and art fans and far beyond Germany, even in countries where he had rarely or never exhibited (for instance, Britain or Georgia).

The editor was Angelika Muthesius, later Taschen's wife. Burkhard Riemschneider, the young art historian who worked with Gisela Capitain at the time, was responsible for the texts and documentation. Riemschneider, who today runs a gallery in Berlin with his former coworker Tim Neuger, remembers working with Martin as being very straightforward and uncomplicated. Martin encouraged him to write the introductory text himself: he was sick of all the professional art writers. Then they put together the artist bio at the end of the volume in a couple of hours one morning at Café Central, using Baselitz's CV as a model. The result was like a parody of an Important Artist Biography.

In fact, the whole book was a bit too didactic for Martin's taste. Works using the same motif were always grouped together, for example. On the other hand, he was excited to have a picture book so different from the books he produced himself: a real coffee-table book for a broad audience. "Everything's in there so that any old train conductor can understand it. It brings something to a close, a book like that, but it also destroys you."

In November of that same year, Martin showed that he wasn't a coffee-table-book artist after all. He opened the *Heavy Fella** show at the Cologne Art Association, his most radical statement on art, authorship, the aura of the work of art, and the art business. Merlin Carpenter had been assigned to paint pictures after motifs from Martin's work, and Martin said that the paintings were "too good," so he had Wilhelm Schürmann photograph them and then destroyed the paintings. The photographs hung framed on the wall while the originals, torn and crumpled, filled a dumpster that Martin exhibited in the same room.

Some responded enthusiastically: Rudolf Zwirner liked "how radically he pursued this anti-attitude against the bourgeois idea of culture and cultural production and the whole apparatus around it." Others wondered if Martin had maneuvered himself into a corner.

THIS IS TO A CERTAIN EXTENT UNBEARABLE

Martin had had enough of Cologne, and vice versa. He was tired of his little Bermuda Triangle of bars, cafés, and galleries; he said in 1991 that he spent the evenings at home with Gabi and Helena more and more often, "although I don't

---

* Sometimes translated *Heavy Lad;* the original title is *Heavy Burschi*. "Heavy" here has the sense of "not easygoing" rather than "overweight"; *Burschi* is dialect for "fellow, little guy, lad." The title plays on an earlier work, *Heavy Mädel: Mädel* means "girl," and "*Heavy Mädel*" sounds almost exactly like "heavy metal." A Heavy *Burschi*, then, is the male counterpart of a Heavy *Mädel*.

really belong at home, but nothing is pulling me out the door either." Domestic life was not the answer, but he often didn't know where else to go.

Meanwhile, many people were starting to find Martin's performances and provocations too formulaic and ritualized. They were annoyed by the jokes, which increasingly came across as sad more than funny, so they avoided him. "Even the people who always defended him," Diedrich Diederichsen said, "tried to get out of going to his endless performances at the opening parties." Speeches that once would have lasted fifteen minutes now went on for two hours; even Werner Büttner says they were "torture."

People were exhausted from the eighties, too, and with increasing age and worsening health they simply couldn't keep up with the endless drinking. Alcohol no longer pepped Martin up—by that point it tended to make him aggressive. "At the end," Charline von Heyl said, "alcohol was not his friend. The last years were mainly about struggle and survival."

The more famous Martin grew and the more attention he attracted, the more pressure he felt. The adventurous agility of the early years was largely gone: "The strain keeps getting worse," Martin said.

WHEN YOU DON'T KNOW WHERE TO GO, GO TO THE NO

Martin wrote in his artist bio for the year 1992: "Moves further and further away from the art world; lives and works in the Black Forest." He had done something he otherwise never did—returned to a place he had already left behind. After his time in Frankfurt and the intensive work with his students, he knew he didn't want to move back to Cologne.

When you don't know where to go, go to the no, he titled one of his pictures.

Ten years had passed since he last lived in Sankt Georgen, though he had visited often and continued to send mountains of postcards there from all over the world. The Grässlin family had diligently collected his work. At one point, when they didn't want to or couldn't buy his works for a while, he painted a series especially for them and called it *The Unbought Pictures*: a smaller example of every series and motif that they didn't have in their collection.

Karola had finished her art history studies and headed the Daxler Art Space in Munich. Sabine, after her culinary education on Lake Constance, was a cook in Munich before returning to the Black Forest to run the marketing department of the family business. Sabine's daughter, Katharina, was no longer a screaming baby but a teenager: she fought bitterly with Martin over which TV shows to watch and cursed him as an "occupier," a "terrorist." He wanted to decide everything, and when he had no other choice he retreated downstairs to watch TV with Grandma. She was over ninety years old by that point and had become even more bitterly set in her ways, but she had continued to set a place at the table for Martin long after he had left. The Eggman song—and only the Eggman himself—could still make her laugh.

Anna Grässlin was still Anna Grässlin, the good mother. "He could spend hours on end tearing apart Bärbel or Karola," Johannes Wohnseifer said, "but Anna! He thought she was really cool." Not surprisingly, Anna remembers Martin as being always in a good mood, not depressed or aggressive. Again she mothered him and tended to him; she usually served his favorites, pasta and noodle casserole. Still, she continued to keep a certain distance from him and didn't go along with everything.

There was no Sahara Program this time, only the Anti-Sahara. Bloody Marys and vodka apple juices in the café in the morning, or red wine. Often he was the only patron: people didn't go to cafés in the morning in Sankt Georgen. In the evenings it was red wine and Ramazzotti liqueur at the Italian restaurant whose walls he had filled with his paintings. Sometimes the party continued back at his studio afterward.

He wanted to stop drinking, or at least that's what he once told Bice Curiger, the co-editor of *Parkett,* when they were together in a car: "He was looking out the window, it was almost like a monologue: 'I'm forty now, it's time for me to become a new person. If you can do that you're an Olympian. I should stop drinking, but I was just in the Black Forest again and I didn't manage it.' You could feel his despair: *I should have, but I didn't...*"

Martin felt like a full member of the family, and it didn't go well when anyone treated him otherwise. One time, Bärbel Grässlin invited her goddaughter Pia and Pia's parents, and Martin's friend Meuser and his wife Nanette Hagstotz, to Frankfurt for Advent. Martin was furious: "Why wasn't I invited too? I'm part of the family too!" When the American artist duo Clegg and Gutman came to take a large photograph of the whole Grässlin family, Martin absolutely wanted to be in the picture and was incredibly insulted when he wasn't included. The sons-in-law were not in the portrait either, but that didn't mean a thing to him. He felt excluded.

He made a family portrait of his own, a lot less formal than the Americans'. Martin called the series *Upside Down and Turning Me*: panels covered with lead, each one the same height and width as the respective family member.

In other ways it was like a real family: he liked to get into fights with the sisters, for example, about things that no one remembers any more. "It felt like kindergarten sometimes,"

Johannes Wohnseifer said. He sometimes brought the sisters to tears, too, making fun of their weight or their ways of talking. Occasionally, he played more serious tricks on them. For example, when he was in Zurich he had a friend call Sankt Georgen and say that the former Israeli Prime Minister, Menachem Begin, was visiting Germany; he wanted to look at the family collection, on the condition that they remove the works by Förg and serve kosher food. (Günther Förg's antics in various bars and restaurants had given him the reputation of being a Nazi, and the Grässlin collection had a few of his pieces on the wall.) Everything was made ready for the Israeli dignitary, who of course never showed up.

But no matter what jokes Martin played on them and how annoyed they got, everything was usually fine the next day.

One of the reasons Martin moved back to Sankt Georgen was his large studio there. It was inexpensive: 2,500 square feet in an old woodworking workshop, where Martin also lived, for a thousand marks a month. Sabine paid the rent, and Martin gave her more art.

A photographer, Thomas Berger, had his studio under Martin's and took a famous picture of Martin peeking through blinds. They talked together a lot—for example, about religion, which meant a lot to Berger. "Martin took it seriously, he didn't make a joke out of it, but left it open whether he himself was a believer."

Berger, who was from Baden, in southern Germany, liked Martin's dry humor and asked him "what he meant by this or that piece. For example, the EuroPallets. I thought it couldn't really be true, that you could get so much money for something like that. But he always had something to say about it, deep things. He always told me something so that I could think the piece was great."

Their lifestyles could not have been more different. In

the morning, when Berger arrived at his photo studio, Martin sometimes was going to bed and the last guest going home. Martin sometimes threw parties in the studio, and Berger surveyed the damage afterward with amazement: "tables full of empty bottles—I've never seen anything like it." There were also phases when Martin did nothing but work for weeks— followed by periods of drinking through the night. "Other than that I'd have to say he was a quiet neighbor. He was a very friendly person. He just indulged in such excesses."

This was the period when Martin was working on his Schreber pieces and painting his series of Kasper paintings— "one after the other," Berger said, "zap zap zap, like piecework." Kasper was a figure he knew well: the clown from the German version of Punch and Judy shows, who was always trying to beat others with his stick and instead landed the blows on his own head.

THE HAPPY END OF FRANZ KAFKA'S "AMERIKA"

"I'm on a mission," Martin told Thomas Grässlin while he was working on *The Happy End of Franz Kafka's "Amerika,"* "I have to carry it out and I don't have much time." Martin often said in this period that he had decided to create his masterpiece, and he knew how poor the condition of his liver was. The doctors had been warning him in the strongest possible terms.

Franz Kafka wrote to his girlfriend, Felice, that his novel, which he called by the working title *The Missing Person* or *The Man Who Disappeared*, was "heading off into endlessness." It remained a fragment, but Max Brod, instead of burning the manuscript after Kafka's death as his friend had requested, published it in 1927. *Amerika, The Trial,* and *The Castle* together formed what Brod called "The Trilogy of Loneliness." Kafka himself may have seen this work as lighter than his others; Martin wrote in the foreword to his book on the Kafka installation, *Conversations with Martin Kippenberger,* that it was the first time something by Kafka suggested a happy ending.

Martin probably never read the book. But he asked other people to tell him about it, and he seems to have found a kindred spirit in Kafka's protagonist, Karl, a young man sent away from home by his parents, totally alone in a foreign land. A sixteen-year-old boy who has gotten the maid pregnant and never finished school; funny and optimistic, someone who believes in people and believes that they're good, no matter how many times they lie to him and betray him; and someone who, in the first paragraph of the novel, discovers freedom—in the shape of the Statue of Liberty—only to learn all too quickly how difficult freedom is. The theme of the book is constant departure, moving around, starting anew over and over again—and, finally, arriving and wanting to be let in. "All welcome!" a poster for the Nature Theater of Oklahoma announces. "Anyone who wants to be an artist, step forward!" Karl reads the sentence again and again: All welcome, so he must be welcome too. Even if he is somewhat disappointed not to get the job he wants, as an engineer, "he kept saying to himself that what mattered wasn't so much the type of work as one's ability to stick it out, whatever it might be." Karl is especially touched that everyone, absolutely everyone, is "so well received and looked after" by the Theater.

Kafka presents the job interviews as grotesque theater, and it is in no way clear whether heaven or hell awaits those who get jobs. The scene is as ambivalent as Martin's relationship to America itself, and in fact Martin's idea of America was very close to the image of America Kafka presents in his novel (even though Kafka was never there in person): the mixture of hope and disappointment, apparent openness and ruthless competition, and the focus on the future and lack of a sense of history that especially irritated Martin, a European artist through and through.

Martin worked longer on his Kafka piece than on any other work, and none of his other works is as big and complex: around fifty tables with two chairs each, as in a job interview situation, clustered together on a painted soccer field. Martin's body of work was also put together "into endlessness," and in *Kafka* he took up many of his themes, methods, and motifs, his own pieces and the works of other artists. The installation returned to the questions of inclusion and exclusion, power relations, solitude, failure, history, and belief (in yourself, in happiness, in other people). More than anything, it was about communication, both within the work itself and in the way it completes and improves on the work of others. Martin said he wanted to "sort of give Kafka a hand, after the fact. Give him a Happy End. His books always end so full of self-doubt, in death, I wanted to give him a Happy End."

The installation is intensely colorful but has something oppressive about it, not unlike the trapped hopelessness of Kafka's other novels. The chairs are empty, and no one is there to sit in them (the museum visitors are not allowed to). In Martin's concept, viewers are supposed to imagine the conversations that might be taking place at the tables.

The *Kafka* installation was presumably not originally intended to be so huge, but it grew over time into the summa of Martin's work. It wasn't even intended to be an installation: Martin had considered actually writing the book to the end, working "with the best ghostwriters in the world to do it," or making a movie based on it.

The whole thing started with the furniture he had bought for his apartment in L.A.: used furniture, both classics of modern design and anonymous pieces from flea markets and the Salvation Army. He continued to collect furniture in New York and Europe, acting fast whenever he found something. He and Elisabeth Fiedler found a whole warehouse of obsolete office furniture owned by the state government in Graz. Martin had been interested in furniture for a long time. He had furnished his Office in Berlin with classic Bauhaus pieces. Thus the *Kafka* piece was, among other things, an encyclopedia of living, of residing: "every decade, everyone has a crystal clear memory of a chair that embodies something for you, you're right back in that time, it's like a visual dictionary you drag around with you." Martin combined the furniture he had bought with artworks left over from other exhibitions, pieces by other artists, and objects built specially for *Kafka,* many of them by Uli Strothjohann and some by Sven Ahrens.

Kafka cost Martin a fortune but was practically impossible to sell, due to its sheer size. Martin's New York girlfriend, Tracy Williams, saw it as a response to the crisis in the art market and especially in his own market value: "It's as if he was saying: OK, you're not buying anyway, so I'm gonna do something really big." On the other hand, the Swiss curator Daniel Baumann (who considers the *Kafka* piece "overvalued and overanalyzed") said that it was just the trend of the time: "to get through to the international market, you had to show gigantic works."

When talks began between Martin and Karel Schampers, the director of the Boijmans Van Beuningen Museum in Rotterdam, Martin was insistent that he wanted to show the Kafka piece there, because so many emigrants had left for America from the Dutch port city. Karel Schampers was uneasy about the undertaking—Martin did, after all, still have the reputation of being difficult and unpredictable—but it turned out that their collaboration was "extremely pleasant, peaceful, and a lot of fun," he said. Every day Martin dragged the museum director to lunch at one of the vending-machine restaurants we had loved so much as children in Holland. There was nothing but "garbage to eat" there, in Schampers's words—everything deep-fried: potatoes, croquettes, meatballs, Indonesian fried rice. Martin also made noodle casserole for Schampers at home once.

The curator was "overwhelmed" by the way Martin installed the show. The soccer field was painted on the floor, "and then he started, and it was like he had a photo in his head of the whole thing. He knew exactly where everything should go, he never had to change a thing. He was totally focused and the whole thing went very quickly." Schampers was also overwhelmed when a truckload of books showed up between the trucks of furniture. "What are these books," he asked Martin, "I didn't order any books." He didn't know that Martin had commissioned (and paid for) nine books on the theme of job interviews by his friends, to display on the tables. "That was a nice surprise."

Martin sent out invitations to Café Loos in Rotterdam for his birthday party, on February 25, 1994. The cards showed the Indian that Wohnseifer had found at the used bookstore in Cologne. The next day was the big exhibition opening, with French fries and croquettes to eat, the authors reading from their books, and the female guests forced to act the part of cheerleaders. Boris Becker and John McEnroe didn't make it, unfortunately. (The tennis stars were at the same hotel in Rotterdam at the same time—apparently, when Martin started telling his jokes there one evening, Becker yelled at him to sit down and shut up. Martin had invitations to the opening put into all the athletes' mail slots in the hotel and was disappointed when they didn't come. The only one who sent his thanks and regrets for not being able to make it was Michael Stich.)

The show went almost unnoticed in Germany but received a lot of attention in the Netherlands, with numerous major interviews and reviews, most of them very positive. Only a couple of newspapers complained that there was too much humor in the show and not enough art.

Martin told Jutta Koether, in the interview that would be his contribution to the books for the installation (on Table 17), that giving Kafka a happy ending "is my life's work." His assistant, Sven Ahrens, thought "Martin made peace with himself" with the Rotterdam show: "He felt that he had done what he wanted to do." His masterpiece—as Martin also called it to Schmapers—was complete.

Two years later, the installation was mounted and shown in Copenhagen. Arno Victor Nielsen wrote in the catalog that "Martin Kippenberger's gigantic office-landscape . . . can be interpreted as a wicked allegory of a hyper-modern society, locked into operations of supervision and control. Everyone is hired, but we have to start to wonder if the price for this universal openness is that no one can escape."

IT JUST MADE SENSE

Johannes Wohnseifer visited the Black Forest often. There was a small guest bedroom at Martin's studio, with a replica of Napoleon's military camp bed to sleep on. They watched a lot of TV together, with the remote in Wohnseifer's hands and Martin giving orders: "Next! Next!" They watched the news and soccer, and "we got worked up over what garbage everything was" on MTV. They rarely watched a single show from beginning to end.

Martin had another assistant in this period: Sven Ahrens, his student from Kassel, who commuted between Frankfurt and Sankt Georgen. Ahrens could drink a lot of wine, an important qualification for Martin's companions at Sankt Georgen; he could behave himself, which was important for Martin at the Grässlins'; and he could talk about art. He was good with his hands, which was of practical use for the Kafka project, and he had a car and a driver's license. "It just made sense." So Ahrens drove back and forth between Frankfurt, where he was painting, and the Black Forest, where they often just sat in front of Martin's new pictures with a bottle of red wine and talked about them. In Ahrens's view, Martin liked his reclusive lifestyle in this period. When he started to feel like there was too much peace and quiet, they permitted themselves little excursions, for example, to Zurich. They stayed for three days and then drove, also on the spur of the moment, to an old hotel in Badenweiler. Martin was a regular there, too, with "his" room, and if another hotel guest was in "his" room, the guest would be transferred to another; Ahrens, meanwhile, slept in a different room every night, on Martin's recommendation, so that he could try them all out. In this hotel, too, Martin bewitched the sizeable crowd of older ladies, arranged swimming races in the pool, and instigated "Glow-Worm" singalongs, writing the notes of the melody in magic marker on the waiters' striped shirts.

After two and a half years as Martin's assistant, Ahrens had the feeling that it was time to move on. "Everything got to be more or less routine," he said; Martin's provocations had gotten to be too mean for him; and so, after another evening when Martin the Punch had made Ahrens his Judy (as Ahrens put it), and taken a fortune off him at pinball and mau-mau to boot, Ahrens got into his car and drove off. First he drove to the highway, where he stopped in a parking lot to sleep and sober up, and then, the next morning, when he had to decide whether to drive back or keep going, he kept going. He had already secretly been preparing to open a gallery in Stuttgart with a friend, Bernd Hammelehle. If he wasn't a real artist (and Martin had told him he wasn't), he certainly knew how to deal with artists. At first Martin was offended. Then he started giving him good advice for his new gallery, which Ahrens gratefully declined. "It was a nice, fatherly side of him, but I wanted to run the gallery my way." At the Art Fair he talked trash about their program ("What shit you guys are showing!"), and then announced, "OK, I'll give you something!" This didn't appeal to Ahrens at first, but when Martin faxed him his collaborators' drawings on hotel stationery, he was enthusiastic.

The show opened at the Hammelehle & Ahrens Gallery in 1995 and was called *Not just anybuddies*. Ahrens later said it was great honor for him, not only that Martin showed there but that he did it with such pleasure. Many people took it as a slap in the face: how could Kippenberger put on a show like that in an unknown gallery in someone's living room in Swabia? But Ahrens said that Martin "liked helping me get started in a place that was once so important for him." They went around together to see the sights and locales he remembered from his Stuttgart days.

FORTY YEARS OF GRATITUDE

The climax of Martin's second period in the Black Forest was February 25, 1993: his fortieth birthday. Martin had always put on big public parties for his birthday, even though for him, as he once said, every day was a birthday: causing a ruckus, putting himself in the center, and giving gifts to himself and others. He always staged big events for his major birthdays—giving himself a sheet of stamps for his twenty-first; a huge party with a catalog for his twenty-fifth (*1/4 Century Kippenberger*); the catalog *Farewell to the Youth Bonus* for his thirtieth.

He never put on anything like his fortieth, though. The invitations read, "On the occasion of henceforth forty years of gratitude, Martin Kippenberger cordially invites you to a celebration in Sankt Georgen, February 24-25." It sounded harmless enough, but it was "murderous," as Anna Grässlin put it: a three-day orgy of drinking and excess. It went late into the night of February 24 at Nachtcafé, continued the next morning with a buffet at the Grässlins', surrounded by Martin's works, proceeded to a studio visit that afternoon and a viewing of his show at the Döbele exhibition space, and then went on to dinner and dancing that night, and the hair of the dog the next morning at Café Kammerer.

At one point, all hundred guests were gathered together for a group photograph—Martin in front and many of the guests, as requested, in folk costume (Karola Grässlin even wore her great-grandmother's original outfit, complete with a Black Forest Bollenhut hat). Martin titled the picture *Say Cheese!* and used it on the invitations for his exhibition at the Pompidou Centre. He had gathered around him many of the people who had been important to him over those forty years: Michel Würthle next to him in front, Cosima von Bonin, Gisela Capitain, Lukas Baumewerd, Albert Oehlen, Friedrich Petzel, Michael Krebber, Sven-Åke Johansson, Charline von Heyl, Jörg Schlick, Meuser, Sabine Achleitner, Sven Ahrens, Hubert Kiecol, Uli Strothjohann, Petra Schilcher, Helmut Seiler, Uschi Welter, Birgit Küng, Christian Nagel, Johann Widauer, Andrea Stappert, Tobias Rehberger, Martin Prinzhorn, Esther Schipper, Matthias

Schaufler, Dr. Peters, Gundel Gelbert, Hans Böhning, Roberto Ohrt, Markus Oehlen, Gabi Dziuba, Nicole Hackert, Heliod Spiekermann, the whole Grässlin family, Nicole Neufert, Veit Loers, Johannes Wohnseifer, and from our family Petra, Babs, Bine, and Moritz.

Martin was overjoyed to have everyone there and to get a mountain of presents—he was always as happy as a little child about presents. Sabine Grässlin gave him a Hunger Family made of marzipan (a reference to Martin's *Hunger Family* works), and the guests received presents, too: signed slices of birch (a reference to Martin's birch forest installations). Martin put many of the photographs from the big event into the catalog he made for the Grässlin collection (*We Always Thought Kippenberger Was Great*), including one that he captioned "M.K. birthday breakfast 1993 (so that he isn't all alone)." The only thing he was in a bad mood about were the people who hadn't attended. "The fortieth birthday was mandatory," Gisela Capitain later said; Rüdiger Carl couldn't come, for example, because he was playing a show that night, and Martin held it against him for years. In fact, "the fortieth birthday was real torture," Veit Loers later said. It was the pinnacle of Martin's *Zwangsbeglücktertum*, or enforcing of mandatory good cheer. Bärbel Grässlin, as the oldest family member present, had to stay at the restaurant to the end on the night of the dinner and dancing, because the owner was afraid of what might happen. And with good reason. He phoned Mother Grässlin in a rage the next day to demand payment for damages: the guests had acted up and gotten violent, and the parquet floors were ruined from broken glasses and stubbed-out cigarettes. Mother Grässlin listened calmly, but when the hotelier added that they had left condoms lying around everywhere in the bathroom, she apparently said, "Well, then it couldn't have been our party, they don't use them," and hung up. She still had to pay to replace the floors.

"Martin's fortieth birthday was a gigantic, epic mania of self-dramatization," Burkhard Riemschneider said. "I've never been through anything like it," said Elisabeth Fiedler from Graz. Others felt they had been through such things only too often and preferred to stay home: Peter Pakesch, for example, since "the huge parties got on my nerves." Isabelle Graw and Merlin Carpenter also refrained from attending. As Graw said,

> because we didn't like that kind of group pressure any more, it had always been a bit much, really. These rituals always had something oppressively stagnant about them—they weren't fun any more, they had turned into something compulsive and depressing. And I hated being constantly reduced to a sex object.

Riemschneider said that Martin's fortieth birthday "took to an extreme what he had already constantly acted out in Cologne. It had a certain redundancy."

By the end of his time in Sankt Georgen, the peace and quiet that had originally sparked Martin's creativity put a damper on it. He painted only a handful of pictures in 1995; by then he knew every bar and street corner. "It's boring here," he wrote to his girlfriend Kazu Huggler, "I get bored + then I have to deal with the everpresent boredom too. Boring or rude arguments spoil the everyday life that I really do take seriously."

Most of the people who visited Martin certainly couldn't comprehend how he had lasted so long in that bourgeois backwater (as they saw it). In 1995, after the Cologne photographer Albrecht Fuchs saw him in Sankt Georgen

40th birthday in St. Georgen

465

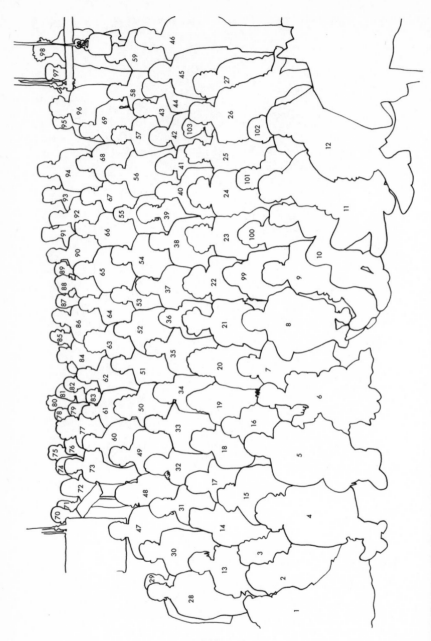

1. Waitress	36. Birgit Küng	71. ?
2. Annette Minnitti	37. Christian Nagel	72. Mimi Hocke
3. Waitress	38. Johann Widauer	73. Mrs. Johansson
4. Ingeborg Gabriel	39. Andrea Stappert	74. ?
5. Rainald Nohal	40. ?	75. Nordenhake
6. Bettina Kölle	41. Ina Weber	76. Sabine Kippenberger-
7. Martin Kippenberger	42. Pia Witzmann	Steil
8. Michel Würthle	43. Michael Krome	77. Esther Schipper
9. Rainald Goetz	44. Tobias Rehberger	78. Christoph Steinmeier
10. Albert Oehlen	45. Nanette Hagstotz	79. Nina Pohl
11. Jörg Schlick	46. Rolf Edler	80. ?
12. Andres Blöchlinger	47. Herbert Fuchs	81. ?
13. Caroline Braun	48. ?	82. Hans Böhning
14. ?	49. Lukas Baumewerd	83. Gundel Gelbert
15. Thomas Grässlin	50. ?	84. Iskender Yediler
16. Hubert Kiecol	51. ?	85. Oliver Brux
17. Claudia Böttcher	52. Sven Ahrens	86. Roberto Ohrt
18. Petra Kippenberger	53. Michael Callies	87. Josef Zehrer
19. Nicole Neufert	54. Kai Helmstetter	88. Gabi Dziuba
20. Frau Hammerstein	55. Beate Kemfert	89. ?
21. Karola Grässlin	56. Veit Loers	90. Axel Huber
22. Ulrike Edler	57. ?	91. Markus Oehlen
23. Anna Grässlin	58. Stefan Fedeler	92. ?
24. Bärbel Grässlin	59. Moritz Kippenberger	93. Axel Zwach
25. Sabine Grässlin	60. Bruno Brunnet	94. Andreas Höhne
26. Meuser	61. Sven-Åke Johansson	95. ?
27. Bernadette Grässlin	62. Michael Krebber	96. Heliod Spiekermann
28. Petra Schilcher	63. Nina Borgmann	97. Stefanie McBride
29. Uwe Gabriel	64. Uli Strothjohann	98. Michael Trier
30. Helmut Seiler	65. Martin Prinzhorn	99. Cosima von Bonin
31. Tatjana Steiner	66. Gerald Just	100. Charline von Heyl
32. Gisela Capitain	67. Matthias Schaufler	101. Mayo Thompson
33. Olaf Hackel	68. Friedrich Petzel	102. Wolfgang Schönrock
34. Uschi Welter	69. Johannes Wohnseifer	103. Milena Vrtalova
35. Werner Peters	70. ?	

to take some pictures, someone asked him back in Cologne: "What, is he still alive?" "For a lot of people," Fuchs said, "Martin was such a Cologne-in-the-eighties figure. He was off people's radar." When Martin found a new place to live in the Burgenland, he packed up his things immediately— "lickety-split" as Anna Grässlin said. He wanted the Grässlins to continue to pay the studio's rent, so he could keep the Kafka piece there, but the family decided not to. Thomas Grässlin felt that "it hurt Martin's feelings. He was dejected."

FRANCE

In 1993, Martin invited Roberto Ohrt, a freelance curator, to join him in putting together a show at the Pompidou Centre, *Candidature à une retrospective* (Application for a Retrospective). There was an official curator at the Pompidou who had invited him: Fabrice Hergott. The French didn't have the best impression of the two German artists, seeing them as rather macho.

The main point of contention was what Ohrt called the "backbone of the show": a long glass display case extending through all three exhibition halls in the museum, filled with all kinds of printed matter. Fifty feet of books, postcards, things Martin copied or alluded to—"the materials and ideas were laid out," Ohrt said, "to make his work transparent, but at the same time still mysterious." The museum felt that the public needed to be warned before entering that Martin had included his collection of erotica: "The public is hereby informed that certain works presented in the Kippenberger exhibition may offend the sensibilities of young visitors. — The administration." Or, as Martin wrote in the catalog: "Children Beware This Man."

The opening-night dinner took place at the restaurant run by Martin's "Chinaman," as he called his friend Davé. They had met through Jenny Capitain back during Martin's earlier stay in Paris, when Davé was still working in his parents' restaurant. Now he and his sister had a restaurant of their own, and it had become the place to meet for the fashion world. Martin knew that Davé was always there—he worked seven days a week, 365 days a year. Martin felt welcomed by Davé, he could talk to him, and he even lived in his apartment while the exhibition was being put up. Martin liked Davé's cooking and, perhaps more importantly, Davé's readings of Martin's tarot cards: he called Davé's style of telling fortunes "fine, truly fine." Davé predicted a splendid future for Martin and was firmly convinced that Martin had something great within him: "Kippi was a true visionary. If he had been a banker, he would have been a great banker."

Martin also had Sylvana Lorenz read the cards for him, though her predictions were sometimes more negative than Davé's. Lorenz was Martin's Parisian gallerist and the wife of the BMW executive Günter Lorenz, although Martin probably liked her better as a fortune-teller than as a gallerist. He had shown work with her several times, individually or as part of the Hetzler group.

At the same time as his Pompidou show, Martin showed his Kaspar paintings at Samia Saouma's gallery. It was hardly a commercial success: "It was very difficult to place Martin's work in Paris," she said. "A lot of people thought he was too German."

What especially intrigued Martin about Paris, aside from the museums, were the big cafés and bistros: he liked to go to La Coupole, and he bought a table, chair, glass, and coffee cup from Café Flore. He was less interested in French artists—he understood their language as little as they did his sense of humor. Still, Martin did have a fan club in France, at the Villa Arson in Nice. Its director, Christian Bernard, had met Martin in 1985 and was a very intellectual Frenchman: "a delicate soul who never drank a sip of beer," as Günter Lorenz said. The driving force behind the Villa was a Swiss man, Axel Huber, who knew Martin from Berlin. He was responsible for taking care of the artists there and was a curator, an artist, and a fan of Martin's. Meuser called the Villa "architecturally a kind of cross between Corbusier and gravel pit."

Martin showed his first exhibition at the Villa in 1987, with Albert and Markus Oehlen and Werner Büttner: *Family Program,* "where their art would relate to each other," Martin said. Later, he showed solo work, including his *Social Pasta* pieces, *Snow White's Coffin,* lampposts, and candleholders. He worked at Villa Arson, taught there, and drank a lot there, too. "It was tough at the Villa," Werner Büttner said, "a week of heavy drinking." For a couple of years, in the opinion of the Viennese artist Hans Weigand, Villa Arson was one of the best locations in Europe: Herold, Kiecol, Schlick, McCarthy, Kelley, and Jason Rhoades, everyone was there. "The moment Axel Huber left, it all collapsed like a hot soufflé."

WE ALWAYS THOUGHT
KIPPENBERGER WAS GREAT

When the Swiss artist Urs Fischer, who was twenty years younger than Martin, was studying art in Amsterdam in 1993, he and a classmate would stay up all night with Martin's monographs: "Kippenberger was a hero to us. The stories circulating about him were like Christopher Columbus's reports from the New World," he wrote in the Tate Gallery's journal. Whether the stories were true or just legends didn't make any difference to Fischer—for him they were as important as Martin's work. "Kippenberger incarnated an unreproducible model, a kind of knight or superhero . . . everyone wants to emulate, though you cannot exactly copy him." It was only a few years later that he lost some of this luster.

A split developed in the nineties. Martin's fans kept growing in number, especially among younger artists, and he won more international recognition. His international shows seemed to follow each other nonstop: *Put your Eye in your Mouth* at the San Francisco Museum of Modern Art and his *Tiefes Kehlchen (Deep Throat)* installation at the Vienna Festival Week, both in 1991; *Candidature à une rétrospective* at the Pompidou in 1993; *The Happy End of Franz Kafka's "Amerika"* at the Boijmans Van Beuningen Museum in Rotterdam in 1994, with full-page reviews in the major Dutch newspapers; *Directions* at the Hirshhorn Museum in Washington in 1995; *Kafka* again in 1996, this time in Copenhagen; and finally the large "Respective" that filled the building at the Musée d'Art Moderne et Contemporain in Geneva in 1997. 1997 was also the year when Martin was finally invited to documenta—by a Frenchwoman, Cathérine David, a woman, a foreigner, *and* an intellectual! During the same period, though, most museum people and critics in Germany ignored Martin at best and heaped abuse upon him at worst.

When the old West Germany came to an end in 1989, it meant the party was over in Germany as a whole. In addition, West Germany's center of power was along the Rhine; now Berlin was in charge, and Berlin hated Martin. Humor was verboten, and everything had to be not only political but also politically correct. The view of the critics seemed to be that after the violence against foreigners in Rostock and Hoyerswerda in the early nineties, and the torching of a synagogue in Lübeck, Germany's image was endangered enough without a Rhineland clown like Kippenberger.

When Josef Strau, a Rhineland artist, moved to Berlin after the fall of the Wall, he was shocked at the level of hatred that the political-artistic bohemians there directed at Cologne. Cologne was demonized as the epitome of the Enemy, and, as Strau wrote in the 2006 catalog for the American show *Make Your Own Life* about Cologne as an art center, it "[stood] for all evil [and was] perceived as the place of old-fashioned hierarchical structures, artist-authorship power-attitude, commercialism, anti-political art, anti-PC, male brotherhoods displaying open anti-feminism—altogether the place of the most reactionary art system."

If this city of evildoers had a Head Mephistopheles, it was Martin Kippenberger: no longer the King of Cologne, but rather "the King of the Cologne mafia," as Marius Babias labeled him. It was as though they had been waiting to come out of the woodwork and batter him with the club of morality—an artist who didn't follow the ideological rules and who had repeatedly attacked liberal self-congratulation, unreflective do-gooderism, and bourgeois hypocrisy with works like *War Bad*. Even his humor was taboo.

The hatred directed at Martin had a history going back to the late seventies and early eighties, when Martin still lived in Berlin and "the whole Kreuzberg scene was a thorn in people's sides," according to Uli Strothjohann, who himself lived in Berlin at the time. They didn't like that Martin refused to toe any group's line, zoomed through the streets on a moped in a suit, played punk music *and* boogie-woogie at S.O.36, and ran a dive in Kreuzberg while being a regular at establishments like the Paris Bar and Fofi's in Charlottenburg. "They had it in for him from the start."

The Berlin establishment had just as little sympathy for

Martin as an artist. He was excluded from the two major generational exhibitions in the Martin Gropius Building—*Zeitgeist* and *Metropolis*—and the established gallerists didn't care for him any more than the curators. As of 2010, no Berlin museum owned a single work by him.

Martin had already written off Berlin, especially after the fall and subsequent complete eradication of the Wall. He was angry that Berlin, which in his day had showed the wounds of the past more openly than any other city, had now wiped out its own history as though it had never been. How could Berlin just tear down such an important monument? Martin couldn't understand it: "stone by little stone, that's so German," he told Marius Babias in an interview for *Artscribe*. "History is something you need to feel. First they weren't Nazis, then they weren't Communists. So what are they?" In his opinion, the Wall needed to be preserved. "We don't need exvacations like in Greece—in this country history happens at your front door."

In 1991, at Literature House Berlin, the journal *Texts on Art* published an issue that contained a long excerpt from Martin's conversation with Jutta Koether—a quote from the interview was even on the cover. This was the very journal dedicated to the identity politics, multiculturalism, and anti-racism of contemporary American art. "People hated us," Isabelle Graw said. "Kippenberger was like a red flag in front of their faces."

Later that year, he appeared in the small Wewerka & Weiss gallery in the Wilmersdorf area of Berlin with his—or at least his representative's—Africa campaign: the *William Holden Company* show, which only confirmed all the prejudices of his enemies in Berlin. Hadn't Martin abused his student by sending him across Africa? Martin sat at the table, forced the women there to kiss him on the lips, signed books, and had a comment for everyone.

The witch-hunt was really on by the time the Brandenburg Art Association in Potsdam showed the Grässlin family's Kippenberger collection in 1994. The day of reckoning had arrived, and all the debts were paid off: even those who had kept a timid silence before now dared to speak up, because they knew they had nothing to fear. The critics from the *FAZ* and the *taz* were united in their Kippenberger-bashing.

"Panty-Raider" was the headline of Harald Fricke's article in the journal *Concrete* on the occasion of "the red-carpet treatment he received" in Potsdam.* While Uli Strothjohann calls these attacks "left-wing-fascist," Harald Fricke labeled Martin's mottos, pictures, and attitudes as "right-wing-anarchist," portraying Martin as a misogynist, Nazi, porn star, racist, and cynic who liked nothing better than to eat linguini and mozzarella salad in Italian restaurants (fashionable dishes that Martin held in the deepest contempt). The article presented Martin as a fraud trying to milk Potsdam dry and said that the Grässlins ("Kippenberger's steady customers since the mid-eighties") had "paid for an expensive catalog," too. Fricke called Kippenberger "a German allotment gardener" and a child of the Helmut Kohl era: "Kohl took power at the same time the 'Hetzler Boys' achieved their breakthrough in the art market." Fricke's conclusion: "His painting is a stockpile of banalities from seventies Karstadt culture."

"Kippenberger doesn't hurt anyone in Potsdam any more" wrote the same author in the *taz* about the Potsdam exhibition. "He has outlived himself. Not with his provocation-pictures and dented sculptures, which in large part he has assistants paint, build, or find, but in his anti-attitude toward history. The wild and crazy eighties seem just

* The German is *"Schlüpfer-Stürmer,"* literally "panty stormer" but in this case also suggesting *Der Stürmer,* a Nazi propaganda weekly

as hopelessly far removed from the nineties as the middle-class fifties. And Kippenberger is the concierge in the social housing project on the outskirts of Cologne."

Meanwhile, Marius Babias described Martin in the city magazine *Zitty* as "a society man somewhat advanced in years, for a jet set bored by just one event after another"; as "a bellwether for a herd of sheep with delusions of avant-gardeur" who "managed to have a mediocre career with his 'underground' attitudes. The adolescent muscleman threatened to go under in the theory mess of the late eighties, but the Cologne circle around Christian Nagel, Diedrich Diederichsen, and Jutta Koether continued to stand up for the reprobate." Babias continued his scolding in the pages of *Junge Welt* (the official paper of the German socialist youth movement until 1989):

This champion of shocking the bourgeoisie has long since turned bourgeois himself, overtaken by reality. Granted, his career, based on provocations aimed against already marginal groups, remains merely average—true to the artist's motto, "I want to be the best of the second-rate." Serious German museums continue to refrain from including Kippenberger in their retrospectives.

Fricke had called the curator of the Potsdam show, Christoph Tannert (an East Berliner and by then head of the Bethanien international artist house in Kreuzberg), a "Zampano of the East" after the itinerant strongman in Fellini's *La Strada*; Babias called him "the latest ticket-collector in Kippenberger's peep show.... Tannert now expects the Potsdam public to put up with Kippenberger's late-pubescent erections."

Andreas Quappe summarized him as follows in the *Neue Zeit* from East Berlin:

> With Kippenberger it is always and only ever about Kippenberger. He remains a major artist of the eighties, an entertainer for yuppies who are sick of feeling awkward. A narcissus.... The painter first caused a real sensation when he had someone else work for him: in 1981, when a billboard painter painted the *Dear Painter, Paint For Me* cycle following his designs. A man in secure financial circumstances can obviously afford such investments in his career.

The press outside Berlin, too, which usually preferred to ignore Martin's shows, took the opportunity to proclaim, with a visible sense of relief, that the party was over. "In retrospect, Kippenberger's call to hedonism reads like the economic news from the eighties," Annette Tietenberg wrote in the *FAZ*. "But since luxury, extravagance, and waste have taken a downturn since then, so too has the appeal of perpetual puberty. Even art isn't all milk and honey any more." As an artist, Kippenberger was passé, Tietenberg wrote, and he should take a break, for his own sake and that of the public.

"Kippenberger's clowning plays a cynical game with the values of social and political propriety," Sabine Vogel reprimanded in the *Week*. In the eighties, she wrote:

> artists such as Kippenberger stood boldly on tables and bars and undertook excessive boozing and carousing while singing dirty songs. No sexism was too ordinary for this yuppie-existentialism to turn into an impudent *bon mot*, no racism too malicious, no anti-antifascism too close to the truth.... Today, in

any case, none of that looks quite as fun as it used to. By the end of the eighties, the fun turned serious and people put away childish things: there was the rise of AIDS, and the fall of the Wall, and now adolescent macho games from conceited boys who never grow up, like Kippenberger, only suggest more jackass behavior in store. Present-day reality has overtaken the avant-garde of taboo-breaking artists.... The fall of the Wall has transformed how we look at Kippenberger's works in particular. There is good and bad again. And good and evil. Since the recent debates about granting foreigners asylum, a photographed gravestone for "Our Little Bimbo" the dog is no longer just a dumb boyish prank. Since dumb German boys have started vandalizing [Jewish] cemeteries again, and had a good time with violence against foreigners, Kippenberger's sticker "J.A.F." for "Jesus Against Fascism" isn't funny anymore. The rude gestures of irresponsibility in Kippenberger's chilled-out helluva-guy works have gone flat.

Outraged at this witch-hunt, Roberto Ohrt, the curator of Martin's Pompidou show, published a response in the (leftist) newspaper *Die Beute* (The Spoils). Under the headline "Only Other People Ever Go To Whorehouses," he accused the critics of moral self-satisfaction and humorlessness, "unbelievable assumptions and flagrantly inverting the truth.... These supposedly leftist critics feel, not unjustly, that Kippenberger is talking directly to them when he unmasks their self-righteous moralizing."

The criticism may have reached its high point around the Potsdam exhibition—Martin was never again on the receiving end of such unanimously hateful blows—but it never stopped altogether during his lifetime. Even artists in his circle were tarnished with guilt by association: his former student Tobias Rehberger, for example, said in a 1996 interview that "editors sent critics to my show and they wrote scathing reviews because there was this connection to Kippenberger." When the Berlin Academy of the Arts decided in 1996 to award Martin the Käthe Kollwitz Prize—a decision that Christoph Tannert saw as "a kind of invitation to come home"—Fricke wrote in the *taz* that he was flabbergasted to see someone receive the honor who, in 1982, "had drawn starving Africans on a sheet of paper in a kind of Käthe Kollwitz parody and written 'They say Blacks have longer ones—not true!' underneath as a kind of commentary." When Martin received the prize posthumously, shortly after his death, Fricke wrote in his obituary in the *taz*, "He was not a good person."

SERIOUSLY UNSERIOUS

"Cheerful and relaxed, curious and unconceited": this was Martin as Christoph Tannert saw him during the construction of the exhibition in Potsdam. The curator was the same age as Martin and had lived in Berlin at the same time—on the other side of the Wall. He had become a fan of Martin's as a member of the Prenzlauer Berg art scene: "For me he was a punk, the way I would have wanted to be—functioning outside the system, between the systems." He liked the combination of Martin's snotty analyses of the West and his having his photograph taken with a soldier guarding the Wall in East Berlin, or in front of a *Thirty Years of East Germany* billboard. "To be seriously unserious was really alternative for us. Fun was absolutely alien in the GDR." As a result, the Prenzlauer Berg scene especially enjoyed Martin's slogans, some of which,

Tannert said, took on whole new meanings in the society of scarcity in the East. "We use natural fart heating," for example: "In a place where we had barely the absolute necessities, we liked seeing someone spread the fun with a cheerful/ironic aperçu like that." And they felt validated and energized by the fact that musicians, performers, filmmakers, and artists appeared together at S.O.36: "In Prenzlauer Berg we were cooperating the same way."

Tannert said that he didn't experience much of a culture shock after the fall of the Wall, like so many of his peers did, because he had always had the feeling that the West had its own dark side—dingy Kreuzberg streets and courtyards, for example, which he knew from Martin's photographs. Even the tattered copy of Martin's book *Women* that Tannert had found somewhere was thrilling: "It wasn't tacky like most of what came out of the East, but also not spic and span like stuff from the West—it was different. A book like that would not have been possible in the GDR: photographers at the time were harrassed if they didn't take crisp, clear photos, and they certainly weren't admitted into the Art Union. To see an artist in the West irritate people with these blurry, shaky photos and strange angles confirmed that I was on the right track: that it was really about making conscious conceptual decisions."

Even if some of Tannert's interpretations at the time turned out to be based on projection ("I realized that he didn't care about the GDR, the same way he didn't care about anything else"), he was glad to see Martin's post-1989 openness toward East*ern* Germany, as it was now known: an alien land on German soil.

Martin was interested in everything different, he made fun of it and told jokes too but not as arrogantly as the other West Germans. The nooks and crannies of all this radical change were interesting to him—he wanted to know about it—while many West Germans only performed their pity about the fact that we in the GDR had had to live in such conditions. He wanted to learn about the contexts, he asked and he listened. And didn't go around demanding approval either, acting like he had gone through exactly what the East Germans had. Not at all. The difference was totally clear to him. But there was still this interaction with the other side on completely equal footing.

Johannes Wohnseifer remembers Martin as being depressed during this period, as telling him that he couldn't bear to look at all his old work again. It was certainly a strange re-encounter with the past: more than ten years before, he had fled Berlin for the Black Forest, and now he was coming back with work the Grässlins had collected there. The whole thing may have seemed too backward-looking for him, too closed-off. Anna Grässlin, on the other hand, says he was "enthusiastic" about the exhibition and in good spirits.

Tannert remembers especially Martin's humor, as well as his enthusiasm, during the construction of the exhibition in the enormous old granary. In fact, spending time with Tannert—someone for whom many of the old pieces were new—may have been precisely what Martin found refreshing and encouraging. "Here, you know this one?" Martin would say, pulling one piece after another out of the crate, and they would enjoy it together—the crucified frog, for example.

The Grässlins' Kippenberger collection had never been fully shown, with all the early small pictures and late large ones, the *Rest Center for Mothers* pieces, the birch forest, the collages, the bath mats, the Hunger Family. Certainly not in the East. But that was precisely the place for it, in Tannert's view. Friedrich Meschede of the DAAD (German Academic Exchange Service) in Berlin had arranged it, along with Gisela Capitain; the show took place in a country that for decades had had a single artistic direction imposed on its people, socialist realism, which Martin in turn had referred to stylistically and thematically over and over again, in works like *Likeable Communist Woman, Two Proletarian Inventresses on the Way to the Inventors' Congress,* and *Cultural Peasant at Work Repairing Her Tractor.* Tannert had experienced socialist realism as "fully moralizing, never ironic, never self-reflexive, downright Protestant in its purity," so "it was absolutely essential for me to show, precisely in the former GDR, that a realistic perspective could be different."

For Christoph Tannert the show was a personal triumph.

For the critics it was an insult.

For many of its visitors it was an irritation. One woman from the Potsdam Ministry was outraged at the artist's gall, showing wooden transportation pallets as *Rest Center for Mothers* pieces. And then this dirty artist had had Joop, the flashy perfume manufacturer who was in the process of rediscovering his Potsdam roots, design the posters— "ornamental nonsense," as Tannert described them.

For Martin it was an occasion to run wild with Michel Würthle on the night of the opening, after not having drunk a drop during the construction. He had come to a point where he no longer knew where and how to keep going.

YOU ARE MY WIFE

He stood in the doorway, took a deep breath, and sighed: "Wonnebergstrasse [literally "Merrymount Street"]! What a beautiful name!"

481

Minchie Huggler says that she will never forget that moment. "I liked him from the very beginning."

She was a beautiful Japanese woman—*Japonaise,* as Martin called her—who lived in Zurich, the wife of a successful Swiss banker and mother of three daughters. She was working with Fram Katigawa, a gallerist, to provide public art for Tachikawa, a gigantic, bleak new district on the outskirts of Tokyo. "It was so sad there that we had to give it some poetry." And she had discovered poetry in one of Martin's sculptures: a lamppost in the form of a Santa Claus with a rod. No sooner had she said she was interested in it than Martin and Gisela Capitain showed up at her lovely dream-house. Minchie made sushi and took Martin to the station when he had to leave urgently after the meal. They spoke English with each other since she didn't speak German—though she did, to Martin's great delight, speak Swiss German: her Swiss mother-in-law had insisted on it. He thought that was great, and he kept making her say things for him in her Japanese/English/Swiss-German sing-song voice.

He liked her from the start.

This was in 1993. At the same time, since Zurich is a small town, Martin met Minchie's beautiful daughter Kazu at the house of his friend Andi Stutz, a silk manufacturer. Kazu was sitting next to Martin at dinner, and the first thing he did was build a little sculpture out of the schnitzel, salad, and tomato sauce lying on her plate. He was "charming" to her, she says; he told her her high forehead reminded him of Romy Schneider.

Martin told another story to his friends in Austria: on the night he met Kazu, he was apparently so drunk that his head dropped face-first into a bowl of goulash, and when he looked up, she was just walking past, and he said, "You are my wife."

Kazu didn't know who Martin was. But she was intrigued, and inspired, and a bit afraid.

"Then I went back to Japan and was unhappy again."

Kazu had lived in Japan until she was eleven: a happy childhood, she said, before the move to Switzerland. "If you only grow up in Tokyo, you never learn to communicate. Ask a Japanese what he thinks of something and he'll say 'I don't know,' and everyone will think that's normal." At school, she said, everything was learned by rote, "and it was very hard to stand up and express your own opinion." Kazu returned to Japan after high school in Switzerland, to live in her family home "and get to know the culture." She studied Japanese art history and aesthetics, specializing in kimonos. She remembers herself as being "young and always sad."

A year later, Martin was sitting with Minchie Huggler and Jacqueline Burckhardt, co-editor of the art magazine *Parkett,* at the Kronenhalle restaurant in Zurich, and it came out that Minchie was Kazu's mother. She encouraged him to contact her daughter, and he had her write her daughter's address in his passport, on the page that already had Japanese stamps. Burckhardt suggested that he was much too old for Kazu, wasn't he? Martin just stuck his tongue out at her: no problem, he said, "my girlfriends are always at least fifteen years younger than me." They drank very good red wine at the meal, and eventually the conversation drifted. Martin announced that he wanted to marry Kazu and have Minchie as a beloved mother.

He wrote to Kazu from Syros, in April 1994. A fax came back with a poem from her that he tore up because he thought someone was playing a joke on him: according to Kazu, Martin "thought that the poem was so beautiful, it couldn't have been written by a woman." No matter how many jokes he played on others, he couldn't stand feeling like someone was playing one on him. The correspondence with Kazu continued nonetheless. Martin flew to Tokyo, and the moment he stepped out of the taxi, she said, she felt for the first time like she was in over her head. "I thought: Oh God, a man like that, how will I ever be able to handle him? He was such a big man, it was almost a little scary."

There is a photograph of the two of them in a Japanese courtyard: Martin, tall and looking very German in a hat and a heavy winter overcoat, has his arm around Kazu, looking very Japanese: sixteen years younger, short, very petite in her kimono, with her black hair pulled tightly back. They look almost like father and daughter.

She called him "my barbarian."

He called her "my little feather."

He had come for a few weeks at first. They got engaged, saw each other again in Switzerland, and traveled together to Syros—"for a vacation," Martin announced. In fact, what she needed was a vacation from him, and she went swimming in the sea with Michel Würthle's daughter as often as she could. "Being with Martin was un-be-liev-a-bly stressful." Their trip to Madrid "was the most stressful week of my life. I thought every morning that I was going to die. It was torture, the endless drinking, and you weren't allowed to go home." They were always in company, with large groups, and always, she felt, "there was this pressure—everyone was waiting for him to stand up and put on another show." The next morning, as always, he would get up punctually, "but physically he was totally at his limit."

Minchie Huggler and her daughter both say that that is what they learned from Martin: to be there no matter what shape you're in, and to never give up. "That's what he demonstrated to the end."

In Zurich, Martin had a little family circle. Jacqueline Burckhardt and Bice Curiger from *Parkett* were there, as well as the Swiss artists Fischli and Weiss, who appreciated

Martin's art and his humor as much as he did theirs. They recall him as "insanely fun and inspiring. He had such a refreshing way of looking at all the expressions of the time, whether art, film, or everyday life—he had something to say about everything, even a couple of chairs, that was witty, accurate, and entertaining." As Swiss, they weren't used to someone letting fly so directly at people and things, and they liked his confrontational approach, which struck them as extremely German: "this culture of conflict, this merciless way of treating each other—in Switzerland everything is always expressed diplomatically and in a balanced way." On the other hand, his anarchy and anti-authoritarian behavior didn't fit the image of the German in the least.

The art dealer and collector Thomas Ammann and his partner This Brunner also lived in Zurich. Brunner ran the only repertory cinema in Zurich, and Martin and Kazu stayed for a while in his guest apartment. Martin had made a drawing for him once, *WC Fields at Brunner's Bar* (Brunner himself never drank but admired the notorious drinker, provocateur, and coiner of snappy phrases as much as Martin did.)

Andi Stutz was a good friend of Martin's—formerly a psychiatric nurse and thus used to dealing with difficult people. He turned to manufacturing fine silk handkerchiefs and ties, including one with a motif of one of Martin's lampposts; Stutz liked to cook for Martin, drink with him, and collect his works.

Finally, there was Birgit Küng, the gallerist, who also liked to drink but who ate less and less. (She died in 2005.) He liked it when she mothered him and cooked for him; for her, according to Brunner, Martin was "God: her favorite artist, the most important artist in her gallery. She always lit up whenever he was there or even when she heard his name." He could visit her whenever he wanted, no matter how things were going with him; she also let him exhibit and curate at

Art Space Fettstrasse 7a, her gallery with Albert Oehlen, named after Art Space in Hamburg and the address of Albert Oehlen's and Werner Büttner's studios.

Now, Martin had found in the Hugglers another family—father, mother, and three children—in an open household. He paid court to the whole family, inviting them all out for caviar, drawing their Christmas cards for them (a dog carrying a Christmas tree in his paw), and giving them drawings as presents (a picture with rocks, since the Japanese have rock gardens, and a little feather on the sofa, "for the parents of the little turtledove"). When Kazu was in Tokyo and he was in Switzerland, he felt that he had to look after her sisters—in his own way. He met up with Anna, Kazu's older sister, and raked her boyfriend over the coals; he went out with Joshi, Kazu's thirteen-year-old sister, and her friends, "and he hacked the boys to pieces." He also wanted to paint a family portrait: Anna with a Jewish star, since she had the nose for it (they said); Joshi with a Peruvian hat, since he thought she looked Peruvian; Kazu from behind; the mother another way (that the family no longer recalls); the father naked.

Kazu's father was probably the most skeptical in the family of this potential in-law. Martin was "an unusual man, hard to grasp, hard to understand, but strangely charming," Peter Huggler said. When his wife reminded him that he used to laugh himself silly over Martin's antics, he said that Martin's speeches were wonderful, and the stories he told were very funny. It impressed the banker that Martin could stand up and talk for two or three hours straight. "Fidel Castro can do that, too. But Castro is very boring. Martin was a kind of Fidel Castro of the art world, minus the Marxism."

Kazu's mother, though, was the most important figure for Martin among Kazu's relatives. He adored her, and she adored him as both an artist and a person. She was an elegant, stylish woman from an aristocratic background—related to the Japanese imperial family, as Martin proudly told people—and at the same time warm, unaffected, and open. She took care of him, cooked for him while he sat in the kitchen with her, and calmed him down.

Minchie Huggler knew what people were talking about when they said he was an embarrassment: "But it never embarrassed *me*. There was always truth in what he said." Still, she admits, her German was not good enough to understand a lot of what he was saying, for example when he talked about her marriage. "Mommy," Kazu told her, "it's better if you don't understand."

Martin was at a dinner at their house once with a group of people—bankers, investment people, and the like, talking about politics and business. "That probably bored him," Kazu said. So he stood up, and Kazu cringed ("Now what?!"). Kazu's delicate, extremely traditional Japanese grandmother (whom Martin had taught to play mau-mau in Tokyo) rebuked her for making a fuss, and then Martin invited the whole group to stand up and sing, which they actually did: the whole table, even Madame Butterfly (as Martin called one of the toupeed ladies), held hands and sang "Glow-Worm." Minchie remembers the song as "quite moving": "Shine, little glow-worm, glimmer, glimmer / Shine, little glow-worm, glimmer, glimmer / Lead us lest too far we wander / Love's sweet voice is calling yonder / Shine, little glow-worm, glimmer, glimmer / Shine, little glow-worm, glimmer, glimmer / Light the path below, above / And lead us on to love." "It was very beautiful," Kazu said, "everyone enjoyed it." They didn't know what to think of it, exactly, and were a bit embarrassed but also amused.

"He played with us a lot," Minchie Huggler said. Martin often admonished her for being too serious: "You have no sense of play! You need to play. Play, play! You need to be sillier."

She thought it was too late for that: "I am a finance daughter."

But an artist, he told her, had to be able to play.

He only got angry once, according to Minchie. It was when she asked him about his message as an artist. What do you mean message, he'd said, he didn't have a message. But you are only on this earth for a limited time, she'd replied, at some point you'll die and you should leave a lasting message behind. Martin got terribly angry and screamed at Kazu in her room: "Your mother! She's saying bad things about me!"

A GIANT AT REST

Martin went to see Kazu in Tokyo for three months in the winter of 1994-95. He stayed in the family home, which stood as though fallen from outer space between the skyscrapers and faced inward to an enchanted garden in the courtyard. It was built in the twenties—not especially old, but still one of the oldest houses in the center of Tokyo.

It was not the first time that Martin had been to Japan. He had come for two weeks in 1991 with Uli Strothjohann: a printshop had invited them to work there and given them lots of money and a show at the end. Martin made cold-point engravings and a very expensive artist book (*One Flew Over the Canarybirds Nest*), and Uli made latex pictures. They didn't see much of the city—they worked all day and otherwise felt a bit like the Bill Murray character in *Lost in Translation.* Even Martin, who usually had something to say about everything, was speechless when he ordered spaghetti and saw what arrived on his plate. He was not doing well when he moved to Tokyo to be with Kazu. A fortune-teller in Frankfurt had suggested he might have cancer, but that wasn't enough to get him to go see a doctor. His hands were red from alcohol to an extent that could not be ignored, his feet so swollen that he couldn't wear normal shoes—Gisela Capitain had to send him felt slippers.

Kazu had laid down the rules: that she "could not take care of him as a foreigner in my country with all of his usual energy and personality... I have to work, and you have to work." Martin settled into her mother's writing room and drew while Kazu worked in the library. The house was near a lively neighborhood with lots of bars, restaurants, and stores. For lunch they went to a schnitzel place where they had Japanese-style schnitzel: breaded and fried, with very finely chopped cabbage, rice and miso soup, and a small bottle of sake. Then back to the house for his afternoon nap, more work, and out again in the evening, but not for too long. "It was a nice rhythm." They had dinner at a traditional restaurant, the Crane, sitting at the counter and eating fish, and then moved on to an old lady's tiny jazz bar that was usually empty. He drew in some of the bars and in one miniscule karaoke bar sang "My Way," big and loud, Martin-style, in his hat and coat. The Japanese clapped and thought it was great; Martin was in tears as he sang.

He seemed "calm" to her in Tokyo, "calm in a beautiful way." They drove to the ocean, to her traditional, straw-roofed house. "He probably liked not understanding anything, just sitting there and observing." Martin had said in the *Artfan* interview that it was an advantage not to speak a language or to speak it badly: "You can pop into a café and not hear any of the shit being whined all around you unless you want to listen and try hard. You hear fragments and make a little rhyme out of them. You are in an isolation but with lots of people, I always need lots of people around me."

He sometimes managed a made-up Japanese of his own,

by copying what he heard. "What he could do well was order: 'One sake!'"

It didn't bother the Japanese that he was sitting so quietly in the corner, "they don't say much themselves, after all." Kazu believes that if he had understood everything he would have gotten more worked up; if he had been able to communicate, the whole stay in Japan would have been more dramatic. But he couldn't express himself. "So he was like a giant at rest. And so they respected him. They probably knew that you really shouldn't wake this man up. He was in a quiet phase."

Even when they got engaged, they did so quietly and without a big celebration. Martin had already imagined the wedding party: it would take place in Japan, where couples always got gifts of money in an envelope, two hundred dollars minimum, and he would invite "everybody."

He thought Kazu looked beautiful when she wore a kimono. On the other hand, he made fun of the tea ceremony she studied and attended in her kimono. He thought the whole fuss and ultra-respectfulness was exaggerated. And it was too expensive. "Come on, you don't need to pay that much for a tea bag!"

After a few weeks, the idyll began to crumble. At first Martin had liked sitting and drawing in the schnitzel restaurant, but "it just wasn't working any more. Martin started acting up again, he was dissatisfied and aggressive. At some point it just wasn't enough for him. Everything was too perfect." Perhaps it was their idyllic coupledom, perhaps the boredom that took hold of him everywhere eventually and made him move on down his highway, perhaps he realized that his dream was about to collapse, or perhaps he felt that Kazu in Japan was too Japanese for him ("from another planet") and too concerned with her own friends and social obligations within the imperial family. He was jealous when she went skiing with the Japanese prince;

he couldn't stand her friends. The only one of them he liked was Aki, a gallerist with an excellent knowledge of Japanese culture, who was very fat, very tall, and very gay, "very conspicuous for a Japanese man." He was the son of a famous sumo wrestler who had died young, and he was "hypernervous, hypersensitive, highly intelligent." He arranged to get Martin Japanese comic books as models for his paintings.

Martin felt neglected, and Kazu felt overwhelmed. She told him that he was expecting too much from her. "Eventually it couldn't go on. Then there was nothing to do except run away. Leave him sitting in the restaurant and run out the door." She went out with him at night less and less often.

So Martin found himself staying at home in the evening with Kazu's housekeeper—he thought she was great, and he knew she would always be there. Toshko, almost eighty, was a tiny woman who had once been the family's governess and spoke perfect English and French, having worked at the Japanese embassy in Bern, Switzerland. Martin liked sitting at the big kitchen table with her with the TV on while she was cooking. Once, when he said that he'd like her to make him coq au vin, "it was the coq-au-vin record, every night for two straight weeks. But he didn't say anything. He thought it was funny."

Martin continued to draw—in earnest, Gisela Capitain said, "like a man possessed and with absolute intensity." He had a hundred and fifty drawings by the end, and he faxed them all to Zurich. "It was endless, they came rolling out of the fax machine like toilet paper," Minchie Huggler said. (Martin promised a drawing each as presents to Minchie and her husband, and Peter Huggler picked the exact one that Martin himself thought was the best, which made him insanely angry: it took him a day to get over the fact that "now he's gone and taken the best one!")

491

Martin called the show of his drawings at the Borgmann Capitain Gallery *Beyond the Beyond*, and, Capitain said, "people came in droves, it was like everyone saw the light, even museum people suddenly felt called upon to say that he was a real artist. The whole city was talking about it, Benedikt Taschen bought twenty drawings." After years of doldrums, Martin had the feeling that "the floodgates were opened."

In retrospect, Martin's stay in Tokyo seemed like an experiment to Kazu and she wonders how she could have lasted as long as she did. After the experiment failed, he returned to Germany depressed and in despair. Three glasses were enough to get Martin drunk—he wasn't used to it any more. Capitain put him in a taxi to the Hotel Chelsea. Soon afterward he traveled to Essen to see his friend Meese, who handed him off to Meuser in Düsseldorf after a few days when he couldn't take it any longer. Meuser's wife, Nanette, said she wanted him not to drink alcohol in the mornings, and Martin said, "That's what I want, too."

Germany in winter wasn't exactly designed to cheer him up: "so many gray barbarians here," he wrote to Kazu in Tokyo.

Martin went back to Sankt Georgen; he and Kazu wrote to each other, and in Zurich they spent a little more time together. Eventually Martin told her that he didn't want to wait any longer, she had to decide—and so she did. They were both sad. He gave Kazu his engagement ring and said she should tie a black ribbon around both rings and put them in a box he had given her once. And so, bound with a mourning ribbon, they lay there as in a coffin. For the second time, Martin had to carry to the grave his attempt to start a family.

CHAPTER TEN

JENNERSDORF

We All Need Somebody To Lean On: that's what Martin called his 1986 show at Christian Nagel's in Munich. Bronze broomsticks leaning against the wall.

Ten years later, he drew himself as half-boy (with crew cut), half-old-man, leaning on his wife's shoulder with his arm around her, pencil in his hand. It was a self-portrait on a tablecloth, made in his new regular hangout, the restaurant at the Hotel Raffel in his new home, Jennersdorf. The owner said Martin drew it at 1 a.m. on Christmas night. A couple of days earlier was the first time Martin's new friends had seen him without him cracking any jokes: he was just back from the doctor, who had sent him to the hospital for further tests two days before Christmas. They told him they didn't find anything, but six weeks later, at a hospital in Vienna, came the official diagnosis: liver cancer, cirrhosis, hepatitis.

He was always craving: drugs, alcohol, love, cigarettes, recognition, good art. He was full of longing, an addictive personality. "Addiction [*Sucht*] is just searching [*suchen*]," he said in the interview with Jutta Koether. He was always searching for people who wanted the same thing he did: "something better."

On a sticker that Martin put up all over Berlin in the late seventies, especially in the bar toilets, was his photograph and address with the words "Man Seeking Woman." It was more than just a good joke: he actually was seeking a woman, a home. And in the end, he found her. Maybe he knew that he no longer had time to seek—it was time to find.

"Women are goddesses," Martin said in a 1992 interview, even if he treated them often enough as the opposite. "They are above us in the hierarchy. Who do you see sitting on a bench in the park? Old women. There are no old men. It's the women who survive, not us."

Now he had found his goddess: beautiful, intelligent, charming, and successful, an experienced woman who loved to cook and cooked well, someone he was proud of. When Martin was young, his girlfriends were always older than he was, but the older he got, the younger they got. This time it was different: Elfie Semotan was twelve years older than Martin and the mother of two sons, Ivo (21) and August (13). "She's 53, I was born in '53!" For Martin, it was a sign. She had already been married to an artist: Kurt Kocherscheidt, who had died at 49 after years with a serious heart ailment. This time, when Michel Würthle came up to Martin with his favorite phrase, a running gag between the two—"Fucked yet today?"—Martin answered, "I don't fuck, I love."

Martin and Elfie met at Michel's fiftieth birthday party on Syros. Her husband had been an old friend of Michel's from Vienna; he had died nine months earlier, after the last of a series of heart operations. Elfie, who had become well known for her fashion and advertising photography, had promised to be the photographer at Michel's party. Martin was the only one there she avoided. It wasn't that she wasn't interested in him, but the whole fuss around him got on her nerves: "Everyone bowed down to him so piously and laughed at all his jokes, I thought I sure didn't need to join in." And he noticed. At some point he came up to her and asked if she wouldn't mind taking his picture too. He so liked having his picture taken.

That was in 1993. Two years later, they saw each other again at Club an der Grenze (Club on the Border), at an opening for one of Michel's shows in the Burgenland. "Where's the widow?" Martin asked, and when he saw her, while a club member was in the middle of a speech, he took her hand and kissed it and said, "Ah, you're here, too, how lovely."

He gave another long, meandering speech of his own that night. Most of the people quickly fled; only a few loyal listeners stuck it out, such as Michel, and Elfie. At one point Martin climbed off the table and said to Elfie, "Please, come here, sit with me." "He was drunk and tired, but he told me the most wonderful things: what he wanted to do, how he'd do it, our whole life together. It was unbelievably seductive. The most poetic thing I have ever heard in my life, how he imagined our lives together. It was an idea that developed very quickly, this possibility."

At the end of that night, he told her that they should try to live together. "You're someone, I'm someone, it would have to work." He wanted to go home with her then and there; only after she gave him a kiss on the cheek did he let her go home with her son. He called her the next day, and they spent an hour in Hotel Raffel. They went to dinner the day after that, and the day after that he wanted to meet her sons, but she had to fly to Paris for a fashion show. He went with her.

Elfie worked, and they went to La Coupole together, and Davé's restaurant, where Martin got jealous because Helmut Lang, the fashion designer and Elfie's best friend, was getting all the attention. Martin quickly pulled one of his old turtle jokes out of his sleeve: he wanted to be the center of attention himself.

He had already told her, "We have to get married." She thought they were old enough to just live together. Martin disagreed: "I've never been married." He was a romantic, a fan of Hollywood happy endings. He wanted a honeymoon in Venice.

Elfie had an apartment in Vienna and an old renovated farmhouse in the Burgenland that had gradually become a perfect hideaway, lovely and comfortable but not too neat and tidy. He had found what he needed among the cornfields, trees, flowers, and meadows: a nest that he didn't have to build himself, and a family that he wasn't responsible for.

He immediately took pictures off the wall of Elfie's apartment in Vienna, including ones by Kurt Kocherscheidt, and hung works from his own collection, such as paintings by Büttner and Albert Oehlen. He acted more intrusively than diplomatically with Elfie's sons too, at first.

"He didn't beat around the bush, he asked for what he needed," Elfie said. First and foremost, Kurt Kocherscheidt's studio, with a view of the fields and floorboard heating that he especially liked (he may have already been suffering chills from his illness). Elfie emptied out the studio, and soon he was hauling in two truckloads from Sankt Georgen: a Franz West day bed, a huge pile of photos of Helena, two art cabinets, a leather sofa, a framed photograph of our father from the sixties, our father's books and china cabinet with his collection of schnapps bottles and the Siegerland almanac with contributions from him, as well as Martin's half-finished and primed paintings, models, empty frames, full slide carousels, and more. His household furnishings were smaller in scope: a Braun coffee maker, a bread knife, pasta tongs, and not much else.

Before he married into his new family, he rounded up his old family one more time. He had us spend Christmas 1995 together in Berlin—Martin, we sisters, our families, and Gabi and Helena. It was his farewell to bachelor life. We spent Christmas Eve at my apartment, with a Christmas tree and presents, then Christmas Day at our sister Tina's, with turkey, of course, and the next day at the Paris Bar, for mau-mau and other fun.

The wedding was in February. The civil ceremony took place in Jennersdorf—a very small affair, with Helmut Lang and Jörg Schlick as witnesses. Then came the party, the way Martin had always planned it, according to Kazu Huggler: "big and endless and draining," in three acts with a slightly shifting and ever more intimate cast of characters. It was thoroughly organized, but not nearly as wild as Martin's fortieth birthday—he was much calmer than usual, sometimes almost melancholy.

The first act took place at Café Engländer, Martin's regular hangout in Vienna. There was a crushing crowd that night, with friends and ex-girlfriends. There was a Vienna buffet: "totally easy, no stress" to prepare, according to the host, Attila Corbaci, "his calm had rubbed off on me." The bride and groom, dressed in Helmut Lang, were glowing, and at one point everyone had to go out in the freezing cold night for a group photograph on the church steps. "There were no scandals," Corbaci said. "Except the usual discussions about art."

The next morning, some of the guests reassembled at Café Engländer with suitcases—"it looked like a group of immigrants to America"—and boarded a chartered bus for the Burgenland. For entertainment during the ride, an old German movie from the fifties was shown: *The House in Montevideo,* a comedy about humor, morality (and double standards), human kindness, a big family, and a house full of children.

For lunch, there were pancakes and wedding soup at Martin's favorite inn in the region, the White Cross, where the owners had prepared a reception for the couple, including a trumpet solo and a canvas that Martin had to sit down and paint at. The party went on that night in Jennersdorf, in Elfie's house and Martin's studio: Rüdiger Carl played music for dancing. On the third and last night, an even smaller circle met for dinner at Club on the Border with a Hungarian band playing. Finally, at five in the morning, the photographer Albrecht Fuchs found Martin sitting alone in the snow at a campfire: he hadn't sat there especially for the camera, but "he also knew it looked good."

By the time of his wedding, Martin had realized that his status in Austria had changed. He was no longer a German hooligan, he was the husband of a well-known woman—a "high-class fashion photographer," as one tabloid journalist put it—who was also the widow of an esteemed Austrian artist. In a short newspaper article on the wedding, Elfie was named first, before Martin and the "320 international art-world friends," including John Baldessari, Coop Himmelblau, Gerhard Rühm, and Catherine David.

The wedding also provided Martin with a treasure trove of material that he turned to in his work again and again over the coming months. The photos that Gisela Capitain took on the morning of the second day, in front of Café Engländer, became the invitations to the *Nada Arugula* show; the last issue of the Lord Jim Lodge magazine *Sun Breasts Hammer,* "The Ex-Bachelor Issue," showed photographs from all three days of beaming, talking, dancing, eating, smoking, hugging, and drinking guests and the bride and groom. Martin showed the chairs from the club's courtyard, complete with campfire, at Villa Merkel in Esslingen. The photos Elfie took of him on their honeymoon in Venice ended up in his Academy of Arts catalog together with the drawings he had made from them. He turned one of those photos, of him in front of the German Pavilion of the Biennale, into a poster.

Martin had always avoided Venice on his many trips to Italy. He had once told Jan Hoet in Kassel: "Honeymoon or German Pavilion, otherwise I won't go." He asked for good red wine and a couple of nights at Hotel Cipriani for a wedding present. Elfie said that the trip was very relaxed, with a lot of strolling around, pasta twice a day, bellinis at Harry's Bar, sitting in cafés, and going out dancing, taking pictures the whole time.

In Venice, Martin did what he always did: took a cliché and simply piled another one on top of it. He sat like a gigolo in the gondolas; he went to Piazza San Marco, "where every stone has already been photographed to oblivion," and had his picture taken there with bird food crumbled on his head and in his pockets so that the pigeons were swarming all over him. "Then, after doing the dullest things, I went and made drawings that suddenly resulted in something of my own."

On the Raffel tablecloth, he would draw himself and his wife as a pair of artists: he with a pen in his hand, she with her camera in front of her. He liked having Elfie take his picture. For a magazine she once posed him in a big floral Issey Miyake evening gown (he later painted a picture with that motif). Another time, she asked him if she could pose the young models in front of his canvases—"sure," he said, but in the end he wanted to be in one of the pictures, too, so after the official photos were done he slipped out of his pants and shoes and stood between the boy and the boyish girl, in his white socks and totally unfashionable briefs. (That motif turned into a poster for his show at the Villa Merkel in Esslingen, but the posters were pulped before the opening because they might suggest child abuse. The invitations were withdrawn, too, for the same reason: they showed him with Helena, in a photograph taken by Elfie.)

He liked having his picture taken, Elfie said, but he wanted to be shown "the way he wanted to be shown." At first, his "exaggerated way of posing" annoyed her. But just as he got her to cook things that she normally never would have cooked (fish sticks), he got her to take pictures in ways she never would have done otherwise.

In the countless pictures of himself he had people take or make over the years—which played no small part in his fame—he always looks different and yet always like himself. "Martin knew right away what was important in any situation," Johannes Wohnseifer said. "He was an unbelievably visual person who thought in pictures." Martin was shocked only when he saw a picture that Elfie had taken of him when he wasn't striking a pose: an extreme close-up of his face, showing two deep wrinkles in his forehead. Did she really think he looked good like that? he asked. Yes, she insisted.

Martin spent most of his time in Jennersdorf, not in Vienna, where his wife had her career and August was going to school. Elfie continued to live her life and traveled around the world to photo shoots and fashion shows, while Martin spent most of his time in seclusion, working in the country. Every now and then, they would meet up at one place or the other, travel together, and work together.

His new place couldn't have been farther from home: in the southwestern-most tip of Austria, at the three-way border with Hungary and Slovenia. And it also couldn't have been closer to home: he had ended up in St. Martin, as the village and its chapel were called. He often passed the chapel, which was easy to see from a distance, alone on its hill. Saint Martin himself had been born not far from there, in Hungary.

Martin's move to the Burgenland was a liberation. He was glad to have escaped the German art scene, and also Sankt Georgen. Once again—for the last time—he could build a little world of his own, occupy a place, stir it up, take it over, make friends and enemies, play tricks, and make fun of people, including Helmut Lang, whom he wanted to compete with as a fashion designer named Hans Kurz (*kurz* means "short" in German; *lang* means "long").

He had found a nest where he could really lay his eggs;

his last year would turn out to be one of his most fruitful and successful. He had also finished his masterpiece, the Kafka installation. Zdenek Felix, the curator of *Truth Is Work*, who devoted a big solo show in Deichtorehallen Hamburg to Martin after Martin's death, believed "he could have still discovered a lot of things . . . But he'd said what was most important. He'd done what he'd wanted to do."

Martin worked on countless projects in this period. He had finally been invited to documenta, for which he was preparing a subway station that was to be set up in the middle of the Fulda River until German security regulations had thwarted that plan. Kasper König had invited him to the major sculpture exhibition in Münster, running parallel to documenta, and Martin wanted to show a subway vent there. He found a place to set it up across from a bust of Annette von Droste-Hülshoff, the classic German poet whose Rüschhaus we had seen on weekend trips as children. He was also preparing a subway entrance for the Leipzig Fair and a transportable crumpled subway entrance for Metro Pictures in New York.

Uli Strothjohann was building the Spiderman Studio for Martin, which he would exhibit for the first time in Nice; Martin showed *Forgotten Problems of Furnishing Villa Hügel* at Esslingen's Villa Merkel; he had shows with Eleni Koroneou in Athens (*Made in Syros*), Gisela Capitain in Cologne, Mikael Andersen in Copenhagen, and Bleich-Rossi in Graz; he put out a CD of his *Greatest Hits*; he worked on lithographs in Copenhagen; and he received the first prizes of his career, the Konrad von Soest Prize in Münster, the Arthur Köpcke Prize in Copenhagen, and the Käthe Kollwitz Prize in Berlin.

A regular explosion of work came out of his studio. Valeria Heisenberg recalled that "when he was in Frankfurt, he desperately wanted to step back from the whole machinery he had been resorting to. Everyone wanted more of his drunken lampposts, but he wanted to paint portraits, like a classical painter." In her experience, Heisenberg went on, "A lot of artists talk that way but don't dare do it, because of the pressures of the art market. Martin could do it, because of all the variety and fissures in his work." At the end of his life, he fulfilled that dream of his, too.

When he described to Jutta Koether the funeral he imagined for himself, he said he hoped that his coffin would be floating in a sea of tears. "And everyone will love me for what I did at the end. Everything else was nice, sure, but people forget that too, they're busy thinking about themselves.... The last thing has to be a real bombshell." And so it was. *Jacqueline: The Pictures Pablo Couldn't Paint Anymore* and the *Medusa* self-portraits were his most intense and moving series.

Shortly before his own death, Martin painted portraits of Picasso's sad widow from photographs taken after Picasso's death. "Picasso has died, so she's sad," Martin told the curator Daniel Baumann. "And so I took over his job. The last photographs there are of Jacqueline Picasso are black and white and blurry; I tried to transpose them into color and turn them into Picassos. To complete the work, so to speak." David Douglas Duncan had taken the photographs of Picasso's widow two years after Picasso's death, when she was still numb with grief but was being brought back into the world of the living by a couple she was friends with. In Martin's paintings, Jacqueline bears a certain similarity to Martin himself, perhaps also to our mother, and to Elfie. When the paintings were finished, he wanted to show them immediately in Samia Saouma's Paris gallery, across from the Picasso Museum, during Fashion Week, which Elfie always spent in Paris.

THE RAFT OF THE MEDUSA

The Kafka installation was also shown in 1996 for the first time since its premiere in Rotterdam two years earlier. Annesofie Becker and Willie Flindt, the curators who included it in the Copenhagen exhibition *Memento Metropolis*, ended up giving Martin the greatest gift that any curator ever gave him: they hung a reproduction of Théodore Géricault's famous painting *The Raft of the Medusa* at the entrance to the exhibition because they saw an astonishing similarity between the two works, despite their obvious differences. "Both cases deal with a catastrophic situation, and in both cases it is unclear whether salvation is the actual disaster."

The painting is based on a real event. In 1816, the French frigate *Medusa* ran aground off the coast of Senegal. The officers boarded the life rafts and left the soldiers to fend for themselves; for thirteen days, a hundred and fifty soldiers crowded onto or hung off the edge of a small, hastily built raft, some of them up to their hips in water. Only fifteen people survived the murder, mutiny, and cannibalism on the raft. The case led to a storm of political outrage; two of the survivors wrote an article, which inspired Géricault's painting. More than twenty-three by sixteen feet in size, it is now in the Louvre and considered the first great political painting after the French Revolution. The painting is very true-to-life: Géricault, who himself would die at only thirty-three, made studies of dying patients, corpses, and body parts in hospitals and morgues, brought the head of a dead thief into his studio, and used some of his friends as models.

Martin was electrified and immediately latched onto the connection. He had information about the painting and the historical case sent to him and had Elfie take his picture in the poses of the various people on the raft in Géricault's painting.

During the photo session—where Martin was afraid of only one thing, which was that the pictures might come out too perfect—there was a moment, Elfie said,

> that I will never forget. It was unbelievable. I felt like I was seeing something, another place, in Martin, he was completely in another world, and I saw a drama, a life drama. Martin could play a part very well, but this was different, this was what he wanted to express. He had totally opened up and let everything out, everything that had hurt him in his life, and in the thought that it could all be over. That's what he got to through the *Medusa* project. Everything came out of him—it was everything he was.

In his Jennersdorf studio, he painted and drew himself in those same poses: caught between hope and despair—dying, already dead, and longing to be saved and reach home. He painted himself as he was and as he saw himself, not like the men in Géricault's painting, who were much more muscular. His body comes across as rather shapeless, his hands are swollen, almost gouty. One painting shows him shirtless in bed, in the Thinker pose with his chin resting on his hand; another shows him lying on his back, eyes closed, dead. In one painting he looks like a drowning man, in another he is waving a handkerchief, in one he is lying on a gynecological chair covered with a sheet.

Margarete Heck was there when the pictures were being made. She was a curator at the time at the Wolfsburg Museum and was spending three weeks on vacation in Jennersdorf with her sister. Elfie was working in New York at the time, but Martin didn't want to go to America again: "He was through with that after Los Angeles." So Margarete and her sister saw

Martin every day. "He forced us to come see him in the studio every afternoon," and he showed them what he'd painted; he wanted to hear what they thought. Margarete Heck—not an art historian, but a sociologist whose dissertation was on the art trade—said that the *Medusa* pictures

> really jumped out at me—they were so intense, so personal, they had something so physical about them, real bodily experience. During those three weeks I had the feeling that there was always something new there, it was like a rushing river, the next picture went farther than the last, as though he had looked inside himself and pulled everything out, piece by piece—and then another painting! And then another drawing! It was like he had totally free access to his inner nature, like everything had opened up. Even though the theme was so difficult and heavy, his way of working was so free, totally without a struggle.

Her impression was that Martin was satisfied with his work. "Very satisfied."

CLUB ON THE BORDER

Jennersdorf was ideal for Martin: small, manageable, easy to crack. That's what idyllic places were for, but at the same time, he would lose interest if they got too cozy and comfortable. In Jennersdorf there were enough artists and other people for Martin to challenge and generate some friction with. And so he did, with great delight.

"Martin didn't exactly make things easy for the other people there," Elfie said. "They had to suffer." For example, one night in the Club on the Border, when he told a story that never ended but the others weren't allowed to start eating until he was through. Again and again he added something, or repeated something, until everybody was thoroughly pissed off.

The Club on the Border was founded in Windisch-Minihof not long before Martin's arrival. Over the years, many Viennese artists, set designers, musicians, and the like had bought first or second homes there, and they founded the Club to have a place where they could meet, talk, dance, sing, argue, cook together, or (if they were arriving from the city on a Friday night) have someone cook for them. Among the few non-resident members of the club were Michel Würthle and Reinald Nohal from the Paris Bar in Berlin. The old farmhouse on a hill that held the club belonged to Reinhard Knaus, who lived upstairs and managed it. The low Burgenland building with an inner courtyard had been thoroughly renovated, and its beauty came from its simplicity: unfinished floors, unfinished wooden tables, whitewashed walls, wood-burning stoves to cook on and in. Many of the things in the club had been made by artists: the stove by Pichler, the bar by Kocherscheidt, and accompanying barstools designed by Martin, with wooden seats made to look like Alka-Seltzer tablets.

Martin quickly made an ally of Knaus, who became his companion, chauffeur, and all-around assistant, also building the models for Martin's concrete dwarves with cannons and heaps of cannonballs. Knaus often fetched Martin for lunch, drove him back home, and then fetched him again in the evening, at eight and not a minute later. On Fridays, Martin would sit down with him in the club's open kitchen and watch him cook. "Martin stuck by Reinhard and backed him up," Margarete Heck said. And vice versa: "Whenever anyone breathed a word against Martin, Reinhard went wild." Once, when a judge from the village insulted Martin, Knaus—a very strong man—turned him upside down, carried him out the door, and stuck him head-first into the snow.

One night, the two allies, under Martin's direction, cooked together in the club: noodle casserole, needless to say. "There was more and more," ninety portions for thirty people by the time they were done, so everyone had to take some home with them, which they did with less than total enthusiasm: the noodles were rock-hard. At least the appetizers were soft: After Eight mints. Martin also drew a menu for the occasion: a self-portrait with "our today's great menu" in front of his belly.

I
After choco

II
Vegetable marks not deutsch + oxtail-marrow soupette

III
Mommy's birthdaywishhappy
with
Insalata seed & sweetbird

IV
Dessert al desserto as usual
encl.: vino in very verrytas
costa cordalis 140,– *

Then Martin came up with something that really shattered the peaceful country life of this idyllic artist colony with its tastefully renovated houses and handwritten menus: a helipad in the shape of a giant fried egg on the meadow next to the club. Kurt Kocherscheidt had died of heart failure, after all—not in Jennersdorf, but it might easily have been in

---

* On "Insalata seed & sweetbird," see p.195 above; the pun on "cost" refers to Costa Cordalis, a Greek-German singer; 140,– shillings was a little under $15.

Jennersdorf, in which case he would have had to be flown out by helicopter. Some people saw Martin's landing pad as an affectionate homage to his predecessor, others as the worst possible tastelessness.

Knaus built a model helipad with little lights and all the rest of the paraphernalia. One evening, a model-airplane expert was hired for a test flight, but there was too much wind.

The fried-egg helipad never was built; Merlicek's and Pichler's opposition was too vehement. Over our dead bodies, they said. So Martin produced a drawing of a cemetery with two gravestones bearing the names of his antagonists and declared, "OK then, we'll hire some hit men from Romania, there's a discount for two—only a thousand marks." It became a catchphrase in Windisch-Minihof: even today, whenever Pichler gets bossy, someone says, "We better get some Romanians!"

After Kocherscheidt's death, Pichler was the "big boss," the "pope," the undisputed top dog, as everyone called him. But Martin wanted to be the big boss too, as always. The two artists inevitably collided. Opinions differ today about whether their run-ins had a more sporting character or whether their aversion to each other was too intense to be called a game. But one thing is clear: in his seclusion, Martin needed Pichler as a sparring partner worth the effort.

Their artistic views could not have been more different. Fifteen years earlier, in Martin and Oehlen's "Address to the Brainless," they had already written off Pichler's sculptures as "shit." Pichler represented the noble calling of the Great Artist, holed up in his farmstead in St. Martin an der Raab making unsellable sculptures and structures, which he financed with drawings. "Stereometrically strict cult structures," as the *SDZ* put it in a piece on his seventieth birthday:

one individual enclosure after another in an almost stately rhythm, each one with its corresponding materiality and purposeful lighting giving rise to high sculptural qualities, but at the same time attaining a quality of almost sacred ritual in its formal interchange with the objects introduced into it.

Then Martin showed up with his art created out of the banalities of everyday life, his works churned out one after another in just about the least stately rhythm imaginable.

Martin was constantly thinking up new little pranks, insults, and nasty tricks. Who is the most powerful? Who is Number One? Perhaps most importantly: Who is the best-dressed man in the club? Pichler dressed so that everything matched, so Martin went him one better and covered himself head to toe in Burberry plaid: shirt, pants, umbrella, sports coat, hat, and matching Burlington socks. Or he planned to cross out the "St." and "an der Raab" on the road sign for "St. Martin an der Raab," where Pichler lived, and add "Kippenberger," "so that every time he went home he would have to think about me." When Pichler was preparing for his show at the eminent Stedelijk Museum in Amsterdam, Martin spread the rumor that the Stedelijk's director, Rudi Fuchs, had died.

Sabine Achleitner, Jörg Schlick's wife, was at a party at Club on the Border where "you could feel the kind of aggression being directed at Martin"—until finally Pichler threw a pie in his face. "So Martin took it farther, smeared the pie all over his face and had Jörg take his picture, so that he drew the attention to himself and also calmed the aggressivity in the room. Martin inflated it so far that in the end Pichler felt more insulted than him."

Martin never succeeded in ousting the top dog, even if

the Club did split into two camps to some extent, with the younger members siding with him. But he had his fun.

That summer, Martin was preparing for the major, long-planned but postponed "Respective 1997–1976" at the Musée d'art moderne et contemporain (MAMCO) in Geneva, where his old friends from Nice, Christian Bernard and Axel Huber, were working. It was a powerful show: Martin filled a whole building with his works, from the lampposts to the allotment gardens (a.k.a. Schreber-gardens). Martin gave Daniel Baumann, the young Geneva curator, his last big interview, for the catalog. Baumann said, "The best thing was to sit next to him and just see how the ideas came out—I sat there open-mouthed: boom-boom-boom, how to lay out the catalog, how to hang the show... It was genius, that energy, that richness." Martin was doing well that summer: eating a bit healthier for Elfie's sake, drinking a bit less, spending time outside in the fresh air, swimming, and sometimes walking miles from the studio to the Raffel, so briskly that the much younger Baumann could barely keep up with him.

Veit Loers—who by then had left Kassel to be the museum director at Mönchengladbach—also came to Jennersdorf to work with Martin, preparing *The Eggman and His Outriggers,* the major show in the Abteiberg Museum that would open a few days after the Geneva show. Loers was hoping to stay with Martin and Elfie, but Martin sent him to the Raffel: "Museum directors have to spend the night in hotels." (Loers suspects he was trying to give the hotel some more business.) It was fun anyway: Martin previewed the *Medusa* pictures in his studio, carrying them past Elfie, Loers, and Hans Weigand (the Vienna artist who was doing the catalog with Martin) "like a ring card girl," in Loers's words. In the evenings, the men made inroads into the expensive wine that the Grässlin family had given him for his wedding.

"1996: Returns to the subject of eggs and noodles with renewed interest," Martin wrote in his artist bio. When Daniel Baumann asked him how he had come up with the idea to make egg pictures, Martin said, "In painting you have to be on the lookout: what windfall is still left that you can paint. Justice has not been done to the egg, justice has not been done to the fried egg, the banana was already taken, by Warhol. So you take a form, it's always about sharp edges, a square, this and that format, the golden section, but an egg is white and blah, how can you make that into a colorful picture? If you turn it around, this way and that, you'll come up with something." He had always suffered under the dictatorship of the square in art and architecture—he always felt it was too angular, cool, perfect, straightforward, and closed-off. The only squares he accepted were checks, like the red checked tablecloths in Italian restaurants: he used them in his *Prize Pictures,* brightly colored and obviously hand-painted.

Martin spent months working with Hans Weigand to collect egg motifs for the catalog from anywhere and everywhere and then left the catalog's design up to Weigand. They were planning to do a second book later, about noodles. They met up in the Burgenland, or for lunch at Café Engländer in Vienna, and talked about everything, all the exhibitions— Martin laid into the whole art scene. "Schmalix is worthless!"* he shouted across the coffeehouse.

Elfie and Martin took several trips together that year. They went to exhibition openings and to Copenhagen, also to Greece a few times—they wanted to build a house for themselves on Syros. The spartan tower Martin had dreamed of as a bachelor (a room to work in and a room to sleep in) had grown in his mind to a whole house, with a darkroom, studio,

---

* Hubert Schmalix, Austrian artist. The original German is cleverer: "*Schmalix mal nix.*"

kitchen, shady inner courtyard, and rooms of their own for Ivo, August, and Helena. Lukas Baumewerd, the architect who had worked on the large METRO-*Net* sculptures for Kassel and Münster, was drawing up plans. Martin also wanted to do more work with his Modern Art Museum on Syros: that year he invited Johannes Wohnseifer and Michel Majerus, the young artist from Luxembourg who would die in a plane crash only a few years later. Martin's Athens gallerist, Eleni Koroneou, said that with Elfie at his side "he was calmer, he felt safe and secure." "Elfie!" he would cry out when she wasn't next to him, "Where is my Elfie?"

At an Athens event hosted by Dakis Ioannidis, a major Greek collector, Martin once again appeared as a provocateur: on the podium with such famous artists as Jeff Koons and Joseph Kosuth, he suddenly pulled out a red wooden cellphone and pretended to talk into it, totally seriously, for ten minutes, without anyone trying to stop him. He also criticized Paul McCarthy and complained about his hotel. In the fall he became tired and his back started to ache—from all the work he had been doing, he said. When Martin Prinzhorn met him at Café Engländer shortly before Christmas and was shocked at how terrible he looked, Martin said calmly and with few words that it would all be over soon, he was going to go meet his dead mother on cloud nine. "He was acting very strange and seemed very depressed."

We celebrated Christmas together again, as he wanted. The family came to him: our sister Tina, with Lisa, Philipp, and Lars; Gabi with Helena. He wanted us to come even though he was in a lot of pain and was tired; he had tests to undergo in the hospital two days before Christmas. Even though he was not in good shape, there was no mercy: the rituals had to be carried out—Christmas tree, presents, turkey, plus the Jennersdorf tour from the Raffel to the Club on the

Border. (He had called it "furnishing proof" in our father's case, when our father had gathered all his energies for one last Christmas shortly before his own death.)

It was Christmas night, 1 a.m. on December 26, when he drew himself leaning on Elfie's shoulder in the Raffel. The Raffel was his second home, so he had had business cards printed, complete with his office hours ("Mo.–Sa. 12.00–13.30"). It was central located, though not particularly nice, and the farthest thing imaginable from a trendy restaurant: a conference hotel with fake-leather benches and fake plants on columns, the waitresses dressed in black with little white aprons.

The tablecloth drawing doesn't only show Martin with Elfie: leaning against their table is a chicken ladder with Frau Martha, the waitress, standing on it holding a cigarette box. Next to her is written "Now after 43 minutes the HB" (a brand of cigarettes). Behind Elfie and Martin, who are drawn small, like children, stands the Great Father Kampel, a balloon in each hand: one says "Old but goody," the other says "No way Nouvelle Cuisine." Raffel served hearty traditional dishes, just like Martin liked. And when the food didn't come to the table fast enough, he would march into the kitchen to spur them on.

Old but Goody: Herr Kampel still works in the restaurant every day except Christmas and plans to keep working full-time until he's ninety (then switch to half-days). He is an old-school Austrian innkeeper with all the polite finesses, down to kissing ladies' hands. He and Martin adopted each other, as father and son, without the conflicts, complexes, and problems—and the common history—that usually go with that relationship. Reinhard Knaus said that Kampel almost never sat down at the table with the other Club members in all the years he was there, or if he did, it was for five minutes at most. But with Martin he sat for hours, and he also stood up to Martin when his guests couldn't take any more of his endless speeches. Kampel gave Martin what he wanted: homemade noodle soup and special treatment for being an artist. "I had to be with him all the time," Kampel said. "He was very grateful for the attention. He needed warmth."

Sometimes, when he came home from the Raffel at two or three in the morning, Martin went to the studio and painted through the night, and then appeared at the hotel for breakfast the next morning. When he didn't hike to the Raffel on foot or have Knaus fetch him, he drove his egg wagon. In this isolated setting he needed a vehicle, but he couldn't drive a car without a license—only a three-wheeler. He got a little Italian vehicle and then, on its cargo bed, had an enormous egg built. That is what he drove through the village, with his theme song blaring from a loudspeaker: "Ding-a-ling-a-ling, Here Comes the Eggman." (Or AC/DC, or Wagner's *Flight of the Valkyries,* depending on his mood.) He planned to keep surprise eggs for the village children in a drawer of the big egg, and he wanted to have ads for the Raffel painted on the egg in mirror writing (for rear-view windows), in exchange for the good bordeaux he liked so much. But he was not able to carry out those plans. Elfie's photograph of the egg wagon in the snow would become the last of Martin's 178 posters, for steirischer herbst 1997—he arranged it with Jörg Schlick before he died.

Martin "was always up for anything fun," Kampel said. Since Kampel spent a lot of time during the summer at the public pool, where he ran a second restaurant, and since Elfie went swimming every day when she was there, they came up with the idea of a Raffel Relay Race (*Raffel-Staffel* in German). The training consisted of drinking Ramazzotti, and Knaus (who didn't swim) was supposed to pull a bottle of Ramazzotti on a string through the water ahead of the swimmers, like the rabbit in a greyhound race; it would be a hundred-meter race, and the loser would owe the winner a bottle of champagne.

But again, it never took place. Still, Kampel often wore the red baseball cap that they had had made for the race.

Kampel has never washed the tablecloth with Martin's drawing and the food stains still on it, and every time I see him he asks after Helena, because, he says, Martin loved her so much. On the wall, between the plastic flowers and columns, still hangs Martin's fake Biennale poster, showing him in front of the German Pavilion in Venice in Elfie's honeymoon photograph. At one point on the night before Martin set out for his last exhibition marathon in January 1997—Zurich, Geneva, Mönchengladbach—he rushed out to the car to get the poster, right away, right now, Knaus had to frame it and hang it. "He left the next day, and he never came back."

"He was a truly special person," Ernst Kampel said. "I miss him very much."

THE END

> But time —
> But time —
> But time.

As a young man, Martin printed these lines by the French singer Gilbert Bécaud in *Through Puberty to Success*. He often said that he didn't have much time. "I dont have time to wait eight years to hang in the Ludwig Museum," he had said; that's why he had to get attention right away with his extreme behavior. "I always have to work for the present moment because of this short span of time that you have as an individual."

He didn't have time because he would die of cancer; he was convinced of that quite early on—an old fortune-teller in Frankfurt had predicted it. One Family One Line: Our mother had breast cancer, our father died of skin cancer, our grandfather died of cancer of the jaw.

"If someone didn't understand him right away, he just packed up his fliers and left," says Attila Corbaci, the Viennese restaurant owner. "He had no time for people to request permits or call meetings." So he did whatever it was and pushed and shoved and got on everyone's nerves with his impatience. Corbaci was no longer surprised when he heard how quickly Martin had decided to get married: "He was a man who painted a picture in a day, married his wife in a day, lived his life in a day." In most of the *Medusa* pictures, Martin painted himself with a naked upper body: the only thing he was wearing was a wristwatch.

"Never give up before it's too late" is a line in "Ciao Mega Art Baby," a poem that Martin put on all the guests' tables at the opening for the Geneva exhibition in January 1997 and that the museum director bound as a little booklet and gave to Martin's friends at his burial two months later. He called one of his early pictures *Work Until Everything's Cleared Up*, and that is exactly what he did. "Cirrhosis of the liver is no excuse for bad art" is another line from his poem.

At the end, everything went quickly. There was an opening in Zurich at Birgit Küng's on January 28, marking the end of a year-long exhibition project: *Albert Oehlen presents Martin Kippenberger. Martin Kippenberger presents Noodles. Noodles represent the end of Fettstrasse 7a*. The invitation showed a plate of spaghetti bolognese. Two days later, on January 30, when he already was in a lot of pain and could barely walk, *Kippenberger sans peine* ("Kippenberger Made Easy" but literally "Painless Kippenberger") opened in Geneva; on February 1, *The Eggman and His Outriggers* opened in Mönchengladbach, near the Dutch border by Düsseldorf.

Martin "really pulled himself together" for the construction of that exhibition, the museum director Veit Loers said. He didn't talk much but still cracked jokes. Daniel Buchholz, shocked like many people to see Martin grown so small and sitting in a wheelchair at the opening, asked him what had happened. "Don't drink so much and don't smoke so much. Not worth it," Martin answered—with a cigarette in his hand, even in the museum. "Hey, tall girl," he greeted Andrea Stappert, "how's the air up there?" Then he rolled with her through the show and into the Spiderman Studio, where he had his picture taken in the wheelchair. He told everyone who asked that he was having back troubles. When Anna Grässlin looked over at him at one point during the meal after the opening, he rolled his eyes upward and pointed up at Heaven.

"Cant mak it," Martin wrote in his egg book in shaky handwriting on that February 1, to a museum employee who was in the hospital and had asked for a signed catalog, "tomorrow in the hospital too." On March 7, he was dead.

Martin had always bounced back and was never sick. Johannes Wohnseifer couldn't believe that he would die: "I had such faith that nothing would happen to him." He'd had headaches or toothaches or stomachaches, of course, but just took aspirin, got up, and went back to work. He didn't get sick because he didn't want to get sick, which was also why he went on his cures so regularly: so that he could keep going. He was afraid of getting really sick, of being helpless, and also of going to the doctor and finding out the truth. The only medical treatment he got regularly was from Heliod Spiekermann, his dentist, which may have been out of vanity more than anything else.

Martin always revealed his weaknesses and injuries, his "Alcohol Torture" (to use the title of one of his early self-portraits) and bloated belly—he exposed them, turned them into art. As an artist, he held the reins himself. He put off as long as he could the need to give them up—he was horrified at the prospect, since he knew what it would mean. "Super-Childhood," as he put it in one of his songs, "Back to the Super-Childhood." He said to Jutta Koether:

> I have seen it, the summit of super-childhood. When my father died of cancer, he was just like my baby. And I'll die of cancer the same way. I don't know if cancer is more pleasant than being run over by a bus. I don't know yet how it feels inside. I don't insist on having it long and dirty, but my father also thought he'd survive. It took him six years, with all these heart attacks, and whatever else goes with it—and beat it! And, of course, you are there all the time. And suddenly he can dress himself, at Christmas, by way of exception. Just to furnish proof. It's about proof. In that I'm quite similar to my father.

For Beuys, according to his biographer Heiner Stachelhaus, death was a "mythical event, a magical ritual." For Martin it was something to get through as quickly and unobtrusively as he could. "The moment he got to the hospital," Elfie said, "he gave up."

Hospital, school, jail, army—for Martin, they were all the same, institutions that rob you of your freedom. He sometimes put apartments and museums in the same category. That was why he always tried to avoid institutions and authorities, why he always behaved well (as he saw it), at least well enough not to end up in jail. That would have been a "creeping death": "Say 20 years, no life, no rights, no nothing, it's the worst thing anyone could wish on you." As a result, he was always polite to the police: "I never do anything that's not allowed."

He could never handle "bureaucracy," as he called it, "not with cars or planes or electronic devices. So I keep quiet. Or find someone to start the motor or screw in the light bulb." He never officially left the church for the same reason: "I toe all the lines so that no one will catch me. So as far as my file goes, too, I'm a dear boy." He wanted to make it to Heaven after all. Just not Hell. That would be even worse than a life sentence. No one comes back from Hell.

Then, at the end of his life, he ended up where he never wanted to be: in a closed institution. At the AKH general hospital in Vienna, his worst nightmares came true and, deathly ill, he was criticized, reprimanded, ordered around. The cleaning lady kicked his wife out of his room; the caregiver was nowhere to be found; the nurses were hidden away in their room at the farthest end of the hallway. They had no interest in starting a motor for him, screwing in a light bulb, easing his pain. They helped grouchily and reluctantly, if at all. When a visitor wanted to lift Martin into his wheelchair and needed help, they said, "he was already out today." Then, when he got back from his trip to the smoking room (he smoked to the end, even when he could barely hold the cigarette), too late for the dinner he couldn't eat anyway, they scolded him like he was a first-grader again. What he always demanded and often gave others, respect, was denied him at the AKH.

His liver had poisoned his body. He was confused and crystal clear at the same time—sometimes aggressive but still always concerned about others. When our sister Bine came to visit him, the most important thing for him was to find out where she was staying, to make sure that she didn't have to go to a hotel but could stay in his and Elfie's apartment. Past and present, fantasy and reality blurred together: "They've stuck me in a haunted-house ride," he said, after he was sent for another MRI, and he described exhibitions he had seen in the more or less distant past as though he had just been there.

He knew that no one could help him there, that no one could cure him anymore, so there was only one thing he wanted: "to go home," like E.T., whom he had so often felt like in his life. On a high floor of the hospital ward he thought he was in a New York skyscraper and that it was time to go downstairs to the hotel bar. "Get me out of here," he begged everyone who visited him. Even when he had tubes in him, he tried to run away. So they tied him down.

Ten days after his death, at the posthumous awarding of the Käthe Kollwitz Prize, his *Medusa* exhibition opened at the Berlin Academy of Arts. The critic Dieter Bachmann described Géricault's painting as a wake: "Does the catastrophe he is painting lie behind him or ahead of him?" Martin looked in his *Medusa* pictures the way he looked while he was dying in the hospital. The catalog presented another, happier picture: Elfie's photos of their honeymoon, his dance with the pigeons. Pictures of a Happy End.

Martin chose his last resting place: when he came to Jennersdorf he told his stepsons, August and Ivo, that he wanted to be buried up on the top of the hill there, in the small village cemetery where their father was already buried. A few years earlier, Martin had spoken of his own death notice and funeral as part of his art, of his total body of work, along with the painting and sculpture and dance, wondering "whether it would add up to a respectable Kippenberger or not." He cared how the public would react—"what expressions people would have on their faces"—who would cry and who wouldn't. He imagined his funeral as a day of reckoning.

But when the time actually approached he didn't have the strength—and maybe didn't even want—to stage-manage his own burial the way our father had. It was a ghastly day, gloomy and freezing cold, and a silent funeral: no ceremony, no music, no funeral sermon. At some point we set out for the cemetery, the church bells tolled, and when they stopped it was even more silent than before. Heimo Zobernig captured it all on film, in place of the movie he had wanted to make with Martin. Karel Schampers, the director of the Rotterdam Museum, spoke a few words at the grave, and then the line of waiting friends filed past, "like a penitent's pilgrimage," Isabelle Graw said. Werner Büttner said later, "We waited, frozen stiff and morbid, to walk past the grave." Eventually it got to be too much for the gravediggers. Dressed in scruffy rags like caricatures of themselves, they decided it was taking too long—it was Friday afternoon, they wanted to go home and eat their roast pork—so they started shoveling dirt into the grave in the middle of the funeral. Quitting time, they said. An argument started, it almost came to blows, and only the prospect of an additional special fee calmed them down.

Everyone said afterward that it was as if Martin had scripted it. As though he had taken the reins one last time, played a little joke, shocked his audience, and had his fun. Then everyone went to the Raffel for the wake.

In his speech by the grave, Karel Schampers recalled the words on Martin's *Opinion Picture: Spiral* from 1985. "Embarrassment" is written in the middle of the picture, and around it "indecisiveness, politeness, mess, inanity, security, gaiety, eternity, freedom of expression, insecurity, humanity, clarity, triviality, unity, willingness to take risks." "That is Martin all over," Schampers said, "so basic and yet so vulnerable."

CHAPTER ELEVEN

THE ART OF BEING A PERSON

Martin once reflected on what it might mean to be old. He wanted to grow old and was convinced that he would, despite his fear that he would die young: "My chips are on seventy-two years." He imagined how he would sit in a café in Italy as an old man telling stories about his life. He enjoyed the peaceful picture for a moment, and then his doubts came back: "But then no one believes you and you're alone again."

Those were always the issues with him: Belief. Struggle. And being alone.

He told Diedrich Diederichsen in an interview for the book *B* that as a boy in boarding school he had once stood all alone on a hilltop, howling; he had once again been "jerking off so that the bed shook" and his schoolmates had tattled, and he'd gotten a thrashing, and it was "really going like shit" for him. "Then a lightning flash came and I thought: Don't worry about it, you're one of the chosen.... Since then it's easy to deal with everything, no problems with anybody.... Since then I've been above it all. Sounds stupid but that's how it is." A few years later, Martin told another story of his childhood to people around the pool at a Greek collector's house: once, when his sisters had tormented and spanked him yet again, he saw a light, and on the next day his mother had told his sisters to leave Martin alone. Nothing ever happened to him after that.

He had his camouflage outfit, and as a result he was a free man.

He believed in himself and in art from the beginning—as a child he thought he would become a famous artist; as a teenager he thought he'd make millions. This belief gave him the strength to work like a man possessed and to get up again every time he was knocked down. His enormous self-confidence seemed to give him the sense of being on a mission, according to Angelika Margull, his friend from the Berlin days. Other friends from those early years—when Martin had not yet produced much in the way of visible works of art—put it in the same terms: they believed in him. From the start.

And Martin expected them to. "If you take two aspirin and are constantly saying 'It's not working, it's not working!' then of course it won't work." Martin liked believing in things too, from the herbal medicine a healer prescribed for him ("one drink for the heart, another for the kidneys, another for the liver, another for the spleen, another for the brain—I had to build a whole bar"), to "soul drops" (a German health product made from green walnuts), to Tarot cards. And in people: "Because they make such beautiful things. Make such beautiful mistakes." Belief, for him, was love—and love was belief, in life as in art. "There was an almost religious side to him," Barbara Straka said: "If you're not with me you're against me." That was the source of his crushing disappointment whenever he felt that someone wasn't believing in him. He always said, "They don't love me."

And so he furnished "proof" for everyone who doubted him—and there were a lot of those people in his lifetime. Vast quantities of proof: pictures, cards, posters, exhibitions, appearances, books, sculptures, editions, and records, for a start.

He himself believed in art and loved it, "I mean really, from the heart, I love art with all my heart. That will never change no matter how idiotic it gets, I'll only have to put it on a higher and higher pedestal." Albert Oehlen said, "He loves art like no one else—he likes it and likes to make it. I think that's why he puts on ninety exhibitions, because he wants to be working every minute." In one of his last shows, *Nada Arugula*, he called himself Martin Kunst Kippenberger— Martin Art Kippenberger. He left no inheritance behind except art: no manor house, no trust fund, no stock portfolio. Even on his grave there is art: his friend Hubert Kiecol, the sculptor, who had previously made our father's gravestone with Martin, designed a simple stele out of pale stone, classical and modern at the same time. There is only one word or number on each of the four sides: Martin Kippenberger 1953 1997.

"I am Salvador Dalí the divine," the Spanish artist used to declare. I am a human being, Martin proclaimed with every one of his works and performances. One of You – Among You – With You.

He didn't want to be God. He preferred to play the part of an imp. For him, the artist is not a solitary genius pursuing his divine gift—Sigmar Polke had already mocked that idea in 1969: "Higher beings order me to paint the top right corner black!" Martin often didn't even hold the brush himself.

Of course he wanted to end up on Parnassus—he thought he belonged there. But he wanted to get there his own way: keeping both feet on the ground. Playing all kinds of jokes on and with himself and everything else in the world.

Martin sought the heights among earthly valleys and degradations; he found beauty in garbage. One of his most romantic self-portraits shows him on a New York street corner, sitting elegantly on a sofa surrounded by garbage bags that had been left out on the street. "The morality always takes care of itself," wrote F. T. Vischer, the nineteenth-century Swabian professor of aesthetics whose book *Auch Einer* Martin and Jörg Schlick reprinted in *Broken Neon*. The quotation continues:

A real fellow seeks and strives and does not complain about it but is happy in the unhappiness of the rising but never arriving line of life. That is the highest floor we can reach. But everything else, the dog shit on the ground floor of life—that's what we're talking about... We are born to seek, to unravel knots, to see the world from a worm's eye point of view.

Bath mats, oatmeal flakes, Opel-Manta driver jokes: these were the materials of Martin's art. The American critic Stephen Ellis said about him that "he brings the junk that society churns out to our attention with the pride of a cat dragging the carcass of a mouse into the living room." For many critics, even now, this material is too banal to qualify as art. But in my view, his art is only as banal as life itself is—exactly as dirty and ridiculous and elemental. Another reason why Martin turned EuroPallets into a whole series of sculptures—the *Rest Center for Mothers* pieces and *Design for Administration Building for Rest Center for Mothers*—was that our mother had been killed by a EuroPallet that the truck driver hadn't fastened properly.

Quite early on, Martin turned Beuys's maxim, "Every human being is an artist," upside down: "Persistent analysis has resulted in the finding that every artist is a human being," he wrote on a postcard from Italy in 1981. He gave a picture from that year the same title: *Every Artist Is a Human Being*. The picture shows an artist painting on the naked body of a man who is hanging above the canvas as though crucified. His portrait of Harald Juhnke from that period is called *The Art of Being a Person*: Juhnke was an entertainer and heavy drinker who always put his pleasures and sorrows on public display.

"I don't know a single bad person," Martin told Joachim Lottmann in an interview. "There aren't any. There are no good people or bad people. They're always both together." That was why he always held up a criticial mirror to the self-proclaimed good people and why he always included himself as the target of the ironic critiques he directed at others.

Wols and Blinky Palermo "knew they were big, but that is a hard cross to bear," Martin said. To be an artist was not to be God, but more like his son, who was also human. And that means to suffer (Martin liked to make people suffer). He nailed a wooden Fred the Frog to the "Artist Cross," its tongue sticking out of its mouth, with a beer stein in one hand and a fried egg in the other.

He knew that pleasure and suffering were not far apart: "What is the difference between Casanova and Jesus?" he wrote under the crucified frog. "The look on their faces when it goes in." Martin wasn't a martyr, or at least never wanted to be—he loved eating his noodles and drinking his wine. But for him there was no such thing as art without suffering. "He has never offered himself up," he said about Gerhard Richter. "He doesn't know any altar, only techniques."

The wild life that seemed so exciting from the outside was itself, as he said, "insanely stressful: life on the move all the time with absolutely no private life.... I've always done art, that was my private life, in a way. And so I missed out on a lot, let's say my Holy Spirit in me made me do it." He couldn't cut off his ear every day, he said once. But he managed to do it on a lot more days than most people.

Jutta Koether suggested in her conversation with him that by influencing other artists he made them into Kippenbergers, to some extent. Martin answered, "I wouldn't recommend that to anyone. See it's very stressful... I've gotten used to it, physically, the way I treat myself. No matter how hard it gets I can handle it, more or less. Later it's a gigantic effort to even stay alive, never mind still have fun with thinking and working."

"It sounds idiotic," Albert Oehlen said, "but in a way he sacrificed himself for the art world," so that others wouldn't have to go to these extremes themselves. Albert painted him as Mahatma Gandhi back in 1984—to emphasize, he said, the message of human kindness in Martin's work. Susan Sontag wrote about "The Artist as Exemplary Sufferer"; Wolfgang Max Faust turned that into "The Artist as Exemplary Alcoholic" in his article about Martin, as though alcohol were not also part of suffering.

As an artist, Martin himself said, he was a salesman—in other words, someone who constantly travels around, knocks on strange doors, asks to be let in, and tries to convince people. Someone who sells his wares—or doesn't. Even when someone slams the door in the salesman's face, he has to keep moving and try again to get in somewhere else. It is a stressful life, a lonely business. Martin described art once as a "One-Man-Business." He had a lot of support, from friends, colleagues, gallerists, his family, and his substitute families—he spun his net in all directions. But in the end, the spider sits in his net alone, like the Spiderman in his studio, whose mouth is open in fear as though he himself is caught in a net. When the curator Daniel Baumann asked Martin at the end of his life whether he was a loner, Martin answered, "I've become one."

He was not just a sales rep but a representative as such: a proxy, a substitute. He portrayed himself in his *Medusa* pictures taking on the suffering of every single person on the raft. That is how the collector Wilhelm Schürmann saw him: "We would have been too scared to live that." Thomas Bayrle said, "We all try to make sure it doesn't cost us our own skin. Most artists still cling to self-protectiveness." One of Martin's *Picture Titles for Artists to Borrow* runs: *Go ahead and keep painting, just don't hurt yourself.*

Martin chose a frog as an alter ego—a creature that disgusts a lot of people but which, as every child knows from fairy tales, might turn out to be a prince. You just have to believe in it. Martin's whole art was to see the frog as a prince suffering for his beliefs and simultaneously as a frog, a comic figure in shorts, a drinker sticking out his tongue.

Peter Pakesch thought Martin's "switching back and forth between a game and an almost religious seriousness was one of his greatest strengths." Or, as Martin said in the *Artfan* interview, "I always say I haven't decided yet whether I'm Jesus, God, or the Holy Spirit, but I'm defnitely destined for something good. If Michael Landon can be an angel on earth, what am I. In presentation or reality."

He simply could not understand why the Austrian Catholic church got so outraged over *Fred the Frog on the Artist Cross*, with the archbishop calling it blasphemous. Martin thought the real insult was the Jesus kitsch that the carver cranked out the rest of the time, not the frog he made following Martin's instructions.

The church was the only organization Martin belonged to, and he set great store in the fact that he never left it. He wanted to go to Heaven in the end. That doesn't mean that he went to church on Sunday—he preferred fortune-tellers to preachers. But he wanted to believe. If he couldn't believe in God—and his time at a pious boarding school had probably driven that out of him—then he would believe all the more in what he called prophecy: in creation, in something higher, which for him was nonetheless something human. "Let's talk about higher things," he told Jutta Koether. "Higher things, those are very decisive. What we mean by love and affection and security. Warmth, is that the overarching concept?"

No, he wasn't making fun of the man on the cross, only of what people did with him. The Holy Family fascinated him, of course, and the father-son relationship was always a burning issue for him—both his own relationship with his father and others' relationships with theirs (Preller's, Krebber's, Nagel's, Schreber's). And let us not forget mothers. He held it against the church that they left out the mother. He had no patience for the Immaculate Conception: "We all come from the mother's womb, and fathers all stick it in." Nothing was ever spotless, and he thought you shouldn't try to wash the spots away or cover them up. "How would I ever cope with a brown room?" he asked in one of his sayings. "Not by whitewashing it."

"To be good without sin, doesn't happen," Martin said. "That's how you grow." The theme and motive force of his work is seeing mistakes not as crippling failures but as productive strengths. With Büttner and Oehlen, he made "Broadening Knowledge through Failure" into his mission. Wilfried Dickhoff describes the fundamental idea of Martin's work as "affirming the world as error."

Celebrating human flaws: Martin praised our mother for the noodle casseroles he so loved by saying, "She can't cook, but she does it right." Rather than sweeping his own mistakes and weaknesses under the carpet, he put them up on display, turning the sweatiness of his feet into an edition of shrink-wrapped socks, his alcoholism into paintings, his braggadocio into posters, his inability to speak French into a movie.

Andy Warhol once said, "Anybody can make a good movie, but if you consciously try to do a bad movie, that's like making a *good* bad movie." Every exhibition, Martin thought, should contain bad pictures, too, so that the good ones would be easier to recognize and in order to provoke controversies, not just silent worship. "Lüpertz like Knoebel is just about perfect. That's what's miserable," he said to Jutta Koether in their interview. "If everything's good it doesn't count. For some reason God above in the beginning decided differently, didn't he: there should be both good and evil! But you don't find dialectical approaches in art any more." For him, art didn't arise from ability. Some people were amazed to discover after his death that he really knew how to draw, how to paint! But ability was what he was most afraid of.

The world of pure beauty and harmony bored him—he wanted people to have something to look at, for a long time, and in his opinion the best way to accomplish that was through aggression, something that catches the eye. That is what he told Karel Schampers, director of the Boijmans Van Beuningen Museum in Rotterdam. Content, color, form—the artist has lots of ways to hurt people. "But my aggression is never destructive, I have a positive attitude, I see it as proof of engagement. I want to unmask double standards and false hopes."

That was also why he trumpeted other people's weakness, sticking his finger in open wounds and really twisting it around. It wasn't nice. But it was meant well: work in the service of truth. Peter Pakesch put Martin in the same category as the philosophers of the Enlightenment: "He wanted to make people better." Pakesch felt that "there was great despair about the condition of the world. To have hope, on the one hand, that there could be a better world, but to be smart enough on the other hand to realize that it wasn't working out that way—that's what produces the 'cynicism' that is actually moral. He made very high demands: on himself, on others, on art, on society."

Not Knowing Why but Knowing What For was the title of one of Martin's pictures. He reacted angrily when Minchie Huggler asked him what his artistic message was—"I don't have one!" He wasn't a messiah, he said, "I'm the nice, fat uncle." Or "I am St. Martin," a saint who showed his humanity with modest means, by sharing what he wore with another.

Werner Büttner described Martin's work as "a gigantic hymn to human kindness." Martin lovingly took in whatever was left behind, had failed, or gone wrong. His melancholy yet comic painting of a Ford Capri sitting abandoned on the street at night in the snow is called *No Capri*. "The aura of something gone terribly wrong dominates his work," according to Nilas Maak in the *FAZ*, "and it is Kippenberger's art to extract an inimitable good mood from these ruins."

He wanted to heal the art of his time, not heal himself. Martin never took a vacation. "Kippenberger was always on duty," Gisela Capitain said. Even on his honeymoon. One of his favorite sayings was "Life is no holiday." And he wrote in his book *Joints I*, "I don't give a shit whether art or I suffer more, because a tile isn't scared of shit: it just sticks where it's put." Martin was Protestant through and through in his discipline and sense of duty, including his duty to make sure people were having a good time. As Bärbel Grässlin said, "However he felt, he still shined his shoes and put on his hat and went out. Even in despair he was the class clown."

On Martin's tenth birthday, our father wanted him to have "a lot of time": among all the pens and colored pencils and drawing paper and the easel and camera and long pants he got, that seemed to our father "the most important birthday present that God above has given you: the time you still have, in which you can do something, and should." He had no choice. He was born an artist. As he said in an interview, "All that matters is that you not defend yourself, on the contrary, that you go along with it, that saves you a huge amount of energy, just obey your genes so that you can develop freely and get wilder and have fun."

He thought that by the time you were thirty, you needed to have made it as an artist enough to support yourself with your work, but when an interviewer asked him if you should give up on art if you haven't reached that point by thirty, Martin answered, "No, then you need to work in order to pay for your art and the ideas in your head.... Just don't suffer and say 'Nobody loves me.'"

Even when he was dying, Martin didn't complain. In Zurich, a few weeks before his death, Birgit Küng made a meal for him on the occasion of his last show with her—one of her her "magical country meals" that he loved so much. "He was as happy about it as ever," This Brunner said. "It was so clear that he was sick, he was extremely depressed—but not whiny. He was still cheerful."

Michel Würthle called him brave: "tremendously brave." Because over and over, when he was depressed, "he pulled himself up out of the shitpile by his own bootstraps." It was always a struggle. "You have to haul yourself over the coals," Martin said. "It's a lonely job." Jutta Koether said that she admired his persistence: "This idea that you have to struggle for what you want in the world, through continuous hard work. That you can't abdicate responsibility and say it's someone else's fault, or God's fault, or whatever. That you can't withdraw into private things and say, 'OK, time for a vacation,' or, 'Now I'll let myself be depressed.' That you always try to get over it."

"It's an incredible attitude," his New York gallerist Janelle Reiling said, "to think that you can do whatever you want. That if you want something you just go ahead and do it and don't bitch and moan if it doesn't work out." During an exhibition at Metro Pictures in New York, when Martin was supposed to sign copies of his catalog at the art bookstore Printed Matter, he asked if they thought a lot of people would come; they told him probably not. He turned the gloomy afternoon into an event where he would not only sign each catalog but also draw a real little drawing in every one. Soon the line stretched almost out the door.

He used to say, "The spark of hope doesn't come in the mail." But equally naturally, he didn't repress his doubts—he put them on show. He not only experienced exclusion, he constantly provoked it. He knew that others' dislike would only give him more energy. "You need your tender loving care, and you can't let yourself get sucked in. Success is the deadliest thing for an artist or his art." That was one of the things he explicitly liked so much about the other Hetzler artists: that none of them rested on his laurels. "They all doubt themselves."

His artistic policy was to believe: to accept not only himself but the whole world, as it is, and "to take action accordingly." With Martin, the concrete was always metaphysical and metaphorical—and vice versa. So this was how he described the difficult, overgrown path by the foundries through a landscape that wasn't one, around the ugly house where he was staying in Andalusia:

> To follow the right path was always, even in the good old days, embellished with rough patches. Thank God I never avoided paying my tithe to the church, so sometimes on my walks I find sculptures on the hard (as long as it's not raining) path, put there from Above (or sometimes not from Above). The bulldozer-driver on the edge of the garbage dump understands his craft: he actually built me a real giant ramp out of clay & and a photobackdrop hill for free & without obligation.

That was also why he seized on anything he found by the roadside, without delay or hesitation, or scruples. If it lay along his path it must be meant for him. "Make good use of chance," he wrote in *Joints I*, "it never comes back."

Living in the here and now also meant that he was never

interested in posthumous fame. He wanted to make money—a lot of money—so that he could turn around and spend it again for a life in the service of art. He wanted success, even if it was dangerous, and wanted it right away so he could enjoy it. And he paid the price. In Florence, he was thrown out of the Villa Romana once for arguing too violently against a critic who thought that an artist should be happy to become famous after his death. "That's such nonsense," Martin answered. "It's such an effort to do anything as an artist." It annoyed him whenever someone said that an artist survives in his work: "No one survives. We're not clever enough to survive. Everyone dies. Life always ends with death."

He knew that posthumous canonization meant being made harmless. Today, collectors snap up his work at monstrous prices, even the Americans who wanted nothing to do with him when he was alive: "The pigs of yesterday are the ham of tomorrow," he prophesied in his very first book, *al Vostro servizio*. In today's booming art market, Martin is hotly sought after as a painter, especially a painter of self-portraits— but the rest of his work, unmanageable and often ugly as it is, has receded into the background.

What remains is a domesticated Kippenberger— Kippenberger without the embarrassment. But without embarrassment there's no Kippenberger left. The critic Patrick Frey wrote about Martin that "the experience of embarrassment is painful, lacking any noble greatness or sublimity, which is precisely why that pain can be turned into gladness." The Austrian writer Walter Grond, who wrote for Martin as well as about him, remarked that "*Peinlichkeit,* or embarrassment, contains *Pein,* torment, but torment is not just pain, anguish, and sorrow, it is also punishment and effort. Embarrassment contains the search for the meaning of suffering."

Kippenberger sans peine was the title of his "Respective

1997-1976" in Geneva that opened six weeks before his death. He longed for a life without pain and suffering himself: he called one of his paintings *For a Life without a Dentist,* having suffered his share of agony in the dentist's chair. But he also knew how you ended up if you led such a life: toothless.

In his book *Café Central,* Martin described a dream he had once about peanut doodles forming words on a pink particleboard table. "As far as I can remember there were sentences like: 'Today you don't need to clean your fingernails any more! Starting tomorrow you will never run out of toilet paper again! Starting the day after tomorrow, cavities are no longer an issue! Starting the day after the day after tomorrow, everyone will like what you do! Starting the day after the day after the day after tomorrow, everyone will also like what you don't do!'"

Art, he thought, should hurt. Life did too, after all. Whenever things got too cozy, he made sure to make them uncomfortable: he moved to a new city where he had to start over, or made sculptures as a slap in the face to people who had just gotten used to his paintings. Whenever a painting got too pretty, he spray-painted letters on it or plastered it with stickers like "I love no go home." He stuck a torn-out, incomplete quotation from Paul Valéry on one of his photographs: "a sun that only he has. Rembrandt knows that the flesh is filth that the light makes golden."

In 1981, in the program for his appearance at Café Einstein, he wrote, "Jesus the scamp really only confused all of us." An outraged Berlin man, one Curt Pinkert, sent him a letter afterward, which Martin happily printed in his *Bankruptcy Book*: "Doesn't every great spirit have to confuse his existing environment first if he wants to achieve success?"

"We're spreading confusion," Martin explained once. "But fundamentally, we don't intend confusion at all, only the truth." For him, the truth could only be reached through humor—without humor, pathos would be merely pathetic, even kitschy. He used his humor to launch an assault against all forms of mendacity, whether Alpine-style Christian kitsch, political self-righteousness, or art-world hypocrisy.

Martin titled his painting of the Guggenheim Museum *The Modern House of Believing or Not*. If art for him was a matter of faith—and it remained that to the end—it was nonetheless a religion without haloes and incense. He brought art out of the sacred halls of the museum and into the Italian restaurant, because for him art was as ordinary as noodle casserole, as fundamental as eating and drinking. People didn't have to get down on their knees and worship art—they should grapple with it, with all the necessary seriousness, humor, and respect. One of his last exhibitions was called *Please Don't Sit on the Pictures*; the multiple for the 1997 documenta was called *Watch Yourself into the Show* and consisted of cast-lead soles for attendees' shoes, since they usually raced past the works of art. "If anyone says that a painting was painted too fast, you can reply that they looked at it too fast," Vincent van Gogh once wrote to his brother Theo.

Martin's art was always about looking—about how you perceive the world, which is what he so admired about Krebber and Meuser and what others so admired about him. Meuser said Martin had x-ray vision uninhibited by reality—he saw things that no one else saw. He saw a mountainous landscape in a plate full of bratwurst, dumplings, and sauerkraut; he discovered funny patterns in the way the wires ran from the corner of a restaurant's roof; even the remains of food on his plate seemed like a still life to him. "And you can't paint anywhere near as beautifully as what you see around you." He left behind a joke postcard in his studio in Jennersdorf, showing a rabbit in front of an empty canvas: "The prettiest picture

that Moll ever made / was the picture he only imagined."
If he did have a mission after all, it was this:

> To take the things a person sees on the street and
> see them differently. And! Very Important! It can't
> be educational! That's the special art of it. You can't
> hammer it into someone. To do that you need to turn
> your whole life into the foundation! And that's where
> you have to start from yourself. That's hard. That has
> nothing to do with the art market any more.

Martin answered the question of what art is by saying:
"Everything that moves you. The visualization of being."
His favorite nonsensical construction project of all was one
he conceived with Albert Oehlen and Werner Büttner, but it
was much too expensive to make: a three-foot-long divided
highway. "You could exit the highway and park your car and
relax and look at this three-foot little highway. But it would
have to be three lanes wide in each direction, with a median
strip. With lots of little flowers."

One of Martin's friends said that even after he died, he was more alive than most people who actually are alive. Posthumous fame, as he angrily said in his early years, didn't interest him, but it would still have made him happy to learn that eleven years after his death a large photograph of him would appear in the *Bild* next to the Pope's. On the left: Benedict XVI, praying. In the middle: Martin, an ironic, melancholy look on his face, his palms pressed together as though asking something from the Lord above—a photograph from his Helmut Berger phase. On the right: the garish green frog on the cross, with a beer stein in one hand and an egg in the other. The headline: "Art or Sacrilege? Pope Wants to Ban Crucified Frog from Museum." The frog was hanging in the opening exhibition of the new Museum for Modern and Contemporary Art in Bolzano in the summer of 2008, and it was enough to generate an enormous controversy, lasting for months, in the conservative South Tirol region of Italy. A politician went on a hunger strike, protestors stood praying in front of the museum's doors, other Catholics spoke up for artistic freedom; the director had to leave the museum a couple of months later (for exceeding the budget, supposedly).

In the end it turned out that the Pope himself was not the one who had answered the South Tiroleans' pleas and personally protested the crucified frog—it was the Vatican Secretariat of State. But what difference did that make? Martin had gotten pretty far up the ladder toward Heaven either way.

And then he ended up on Olympus. "Kippenberger doesn't hurt anyone in Potsdam any more," the critic Harald

Fricke had written in 1994 on the occasion of the Potsdamer Kunstverein show: "He has outlived himself." On February 24, 2009, a day before what would have been Martin's fifty-sixth birthday, a phenomenal retrospective opened at the Museum of Modern Art in New York after having first showed in Los Angeles: *The Problem Perspective*. Ann Goldstein of L.A.'s Museum of Contemporary Art curated the exhibition (and would soon afterward be named general artistic director of the Stedelijk Museum in Amsterdam), with the support of MoMA's Ann Temkin; Martin's Santa Claus with a streetlamp greeted visitors to MoMA, surrounded by works by Miró, Picasso, and Max Ernst. Out of all his shows and openings, this was probably the most moving moment: the high school dropout, whose painting Fricke had described as "a stockpile of banalities from seventies Karstadt culture," among the great masters of modern art. *The Happy End of Franz Kafka's "Amerika"* was shown to best effect in the giant lobby of the museum annex, and upstairs in the exhibition proper, his work was laid out in all its breadth, a web of paintings and drawings, sculptures (a reconstruction of the *Peter* exhibition), posters, books, postcards, photographs, and more.

The show was a blockbuster, with reviews to match. The critics were overwhelmed—they praised Martin's radicalism and the uncomfortable, contradictory complexity of his work and personality. "A League of His Own" was the headline in the *Los Angeles Times*; in the *New York Times,* he was praised for being the artist for our time, "meaning the model he sets for what an artist can be and do. His multitudinous recyclings, insubordinate temperament and generosity seem unexpectedly right for a non-party-time time." In *New York* magazine, in a review called "The Artist Who Did Everything," Jerry Saltz said that if Robert Rauschenberg was the American Picasso, Kippenberger is the German Rauschenberg. Even Peter

Schjeldahl, whose review in *The New Yorker* was as hard on Martin as he had been during Martin's lifetime (see p. 372 above), called the show one of the best of 2009 in his end-of-year list.

The public was just as excited about this artist who seemed so fresh, vital, and full of ideas. For many of them, Martin was a real discovery. He had had various exhibitions in the U.S., but his work had never been shown there in anything like the abundance offered by what the *Süddeutsche Zeitung* called "the first big American Kippenberger retrospective, overflowing and bursting with vitality." He took another step toward Olympus in 2011, with the show "Kippenberger Meets Picasso" at the Picasso Museum in Malaga, Spain: the culmination of Martin's lifelong engagement with Picasso's work.

A happy ending?

Not entirely. A few months after the retrospective, Martin's picture of the Paris Bar was auctioned at Christie's for over $3.7 million. That was a wake-up call for *Der Spiegel*, which had never published a major piece about the artist now credited with producing "one of the most significant, and prescient, bodies of work from the postwar era" (*Artforum*) and "one of the most inventive and influential bodies of artwork" of his time (*Art in America*). So *Der Spiegel* put out a four-page hit piece by Nora Reinhardt, with all the old clichés about Martin as bad boy and boozer, someone who got others to make his work for him and was a petty and bad-tempered boss while doing it. She even called 2009 "the most successful year of his artistic activity," not because of the major retrospective in L.A. and New York—which was not even mentioned—but because of the record prices his paintings were fetching at auction. As an artist, she wrote, he was a "punch-line manufacturer."

It's a good thing that there is no Happy Ending here—no ending at all. That Martin, even now, almost fifteen years after his death, can still disturb and provoke, still be misunderstood. Mistakes and misunderstandings were, in the end, closest to his heart. He continues to achieve, with his life and his art, what he always wanted: confusion.

ACKNOWLEDGMENTS

We don't see things the way they are, we see things the way we are—and as subjective as perception is, memory provides an additional filter. It is impossible to give an objective portrait of Martin and his life, we can only give approximations from our own perspectives. The perspective of this book is mine, but the picture I have made is a mosaic assembled from numerous documents and interviews.

I had the good fortune to come from a family of collectors. Nothing was thrown away. In Martin's posthumous papers there are cards of congratulation he received after his confirmation, report cards, apartment leases, postcards, models for his artworks, the official document attesting to the Hamburg Shipping Board in 1969 that Martin had no criminal record; on my own bookshelves I discovered things I never knew I had, such as our parents' love letters. The great pleasure that both our parents took in expressing and dramatizing themselves resulted in a wealth of photographic, visual, home-movie, and written material, including our father's books and letters and our mother's letters and articles (many of them given to me by her friends Wiltrud Roser and Christel Haasis). Much of what I learned about our mother's family came from the writings of her youngest brother, Erich Leverkus.

Given his own enormous drive to communicate, Martin left relatively few original recordings of his life after his many letters from childhood and adolescence. He never appeared on talk shows, appeared only briefly on film recordings, and gave hardly any interviews. The most important source for me was the collection of conversations he had with Jutta

Koether, and sometimes with Diedrich Diederichsen, for the book *B. Gespräche mit Martin Kippenberger* (B.: Interviews with Martin Kippenberger), edited by Gisela Capitain (Reihe Cantz, 1994). In addition, I have taken many quotes from his three other extensive interviews: the anonymous interview at the White Cross near Thomasburg in *Artfan*, No. 5, November 1991 ("collective editorial responsiblity is the rule in this fanzine"), which has now appeared in book form in English as *Picture a Moon, Shining in the Sky: Conversation with Martin Kippenberber*, tr. Micah Magee, with an editorial note by Ariane Müller (Starship, Berlin, rev. and ill. ed. 2010); "Martin Kippenberger Clean Thoughts," with Marius Babias, in *Artscribe* No. 90, Feb./March 1992; and the interview with Daniel Baumann for the 1996 "Respective" in Geneva, reprinted in the catalog *Martin Kippenberger*, ed. Doris Krystof and Jessica Morgan (Kunstsammlung Nordrhein-Westfalen, Hatje Cantz Verlag 2006).

Among Martin's own books, I found the following especially helpful: *Durch die Pubertät zum Erfolg* [Through Puberty to Success] (Neue Gesellschaft für Bildende Kunst, Berlin, 1981); *1984. Wie es wirklich war am Beispiel Knokke. Mit einem Nachwort von Sophia Ungers: Der Tanz des Kippenbergers* [1984: How It Really Was, Using the Example of Knokke. With an afterword by Sophia Ungers: "The Dance of the Kippenberger"] (Galerie Bärbel Grässlin, 1985); *Café Central* (Meterverlag, 1987); and *Gelenke I* [Joints I] (Edition Patricia Schwarz, 1989). They are all out of print (and have not been translated into English), but excerpts from the first three appear in the new volume *Martin Kippenberger, Wie es wirklich war—am Beispiel Lyrik und Prosa* [Martin Kippenberger, How It Really Was: Using the Example of Poems and Prose], ed. Diedrich Diederichsen (Suhrkamp Taschenbuch, 2007).

From his catalogs and illustrated volumes: *Miete Strom Gas* [Rent Electricity Gas] (Hessisches Landesmuseum Darmstadt, 1986); Werner Büttner, Martin Kippenberger, and Albert Oehlen, *Wahrheit ist Arbeit* [Truth Is Work] (Museum Folkwang Essen, 1984); *Input-Output. Umzüge 1957–1988* [Input-Output: Moves, 1957–1988] (Galerie Gisela Capitain, 1989); *Kippenberger*, ed. Angelika Taschen and Burkhard Riemschneider (Taschen Verlag, 1991/1997/2003); *Das 2. Sein/Kippenberger fanden wir schon immer gut* [The 2nd Being/ We Always Thought Kippenberger Was Great] (Sammlung Grässlin im Brandenburgischen Kunstverein Potsdam, 1994).

From the books and catalogs that have appeared since his death: Uwe Koch, *Kommentiertes Werkverzeichnis der Bücher von Martin Kippenberger 1977–1997* (Buchhandlung Walther König, 2002), translated as *Annotated Catalogue Raisonné of the Books by Martin Kippenberger* (D.A.P., 2003); *Martin Kippenberger: Die gesamten Plakate, 1977–1997* [Collected Posters] (Offizin Verlag, Buchhandlung Walther König, Kunsthaus Zürich, 1998); *Martin Kippenberger* (Kunsthalle Basel, Deichtorhallen Hamburg, 1998); *Bei Nichtgefallen Gefühle zurück. Die gesamten Karten 1989–1997* [Satisfaction Guaranteed Or Your Feelings Back: The Collected Postcards, 1989–1997] (Verlag der Buchhandlung Walther König, 2000); *Gitarren, die nicht Gudrun heißen* [Guitars Not Named Gudrun], ed. Thomas Groetz (Galerie Max Hetzler/Holzwarth Publications, 2002); *Kippenberger: Multiples* (Kunstverein Braunschweig, Museum van Hedendaagse Kunst Antwerp, Buchhandlung Walther König, 2003); and *Nach Kippenberger* [After Kippenberger], ed. Eva Meyer-Hermann and Susanne Neuburger (Sammlung Moderner Kunst Wien, Van Abbemuseum Eindhoven, 2003).

People were Martin's true context. That is why the illustrations in this book are primarily of people; images of his work can be found in his many catalogs.

The following published memoirs, reminiscences, and statements about Kippenberger by artists and friends were also important sources for me: those in *Texte zur Kunst* [Texts on Art], No. 26, June 1997; *Tschau Mega Art Baby!* [Ciao Mega Art Baby!], ed. Christina Thomas (www.christina-thomas. de); "The Happy End of Kippenberger's Amerika as told to Gregory Williams" (*Artforum*, Feb. 2003); "A Cacophony for a Formidable Artist" (*TATE ETC.*, Issue 6, Spring 2006); "Er wollte Picasso, Warhol und Beuys zusammen sein" [He Wanted to Be Picasso, Warhol, and Beuys Put Together] (*Die Welt*, Feb. 5, 2006); *Kippenberger: Der Film* [Kippenberger: The Movie] by Jörg Kobel (2006).

Informative background information about various phases of Martin's life can be found in Helge Schneider's autobiography, *Guten Tach. Auf Wiedersehn* [Hallo. G'bye.] (KiWi, 1992), on his childhood in Essen; Jürgen Teipels, "Doku-Roman über den deutschen Punk und New Wave" [Docu-Novel on German Punk and New Wave], in *Verschwende Deine Jugend* [Waste Your Youth] (Suhrkamp Taschenbuch, 2001); in the catalog *lieber zu viel als zu wenig* [Better Too Much Than Not Enough] (NGBK, 2003), on the Berlin years and the Düsseldorf scene; Michel Würthle's *Paris Bar Berlin* (Quadriga Verlag, 2000); Siegfried Pater's biography of Hans-Jürgen Müller (RETAP Verlag, 2006) on the Stuttgart and early Cologne period; *Make Your Own Life: In and Out of Cologne*, ed. Bennett Simpson (ICA Philadelphia, 2006), on Cologne; and "Mythos Lord Jim Loge" [The Legend of the Lord Jim Lodge] by Daniela Jauk and Andreas Unterweger, in *Sexy Mythos* (NGBK Berlin, 2006).

The most important sources for this book, however, were the interviews and conversations I conducted with the people who knew Martin. I was overwhelmed by the openness with which most of these people, many of whom I had never met or knew only from a distance, talked to me—not just about Martin but about themselves. Only two of his friends expressly refused requests for interviews, and a few other interviews were not able to take place for reasons of time. Note that several people, despite their important roles in Martin's life, appear only marginally in this book, either because they feel more comfortable remaining in the background or because I could not do them justice: the closer the people who knew Martin were to me, the harder I found it to question them and to describe them impartially. Thus the frequency with which someone is quoted in this book does not necessarily reflect how close they were to Martin.

I spoke with Christel Haasis, Wiltrud Roser, Sebastian Roser, Jens Mendak, Christine Wansel, Tobias von Geiso, Dörte Warning, Klaus and Agnes Kippenberger, Christoph Kippenberger, Margit Kippenberger, Michael Kippenberger, Ulla Hurck, Lucia Avar, Barbara Avar, Ralph Drochner, Hanno Huth, Herbert Meese, Hans Meister, Jochen Krüger, Ina Barfuss, Thomas Wachweger, Gil Funccius, Inka Büttner (Hocke), Gisela Stelly-Augstein, Peter Preller, Brigitta Rohrbach, Claudia Skoda, Jenny Capitain, Klaus Krüger, Angelik Riemer, Reinhard Bock, Ulrike Ottinger, Achim Schächtele, Michel Würthle, Catherine Würthle, Uschi Welter, Attila Corbaci, Sven-Åke Johansson, Rüdiger Carl, Jutta Henglein, Barbara Straka, Peter Gente, Bruno Brunnet, Hans-Peter Feldmann, Rudolf Kicken, Uli Strothjohann, Rudolf Springer, Helmut Middendorf, Meuser, Carmen Knoebel, Imi Knoebel, Angelika Margull, Christel Buschmann, Albert Oehlen, Werner Büttner, Georg Herold, Hubert Kiecol, Max Hetzler, Hans-Jürgen Müller, Uli Knecht, Tanja Grunert, Bärbel Grässlin, Thomas Grässlin, Karola Grässlin, Anna Grässlin, Sabine Grässlin, Zdenek Felix, Rosemarie Trockel, Wilhelm Schürmann, Thomas Borgmann, Rudolf

Zwirner, Walther König, Reiner Opoku, Andreas Schulze, Jutta Koether, Nanette Hagstotz, Charline von Heyl, Franz Keller, Vincent Moissonnier, Johann-Karl Schmidt, Klaus Honnef, Gabriele Honnef-Harling, Ursula Böckler, Andrea Stappert, Michael Krebber, Merlin Carpenter, Werner Peters, Christian Nagel, Daniel Buchholz, Esther Schipper, Gundel Gelbert, Hans Böhning, Heliod Spiekermann, Hubertus Spiekermann, Isabelle Graw, Johannes Wohnseifer, Burkhard Riemschneider, Tim Neuger, Günter Lorenz, Roberto Ohrt, Albrecht Fuchs, Peter Pakesch, Martin Prinzhorn, Didi Sattmann, Elisabeth Fiedler, Sabine Achleitner, Isabella Bleich-Rossi, Petra Schilcher, Alex Witasek, Christine Hahn, Janelle Reiring, Helene Winer, Friedrich Petzel, Thea Westreich, Jeff Koons, Roland Augustine, Lawrence Luhring, David Nolan, Stephen Prina, Jory Felice, Tracy Williams, Ann Goldstein, Christopher Williams, Julian Schnabel, Louise Lawler, Betsy Wright Millard, Sigrid Rothe, Veit Loers, Tobias Rehberger, Thomas Bayrle, Valeria Heisenberg, Barbara Weiss, Nicole Hackert, Sven Ahrens, Ina Weber, Christoph Tannert, Thomas Berger, Karel Schampers, Eleni Koroneou, Alexandra Koroneou, Davé, Samia Saouma, Kazu Huggler, Minchie Huggler, Peter Huggler, Peter Fischli, David Weiss, Bice Curiger, This Brunner, Hans Weigand, Margarete Heck, Reinhard Knaus, Ernst Kampel, Rogelio Campos, and Daniel Baumann.

It was Gisela Capitain who showed me the way to many of these people. We had countless conversations with each other, and she assisted me with stories, information, texts, pictures, names, addresses, and telephone numbers, with the support of her colleagues Regina Fiorito, Margarete Jakschik and Nina Kretzschmar. They patiently and promptly answered every one of my questions, no matter how often I came to them with more. It is a rare stroke of luck for the best friend and gallerist of a deceased artist, who was there for the creation of his works and exhibitions almost from the beginning, to manage his estate. Without the help of this friend, Martin would not have been able to make the work he made while he was alive; without her intelligent and loving commitment to his work since his death, he would not have achieved the posthumous fame that he has achieved.

Doris Krystof and Jessica Morgan gave me the opportunity to write a piece for the catalog for their 2006 exhibition *Martin Kippenberger* at the K21 in Düsseldorf and the Tate Modern in London, which for me was a second step on the path to this book. The first step was an article in the newspaper *Der Tagesspiegel* about the fifth anniversary of Martin's death, which I would not have written if Christoph Amend and Stephan Lebert had not so stubbornly asked me. After that essay (which is now incorporated into the introduction of this book), I swore never to write anything about my brother again, and so this book would not exist without my agent, Barbara Wenner, who, with her usual restraint, asked me if I couldn't imagine doing it nonetheless. She was patient enough to wait until I was ready, and she accompanied and assisted me through all the crises on this long path. Her trust gave me the confidence I needed when I had lost it myself.

In Elisabeth Ruge, she found a publisher who welcomed this project with an extraordinary amount of pleasure, enthusiasm, and new ideas. My editor at Berlin Verlag, Matthias Weichelt, could not have been more pleasant: he worked gently and intelligently on the text and patiently welcomed one chapter after another. His calm gave me the feeling, even in the difficult last weeks of the project, that everything would turn out all right.

The editor of my second book, Friederike Schilbach, introduced me to Leanne Shapton—and that is how this

American edition came about, thanks to the enthusiasm and courage of Jason Fulford and Leanne Shapton. They threw themselves into the project of bringing this doorstopper of a book to America, something that far bigger publishing houses with much more money wouldn't tackle. Their relentless commitment is astounding. In Damion Searls they found a sensitive and original translator with a wonderful sense of humor, who was able to hit the right tone and who mastered the challenge of Martin's very own language. Meticulous as he is, he even proved me wrong sometimes. And Martha Sharpe was as gentle and intelligent an editor as Matthias Weichelt.

I could not have written this book without the generosity and understanding of my colleagues at *Tagesspiegel* and the encouragement, support, and accommodation of my friends, especially Edmund, Christiane, Lukas, Linus, and Nelly Labonté, Monika and Andreas Bartholomé, Jan Schütte and Christina Szapáry, Nicola Kuhn and Jörg Rüter, Adelheid Scholten and Paul Stoop, Iris and Oliver Merz, Ilse-Maria Bielefeld, Katharina Körner, and all my neighbors.

"There is no such thing as loneliness for a family man," Martin once said. The cohesion of our family has supported me throughout my life, and it is they above all who helped me with this book: with memories, letters, books, advice, trust, anticipation, curiosity, enthusiasm, and some skepticism when needed, too. My deepest thanks to Sabine Kippenberger-Steil and Andreas, Benjamin, Charlotte and Elena Steil, Bettina, Lars, Lisa and Philipp Herfeldt, Barbara Kippenberger, Petra Kippenberger-Biggemann, Klaus and Jochen Kopp, Moritz Kippenberger, Gabi Hirsch-Könen and Helena Hirsch, Elfie Semotan with Ivo and August Kocherscheidt and everyone with them—including Bruno. Bine happily threw herself into our joint trip back into our childhood and beat the drum for this project, together with Andreas, my very first reader; Tina was always there to urge me back to my desk, along with Babs, who warned me not to get lost in too much research. And it was Babs who, with failing strength, pulled every possible string to retrieve an object that Martin had made for our mother—as a favor to me.

Life goes on, as several people said by way of consolation after Martin's death. What no one said was that death goes on, too. On the very day that I officially started working on this book, our oldest sister, Babs, learned that she had kidney cancer. On December 17, 2006, the day before I was due to turn in the manuscript, she passed away. She fought like the lioness she was and firmly believed that she would recover. When she was taken to the hospital the day before she died, she was committed to being back home again for Christmas. She had already bought presents. She never complained, and she took pleasure in many things right up to the end: that Andreas went for walks with her when she could hardly walk herself, being wheeled around in a wheelchair, that Philipp, her hero, would pick her up off the ground and lead her to the bath so that she felt like a figure-skating princess. That Bine cheered her up, and Tina and Lars gave her comfort, trust, and a home. Although everyone acknowledged her sharp, quick thinking and absolute professionalism in her work, Babs was not especially happy as a lawyer. Then, a few years ago, when she overcame her Kippenbergerian fear of machines and got herself a computer, she discovered what she really loved to do besides travel: write. Some of her letters and other pieces can be read on her website, www.barbara-kippenberger.de—all written with the dry humor she maintained until right before her death.

Martin once said that he hated the past perfect tense: "To have had that."

The publishers would like to thank Friederike Schilbach for introducing us to Susanne Kippenberger and Damion Searls for a sensitive and rigorous translation. Thank you to John Wray, Robin Bellinger, Martha Sharpe, Gisela Capitain, Lisa Franzen, Rebecca Nagel, Lorin Stein, and Luise Stauss. Our deepest thanks to Susanne Kippenberger for trusting J&L with this special book. The translation of this work was supported by a grant from the Goethe-Institut, which is funded by the German Ministry of Foreign Affairs.

INDEX

Achenbach, Helge 332
Achleitner, Sabine 320, 323, 331, 461, 509, 547
Adamski 237
Ahrens, Sven 314, 418-420, 424, 456, 458-461, 467, 547
Aizpuru, Juana de 343-344
Albig, Jörg-Uwe 241
Ammann, Jean-Christophe 401
Ammann, Thomas 485
Andersen, Mikael 501
Artmann, H.C. 267, 273
Attersee, Christian Ludwig 270, 279-280, 329
Augstein, Rudolf 10, 115-116, 337
Augustine, Roland 182, 308, 312, 334, 364, 369, 377, 385, 547
Avgikos, Jan 371

Babias, Marius 323, 472-473, 475, 543
Bacon, Francis 229
Baldessari, John 271, 329, 374, 384-385, 498
Barfuss, Ina 100-102, 104, 107, 111, 114, 148, 163, 167, 204, 207, 248, 546
Baselitz, Georg 200, 246, 297, 375, 447
Bauer, Wolfgang 185, 273, 282, 320, 324-325, 331, 336
Baumann, Daniel 64, 70, 116, 441, 456, 502, 510-511, 527, 543, 547
Baumewerd, Lukas 440, 461, 467, 512
Baviera, Silvio 281
Bayer, Konrad 204

Bayrle, Thomas 261, 298, 310, 393, 414, 416, 418, 527, 547
Becker, Annesofie 503
Becker, Ben 2, 174
Beckett 196
Berger, Helmut 12, 110, 119, 538
Berger, Thomas 452, 547
Bernard, Christian 470, 510
Beuys, Joseph xiii, 7, 144, 147, 164, 169, 203, 228, 237, 240, 263, 297, 321, 362, 364, 370, 410, 425-427, 518, 525, 545
Bleich-Rossi, Aki, Gabriella, Isabella, Stefan 270, 295, 318-319, 325-326, 328, 331, 414-415, 501, 547
Block, René 203
Blum, Heiner 316, 329
Blumenschein, Tabea 134, 142, 143, 146, 166
Bock, Reinhard 140, 155, 546
Böckler, Ursula 283, 286, 288, 547
Böhning, Hans 434, 462, 467, 547
Bömmels, Peter 237
Bongard, Willi 332
Bonin, Cosima von 186, 300, 304-305, 309, 315-316, 322, 325, 391, 423, 440, 443, 461, 467
Borgmann, Thomas 220, 241, 244, 402, 434, 547
Bormann, Martin 286, 289, 374
Bötel, Hans (Hajo) 114, 150
Bowie, David 172, 366, 370
Brandl, Herbert 268
Braun, Matti 409

555

Breslauer, Herr 213
Brock, Bazon 282
Brunner, This 253, 485, 532, 547
Brunnet, Bruno 145, 147, 179, 209,
    240, 294, 346, 419, 467, 546
Brus, Günter 211, 316
Buchholz, Daniel 163, 310, 347, 351,
    432-433, 442, 517, 547
Burckhardt, Jacqueline 483-484
Buschmann, Christel 208, 546
Büttner, Werner 7, 121, 163, 175, 184-
    185, 187, 207, 217, 223, 235, 237,
    246-248, 252, 263-265, 268, 271,
    290, 295, 305, 310-312, 316, 349-
    350, 387, 420, 424, 449, 470, 486,
    496, 521, 529, 531, 537, 544, 546
Capitain, Gisela vi, xvi, 8, 148, 160-161,
    169, 172, 177, 241, 245, 261, 263,
    284, 291, 293, 295, 308, 314, 334,
    355-356, 369, 371, 386, 390, 397,
    425, 430-431, 441, 447, 461-462,
    467, 481-482, 489, 491, 498, 501,
    531, 543-544, 547, 551
Capitain, Jenny 140-141, 147, 469, 546
Carl, Rüdiger 160, 174-176, 254, 261,
    311, 336, 386, 395, 401, 462, 497,
    546
Carpenter, Merlin 305, 414, 443, 448,
    463, 547
Caldwell, John 385
Castelli, Leo 415
Chagall, Marc 64, 70
Claramunt, Luis 322, 345
Clark, Larry 333
Clegg & Guttmann 316, 451
Copley, William 316
Corbaci, Attila 144, 213, 250, 253, 266-
    267, 278, 497, 516, 546
Costard, Hellmuth 150
Crone, Ascan 121, 281, 293
Curiger, Bice 310, 424, 451, 484, 547
Czurda, Elfriede 267

Dahn, Walter 163, 237, 248, 251, 301,
    331
David, Catherine 498
Debschitz, Hildegund von 59
Delefant, Luis 59
De Maria, Walter 420-422
Deissen, Eva 269-270
Dickhoff, Wilfried 529
Diederichsen, Diedrich xvi, 5, 74, 171-
    172, 185, 189, 193, 201, 272, 282,
    295-296, 299, 303-304, 341, 444-
    445, 449, 475, 522, 543
Dokoupil 193, 237, 245, 248, 251, 272,
    296, 321
Donner, Wolf 143
Dürr, Christoph 298, 442
Duchamp, Marcel xii, 333, 424, 429
Duchow, Achim 103, 114, 121
Duncan, David Douglas 502
Dziuba, Gabi 462, 467

Eden, Rolf 137, 181
Eglau, Otto 82
E.T. 226, 520

Fallaci, Oriana 118
Fassbinder, Rainer Werner 147, 187,
    209, 294, 381-382, 425
Faust, Wolfgang Max 234, 244, 363,
    527
Feldmann, Hans-Peter 193, 240, 313,
    368, 546
Felice, Jory 172-173, 176, 378-380,
    383-384, 453, 547
Felix, Zdenek 3, 235, 264, 501, 546
Fetting, Reiner 145, 149, 167, 281, 367
Fiedler, Elisabeth 254, 262, 309, 329-
    331, 414, 456, 463, 547
Fiedler, Peter 331
Fiedler, Stefan 329-330
Fischer, Urs 270, 470-471
Fischli, Peter 214, 254, 321, 484, 547

Flindt Willie 503
Förg, Günther 176, 217, 223, 237, 246, 248, 316, 329, 349-350, 364, 385, 452
Fraser, Andrea 214, 443
Frey, Patrick 534
Fricke, Harald 474-475, 478, 539
Fuchs, Albrecht 441, 463, 498, 547
Fuchs, Rudi 509
Funccius, Gil 98, 101, 103, 109, 113-114, 118, 546

Gazarra, Ben 382
Gelbert, Gundel 434, 462, 467, 547
Gente, Peter 180, 184, 546
Géricault, Théodore 318, 503-504, 520
Germer, Stefan 444
Giehse, Anna 404
Gilbert & George 328
Goetz, Rainald 185, 467
Grässlin, Anna 223, 228, 395, 450, 461, 467-468, 480, 517, 546
Grässlin, Bärbel 3, 7, 11, 158, 160, 184, 219, 222, 225, 245, 281, 311, 395, 401-402, 408, 416-417, 451, 462, 467, 531, 543, 546
Grässlin, Karola 222, 225, 236, 299, 443, 461, 467, 546
Grässlin, Katharina 222, 450
Grässlin, Sabine 225, 261, 337, 395, 462, 467, 546
Grässlin, Thomas 222, 225, 227, 255, 395, 409, 453, 467-468, 546
Graetz, Thomas 173
Graubner, Gotthard 237
Graupner, Ernst and Annemarie 59
Graw, Isabelle 196, 250, 255, 391, 405, 411, 443-444, 463, 473, 521, 547
Grilj, Mathias 321, 323
Groh, Dr. Hans 76-77, 81
Grond, Walter 6, 185, 189, 534
Grotkasten, Annette 184

Grunert, Tanja 3, 177, 219, 235, 245, 313, 380, 546
Gundlach, F.C. 258

Haasis, Christel 542, 546
Hackert, Nicole 407, 462, 547
Häfner-Mode, Ilse 59
Hagstotz, Nanette 451, 467, 547
Hahn, Christine 161, 170, 366-368, 382, 547
Hamilton, Richard 211
Hammelehle, Bernd 460
Haselhorst-Lützkendorf, Petra 53, 59, 65, 77, 125
Hauser, Erich 228
Hausner, Rudolf 101, 423
Heck, Margarete 504-506, 547
Heinzmann, Thilo 329
Heisenberg, Valeria 173, 290, 300, 407, 412, 415, 501-502, 547
Henglein, Jutta 178-180, 546
Hermes, Manfred 200, 317
Herold, Georg 163, 204, 237, 246, 260, 282, 343, 350, 371, 423, 444, 546
Hetzler, Max 145, 158, 171, 175, 180, 182, 215-220, 222, 230, 232-233, 235, 240, 243, 245-247, 249, 251, 263-264, 271, 277, 281, 283, 290, 293, 298, 305, 308, 333-334, 346-347, 349, 355, 364, 369, 371, 377, 383, 385, 387, 389, 401, 416, 428, 430-431, 442-443, 445, 469, 474, 533, 544, 546
Heyl, Charline von 310, 391, 449, 461, 467, 547
Hickey, David 429
Hirsch-Könen Gabi 345, 358-362, 378, 380, 394, 403, 434, 445, 448, 496, 512, 549
Hirsch, Helena vii, 11, 178, 352, 358-362, 380, 394, 403, 434, 448, 496, 499, 512, 515, 549

Hödecke, Karl Horst 147
Höhne, Andreas 407, 409, 414, 467
Hoet, Jan 411, 420, 422, 426, 498
Hocke, Inka (Büttner) 109, 129, 265,
    360, 467, 546
Hoffmann, Hilmar 80-81, 83-84, 401
Holden, William 413, 473
Honnef, Klaus 281, 547
Huber, Axel 321, 467, 470, 510
Huggler, Kazu 252, 393, 463, 482-492,
    497, 547
Huggler, Minchie 482-484, 487-488,
    491, 530, 547
Huggler, Peter 486, 491, 547
Humpe, Annette 144
Humpe, Inga 253
Hurck, Ulla 29, 69, 186, 546
Huth, Hanno 88-89, 91, 114, 155, 201,
    284, 546

Immendorff, Jörg 5, 164, 237, 246, 251,
    375

Jacobsen, Arne 60
Janosch, 59-60, 82
Joachimides, Christos 207
Johansson, Sven Åke 145, 149, 170-
    171, 174-175, 200, 316, 322, 461,
    467, 546
Jones, Ronald 316, 374
Judd, Donald 294
Juhnke, Harald 5, 525

Kafka, Franz xvi, 10-11, 157, 188, 204,
    261, 268, 313, 315, 317, 376, 381,
    413, 433, 453-456, 458-459, 468,
    471, 501, 503, 539
Kalb, Kurt 266, 268-271, 389
Kampel, Ernst 513-515, 547
Kapielski, Thomas 204
Keller, Franz 258-260, 317, 351, 547
Kelley, Mike xii, 271, 316, 322, 350,

374, 377
Kiecol, Hubert 161, 176, 217, 223, 237,
    246, 248, 271-272, 282, 284, 297,
    353, 356, 439, 461, 467, 470, 524,
    546
Kiefer, Anselm 375
Klauke, Jürgen 237
Klein, Astrid 237
Klein, Erhard 263, 281, 287, 289, 387
Knaus, Reinhard 506, 513, 547
Knecht, Uli 217-218, 230-232, 288,
    402, 546
Knoebel, Carmen 353, 546
Knoebel, Imi 164, 287, 353, 546
Koberling, Bernd 147, 209
Kocherscheidt, Kurt xi, 494, 496, 506-
    508, 549
König, Kasper 243, 248, 416, 501
König, Walther 183, 186, 242-243, 390,
    400, 544, 547
Köpcke, Arthur 159, 501
Koether, Jutta xv, 10, 13, 154, 163, 171,
    174, 185, 194-196, 220, 247, 262,
    285, 294, 297, 316, 322, 347, 349,
    352, 363, 386, 391, 405, 416, 421,
    444-445, 458, 473, 475, 493, 502,
    518, 526, 528-529, 532, 542, 547
Kokoschka, Oskar 70, 211
Koons, Jeff xiii, 154, 294, 306, 308,
    316-317, 322, 333, 350, 374-375,
    380, 383, 385, 512, 547
Koroneou, Eleni 261, 438-439, 501,
    512, 547
Koroneou, Alexandra 438, 547
Kraus, Elisabeth and Bernhard 59
Krebber, Michael 154, 156-157, 185-
    188, 192, 195, 223, 272, 296-307,
    309, 318, 322, 325, 347, 363, 380,
    391, 407, 411, 423, 434, 442-443,
    461, 467, 529, 536, 547
Krüger, Jochen 101, 105-108, 114, 121,
    150, 163, 367, 546

Krüger, Klaus 140, 142, 146, 148-149, 368, 546
Kubinski, Achim 219
Kuczynski, Adam 409, 414
Küng, Birgit 193, 322, 461, 467, 485, 516, 532
Kuhlenschmidt, Richard 281

Lampersberg, Gerhard 204, 267
Lang, Helmut 495, 497, 500
Lange, Werner 149
Lawler, Louise 214, 316, 329, 443, 547
Leonard, Zoe 214, 380
Lichtenstein, Roy 238
Loers, Veit 283, 423, 425, 462, 467, 510, 517, 547
Lorenz, Günter 261, 469-470, 547
Lorenz, Sylvana 469
Lottmann, Joachim 156, 185, 248, 300, 362-363, 525
Lüpertz, Markus 147, 209, 246, 251, 297, 375, 529
Lützkendorf, Petra and Pippus 53, 125
Luhring, Lawrence 308, 334, 364, 369, 377, 383-385, 547
Lunch, Lydia 149
Lunkewitz, Bernd 402-403

Maak, Niklas 191, 531
Maenz, Paul 233, 237, 244-246, 259, 346
Majerus, Michel 440, 512
Margull, Angelika 177, 204, 206-207, 382, 523, 546
Marzona, Gabi 339
Matussek, Matthias 205-206
Meese, Herbert 120, 313, 492, 546
Meister, Hans 96-97, 546
Merlicek, Jackie 508
Meschede, Friedrich 481
Metzger, Helmut 217, 219
Meuser 13, 150, 155, 157, 163, 190,

208-209, 217, 223-224, 240, 246, 254, 271, 361, 367, 425, 427, 451, 461, 467, 470, 492, 536, 546
Middendorf, Helmut 145, 149, 167, 178, 199, 206, 214, 367, 437-438, 546
Mitchell, Eric 170, 367-368
Moore, Henry 239
Mucha, Reinhard 246, 271, 294
Muehl, Otto 322
Müller, Hans Jürgen 193, 216, 218-219, 223, 238, 245, 281, 333, 545-546
Müller, Heiner 209
Muthesius, Angelika 447

Nagel, Christian 243, 336, 348, 442-444, 461, 467, 475, 493, 529, 547, 551
Nauman, Bruce xii, 426
Neufert, Nicole 431-432, 462, 467
Neuger, Tim 260, 447, 547
Nielsen, Arno Victor 458
Nitsch, Hermann 268
Nohal, Reinald 209, 267, 441, 467, 506
Nolan, David 315, 334, 369, 394, 410, 415, 419, 547

Oehlen, Albert 7, 121, 163, 169-170, 172, 175-176, 178, 187, 192, 195, 207, 220, 233-234, 246, 248, 255, 263-265, 271-272, 275, 279, 284-285, 287-288, 290, 295, 297, 305, 311, 316, 319, 321, 324-325, 329, 343-344, 346, 349, 353, 378, 387-389, 403, 423, 461, 467, 486, 496, 516, 524, 527, 537, 544, 546
Oehlen, Markus 163-164, 174, 185, 217, 233, 240, 246, 248, 316, 332, 462, 467, 470
Ohrt, Roberto 185, 187, 195, 264, 291, 462, 467-468, 477, 547
Oliver, Jay 175

Opoku, Reiner 193, 251, 254, 259, 296, 358, 378, 547
Oppermann, Anna 114, 119
Oswald, Evelyn 269-270
Ottinger, Ulrike 134, 142-143, 145-146, 199, 546

Pakesch, Peter 232-233, 247, 249, 267-273, 275, 279, 295, 323, 326-327, 348, 356, 389, 405, 443, 463, 528, 530, 547
Palermo, Blinky 107, 307, 427, 526
Paris, Heidi 184
Parker, Charlie 254
Pasch, Clemens 82
Penck, A.R. 246, 316, 332
Peters, Werner 334-335, 467, 547
Petersen, Tony 113
Petersen, Jes 163, 203-204, 281, 340
Petzel, Friedrich 172, 369, 411, 461, 467, 547
Picabia, Francis 263, 429
Picasso, Jacqueline 502
Picasso, Pablo, 2, 11-12, 64, 70, 166, 204, 315, 328, 426, 428-429, 438, 502, 539-540, 545
Pichler, Walter 280, 506, 508-509
Polke, Sigmar 102-104, 141, 149, 237, 240-241, 246, 263, 287, 316, 386, 423-425, 524
Pop, Iggy 140, 148, 167, 366
Preller, Peter 114-115, 139, 546
Pretzell, Rainer 186, 267
Prigann, Hermann 97
Prina, Stephen 196, 249, 271, 333, 374, 384, 439-440, 547
Prince, Richard 317
Prinzhorn, Martin 161, 185, 187, 196, 251, 268-269, 272-274, 276, 282, 292, 314, 318, 320, 357, 359, 403, 444, 461, 467, 512, 547

Puvogel, Renate 182

Qualtinger, Helmut 267
Quappe, Andreas 476

Raab, Kurt 187, 508-509
Rainer, Arnulf 147
Rakete, Jim 167-168, 170, 173
Rauschenberg, Robert 218, 239, 539
Rehberger, Tobias 252, 260, 329, 407-412, 414-415, 417, 461, 467, 478, 547
Reiring, Janelle 253, 369, 416, 547
Richter, Gerhard 237, 263, 294, 316, 386, 428, 526
Rickey, George 144
Riemer, Angelik 140-141, 546
Riemschneider, Burkhard 249, 440, 447, 463, 544, 547
Rohrbach, Brigitta 161, 163, 240, 546
Rosen, Andrea 415
Rosenthal, Norman 207
Roser, Albrecht 19
Roser, Sebastian 81, 546
Roser, Wiltrud 16-18, 20, 41, 59, 81-82, 87, 94, 542, 546
Roth, Dieter 147, 183, 209, 211, 428
Rückriem, Ulrich 237
Rühm, Gerhard 167, 204, 498
Ruscha, Ed 364
Ryman, Robert 331

Saatchi, Charles 404
Salomé 145, 248
Samba, Chéri 322, 414
Sander, Otto 209
Saouma, Samia 430, 469, 502, 547
Sattmann, Didi 270, 279-280, 547
Schächtele, Achim 147, 165-166, 170, 178, 180, 203, 205-206, 215, 245, 370, 383, 546

Schampers, Karel 456-457, 521, 530, 547

Schaufler, Matthias 316, 407, 409, 413, 462, 467

Schilcher, Petra 320, 327-328, 461, 467, 547

Schilcher, Ralph 327

Schily, Otto 201

Schipper, Esther 163, 294, 351, 442, 461, 467, 547

Schjeldahl, Peter 372, 540

Schlick, Jörg 272, 278, 309, 316, 320-326, 329, 331, 371-372, 411, 440, 461, 467, 470, 497, 509, 514, 524

Schlippenbach, Alexander von 175

Schmidt, Johann-Karl 150, 206, 239, 281, 426, 547

Schmitz, Rudolf 261

Schnabel, Julian 333, 374, 547

Schneckenburger, Manfred 329, 422

Schneider, Helge 88-89, 144, 545

Schneider, Romy 187, 482

Schultheis, Jo 287

Schulze, Andreas 247, 252, 547

Schürmann, Wilhelm 211, 217-218, 248, 369, 448, 527, 546

Schurr, Ursula 219

Seiler, Helmut 217, 461, 467

Semotan, Elfie, xi, 1, 172, 291, 320, 322, 329, 361, 399, 494-500, 502-505, 510-515, 518-520, 549

Sherman, Cindy 333

Siemens, Jochen 242

Simmons, Laurie 214

Sinatra, Frank 3, 227, 351

Skoda, Claudia 140, 142, 207, 546

Skoda, Jürgen 140

Smith, Roberta 374

Speck, Rainer 244

Spiekermann, Heliod 313, 424, 434, 462, 467, 517, 547

Spiekermann, Hubertus 434, 547

Springer, Rudolf 203, 266, 546

Sprüth, Monika 245, 247, 251

Stachelhaus, Heiner 518

Stappert, Andrea 162, 183, 251, 256, 260, 284, 288, 313, 352, 461, 467, 517, 547

Steiner, Tatjana 409, 414, 467

Stelly-Augstein, Gisela 114-115, 546

Straka, Barbara 202, 206, 314, 523, 546

Strau, Josef 472

Strothjohann, Uli 146, 306-310, 316, 322, 361, 363, 371, 404, 423, 432, 434, 440, 456, 461, 467, 472, 474, 488, 501, 546

Stünke, Hein 237

Stutz, Andi 482, 485

Sylvester, Julie 295, 369

Tannert, Christoph 475, 478-481, 547

Taschen, Benedikt 244, 376, 447, 492

Teipel, Jürgen 144

Trebes, Klaus 404

Trockel, Rosemarie 160, 178, 187, 189, 251, 256, 291, 316, 546

Twombly, Cy 219

Ungers, Oswald Matthias 349, 430

Ungers, Sophia 177-178, 351, 543

Utesch, Hella 142, 148, 151

Vischer, Friedrich Theodor 188, 321, 524

Vogel, Sabine 476

Wachweger, Thomas 13, 75, 100-104, 107, 111, 114, 149, 163, 167, 204, 207, 248, 546

Walther, Karin 59

Warhol, Andy xiii, 141-142, 148, 168, 238-239, 263, 315, 365, 370, 376, 425-426, 511, 529, 545

Weber, Ina 373, 419-420, 467, 547
Weibel, Peter 268, 279, 322
Weigand, Hans 377, 470, 510-511, 547
Weiss, Barbara 314, 547
Weiss, David 193, 214, 254, 321, 484, 547
Welter, Uschi 207, 225-226, 336, 371, 442, 461, 467, 546
Werner, Michael 238, 246, 334
West, Franz 223, 268, 316, 321, 329, 402, 496
Westreich, Thea 369, 380, 547
Widauer, Johann 291-292, 461, 467
Wiener, Oswald 147, 149, 185, 211, 297, 441
Wiener, Ingrid 181, 267
Williams, Christopher 374, 440, 547
Williams, Tracy 369, 456, 547
Winer, Helene 369, 547
Witasek, Alex 290, 547
Wohnseifer, Johannes 6, 157, 162, 193-194, 211, 223, 262, 312, 322, 351, 404, 423, 432-435, 450, 452, 457-458, 462, 467, 480, 500, 512, 517, 547

Wols 281, 526
Wool, Christopher 196, 271, 316, 333, 374, 439
Wright Millard, Betsy 346, 372, 431, 547
Wullems, Ronald 409
Würthle, Carolina 436-437
Würthle, Catherine 398, 435, 546
Würthle, Michael 8, 20, 88, 133, 149, 158, 193, 209-212, 229, 266, 270, 295-296, 316, 319, 343, 392, 398, 414, 428, 435, 441, 461, 467, 481, 484, 494, 506, 532, 545-546

Zickler, Christian 409
Zimmer, Bernd 145, 147, 167
Zimnik, Reiner 51-52, 55, 57-59, 82
Zobernig, Heimo 268, 271, 316, 321-322, 329, 440, 521
Zwirner, Rudolf 218, 237-239, 243, 262-263, 333, 346, 416, 448, 547

ILLUSTRATION CREDITS

14   © Estate of Martin Kippenberger, Galerie Gisela Capitain, Cologne
18   © Wiltrud Roser
27   © Gerd Kippenberger
30   © Gerd Kippenberger
43   © Estate of Martin Kippenberger, Galerie Gisela Capitain, Cologne
45   © Estate of Martin Kippenberger, Galerie Gisela Capitain, Cologne
48   © Gerd Kippenberger
51-52, 55, 57-58 © Reiner Zimnik
123 Kippenberger Family © Ilse Pässler
124 MK in the Kinderhaus in Frillendorf © Ilse Pässler
126 Monkeys © Gerd Kippenberger/Estate of Martin Kippenberger, Galerie
     Gisela Capitain, Cologne
129 With father in photo booth © Estate of Martin Kippenberger, Galerie Gisela
     Capitain, Cologne
130-131 Feldbrunnenstrasse © Gil Funccius
132 1978 World Cup © Estate of Martin Kippenberger, Galerie Gisela Capitain,
     Cologne
132 Paris Bar © Lepkowski
133 Self-portrait from Florence © Estate of Martin Kippenberger, Galerie Gisela
     Capitain, Cologne
135 With Tabea Blumenschein © Ulrike Ottinger
134 In East Berlin © Estate of Martin Kippenberger, Galerie Gisela Capitain,
     Cologne
135 With Skoda Family © Estate of Martin Kippenberger, Galerie Gisela
     Capitain, Cologne
136 In front of S.O.36 © Estate of Martin Kippenberger, Galerie Gisela Capitain,
     Cologne
136 Ratten-Jenny © Jürgen Gässler
137 With Rolf Eden © Estate of Martin Kippenberger, Galerie Gisela Capitain,
     Cologne
137 In the hospital © Jutta Henglein
138 Poster for the 25th birthday © Estate of Martin Kippenberger, Galerie Gisela
     Capitain, Cologne
138 Catalog for the 30th birthday © Estate of Martin Kippenberger, Galerie
     Gisela Capitain, Cologne
210 © Michael Würthle
212 © Michael Würthle

387 With Max Hetzler © Wilhelm Schürmann
387 Singing at exhibition opening © Galerie Klein
388 Vienna carriage race © Dietrich Sattmann
389 Vodka drinking contest © Dietrich Sattmann
389 With Kurt Kalb © Dietrich Sattmann
389 In the Vienna Gallery © Dietrich Sattmann
390 With Gisela Capitain © Martin Lutz
391 Group photo © Hans-Jörg Mayer
391 With Michael Krebber ©Andrea Stappert
392 MOMAS ©Lukas Baumewerd
392 With Michael Würthle in Rotterdam © Jannes Linders
393 With Kazu Huggler © Estate of Martin Kippenberger, Galerie Gisela Capitain, Cologne
393 With Thomas Bayrle © Helke Bayrle
394 With Gabi Hirsch and Helena © Estate of Martin Kippenberger, Galerie Gisela Capitain, Cologne
394 Kippenblinkys © Estate of Martin Kippenberger, Galerie Gisela Capitain, Cologne
395 Grässlin Family © Grässlin Family
395 With slot-car racetrack © Grässlin Family
396 With frog © Sammlung Widauer
397 Dancing with Gisela Capitain © Jörg Schlick
398 Wedding photos © Esther Oehlen
399 St. Mark's Square © Elfie Semotan
400 Egg wagon © Elfie Semotan
400 Window display at Walther König's © Andrea Stappert
464-465 40th Birthday © Estate of Martin Kippenberger, Galerie Gisela Capitain, Cologne

Susanne Kippenberger lives and works in Berlin where she is an award-winning writer and editor at the newspaper *Der Tagesspiegel*. She is the author of *At the Table*, a book about Julia Child, M.F.K. Fisher, Elizabeth David, Alice Waters, and today's culinary bohemians from Brooklyn to Berlin: amateurs and iconoclasts who have changed the way we eat. Susanne is the youngest of Martin Kippenberger's four sisters.

Damion Searls is a writer and translator of authors including Proust, Rilke, Robert Walser, and Christa Wolf. His translation of Hans Keilson's *Comedy in a Minor Key* was a National Book Critics Circle Award finalist and a *New York Times* Notable Book of 2010.